Innovation, Unemployment and Policy in the Theories of Growth and Distribution

Innovation, Unemployment and Policy in the Theories of Growth and Distribution

Edited by

Neri Salvadori and Renato Balducci

Professor of Economics, University of Pisa, Italy
Professor of Economics, Polytechnical University of Marche, Italy

Edward Elgar
Cheltenham, UK • Northampton, MA, USA

Published by
Edward Elgar Publishing Limited
Glensanda House
Montpellier Parade
Cheltenham
Glos GL50 1UA
UK

Edward Elgar Publishing, Inc.
136 West Street
Suite 202
Northampton
Massachusetts 01060
USA

Learning Resources
Centre

12978884

A catalogue record for this book
is available from the British Library

ISBN 1 84542 321 6

Printed and bound in Great Britain by MPG Books Ltd, Bodmin, Cornwall

Contents

Figures

Tables

Contributors

Renato Balducci, *Polytechnical University of Marche*

Alberto Bucci, *University of Milan*

Salvatore Capasso, *University of Naples 'Parthenope'*

Maria Rosaria Carillo, *University of Naples 'Parthenope'*

Mauro Caminati, *University of Siena*

Pasquale Commendatore, *University of Naples 'Federico II'*

Guido Cozzi, *University of Rome 'La Sapienza'*

Francesco Drago, *University of Siena*

Luciano Fanti, *University of Pisa*

Davide Gualerzi, *University of Padua*

Massimiliano La Marca, *University of Pisa*

Andrea Mario Lavezzi, *University of Pisa*

Nicola Meccheri, *University of Pisa*

Carlo Panico, *University of Naples 'Federico II'*

Erasmo Papagni, *Second University of Naples*

Carmelo Pierpaolo Parello, *Universityf of Rome 'La Sapienza'*

Antonio Pinto, *University of Naples 'Federico II'*

Luca Spinesi, *University of Rome 'La Sapienza'*

Luca Spataro, *University of Pisa*

Stefano Staffolani, *Polytechnical University of Marche*

Introduction

Renato Balducci and Neri Salvadori

The problem of economic growth and income distribution was a major concern of the Classical economists. Ricardo's argument about what he called the 'natural' course of the economy contemplated an economic system in which capital accumulates, the population grows, but there is no technical progress: the latter is set aside. In Ricardo the rate of accumulation is endogenously determined. The demand for labour is governed by the pace at which capital accumulates, whereas the long-term supply of labour is regulated by the 'Malthusian Law of Population'. The required size of the work force is considered essentially generated by the accumulation process itself. In other words, labour power is treated as a kind of producible commodity. It differs from other commodities in that it is not produced in a capitalistic way by a special industry on a par with other industries, but is the result of the interplay between the generative behaviour of the working population and socio-economic conditions. In the most simple conceptualization possible, labour power is seen to be in elastic supply at a given real wage rate basket. Increasing the number of baskets available in the support of workers involves a proportional increase in the work force. In this view the rate of growth of labour supply adjusts to any given rate of growth of labour demand without necessitating a variation in the real wage rate. Labour can thus set no limit to growth because it is 'generated' within the growth process. The only limit to growth can come from other non-accumulable factors of production: as Ricardo and others made clear, these factors are natural resources in general and land in particular. In other words, there is only endogenous growth in Ricardo. This growth is bound to lose momentum as the scarcity of natural factors of production makes itself felt in terms of extensive and intensive diminishing returns. (Technical change is of course envisaged to counteract these tendencies.) If land of the best quality were available in abundance it would be a free good and no rent would be paid for its use. In this case the system could grow for ever. Ricardo was perfectly aware of this implication (Ricardo, *Works* VI, p. 301). Contrary to Ricardo, Adam Smith's attention focused on the factors determining the growth of labour productivity, that is, the factors affecting 'the state of the skill, dexterity, and judgment with which labour is applied in any nation' (*WN* I.6). Smith maintained that the key to the growth of labour productivity is the division of labour which in turn depends on the extent of the market and thus upon capital accumulation. In his analysis in the first three chapters of book I of *The Wealth of Nations* Smith established the idea that there are *increasing returns*. Smith's analysis foreshadows the concepts of *induced* and *embodied* technical progress, *learning by doing*, and *learning by using*. The invention of new machines and the improvement of known ones is said to be originally due to the workers in the production process and 'those who had occasion to use the machines' (*WN* I.i.9). At a more advanced stage of society making machines 'became the business of a peculiar trade', engaging 'philosophers or men of speculation, whose trade it is, not to do any thing, but to observe every thing; and who, upon that account, are often capable of combining together the powers of the most distant and dissimilar objects'. Research and development of new industrial designs becomes 'the principal or sole trade and occupation of a particular class of citizens' (ibid.). New technical knowledge is systematically created and economically used, with the sciences becoming more and more involved in that process. The accumulation of capital propels this process forward, opens up new markets and enlarges existing ones, increases effectual demand and is thus the main force behind economic and social development (*WN* V.i.e.26). Also Smith saw that the scarcity and potential depletion of renewable and the depletion of exhaustible resources may constrain human productive activity and the growth of the economy (*WN* I.xi.i.3; see also I.xi.d). However his explanation of a falling tendency of the rate of profit in terms of 'competition' (*WN* I.ix.2) does not stand up to close examination.

Neoclassical economists were more interested in the analysis of resource allocation than problems of growth, which was not a main issue on the agenda of economists for half a century. Things changed dramatically after Roy Harrod (1939) tried to re-formulate Keynes's theory of effective demand in a dynamic context. The analysis of steady growth proposed by Harrod (1939) and by Domar (1946) took centre stage in the second half of the 1950s, when Tobin (1955), Solow (1956) and Swan (1956), on the one hand, and Kaldor (1955–56), on the other, presented their versions of the neoclassical and post-Keynesian theories of growth and distribution. Harrod set the conditions that a growing economy needs to satisfy in order to grow in equilibrium and doubted that such conditions could be fulfilled by the actions of agents. Solow provided an endogenous explanation for the condition necessary to ensure Harrod's condition. He postulated a well-behaved aggregate production function satisfying the Inada conditions and showed that there can exist a combination of the capital and labour factors which fulfils the condition of balanced growth with full employment.

Moreover, there exist values of both real wage and profit rate such that 'optimal' technology will be selected by perfectly competitive firms. In the Neoclassical approach developed by Solow capital accumulation sustained by adequate saving is relevant during the transition to steady state whereas the increase in the working-age population and the technical progress which increases the productivity of the production factors determine the steady state growth path but are considered to be beyond the control of private agents and governments. Whatever the values of the propensity to save and of capital output ratio, and therefore whatever the path of the economy out of equilibrium, the natural rate of steady state growth is not influenced by such magnitudes, for the simple reason that it is assumed to be exogenous: 'But of course Solow did not believe this to be so in reality. ... Rather, economists were reluctant to give formal expression to unknown and ill-understood processes such as population growth and the rate of innovation' (Hahn, 1994, p. 2).[1]

After a decade of dormancy, since the mid 1980s, economic growth has become once again a central topic in economic theorizing. New growth theory[2] seeks to provide an endogenous explanation of technical progress able to generate a growth process which does not slow down in time. New growth theorists account for a non-diminishing rate of per capita growth considering externalities of various kinds and origins. Adopting the scheme of rational and optimizing agents, they draw on notions like Arrow's learning by doing, or the importance of human capital accumulation stressed by Uzawa (1965) and that of technical knowledge, to provide an explanation of *technical progress*. As partly public and non-excludable, these 'commodities' (for example, human capital and the stock of 'knowledge'[3], etc.) may generate externalities in the production process tied to the spread of knowledge and scientific discoveries. Firms which undertake research cannot immediately reap the economic results of their efforts because of the diffusion of innovative ideas, the consequence being that private investment in research may be less than optimal for growth. Agents may behave in optimizing fashion, but because they operate in a setting which is not perfectly competitive, they engender a second-best growth path.

> Most of these models are 'closed' in the sense that they have enough relations to determine an equilibrium growth rate. In one, everything hinges on the production of human capital, in another this is ignored and we focus on R&D, while in yet another it is the process by which the variety of goods is increased which makes the world go round. ... The theories I am concerned with, ..., are all intent on models which allow equilibrium growth at constant rate (Hahn, 1994, p. 1).

The closeness of these models mentioned by Hahn is the basis of the link envisaged by Kurz and Salvadori (1998, 1999, 2003) between these models and the models developed by Classical economists. By a simple comparison Kurz and Salvadori draw the following conclusion: the role played by 'labour' in the classical authors is assumed by 'human capital' or 'knowledge'. Both labour, on the one hand, and human capital or knowledge, on the other, are taken to be producible; with constant returns to scale the rate of profit and, therefore, the rate of growth are determined and constant over time. The use of externalities allows the presence of increasing returns similarly to the division of labour found in Adam Smith's reasoning. In another book (Salvadori, 2003) some of the authors of the chapters presented herein explored this point of view from different perspectives.

The aim of this book is different. Taking for granted the not always recognized links between new growth theory and Classical economics the authors of this book seek to go further and develop an analysis of the relation between growth and distribution, with special attention to innovation, unemployment, and policy. Hence, before entering into a description of the chapters presented here we will quickly survey parts of the literature which are relevant to the following studies.

ENDOGENOUS GROWTH AND INCOME DISTRIBUTION

Within the revolution produced by endogenous growth theory, possible interactions between growth and distribution are resumed by shifting the attention from functional to personal income distribution. Persson and Tabellini (1992) argued that there exists a negative correlation between inequality and growth, and they sought a theoretical explanation for it in an overlapping generations model of economic and political equilibrium. Their thesis was that, when inequality exceeds a socially acceptable threshold, it requires redistribution policies financed by an increase in taxation which disincentives investments and slows down growth. Moreover, excessive inequality undermines the social structure, generating political conflicts, uncertainty over the defence of property rights, and an environment unfavourable to investments. Bertola (1990, 1993, 1994) calls into question the ability of redistributive policies to slow down growth. Investment subsidies, by closing the gap between the private return and the social return on investments in intangible goods (education and research), may increase the rate of growth. Alesina and Rodrik (1994) propose a model of endogenous growth in which conflicts between labour and capital play a key role. This conflict determines income redistribution policies and influences the economy's growth rate: the more unequal the distribution of wealth, the lower is growth rate. This model shows that it is possible to establish relations between growth and distribution in endogenous growth theories, especially if these relations are mediated by the government (see Section 4 below). This conclusion contrasts with the traditional neoclassical model, where the distribution of income has no influence on the economy's rate of growth, while it reproduces the relation between income distribution and growth rate proposed in the post-Keynesian and Kaldorian tradition. However, in this last tradition the main result was that a higher growth rate is associated to a greater share of profits to income, from which it is possible to extract a higher percentage of saving and investment.

In conclusion, endogenous growth models show that structural, political and institutional characteristics of countries play a role in explaining the long-period growth rate. Political and social stability, security of property rights, efficiency of the capital market, research, education, investments in physical and human capital, public spending and taxation policies are decisive for the success and stability of a country's development process.

> So even when we accept the relation of saving to an economy's growth which I have discussed,[4] the distribution of wealth and income may be expected to play a role also. ... In any case the distribution of feasible action sets between agents is likely to be pretty relevant to growth (Hahn, 1994, p. 14*)*.

UNEMPLOYMENT, DISTRIBUTION AND GROWTH

During the 1990s two stylized facts attracted the attention of economic policy-makers and economists: persistently high or growing rates of unemployment, and a decrease in the wage share. An explanation for these 'stylized facts' cannot be found in the traditional neoclassical theory, for which employment is determined by the labour demand and supply and should not depend on the capital accumulation and on technology. This is because real wage ensures that the labour supply is always entirely absorbed, while capital and technology determine the real wage compatible with full employment and the distribution of income between wages and profits. Instead, recent theories of endogenous growth supply explanations of the relation between growth and employment which also involve the distribution of income among the production factors. These explanations take account of frictions either in labour markets, or in the goods markets, or in the financial markets, or in a combination of them. Further, they need to assume either limited substitutability between labour and capital, or complementarity between technology and human capital, and so on.

Recent analysis seems to confirms that a more rapid growth of technical progress may have a negative influence on employment in the short period. The effect of creative destruction *à la* Aghion and Howitt (1992, 1994) (that is skills become obsolete since they are replaced by new, more productive occupations) seemingly predominates over the positive effect of greater capital accumulation. In the long period, however, technical progress innovates products and processes and increases employment both directly and indirectly as a consequence of the more rapid growth. But the long-run effect of capital accumulation on the equilibrium unemployment rate is still widely debated. According to some authors (Layard, Nickel and Jackman, 1991; Nickel, 1997), it cannot be ruled out that investment is neutral in terms of employment, because job creation when the investment is made may be counterbalanced by the 'destruction' of jobs caused by the successive increase in real wages. This should be the case in a trade union model, provided that the production technology is a Cobb–Douglas type and unemployment benefit is a constant ratio to wages. Consequently, it is the high degree of factor substitutability that is responsible for the substantial independence of the unemployment rate from capital accumulation. Rowthorn (1996) explicitly considers conflict for distributive shares, which he calls the '*battle of mark-ups*', to put forward a different thesis. An increase in the capital stock gives rise to an excess of productive capacity which makes it difficult for firms to increase their prices. The distributive conflict consequently attenuates, and a stable inflation rate can be combined with a lower rate of unemployment. Gordon (1997) argues that the steeper the fall in the investment rate, the greater the growth of the unemployment rate. A shock to the real wage, due for example to increased trade-union bargaining power, will initially give rise to a decline in employment and to an increase in labour productivity. By contrast, the marginal productivity of capital will diminish, because a given stock of capital is now combined with a smaller number of labour units. This should reduce the demand for new capital and shifts the labour demand downwards. If the production function is of Cobb–Douglas type, in the new equilibrium there will be the same marginal productivity of labour, but less employment, so that the traditional positive relation between productivity and unemployment is reversed.

Recent literature[5] has emphasized the skilled-biased nature of technology change and the existence of complementarities between technology and human capital. These complementarities increase demand for skilled workers and their remuneration at the expense of unskilled ones, and they may give rise to distributive effects and a widening of wage gaps. But explaining the relation between unemployment and growth, and assessing the role of income distribution in that relation, is almost impossible within the neoclassical framework. Even if one includes 'imperfections' in the labour market, it is not possible to establish a stable relation between growth and unemployment. Vice versa, it is possible to 'construct' relations between distribution and growth by resorting to the classical tradition, in particular to

Ricardo; or by returning to the post-Keynesian tradition, with its emphasis of the effect on income distribution on saving and hence on growth and unemployment.

These models (Boyer, 1988, 1997) resume many of the themes treated within the Classical and the post-Keynesian traditions, although to explain relations between growth and distribution requires reference to imperfections of the labour market or to institutional characteristics. These interactions are acted upon by the social system: influential in particular are the structure of trade-union relations and property rights, and the evolution of consumption patterns and education. Economic systems, in short, are characterized by their own cumulative dynamics. They may break with the previous 'mode of growth' and shift to a new equilibrium with different levels in the growth rate, in the unemployment rate, and in the composition of demand.

LABOUR UNIONS, WAGE INEQUALITY AND GROWTH

Since its beginnings, endogenous growth theory is concerned about the relation between growth and the unequal distribution of wealth. It explores the effects of the distribution of resources on the activity of the research and development sector R&D. The model developed by Aghion and Howitt (1998) considers a three-sector economy where the final sector, which operates in conditions of perfect competition and constant returns to scale, produces both consumption goods and an input utilizable in the R&D sector; while monopolistic competition and increasing returns characterize the intermediate goods sector, in which short-period surplus profits create the incentive to introduce new inputs. Blueprints for new intermediate products are developed in the R&D sector by new intermediate firms. Each firm produces a new input, so that the growth rate is defined by the rate of new firms formation. The use of labour is examined in a competitive setting where it is employed to produce intermediate goods. The population is divided between workers and owners – that is, agents with a low level of spending and high saving (which can be invested only in new firms creation). In this context, Aghion and Howitt show that an unequal distribution of wealth may be favourable to growth. In fact, although the owners have high spending capacity, they are able to save a greater percentage of their incomes than workers. This saving fosters the accumulation of capital and more rapid growth through the creation of new firms which innovate in the R&D sector. Onto this analytical structure can be grafted Schumpeter's notion of the creative destruction that sustains endogenous growth through the introduction of new products which replace already existing ones and thus engender qualitative improvements. The engine of growth arises from the allocation of the labour resource between the traditional and the innovative sectors.

Introducing imperfections into the labour market may give rise to a trade-off between the short-period advantages of a fairer distribution of incomes and the long-period cost of less sustained growth. Duranton (2000) proposes an overlapping generations model where capital accumulation is the engine of growth. Increasing returns to scale generate imperfect competition and stimulate growth, creating incentives for monopolists to invest in the R&D sector, and for younger workers to invest in knowledge in order to increase their productivity and their earnings. Moreover, because young people have greater incentives to save than elderly workers, a redistribution of wealth in favour of young people fosters saving and growth through the creation of new firms in the intermediate goods sector.

These considerations on the labour market lead naturally to inquire as to the role of the trade unions. Wapler (2001) presents a model based on Schumpeterian creative destruction with endogenous technical progress and heterogeneous workers. The trade unions represent only low-skilled workers and they define the pay of these workers on the basis of 'fair wage' considerations. The economy produces two goods, one final and the other intermediate, the latter being constantly improved and innovated by the R&D sector. The first result is that an increase in the supply of skills or in human capital accumulation leads to a more rapid growth rate, reducing the cost of research via a fall in the wages of researchers. The second result concerns the effects of trade-union power on growth. Higher real wages of low-skilled workers cause the unemployment of these workers, who tend to move to the research sector. This reduces the productivity of skilled workers in the creation of innovations and dampens the growth of the economy as a whole. De Groot (2001) proposes a two-sector model with a non-competitive labour market which generates a negative cyclical interaction between unemployment and growth: unemployment hampers growth and a slow pace of growth exacerbates unemployment. As in the previous models, the engine of growth is the accumulation of specific knowledge or innovations. The existence of the trade union leads to the formation of a dual labour market with wage differentials not justified solely by equivalent differences in productivity. This distorts the labour supply and creates unemployment. An increase in the union's bargaining power pushes up real wages in the high-tech sector and alters the composition of output in favour of the traditional sector. Hence, because of the presence of the trade unions the relation between unemployment and growth can be negative.

According to Daveri and Tabellini (1997), the higher real wages due to the presence of the trade unions induce firms to intensify their use of capital in production processes, causing a reduction in the marginal productivity of capital and a fall in profits. Since capital is prevalently owned by the more elderly, who manifest a greater propensity to save than young people, a fall in aggregate saving and investments in research and development is obtained.

The effect on growth depends on how aggregate saving is influenced by the distribution of income among the production factors. For example Bertola (1993, 1996) maintains that the propensity to save on wages may be higher than the propensity to save on profits, so that a redistribution of capital in favour of wages may foster development, sustaining the accumulation of capital and innovations. Bertola (1994) emphasizes the hold-up problem arguing that investments are discouraged by an increase in the unions' bargaining power. Lingens (2002) assumes that the trade unions are able to extract rent by means of wage bargaining in the intermediate, imperfectly competitive sector, but not in the perfectly competitive sector of research. Consequently, unemployment in the intermediate sector shifts labour supply to the research sector, in which a fall in relative wages makes it economically convenient for firms to employ a larger number of researchers. There is therefore a positive effect on innovations and growth which outweighs the negative effect due to lower employment in the intermediate sector. Palokangus (2003) uses a model of endogenous growth generated by the research sector to argue that unemployment is caused by efficiency wages: the presence of the trade unions, which bargain the allocation of profits with firms, shifts skilled labour from the intermediate sector to the research sector and reduces profits in favour of wages, with a consequent brake on growth. Parreño and Sánchez-Losado (1999) analyse the relation between endogenous growth and the role of the trade unions, in a model where output depends both on physical capital and on human capital. The latter is reproduced with constant returns and constitutes the true engine of growth. The accumulation of human capital is undertaken by benevolent parents for bequest reasons. In this scheme, the effect of the unions, which are able to extract higher real wages, on growth ultimately depends on the degree of altruism, that is the incentive to educate children, and on the bequest motive, that is the incentive to work more for a higher wage in order to save more to leave as a legacy to the children.

The foregoing survey of recently developed ideas on the role of the labour market institutions and of labour protection rules in economic development shows that the results depend on the hypotheses adopted on certain basic components. Is the marginal propensity to save on wages greater or smaller than the marginal propensity to save on profits? Do older people save more or less than the younger generations? Is the distribution of labour among the sectors rigid or does it respond to marginal allocative criteria? Choosing either one or the other hypothesis leads to conclusions that may be even diametrically opposed, given that growth is led by development of the research sector, and given that the presence of the trade unions may modify the distribution of labour among production sectors and that of incomes between labour and capital.

The book is organized as follows. Section One has two chapters on human capital accumulation, and the functioning of the research sector and innovation. Section Two analyses the role of consumption variety and quality innovation in stimulating growth. Section Three is dedicated to analysing imperfect labour markets, wage inequalities and human and physical capital accumulation. Finally, Section Four examines the opportunities and the possibilities of public policy to ensure more rapid economic growth and a fair income distribution.

SECTION ONE: HUMAN CAPITAL AND INNOVATION

Chapter 1, by Alberto Bucci, focuses on the link between product market competition and economic growth within an economy where the engine for economic development is investment in education. It is assumed that there exist three vertically integrated sectors. A competitive final output sector produces a homogeneous consumption good employing a constant returns to scale technology. The intermediate goods sector consists of monopolistically competitive firms, each producing a differentiated variety employing only human capital. The research activity produces designs (or blueprints) for new intermediate input varieties by employing only human capital, as well. When a new blueprint is discovered in the competitive R&D sector, an intermediate good producer acquires the perpetual patent over it. This allows the intermediate firm to manufacture the new variety and practice monopoly pricing forever. Population is stationary and a representative household invests portions of its fixed-time endowment to acquire formal education. Hence, in the model human capital can be used in every sector in order to produce, respectively, a homogeneous final output, capital goods, infinitely-lived patents and new human capital. The main conclusion by Bucci is that there is a positive relationship between product market power and aggregate productivity growth.

Chapter 2, by Maria Rosaria Carillo and Erasmo Papagni, analyses the effects on economic growth of the basic characteristics of scientific research such as its organization, its reward structure and the social interactions among researchers. It is assumed that a scientist, according to the priority rule, is rewarded not for his effort, but for his achievement. In this sense the race for priority can be compared to the patent race where the winner takes all and the outcome is uncertain. The productivity of researchers depends not only on personal effort but also on the effort of other researchers with whom a researcher interacts. Finally, academic research is chiefly financed by the state due to the public good nature of academic knowledge. The chapter shows that the social interactions between scientists may have an ambiguous effect on effort in the research activity carried out by a single scientist: it may be positive when group size is not too large and it may become negative beyond a critical size. Moreover, an increase in the fixed component of the salary reduces the possibility of the emergence of a no growth trap, where no research activity occurs, but it reduces the effort of a single individual in the research activity; the opposite effect emerges when the priority-based reward is increased. The reward of prestige always has a positive effect on effort and the probability of success.

SECTION TWO: VARIETY AND QUALITY INNOVATION

Chapter 3, by Mauro Caminati, attempts to set some guideposts on the relation between variety, consumption and growth, while abstracting from the well-known effect that variety may exert on productivity, through specialization. A mechanism is first described, through which preference for variety expressed by intertemporally optimizing consumers perfectly predicting the endogenously growing future consumption opportunities can cause faster steady-state growth. The mechanism amounts to a substitution of future for present consumption causing a higher steady-state savings ratio. The chapter shows that this growth-enhancing effect of preference for variety may not be unambiguous if the creation of new goods is endogenous and costly. Some of the results obtained in this part of the chapter hinge upon the assumption that there are constant returns to the endogenous factor, all factors are producible and that each type of variety can be used both as a consumption good and as an intermediate good in the production of capital by competitive firms. Dissatisfaction with the approach to preference for variety and innovation within the mechanism above is then motivated. The approach is oblivious of endogenous preference formation and the relation between innovation, consumption knowledge and consumption activities. Some research implications concerning long-term growth analysis in a world of endogenous preference formation are then drawn.

Chapter 4, by Davide Gualerzi, focuses on the relationship between consumption composition, growth and distribution. Only by focusing on investment and innovative investment in particular, can the issue of changes in consumption composition, both as a structure of expenditure *and* commodity-based forms of needs satisfaction, become fully relevant for growth theory. This has eluded most analysis despite the many efforts to take account of product innovation and more recently variety in consumption. What is required is an independent account of consumption in the framework of a demand-led view of growth. Consumption choice then becomes part of the contribution of consumers to the establishment of new commodities in the transformation patterns of consumption, something that is shown to be implied by the extension of the principle of effective demand to the long run.

Chapter 5, by Carmelo Pierpaolo Parello and Luca Spinesi, is concerned with whether the determinants of patent infringement and declaratory judgement suits may affect both long-term economic performance and income distribution. A quality-ladder R&D-based endogenous growth model is presented, in which the institutional setting devoted to patent protection directly impacts upon the long-run private incentive for R&D. By ruling, the courts' interpretation of patent law generates the coexistence of the leader's and follower's product, especially in those patent suits where lagging breadth is at the core of litigation. For the quality leader, the existence of a positive probability of losing a patent suit against a potential producer of an inferior product constitutes a threat for its monopoly position affecting its strategic behaviour. The chapter shows that both the institutional setting and the court's behaviour actively affect both long-term growth performance and income distribution.

SECTION THREE: EMPLOYMENT AND INEQUALITY

Chapter 6, by Renato Balducci and Stefano Staffolani, examines the relationship between the functional distribution of income and growth. Using an endogenous growth model based on human capital accumulation and on the hypothesis that firms must invest part of their profits in physical capital while households optimally allocate their earnings between consumption and investment in human capital, the chapter determines the labour share that maximizes expected utility. It investigates the determinants of factor shares in a 'short-run' perspective using an efficient bargaining model between firms and unions. Our main result is that the optimal labour share can be higher than that arising from perfect competition in the labour market. Therefore, trade unions are necessary for optimal economic growth.

Chapter 7, by Andrea Mario Lavezzi and Nicola Meccheri, studies the effects of social networks on wage inequality and aggregate production by considering a simplified version of the Calvó-Armengol and Jackson (2003) model, with good and bad jobs and skilled and unskilled workers. The main findings are the following. Firstly, increasing the number of social links increases aggregate output and may reduce inequality; secondly, given a number of social connections, output increases if the average distance among workers decreases; finally, a more mixed and well-integrated society, that is a society in which heterogeneous workers share social links, produces more output and less inequality than a society in which some workers are isolated, when productivity of the most productive agents in the best jobs is sufficiently low.

Chapter 8, by Salvatore Capasso, studies the interactions between crime, incentives to commit crime and economic development and growth. A low level of economic development implies a higher degree of poverty and, to the extent that poverty is the major cause of crime, a high level of criminal activity. Moreover, economic stagnation can further increase the crime rate if it increases inequality in income distribution. Crime can negatively affect economic growth by affecting return on investments and business profitability. The idea is that a high diffusion of criminal offences, like extortion, affects the riskiness of investments and the return on legal activities. This chapter offers an alternative interpretation of the causal relationship between the degree of criminal activity, income distribution and economic growth. The key proposition is that the level of criminal activity in the economy can not only influence the return on private investment, but also the efficiency and the return on public investments. A high level of crime forces the government to invest in security and measures to ensure public order, like the financing of police, courts and prisons. This misallocation of resources, which are diverted from investments in more productive activities like education and research, undoubtedly has a detrimental impact on growth.

Chapter 9, by Francesco Drago, provides a job search model where individuals with the same productivity may have different arrival rates of better jobs because of different degrees of self-confidence. This behavioural trait determines individual investment in social capital through which workers think to signal their ability. Workers with higher degrees of self-confidence experience higher job arrival rates not as a consequence of signalling (since employers do not observe the ability), but because workers who signal provide higher optimal search effort. Self-confidence and search effort turn out to be complements in the performance of the search activity and the effectiveness of self-confidence is endogenously determined. Moreover, the effects of redistributing policies of opportunities that aim to compress the distribution of job arrival rates can be analysed. It is shown how the presence of social norms when redistribution is effective interacts with the efficacy of self-confidence for search activities. Since the adherence to norms is endogenous, multiple equilibria characterized by different degrees of effectiveness of the redistributive policy may be generated.

SECTION FOUR: PUBLIC POLICY

Chapter 10, by Renato Balducci, sets out to verify whether the results obtained by Barro (1990) in relation to the influence of both productive investments and public consumption on the economic rate of growth are correct. As is well known, public expenditure may exert an effect on the economic growth rate through the positive externality in the productivity of the private capital stock induced by public investment. When public consumption in the households' utility function is considered, a further effect operates, which modifies saving and consumption decisions of the household depending on the relative weight of public consumption. In particular, if households evaluate public consumption positively, whatever the exogenous fiscal policy and its composition, the growth rate is always higher than that in the case of productive investments alone. Moreover, when households choose the optimal fiscal policy and its optimal composition, an optimal growth rate γ^* equal to the maximum γ° may be obtained through a different policy which favours not only productive investments but also public consumption.

Chapter 11, by Pasquale Commendatore, Carlo Panico and Antonio Pinto, analyses the connection between government intervention and distribution in the Kaldor–Pasinetti tradition. Their model considers an economy with similar features to that of You and Dutt (1996). The results achieved show that a larger government deficit produces a higher government debt, an increase in the *rentiers'* share of wealth and a reduction in the workers' share. Moving on to the effects on the distribution of income, a larger government deficit produces a higher public debt and an increase in the *rentiers'* total revenues, measured in terms of the net income of the economy. As to the effects on the total revenues of the working class, measured in terms of the net income of the economy, they are the following: if the rate is stabilized at a given level, the pre-tax total revenues remain constant, while the after-tax ones increase, like those of the *rentiers*. Thus, a larger government deficit and debt makes both classes better off, as far as their earnings are concerned. Yet, income inequality increases, since the benefits received by the *rentiers* are greater than those received by the workers. On the other hand, if the rate of interest is not exogenously given, both the pre-tax and the after-tax revenues of the working class decrease. Finally, the model shows that an increase in the government deficit has a positive effect on the rate of growth, while a change in the rate of interest leaves the rate of growth constant.

Chapter 12, by Massimiliano La Marca, investigates the relation between foreign debt, growth and distribution in an investment-constrained open economy. It proposes an alternative framework to contribute to an old debate: the definition of the possible policy tools to achieve debt sustainability, tolerable distribution, growth and employment and the opportunity of rescheduling and/or forgiving part of the outstanding debt. The suggested interpretation is the well-established framework of an investment-constrained economy; the chapter emphasizes the role of effective demand, relative prices, distribution between broadly defined sectors and aggregate demand feeding back onto each other, and can be therefore ascribed to the Keynes–Kaldor–Kalecki and structuralist tradition. Some fairly intuitive outcomes are grounded on a solid analytical basis and suggest major international and non-standard domestic policy implications.

Chapter 13, by Guido Cozzi, shows that in a 'capitalist economy' where there is no 'creative destruction', and in which financial intermediaries collude, if households have perfectly diversified portfolios they will prefer lower R&D investment and growth if they are rich, and higher R&D and growth if they are poor. Hence, the richer the wealthy group that controls the financial sector, the lower the equilibrium innovation: in this sense inequality harms growth. If profit taxation is present, the higher the tax rate the faster is growth no matter whether taxation is purely wasteful or redistributive. In this model profit taxation proves beneficial to growth because it reduces the incentive for rich influential shareholders to resist growth. The equilibrium growth rate always increases with the marginal tax rate of the richer incomes. Of course, taxation may not be efficiency-enhancing: the trade-off is between lower taxation and higher aggregate growth, but it is not claimed that growth is beneficial *per se*.

Chapter 14, by Luciano Fanti and Luca Spataro, adopts the traditional competitive OLG model *à la* Samuelson–Diamond with two-period-living individuals, fixed fertility rates and labour supply, where the government can pursue redistributive policies between generations by levying lump sum taxes or subsidies. By using standard logarithmic preferences and a CES technology with low factor substitution, the authors show that the taxation of the old can be used: 1) to escape from a poverty trap; 2) to increase the per capita income in the positive high steady state. Conversely, the taxation of the young worsens the stationary per capita income and may in fact lead to the explosion of the economy. This result may be applied to policy analysis in developing countries: the introduction of a PAYG social security scheme as a means of redistributing among generations may be detrimental for economic growth and for the poverty trap. This argument may also be applied to rich countries which have escaped from poverty traps. Conversely, the introduction of such instruments as public education or subsidies to children may be positive for both economic growth and the solution to the poverty trap.

This book is one of the main products of a research group. Each chapter was discussed several times by members of the group and at least once within a debate which involved one or two discussants. On the basis of the results of the discussion, one of the discussants, or both, then supervised the editing of the paper. Some papers have been excluded on the basis of this procedure and others have been heavily revised. The process revealed that at times non-anonymous discussants can be much more demanding than anonymous referees.

NOTES

1. Some attempts were made to endogenize both the population growth rate, setting it in relation to the real wage rate and the growth rate of productivity. For a detailed account see Pomini (2003).
2. See Romer (1986, 1990), Lucas (1988), Barro (1990), Rebelo (1991), Mankiw, Romer and Weil (1992), Aghion and Howitt (1992, 1994, 1998), Grossman and Helpman (1991), etc.
3. For a critique on the use of 'knowledge' as a quantity, see Steedman (2003).
4. 'Now different agents or different classes of agents face different feasible action sets. This on its own can be expected to affect an economy's saving behaviour since different groups face different possibilities of transforming foregone into future consumption' (Hahn, 1994, p. 14).
5. Let us recall: complementarity between capital and labour using the CES production function with elasticity less than unity (Rowthorn, 1977); skill-based nature of technological change and the existence of complementarities between technology and human capital (Acemoglou, 1996); non-competitive labour markets in growth models where the propulsive factor is human capital; production externalities, where the scale factor depends on the number of the employed (Stadler, 1990); lower propensity to save of the unemployed, which reduces accumulation; adjustment costs which prevent the updating of old jobs to new technical standards (Aghion and Howitt, 1994; Goldin and Katz, 1996; Redding, 1996).

REFERENCES

Acemoglu, D. (1996), 'A microfoundation for social increasing returns in capital accumulation', *Quarterly Journal of Economics*, **111**, 779–804.

Aghion P. and P. Howitt (1992), 'A model of growth through creative destruction', *Econometrica*, **60**, 323–51.

Aghion P. and P. Howitt (1994), 'Growth and unemployment', *Review of Economic Studies*, **61**(3).

Aghion P. and P. Howitt (1998), *Endogenous Growth Theory*, Cambridge, Mass. and London: MIT Press.

Alesina A. and D. Rodrik (1994), 'Distributive policies and economic growth', *Quarterly Journal of Economics*, **109**(2), 465–90.

Barro, R. (1990), 'Government spending in a simple model of endogenous growth', *Journal of Political Economy*, **98**, S103–S125.

Bertola, G. (1990), 'Job security, employment and wages', *European Economic Review*, **34**, 851–86.

Bertola, G. (1993), 'Factor shares and savings in endogenous growth', *American Economic Review*, **83**, 1184–98.

Bertola, G. (1994), 'Flexible investment and growth', *Journal of Monetary Economics and Growth*, **38**, 215–38.

Bertola G. (1996), 'Factor shares in OLG models of growth', *European Economic Review*, **40**(8), 1541–60.

Boyer, R. (1988), 'Technical change and the theory of "regulation"', in G. Dosi, C. Freeman, R.R. Nelson, G. Silverberg and L. Soete (eds), *Technical Change and Economic Theory*, London: Pinter.

Boyer R. (1997), 'Why does employment differ in the course of time and across nations? An institutional answer in the light of the "regulation" theory', *Metroeconomica*.

Daveri, F. and G. Tabellini (1997), 'Unemployment, growth, and taxation in industrial countries', Discussion Papers del Dipartimento di Scienze Economiche, 9, Brescia.

De Groot H. (2001), 'Unemployment, growth and trade unions', *Growth and Change*, **32**, 69–91.

Calvó-Armengol, A. and M. Jackson (2003), 'Networks in labor markets: wage and employment dynamics and nequality', mimeo.

Domar, E.D. (1946), 'Capital expansion, rate of growth and employment', *Econometrica*, **14**, 137–47.

Duranton, G. (2000), 'Growth and imperfect competition on factor markets: increasing returns and distribution', *European Economic Review*, **44**(2), 255–80.

Goldin, C. and L.F. Katz (1996), 'Technology, skill and the wage structure: insights from the past', *American Economic Review*, **86**(2), May.

Gordon R. (1997), 'Is there a trade-off between unemployment and productivity growth', in D.J. Snower and G. de la Dehesa (eds), *Unemployment Policy: Government Options for the Labour Market*, Cambridge: Cambridge University Press.

Grossman, G.M. and E. Helpman (1991), *Innovation and Growth in the Global Economy*, Cambridge, Mass.: MIT Press.

Hahn, F. (1994), 'On growth theory', *Quaderni del Dipartimento di Economia Politica*, no. 167, Siena.

Harrod, R. F. (1939), 'An essay in dynamic theory', *Economic Journal*, **49**(193), 14–33.

Kaldor, N. (1955–56), 'Alternative theories of distribution', *Review of Economic Studies*, **23**(2), 83–100.

Kurz, H.D. and N. Salvadori (1998), '"Endogenous" growth models and the "classical" tradition', in H.D. Kurz and N. Salvadori (eds), *Understanding 'Classical' Economics. Studies in the Long-Period Theory*, London and New York: Routledge, pp. 66–89.

Kurz, H.D. and N. Salvadori (1999), 'Theories of "endogenous" growth in historical perspective', in M.R. Sertel (ed.), *Contemporary Economic Issues. Proceedings of* the Eleventh World Congress of the International Economic Association, Tunis, vol. 4: 'Economic Behaviour and Design', London: Macmillan, pp. 225–61.

Kurz, H.D. and N. Salvadori (2003), 'Theories of economic growth: old and new', in N. Salvadori (ed.) *The Theory of Economic Growth: A 'Classical' Perspective,* Cheltenham, UK and Northampton, MA, USA: Edward Elgar, pp. 1–22.

Layard R., S. Nickel and R. Jackman (1991), *Unemployment; Macroeconomic Performance and the Labour Market,* Oxford: Oxford University Press.

Lingens, J. (2002), 'The effects of unions in a simple endogenous growth model', University of Kassell Working Paper, February.

Lucas, R. (1988), 'On the mechanics of economic development', *Journal of Monetary Economics,* **22**, 3–42.

Mankiw G.N., D. Romer and D.N. Weil (1992), 'A contribution to the empirics of economic growth', *Quarterly Journal of Economics,* **107**, 407–37.

Nickel, S. (1997), 'Unemployment and labour market rigidities: Europe versus North America', *Journal of Economic Perspective,* 55–74.

Palokangas, T. (2003), 'Labour market regulation, productivity-improving R&D and endogenous growth', IZA Discussion Paper No. 720.

Parreño, J.M.R. and F. Sánchez-Losado (1999), 'The role of unions in an endogenous growth model with human capital', Universitat de Barcelona, Divisio de Ciencies Juridiques, Economiques i Socials, Documents de Treball 57.

Persson, T. and G. Tabellini (1992), 'Growth, distribution and politics', *European Economic Review,* **36**, 593–602.

Pomini, M. (2003), 'Endogenous growth theory as a Lakatosian case study', in N. Salvadori (ed.), *The Theory of Economic Growth: A 'Classical' Perspective,* Cheltenham, UK and Northampton, MA, USA: Edward Elgar, pp. 42–59.

Rebelo, S.T. (1991), 'Long-run policy analysis and long-run growth', *Journal of Political Economy,* **99**, 500–521.

Redding, S. (1996), 'The low-skill, low-quality trap: strategic complementarities between human capital and R&D', *Economic Journal,* **106**, 458–70.

Ricardo, D. (1951 ssq.), *The Works and Correspondence of David Ricardo,* 11 volumes, edited by P. Sraffa in collaboration with M.H. Dobb, Cambridge: Cambridge University Press. In the text referred to as *Works,* volume number and page number.

Romer, P. (1986), 'Increasing returns and long-run growth', *Journal of Political Economy,* **94**, 1002–37.

Romer, P. (1990), 'Endogenous technical change', *Journal of Political Economy,* **98**, S71–S102.

Rowthorn, R. (1977), 'Conflict, inflation and money', *Cambridge Journal of Economics,* 1, 215–39.

Rowthorn, R. (1996), 'Capital formation and unemployment', *Oxford Review of Economic Policy,* **11**, 26–39.

Salvadori N. (ed.) (2003), *The Theory of Economic Growth: A 'Classical' Perspective,* Cheltenham, UK and Northampton, MA, USA: Edward Elgar.

Smith, A. (1976), *An Inquiry into the Nature and Causes of the Wealth of Nations,* 1st edn 1776, Vol. II of *The Glasgow Edition of the Works and Correspondence of Adam Smith,* edited by R.H. Campbell, A.S. Skinner and W.B. Todd, Oxford:

Oxford University Press. In the text quoted as *WN*, book number, chapter number, section number, paragraph number.

Solow, R. (1956), 'A contribution to the theory of economic growth', *Quarterly Journal of Economics*, **70**, 65–94.

Stadler, G.W. (1990), 'Business cycle models with endogenous technology', *American Economic Review*, **80**.

Steedman. I. (2003), 'On 'measuring' knowledge in new (endogeneous) growth theory', in N. Salvadori (ed.), *Old and New Growth Theories: An Assessment*, Cheltenham, UK and Northampton, MA, USA: Edward Elgar, pp. 127–33.

Swan, T.W. (1956), 'Economic growth and capital accumulation', *Economic Record*, **32**, 334–61.

Tobin, J. (1955), 'A dynamic aggregative model', *Journal of Political Economy*, **63**, 103–115. Reprinted in J. Tobin, *Essays in Economics, Volume 1: Macroeconomics*, Chicago: Markham Publishing Company, 1971, pp. 115–32.

Uzawa, H. (1965), 'Optimal technical change in an aggregative model of economic growth', *International Economic Review*, **6**, 12–31.

Wapler, R. (2001), 'Unions, growth and unemployment', University of Tübingen, Discussion Paper No. 206, February.

You, J.I. and A.K. Dutt (1996), 'Government debt, income distribution and growth', *Cambridge Journal of Economics*, **20**, 335–51.

SECTION ONE

Human Capital and Innovation

1. Human capital, product market power and economic growth[*]

Alberto Bucci

1.1. INTRODUCTION

Although an important theoretical research line of the *research and development (R&D)-based* growth literature has already investigated whether or not the presence of imperfect competition in the product market may be growth-enhancing (we discuss this literature more fully later on in this section), such an analysis has not yet been conducted within an integrated economic growth model where agents (firms and individuals) may decide to invest respectively in innovation and education activities and the growth engine is investment in human capital.

This chapter aims to combine in the simplest possible way the basic Lucas (1988) model of human capital accumulation with (a version of) the Grossman and Helpman model of endogenous technical change without knowledge spillovers (1991, Ch. 3, pp. 43–57) in order to fill this significant gap in the literature. The reason why we focus on the version of the Grossman and Helpman model without knowledge spillovers is that we are interested in studying the link between product market competition and economic growth within an economy where the lever to economic development is investment in formal education, and not R&D activity.

Apart from introducing explicitly human capital accumulation *à la* Lucas, the structure of our model economy is similar to that of the basic Grossman and Helpman approach (1991, Ch. 3). In more detail, we assume that there exist three vertically integrated sectors. A competitive final output sector produces a homogeneous consumer good. Depending on the value of a crucial parameter (the share of total income being devoted to the purchase of the available capital good varieties), the final output sector technology may employ (with constant returns to scale) either solely human capital, or solely the existing varieties of intermediates or both as inputs. The intermediate goods sector consists of monopolistically competitive firms, each producing a differentiated variety. With respect to this sector we make the following two assumptions. First of all we postulate that the production of (whatever variety of) intermediate goods requires only human capital. Secondly, we stick to the first-generation innovation-based growth theory and continue to assume that there exists no strategic interaction on the intermediate inputs market. The latter hypothesis, while probably being unrealistic, has the advantage of allowing us to study how the aggregate economic growth rate may respond to changes in the intensity of product market power in Grossman and Helpman's basic contribution (1991, Ch. 3) with human (rather than knowledge) capital accumulation as the sole engine of growth.[1] Finally, research activity produces designs (or blueprints) for new intermediate input varieties by employing only human capital. When a new blueprint is discovered in the competitive R&D sector, an intermediate good producer acquires the perpetual patent over it. This allows the intermediate firm to manufacture the new variety and practice monopoly pricing forever. Population is stationary and a representative household invests portions of its fixed-time endowment to acquire formal education.

In the model the skills being produced in the education sector are generic (and not sector/firm-specific) in nature and, as a consequence, they can be employed to manufacture with the same productivity level a consumers' final output, capital goods and infinitely lived patents, respectively. Given that human capital is (at the sectoral level) a homogeneous input, it is also perfectly mobile across activities and in equilibrium it accrues the same wage rate, irrespective of the sector where it is actually employed.

Our main conclusions are the following. First of all, we find that there always exists (except when the technology for the production of the homogeneous consumer good is linear in human capital) a positive relationship between product market power and aggregate productivity growth. Secondly, we obtain that both the *type of technology* being used in the final output sector (Cobb–Douglas versus CES) and the number of sectors/activities using simultaneously human capital (what we term *inter-sectoral competition for skills*[2]) do affect the relationship between aggregate productivity growth and monopoly power. Lastly, we also show that the *type of technology* being used in the final output sector and the intensity of the *inter-sectoral competition for human capital* also influence the level of the steady state growth rate.

This chapter is closely related to the recent neo-Schumpeterian (theoretical) literature on product market competition and growth. This strand of literature has been largely stimulated by the well-documented empirical finding (see Blundell, Griffith and Van Reenen, 1995; Nickell, 1996 and Nickell, Nicolitsas and Dryden, 1997, among others) that the correlation between product market competition (measured by different proxies[3]) and firm/industry level productivity growth is positive. In order to reconcile this evidence with the basic Schumpeterian growth paradigm of Aghion and Howitt (1992) (in their paper the relationship between product market competition and economic growth is unambiguously negative), this model has been extended along several lines. The main hypothesis introduced in Aghion, Dewatripont and Rey (1997, 1999) is that innovating firms do not necessarily maximize profits. Instead, it is assumed that in firms subject to agency problems between owners and managers, the latter may aim to preserve their private benefit of control over the firm, while at the same time minimizing (innovation) costs. In this framework, more product market competition may enhance growth since it can force managers to speed up the adoption of new technologies in order to avoid bankruptcy and the loss of control rights over the firm (this is the *disciplining effect of product market competition*). With respect to the basic Schumpeterian growth model, Aghion and Howitt (1996) relax the assumption that research and development activity is homogeneous. Instead, the authors explicitly consider them as two different (though complementary) activities. In more detail, it is postulated that the purpose of research consists in inventing a new (intermediate) product line, whereas it is the aim of development to translate the new idea into a workable plan for producing the new good. In the model product market competition is measured by the substitutability between old and new product lines. Hence, an increase in product market competition induces an increase in the adaptability of developers (the rate at which developers are able to switch from old to new product lines). This, in turn, has the effect of: a) reducing the cost of implementing a new successful invention; b) increasing the return from research; c) increasing the number of workers devoted to research and hence the aggregate growth rate (this is the *Lucas effect*). In Aghion, Harris and Vickers (1997) and Aghion, Harris, Howitt and Vickers (2001), a third way for reconciling the Schumpeterian approach with the evidence on growth and product market competition is envisaged. This consists in replacing the *leap-frogging* assumption of the basic Schumpeterian model (according to which incumbent innovators are systematically replaced by outside researchers) with a more gradualist *step-by-step* hypothesis (the firm actually being behind its industry technological leader has first to catch up with the leader before becoming a technological leader itself). The introduction of this hypothesis radically changes the results concerning the relationship between product market competition (as measured by either a greater elasticity of demand or as a switch from Cournot to Bertrand rivalry) and growth, that can now become inverse-U shaped. The intuition is as follows. When product market competition is low, an increase will induce firms to invest more efforts in R&D in order to acquire a lead over rivals and thereby obtain higher profits (this is the 'escape competition effect'). Hence, economic growth rises and its relationship with product market competition is positive. On the other hand, when product market competition is already tough, a further increase may lower innovation through the traditional 'Schumpeterian effect'. In this case more competition means less investment in R&D and a lower growth rate (the relationship between competition and growth becomes negative).

With respect to the second-generation Schumpeterian growth literature, in this chapter we consider a model where innovation is both deterministic and horizontal (such a context is clearly different from the basic Schumpeterian approach, which is taken as a benchmark in all the papers referred to above). Moreover, we analyse the relationship between product market competition and growth within a framework where the engine of growth is human (and not technological) capital accumulation. It is also to be stressed that it is outside the scope of this contribution to reconcile theory with the positive empirical relationship linking competition and growth. On the contrary, it is our objective here to analyse theoretically such a relationship under the explicit hypothesis that economic growth is driven by an engine different from R&D.

In two recent companion papers, Smulders and van de Klundert (1995) and van de Klundert and Smulders (1997) analyse the link between competition and growth using a model in which high-tech firms can rely on 'in-house R&D' in producing innovations and knowledge spillovers across firms in R&D are explicitly taken into account. In-house R&D means that '... each firm has to do its own research for the product it produces' (Smulders and van de Klundert, 1995, p. 150). Unlike these works, here we continue to hypothesize both that there exists an aggregate R&D sector that produces ideas for the benefit of the whole economy and that innovation generates no pecuniary externality at the aggregate level.

Finally, this chapter is also related to other strands of endogenous growth literature. Bucci (2003b) also develops an endogenous growth model that integrates purposive R&D activity with human capital accumulation and where the engine of growth is represented by the investment in schooling. The present chapter represents a generalization of Bucci (2003b). The generalization we propose here consists in writing the production technology in use in the downstream sector in such a way as to disentangle the (equilibrium) monopolistic mark-up set in the intermediate sector and the degree of returns to specialization.[4] Due to this generalization, in the present chapter we have the possibility of studying in detail, and within the same framework, the relationship between imperfect competition in the product market and economic growth as emerging from two different classes of endogenous growth models: a) Rebelo's model (1991) with human (instead of physical) capital accumulation (or 'AH model'), and b) Grossman and

Helpman's model (1991) of endogenous technological change without knowledge spillovers *and* human capital investment (or 'Lucas, Grossman and Helpman's model'). In other words, the model we present in this chapter enables us to analyse the potential implications (as for the equilibrium relationship between monopoly power and economic growth) of the seminal Rebelo (1991) and Grossman and Helpman (1991) models when a positive supply of skills is explicitly introduced and to compare such implications with those from Bucci (2003b).

The other paper that comes closest to ours is Bucci (2003a). The latter examines what happens to the market power–growth nexus within a model where there is no human capital accumulation (human capital is in fixed supply) and the engine of growth is the externality in the R&D activity. Unlike Bucci (2003a), in this chapter we take an importantly different view, by considering an economy where the lever to economic growth lies in the deliberate choice of investing in formal education by utility-maximizing agents.

The rest of the chapter is organized as follows. Section 1.2 introduces the basic model. In Section 1.3 we study its general equilibrium and examine its steady-state properties. In Section 1.4 we compute the equilibrium output growth rate of the economy and solve for the inter-sectoral distribution of human capital. Section 1.5 presents the results concerning the steady-state predictions of the model about the relationship between the type of production function employed in the downstream sector, the inter-sectoral competition for skills, product market power and economic growth in some special cases. Section 1.6 concludes.

1.2. THE MODEL ECONOMY

In this economy three vertically integrated sectors produce respectively a homogeneous consumer good, intermediate inputs (capital goods) and ideas. In order to produce the undifferentiated consumer good, an aggregate production function combines with constant returns to scale human capital and intermediate inputs. These are available, at time t, in n_t different varieties and are produced by employing only human capital. In the research sector, firms also use human capital to engage in innovation. Innovation consists in discovering new designs (or blueprints) for firms operating in the intermediate sector. The number of designs existing at a certain point in time coincides with the number of intermediate input varieties and represents the actual stock of *non-rival* knowledge capital available in the economy. Finally, unlike the traditional *R&D-based growth models*, we assume that the supply of human capital may grow over time. In this respect, and following the ground-breaking papers by Uzawa (1965) and Lucas (1988), we postulate the existence of a representative household that devotes part of its own fixed-time endowment to educational activities. Thus, in this economy human capital can be employed to produce consumer goods, intermediate inputs, ideas and new human capital. A complete description of each of these sectors follows.

1.2.1.   Final Output

In this sector atomistic producers engage in perfect competition. The technology to produce final goods (Y) is given by:

$$Y_t = FH_{Yt}^{1-\lambda} \left[\int_0^{n_t} (x_{jt})^{\alpha} dj \right]^{\frac{\lambda}{\alpha}}, \quad F > 0, \quad 0 \le \lambda \le 1, \quad 0 \le \frac{\lambda}{1+\lambda} < \alpha < 1. \quad (1.1)$$

As in Bucci (2003a), we have written the production technology in use in the downstream sector in such a way as to disentangle the (equilibrium) monopolistic mark-up set in the intermediate sector and the degree of returns from specialization.[5]

Another reason why we employ the production function of equation (1.1) is that this technology allows us to encompass as particular cases (and depending on the value of λ) two recent models of endogenous growth[6] (one of which is not *R&D-based*) that in their original version do not include human capital accumulation. With respect to these models in this chapter we are interested to study their potential implications (for the monopoly power-growth relationship) when a positive supply of skills is explicitly considered. As already mentioned, unlike Bucci (2003a), we take here a different view by looking at an economy where the lever to economic growth is human capital accumulation (and not the R&D externality).

According to equation (1.1), output at time t, Y_t, is obtained by combining, through a constant returns to scale technology, human capital, H_{Yt}, and n different varieties of intermediate inputs, each of which is employed in the quantity x_j, where α, λ and F are technological parameters. The latter (total factor productivity) is strictly positive, whereas λ is (not strictly) between zero and one. In a moment we shall see that the restriction on α ensures that in a symmetric equilibrium the instantaneous profit accruing to a generic intermediate producer at a given point in time is inversely related to the number of varieties existing at that date.

Since the industry is competitive, in equilibrium each variety of intermediates receives its own marginal product (in terms of the numeraire good, the final output):

$$p_{jt} = F\lambda H_{Yt}^{1-\lambda} \left[\int_0^{n_t} (x_{jt})^\alpha dj \right]^{\frac{\lambda}{\alpha}-1} (x_{jt})^{\alpha-1}.$$ (1.2)

In equation (1.2) p_{jt} is the inverse demand function faced, at time t, by the jth intermediate producer. As is common in the first generation *innovation-based* growth literature, without any strategic interaction between intermediate input producers (which we assume henceforth) the price-demand elasticity faced by each intermediate firm coincides with the elasticity of substitution between two generic varieties of capital goods and is equal to $1/(1-\alpha)$.

1.2.2. Intermediate Goods

In the intermediate sector, capital good producers engage in *monopolistic competition*. Each firm produces one (and only one) horizontally differentiated intermediate good and must purchase a patented design before producing its own specialized durable. Following Bucci (2003b), we continue to assume that each local intermediate monopolist has access to the same technology:

$$x_{jt} = Bh_{jt}, \quad \forall j \in (0, n_t), \quad B > 0.$$ (1.3)

This production function is characterized by constant returns to scale in the only input employed (human capital) and, accordingly, one unit of skills is able to produce (at each time) the same constant quantity of whatever variety. B measures the productivity of human capital employed in this sector. The jth intermediate firm maximizes (with respect to x_{jt}) its own instantaneous profit function under the (inverse) demand constraint (equation 1.2), and taking as given the human capital input wage rate. Under the assumption that in the intermediate sector there exists no strategic interaction among firms,[7] the resolution of this maximization program gives the optimal price set by the generic jth intermediate producer for one unit of its own output:

$$p_{jt} = \frac{1}{\alpha} \frac{w_{jt}}{B}.$$ (1.4)

From equations (1.4) and (1.2), the wage rate accruing at time t to one unit of human capital employed in the capital goods sector (w_{jt}) is equal to:

$$w_{jt} = FB\alpha\lambda H_{Yt}^{1-\lambda} \left[\int_0^{n_t} (x_{jt})^\alpha \, dj\right]^{\frac{\lambda}{\alpha}-1} (x_{jt})^{\alpha-1}. \qquad (1.4')$$

In a symmetric equilibrium (where $x_{jt} = x_t$, $\forall j \in (0, n_t)$), each local monopolist faces the same wage rate ($w_{jt} = w_t$, $\forall j \in (0, n_t)$) and equation (1.4) can be recast as:

$$p_{jt} = \frac{1}{\alpha}\frac{w_t}{B} = p_t, \qquad \forall j \in (0, n_t). \qquad (1.4'')$$

The hypothesis of symmetry is suggested by the way each variety of intermediates enters the final output technology and by the fact that all the capital good producers use the same production function (equation 1.3). Hence, when all intermediate firms are identical, they produce the same quantity (x_t), face the same wage rate accruing to intermediate human capital (w_{jt}) and fix the same price for one unit of their own output. This price is equal to a constant *mark-up* ($1/\alpha$) over the marginal cost (w_{jt}/B). In equilibrium the wage rate accruing to one unit of human capital employed in the intermediate sector (w_{jt}) will be the same (and equal to w_t) for all the sectors where this factor input is employed. This is due to the hypothesis that human capital is homogeneous in this model economy and is perfectly mobile across sectors.

Defining by $H_{jt} \equiv \int_0^{n_t} h_{jt} dj$ the total amount of human capital employed in the intermediate sector at time t, and under the assumption of symmetry among capital goods producers ($x_{jt} = x_t$, $\forall j \in (0, n_t)$), from equation (1.3) we obtain:

$$x_{jt} = \frac{BH_{jt}}{n_t} = x_t, \qquad \forall j \in (0, n_t). \qquad (1.5)$$

Finally, the instantaneous profit function of a generic jth intermediate firm will be:

$$\pi_{jt} = F\lambda(1-\alpha)H_{Yt}^{1-\lambda}(n_t)^{\frac{\lambda-\alpha}{\alpha}}\left(\frac{BH_{jt}}{n_t}\right)^\lambda = \pi_t, \qquad \forall j \in (0, n_t). \qquad (1.6)$$

Note that π is decreasing in n (the number of intermediate firms existing at time t) if and only if $\alpha > \lambda/1+\lambda$. This restriction (that we already introduced in equation 1.1) serves the purpose of guaranteeing that the intermediate sector is monopolistically competitive .

Equation (1.6) states that, just like x and p, so too the instantaneous profit is equal for each variety of intermediates in a symmetric equilibrium.

1.2.3. Research and Development

There are many competitive research firms undertaking R&D. These firms produce designs indexed by 0 through an upper bound $n \geq 0$ that measures the total stock of society's knowledge. Designs are patented and partially excludable, but non-rival and indispensable for capital goods production. With access to the available stock of knowledge n, research firms use human capital to develop new blueprints. The production of new designs is governed by:

$$\dot{n}_t = CH_{nt}, \qquad C > 0, \qquad (1.7)$$

where n_t denotes the number of capital goods varieties existing at time t, H_n is the total amount of human capital employed in the sector and C is the productivity of the research human capital input. The production function of new ideas in equation (1.7) coincides with that employed by Grossman and Helpman (1991) in their Chapter 3 growth model *without knowledge spillovers* (pp. 43–57). In their model such a specification of the R&D process implies the cessation of growth in the long run. In our model, instead, this cannot happen since in our economy the engine of growth is human capital accumulation. In this last sense the model we present here shares the same conclusions of many other works with purposive R&D and skill accumulation.[8]

As the research sector is competitive, imposing the zero profit condition amounts to setting:

$$\frac{1}{C} w_{nt} = V_{nt}, \qquad (1.8)$$

with:

$$V_{nt} = \int_t^\infty \exp\left[-\int_t^\tau r(s)\,ds\right] \pi_{j\tau}\,d\tau. \qquad (1.9)$$

In equations (1.8) and (1.9), w_n represents the wage rate accruing to one unit of human capital devoted to research; $r(\tau)$ is the instantaneous real rate of return on the consumers' asset holdings; π_j is the profit accruing to the jth intermediate producer (once the jth infinitely-lived patent has been acquired) and V_n is the market value of one unit of research output (the generic jth idea that allows the jth variety of capital goods to be produced). Note that V_n is equal to the discounted present value of the profit flow a local monopolist can potentially earn from t to infinity and coincides with the market value of the jth intermediate firm (in this economy there is a one-to-one relationship between the number of patents and the number of the producers of capital goods).

1.2.4. Households

Total output produced in this economy (Y) can be only consumed. Population is stationary and the available human capital is fully employed. For the sake of simplicity, we normalize the population size to one and postulate the existence of an infinitely-lived representative consumer with perfect foresight. This consumer owns, in the form of assets (a), all the firms operating in the economy and is endowed with one unit of time that he/she allocates (in the fraction u) to productive activities (research, capital goods and consumer goods manufacture), and (in the fraction $1 - u$) to non-productive activities (education). The representative consumer maximizes under constraint the discounted value of his/her lifetime utility:[9]

$$\underset{\{c_t, u_t, a_t, h_t\}_{t=0}^{\infty}}{Max} \quad U_0 \equiv \int_0^\infty e^{-\rho t} \log(c_t) dt \;, \tag{1.10}$$

s.t.:

$$\dot{a}_t = r_t a_t + w_t u_t h_t - c_t \tag{1.11}$$

$$\dot{h}_t = \delta(1 - u_t) h_t \;, \tag{1.12}$$

a_0, h_0 given.

The parameters ρ and δ are strictly positive.

The control variables of this problem are c_t and u_t, and a_t and h_t are the two state variables. Equation (1.10) is the intertemporal utility function; equation (1.11) is the budget constraint and equation (1.12) represents the human capital supply function.[10] The symbols used have the following meaning: ρ is the subjective discount rate; c denotes consumption of the homogeneous final good; w is the wage rate accruing to one unit of human capital[11] and δ is a parameter reflecting the productivity of the education technology. With μ_{1t} and μ_{2t} denoting respectively the shadow price of the consumer's asset holdings (a) and human capital stock (h), the first order conditions read as:

$$\frac{e^{-\rho t}}{c_t} = \mu_{1t} \tag{1.13}$$

$$\mu_{1t} = \mu_{2t} \frac{\delta}{w_t} \tag{1.14}$$

$$\mu_{1t} r_t = -\dot{\mu}_{1t} \tag{1.15}$$

$$\mu_{1t} w_t u_t + \mu_{2t} \delta (1 - u_t) = -\dot{\mu}_{2t} . \tag{1.16}$$

Conditions (1.13) through (1.16) must satisfy the constraints (1.11) and (1.12), together with the two transversality conditions:

$$\lim_{t \to \infty} \mu_{1t} a_t = 0 ; \qquad \lim_{t \to \infty} \mu_{2t} h_t = 0 .$$

This closes the description of our model economy.

1.3. GENERAL EQUILIBRIUM ANALYSIS AND THE STEADY STATE OF THE MODEL

In this section we solve for the general equilibrium of the model and characterize its steady state properties under the symmetry hypothesis $(x_{jt} = B \cdot H_{jt} / n_t = x_t, \ \forall j \in (0, n_t))$. To this aim, after defining by u^* the optimal fraction of skills devoted by the representative consumer to production,[12] the general equilibrium distribution of human capital between research, capital and consumer goods production can be obtained through solving simultaneously the following equations:

$$H_Y + H_j + H_n = u^* H , \qquad \forall t \tag{1.17}$$

$$w_j = w_n \tag{1.18a}$$

$$w_j = w_Y . \tag{1.18b}$$

Equation (1.17) is the resource constraint, stating that at any time t the sum of the human capital demand from each production activity must be equal to the total stock of productive human capital available at the same time. Equations (1.18a) and (1.18b) together state that, due to human capital mobility across sectors, in equilibrium the wage earned by one unit of human capital is to be the same irrespective of the sector where it is actually employed.

Moreover, since the total value of the representative agent's assets (a) must equal the total value of firms, the next equation also has to be checked in a symmetric equilibrium:

$$a = n V_n \tag{1.19}$$

where V_n is given by equation (1.9) above and satisfies the asset pricing condition:

$$\dot{V}_n = rV_n - \pi_j,$$ (1.19a)

with:

$$\pi_j = \frac{\lambda}{1-\lambda}(1-\alpha)\frac{H_Y w_Y}{n},$$ (1.19b)

and

$$w_Y = \frac{F(1-\lambda)}{H_Y^\lambda}n^{\frac{\lambda}{\alpha}}\left(\frac{BH_j}{n}\right)^\lambda.$$ (1.19c)

In the model one new idea allows a new intermediate firm to produce one new variety of capital goods. In other words, there exists a one-to-one relationship between the number of ideas, the number of capital good producers, and the number of intermediate input varieties. This explains why in equation (1.19) the total value of the consumer's assets (a) is equal to the number of profit-making intermediate firms (n) times the market value (V_n) of each of them (equal, in turn, to the market value of the corresponding idea). Equation (1.19a), instead, suggests that the interest on the value of the jth generic intermediate firm (rV_n) should be equal, in equilibrium, to the sum of two terms:

1. the instantaneous monopoly profit (π_j) coming from the production of the jth capital good;
2. the capital gain or loss matured on (V_n) during the time interval $dt(\dot{V}_n)$.

In order to characterize the steady-state equilibrium of the model presented so far, we start with a formal definition of it:

Definition: Steady State Equilibrium

A steady state equilibrium is an equilibrium where:

a) *the growth rate of all variables depending on time is constant;*
b) *the ratio (R) of human (H) to knowledge (n) capital is constant, and*
c) H_Y, H_j, H_n *all grow at the same constant rate as H.*

With this definition of steady state equilibrium in mind we note that, when g_H (the growth rate of H) is constant, then u is constant as well (see equation 1.12).[13] This means that in the steady state the household will optimally decide to devote a constant fraction of its own fixed-time endowment to work (u^*) and education ($1 - u^*$). Solving explicitly the representative consumer's problem, we obtain the following results:

$$r = \frac{\alpha\delta + \lambda(1-\alpha)(\delta-\rho)}{\alpha} ; \qquad (1.20)$$

$$g_{H_Y} = g_{H_j} = g_{H_n} = g_n = g_H = \delta - \rho ; \qquad (1.21)$$

$$g_c = g_a = (\delta - \rho)\left[\frac{\alpha + \lambda(1-\alpha)}{\alpha}\right] ; \qquad (1.22)$$

$$\frac{H_j}{n} = \frac{\alpha\delta}{C(1-\alpha)} ; \qquad (1.23)$$

$$\frac{H_Y}{n} = \frac{(1-\lambda)\delta}{\lambda C(1-\alpha)} ; \qquad (1.24)$$

$$u^* = \frac{\rho}{\delta} . \qquad (1.25)$$

According to result (1.20), the real interest rate (r) is constant. Equation (1.21) states that in the steady state equilibrium the number of new ideas (n), the consumer's total human capital stock (H) and the human capital stocks devoted respectively to the final output production (H_Y), to the intermediate sector (H_j) and to research (H_n) all grow at the same constant rate, given by the difference between the schooling technology productivity parameter (δ) and the subjective discount rate (ρ). Equation (1.22) gives the equilibrium growth rate of consumption and the consumer's asset holdings. Equations (1.23) and (1.24), instead, give respectively the equilibrium values of the constant H_j/n and H_Y/n ratios, whereas equation (1.25) represents the optimal and constant fraction of the representative agent's time-endowment that s/he will decide to devote to work (u^*). Since the term in square brackets in equation (1.22) is positive for each value of $\lambda \in [0;1]$ and $\alpha \in (0;1)$, the growth rate of the variables in equations (1.21) and (1.22) is positive if δ is strictly greater than ρ. The condition $\delta > \rho$ also assures that $0 < u^* < 1$. In words, the condition $\delta > \rho$ guarantees that in the steady state equilibrium: 1) the rate of human capital accumulation and (as we shall see in a moment) the aggregate output growth rate are both positive; 2) a positive fraction of the agent's time endowment is indeed devoted to work ($0 < u^* < 1$) and education ($0 < 1 - u^* < 1$).

1.4. ENDOGENOUS GROWTH AND THE SHARES OF HUMAN CAPITAL DEVOTED TO THE DIFFERENT ACTIVITIES

To compute the output growth rate of this economy in a symmetric, steady state equilibrium we first rewrite equation (1.1) as follows:

$$Y_t = FH_{Yt}^{1-\lambda} n_t^{\frac{\lambda}{\alpha}} \left(\frac{BH_{jt}}{n_t} \right)^{\lambda} = \Psi H_{Yt}^{1-\lambda} n_t^{\frac{\lambda}{\alpha}}, \quad \Psi \equiv F\left(\frac{BH_{jt}}{n_t} \right)^{\lambda}.$$

Then, taking logs of both sides of this expression, totally differentiating with respect to time and recalling that in the steady state equilibrium $g_{H_Y} = g_n = g_H = \delta - \rho$ (see equation (1.21) above), we obtain:

$$\frac{\dot{Y}_t}{Y_t} \equiv g_Y = g_c = g_a = \left[\frac{\alpha + \lambda(1-\alpha)}{\alpha} \right] g_H = [1 + \lambda(\beta-1)](\delta - \rho), \quad \beta \equiv \frac{1}{\alpha} > 1. \quad (1.1a)$$

Hence, economic growth depends only on α (the inverse of which can be easily interpreted as a measure of the monopoly power enjoyed by each intermediate local monopolist[14]), λ (which represents the share of total income being devoted in a symmetric equilibrium to the purchase of the available capital goods varieties[15]) and the accumulation rate of human capital (g_H). In this last respect the model supports the main conclusion of that branch of the endogenous growth literature pioneered by Uzawa (1965) and Lucas (1988).

In equation (1.1a), the term $\lambda(\beta-1)$ measures the *returns to specialization*. Such returns positively depend not only on β (the monopoly power), but also on λ. The intuition behind this result is as follows: the higher the mark-up rate that can be charged over the marginal cost in the monopolistic sector and the higher the share of national income spent on the intermediate inputs, the higher the return an intermediate producer may obtain from specializing in the production of the marginal variety of capital goods. Moreover, it is also worth pointing out that β enters the equilibrium growth rate when (and only when) λ is not equal to zero (that is when capital goods are an input in the production of the final good). The reason why it is so transpires when one recalls that the only product market where imperfect competition prevails in the model is the intermediate one.

Before computing the shares of human capital devoted to the different economic activities, we first need to determine an expression for the equilibrium human to technological capital ratio ($R \equiv H/n$). For this purpose, we use equation (1.17), with $u^* = \rho/\delta$, $H_j/n = \alpha\delta/(1-\alpha)C$ and $H_Y/n = (1-\lambda)\delta/\lambda C(1-\alpha)$, and obtain:

$$\frac{H_n}{n} = R\frac{\rho}{\delta} - \frac{\alpha\delta}{C(1-\alpha)} - \frac{(1-\lambda)\delta}{(1-\alpha)\lambda C},$$

which, in turn, implies:

$$g_n = C\frac{H_n}{n} = RC\frac{\rho}{\delta} - \frac{\alpha\delta}{(1-\alpha)} - \frac{(1-\lambda)\delta}{\lambda(1-\alpha)}. \tag{1.26}$$

Equating this last expression to equation (1.21) yields:

$$R \equiv \frac{H_t}{n_t} = \frac{\delta[\delta - \lambda\rho(1-\alpha)]}{\lambda\rho(1-\alpha)C}, \quad \forall t. \tag{1.27}$$

Given R, the shares of human capital devoted to each sector employing this factor input in the decentralized, symmetric, steady state equilibrium can be easily determined as follows:

$$s_j \equiv \frac{H_j}{H} = \frac{H_j}{n}\frac{n}{H} = \frac{H_j}{nR} = \frac{\alpha\lambda\rho}{\delta - \lambda\rho(1-\alpha)}; \tag{1.28}$$

$$s_Y \equiv \frac{H_Y}{H} = \frac{H_Y}{n}\frac{n}{H} = \frac{H_Y}{nR} = \frac{\rho(1-\lambda)}{\delta - \lambda\rho(1-\alpha)}; \tag{1.29}$$

$$s_n \equiv \frac{H_n}{H} = \frac{H_n}{n}\frac{n}{H} = \frac{H_n}{nR} = \frac{\lambda\rho(\delta - \rho)(1-\alpha)}{\delta[\delta - \lambda\rho(1-\alpha)]}; \tag{1.30}$$

$$s_H \equiv \frac{H_H}{H} = 1 - u^* = \frac{\delta - \rho}{\delta}. \tag{1.31}$$

Thus, the shares of human capital devoted to each activity depend on the technological (λ and δ) and preference (ρ) parameters and also on the degree of competition in the capital goods sector (α).[16]

Innovation, unemployment and policy

1.5. TECHNOLOGY, SECTORAL DISTRIBUTION OF HUMAN CAPITAL AND THE INTERPLAY BETWEEN PRODUCT MARKET POWER AND ECONOMIC GROWTH

All the results stated up to now have been obtained under the assumption that δ is strictly greater than ρ. As already mentioned, this assumption guarantees that in the steady state equilibrium the growth rate of the main variables of the model is positive. In the present section, while continuing to keep this assumption, we study how the sectoral shares of human capital and the relationship between product market power and economic growth may change when λ is assumed to be respectively equal to zero, one and α (that is, when we allow the production function in the downstream sector to change).

Case (a): $\lambda = 0$
In this case the technologies adopted in each economic sector (in the symmetric, steady state equilibrium) are:

$$Y_t = AH_t, \qquad A \equiv \frac{F\rho}{\delta} \qquad \text{(for final goods production);}$$

$$x_{jt} = Bh_{jt}, \qquad \forall j(0, n_t) \qquad \text{(for capital goods production);}$$

$$\dot{n}_t = CH_{nt} \qquad \text{(for research);}$$

$$\dot{h}_t = (\delta - \rho)h_t \qquad \text{(for human capital supply).}$$

Accordingly, when $\lambda = 0$ the model we are dealing with is the *AH*-model. The main variables of the model take on the following values:

$$s_j = 0; \quad s_Y = \frac{\rho}{\delta}; \quad s_n = 0; \quad s_H = \frac{\delta - \rho}{\delta}; \quad r = \delta;$$

$$g_{H_Y} = g_{H_j} = g_{H_n} = g_n = g_H = g_c = g_a = g_Y = \delta - \rho. \qquad (1.32)$$

As is well known, both in Rebelo (1991) and Lucas (1988) technical progress occurs through devoting resources to physical (human) capital accumulation rather than a deliberate R&D activity aimed at expanding the set of available (horizontally differentiated) capital goods. In the case under analysis this is reflected in the fact that the intermediate inputs do not enter the final goods production technology and $s_j = s_n = 0$. Thus, all the human capital is distributed between the final output (s_Y) and education (s_H)

sectors. Since capital goods are not productive inputs, market power $(1/\alpha)$, which in the model outlined in the previous sections arises from the intermediate sector, does not play any role on the growth rate of output (g_Y). As in Lucas (1988), the latter coincides with the growth rate of human capital and is equal to the difference between the productivity of the schooling technology $(\delta = r)$ and the subjective discount rate (ρ).[17] Finally, it is worth noting that in the steady state equilibrium (when each sector gets a constant fraction of the available stock of human capital) s_Y affects only the level of output $(Y_t = F s_Y H_t)$, whereas its growth rate is solely driven by s_H $(g_Y = \delta s_H)$.

Case (b): $\lambda = 1$
When $\lambda = 1$ the technologies employed in each economic sector (in the symmetric, steady state equilibrium) can be recast as:

$$Y_t = F \left[\int_0^{n_t} (x_{jt})^\alpha dj \right]^{\frac{1}{\alpha}}, \qquad \text{(for final goods production)};$$

$$x_{jt} = B h_{jt}, \qquad \forall j(0, n_t) \qquad \text{(for capital goods production)};$$

$$\dot{n}_t = C H_{nt} \qquad \text{(for research)};$$

$$\dot{h}_t = (\delta - \rho) h_t \qquad \text{(for human capital supply)}.$$

Accordingly, when $\lambda = 1$ the model we deal with is that of Lucas, Grossman and Helpman. The main variables of the model now take on the following values:

$$s_j = \frac{\alpha\rho}{\delta - \rho(1-\alpha)}; \qquad s_Y = 0; \qquad s_n = \frac{\rho(1-\alpha)(\delta - \rho)}{\delta[\delta - \rho(1-\alpha)]};$$

$$s_H = \frac{\delta - \rho}{\delta}; \qquad r = \frac{\alpha\delta + (1-\alpha)(\delta - \rho)}{\alpha}; \qquad g_{H_Y} = g_{H_j} = g_{H_n} = g_n = g_H = \delta - \rho;$$

$$g_c = g_a = g_Y = \frac{\delta - \rho}{\alpha} \qquad (1.33)$$

In this case human capital enters only indirectly (through the capital goods) the final output technology, whereas it continues to be employed in all the remaining sectors ($s_Y = 0$ and s_j, s_n and s_H are all positive). As in the previous case, the accumulation rate of human capital is equal in equilibrium to $\delta - \rho$, but now the growth rate of output (g_Y) depends positively on the mark-up rate $(1/\alpha)$. The reason is that in the present case g_Y is a function not only of s_H, but also of s_n:

$$g_Y = \frac{(1-\alpha)\rho\delta s_n}{\rho(1-\alpha) - \delta s_n} + \delta s_H,$$

and it is easy to show that $\partial s_n/\partial(1/\alpha) > 0$ and $\partial g_Y/\partial s_n > 0$. In other words, in this particular case it is through allocating a higher share of human capital from the intermediate sector $(\partial s_j/\partial(1/\alpha) < 0)$ towards the research sector that monopoly power positively affects aggregate economic growth.

Case (c): $\lambda = \alpha$
The last special case we wish to deal with in this section is the case where $\lambda = \alpha$.[18] Under this assumption the technologies adopted in each economic sector (in the symmetric, steady state equilibrium) become:

$$Y_t = FH_{Yt}^{1-\alpha} \int_0^{n_t} (x_{jt})^\alpha dj,\qquad \text{(for final goods production)};$$

$$x_{jt} = Bh_{jt},\qquad \forall j(0, n_t)\qquad \text{(for capital goods production)};$$

$$\dot{n}_t = CH_{nt}\qquad \text{(for research)};$$

$$\dot{h}_t = (\delta - \rho)h_t\qquad \text{(for human capital supply)}.$$

The main variables of the model take on the following values:

$$s_j = \frac{\alpha^2\rho}{\delta - \alpha\rho(1-\alpha)};\quad s_Y = \frac{\rho(1-\alpha)}{\delta - \alpha\rho(1-\alpha)};\quad s_n = \frac{\alpha\rho(1-\alpha)(\delta-\rho)}{\delta[\delta - \alpha\rho(1-\alpha)]};$$

$$s_H = \frac{\delta-\rho}{\delta};\quad r = \delta(2-\alpha) - \rho(1-\alpha);\quad g_{H_Y} = g_{H_j} = g_{H_n} = g_n = g_H = \delta - \rho;$$

$$g_c = g_a = g_Y = (2-\alpha)(\delta-\rho)\qquad\qquad\qquad (1.34)$$

In the present case human capital is employed in each economic sector. Thus, we can identify this case (unlike the two previous ones) as that where the inter-sectoral competition for human capital is tougher $(s_j, s_Y, s_n$ and s_H are all positive). As before, the accumulation rate of human capital is equal in equilibrium to $\delta - \rho$, but now (unlike case b) the relationship between s_n and $1/\alpha$ is non-monotonic and the growth rate of output (g_Y) is a positive and non-linear (concave) function of the mark-up rate $(1/\alpha)$.

The main results of the model concerning the relationship between the shape of the production technology in use in the downstream sector, the sectoral distribution of human capital, the degree of product market power and the aggregate economic growth rate can be summarized as follows.

Result 1: *Within a generalized growth model of deterministic and horizontal R&D where economic growth is sustained by a supply function of skills à la Lucas (1988), as that described by the steady state equilibrium equations (1.20) through (1.31) and (1.1a), there always exists (except when $\lambda = 0$) a positive relationship between product market power $(1/\alpha)$ and aggregate economic growth (g_Y).*

Proof: *See equations (1.1a), (1.32), (1.33) and (1.34).*

The reason why there exists no relationship between market power and growth when $\lambda = 0$ is that in this case there is neither an intermediate sector, nor a research one (accordingly, the output growth rate is completely independent of the mark-up that in the model arises from the capital goods sector).

We consider this result extremely interesting since it suggests that, as regards the steady state equilibrium relationship between the degree of product market power and aggregate economic growth, we can replicate one of the most important conclusions obtained in the basic neo-Schumpeterian model[19] by using a horizontal product differentiation approach where: 1) human and technological capital may grow at the same constant and positive rate; 2) the engine of growth is human capital accumulation, and 3) there exists no pecuniary externality from purposive R&D activity.

Result 2: *Within a generalized growth model of deterministic and horizontal R&D where economic growth is sustained by a supply function of skills à la Lucas (1988), as that described by the steady state equilibrium equations (1.20) through (1.31) and (1.1a), both the type of technology being used in the final output sector and the intensity of the inter-sectoral competition for the (growing) human capital affect the shape of the relationship between aggregate economic growth (g_Y) and the monopoly power $(1/\alpha)$.*

Indeed, such a relationship is linear in the Lucas–Grossman and Helpman model (case b) – where human capital is not directly employed in the final output sector, whose technology is of the CES type – and concave in case (c), where human capital is used everywhere and the final output technology is (an extension of) Cobb–Douglas. Similar results can be obtained using a model where the growth engine is R&D and there is no human capital accumulation (see Results 1 and 2 in Bucci, 2003a).

Result 3: *Within a generalized growth model of deterministic and horizontal R&D where economic growth is sustained by a supply function of skills à la Lucas (1988), as that described by the steady state equilibrium equations (1.20) through (1.31) and (1.1a), both the type of technology being used in the final output sector and the intensity of the inter-sectoral competition for the (growing) human capital affect the steady state equilibrium growth rate. The latter is higher whenever the final output technology is CES and does not employ human capital.*

Proof: *From equations (1.32), (1.33) and (1.34) one easily concludes that:*
$g_Y (case\ b) > g_Y (case\ c) > g_Y (case\ a).$

This result parallels Results 3 and 4 of Bucci (2003a). Therefore, even when human capital is allowed to grow over time, the highest possible steady state economic growth rate is obtained within a *Grossman and Helpman-type economy*. On the contrary, the lowest steady state economic growth rate prevails in an *AH-type economy*, where the final output technology is linear in human capital input and all the existing markets (final output and education) are perfectly competitive.

1.6. CONCLUDING REMARKS

In this article we presented a generalization of Bucci (2003b). The generalization we proposed consisted in writing the production technology in use in the downstream sector in such a way as to disentangle the (equilibrium) monopolistic mark-up set in the intermediate sector and the degree of returns to specialization. Depending on the value of a specific parameter (the share of total income being devoted to the purchase of the available capital good varieties), we were able to study the relationship between product market power and economic growth as it emerges from two different classes of endogenous growth models: a) Rebelo's model (1991) with human (instead of physical) capital accumulation, and b) Grossman and Helpman's model (1991, Ch. 3) of endogenous technological change without knowledge spillovers *and* human capital investment. At the same time, the proposed generalization allowed us to encompass the model of Bucci (2003b) as a special case and to analyse the impact that both the kind of technology in use in the downstream sector and the degree of *inter-sectoral competition for the (growing) human capital* have on the market power/economic growth nexus and the level of the steady state equilibrium growth rate in the presence of human capital accumulation, the growth engine. In this last respect, we compared our results with those obtained in Bucci (2003a), where human capital is in fixed supply and economic growth is driven solely by the positive externality from the R&D activity.

Our main findings were threefold. First of all, we found that the presence of more intense product market power within the sector producing capital goods turns out to have always-positive growth effects (except when the share of national income spent on the purchase of capital goods is exactly equal to zero). This confirms one of the results found by Bucci (2003b), according to which it is possible to restore the *Schumpeterian growth paradigm* provided that: 1) human capital accumulation (*à la* Lucas) is the engine of growth; 2) there exists no pecuniary externality from purposive R&D activity, and 3) human and technological capital may grow at the same constant and positive rate in the steady state equilibrium. Secondly, we obtained that, though positive, the relationship linking product market power and economic growth may be linear or concave depending on the type of technology employed in the final output sector (CES versus Cobb–Douglas) and the way human capital is distributed across sectors (whether this factor input is employed in every economic activity or not). Finally, we showed that these two elements (the type of technology in use in the final output sector and the intensity of the inter-sectoral competition for human capital) are also able to affect the level of the steady state growth rate. This is higher within a *Grossman–Helpman–Lucas-type* economy where the final output technology is CES and does not employ human capital directly.

Our findings depend on the hypothesis (common to all the first-generation innovation-based growth models) that there exists no strategic interaction among rivals on goods and factor markets. In the future it could be interesting to analyse how, within the framework proposed in this chapter, the market power–growth relationship might change when one explicitly allows for the presence of some kind of interaction among firms.

NOTES

* I am extremely indebted to N. Meccheri and C. Parello for having carefully read and commented on a previous draft of this paper. I also thank, without implicating, G. Bognetti, R. Boucekkine, D. Checchi, D. de la Croix, M. Florio, O. Garavello, A. Missale, J. Ruiz and C. Saglam for very insightful discussions.

1. In the third chapter of their 1991 book, Grossman and Helpman rule out the possibility of strategic interaction among firms producing intermediate inputs. In the present chapter (Section 1.5, case b) we shall analyse the relationship between product market power and

growth when the underlying model is Grossman and Helpman's, with investment in human capital sustaining economic growth in the long run.

2. The higher this number, the tougher the inter-sectoral competition for human capital.

3. In Nickell (1996), for example, product market competition is measured by increased number of competitors in the same industry or by lower levels of rents accruing to firms operating in the same sector. Other indicators of product market competition used in empirical studies include manager-based assessments, profit and industry concentration measures and firms' market shares.

4. This point is made clear by Benassy (1998, p. 63), according to whom the degree of returns to specialisation '... measures the degree to which society benefits from specialising production between a larger number of intermediates n'.

5. Indeed, in a moment we will show that (under additional assumptions) the mark-up charged over the marginal cost by the monopolistic producers of intermediate inputs is $1/\alpha$. At the same time, from equation (1.1), it is possible to see that in a symmetric equilibrium (in which the total production of intermediates, X, is spread evenly between the n brands) the degree of returns to specialization (the exponent of n) is equal to $\lambda(1/\alpha - 1)$. This is clearly different from the monopoly power measure $(1/\alpha)$ and, more importantly, depends not only on α but also on λ. It is in this specific sense that the model we present here represents an extension of Bucci (2003b).

6. Namely Rebelo's (1991) and Grossman and Helpman's (1991, Ch. 3, pp. 43–57) models.

7. Namely, that

$$\frac{\partial}{\partial x_{jt}} \int_0^{n_t} x_{jt}^\alpha \, dj = 0 \,.$$

8. Notably Arnold (1998) and Blackburn, Hung and Pozzolo (2000).

9. Following Grossman and Helpman (1991) we assume that the instantaneous utility function of the representative agent is logarithmic. Using a more general isoelastic function does not alter the main results of this chapter.

10. We assume no depreciation for human capital. This hypothesis is completely harmless in the present context and serves the purpose of simplifying the analysis.

11. The equilibrium wage rate accruing to human capital is unique since this factor input is perfectly mobile across sectors.

12. u^* is endogenous in the model and, as such, has to be determined.

13. Given our assumptions on the size of the representative household and the population growth rate, we can easily conclude that $h \equiv H$ (which implies that we can use g_H instead of g_h).

14. The higher the value of α, the higher the elasticity of substitution between two generic intermediate inputs. This means that they become more and more alike when α grows and, as a consequence, the price elasticity of the derived demand curve faced by a local monopolist tends to be infinitely large when α tends to one. Thus, the inverse of $\alpha(1/\alpha)$ can be considered as a measure of how uncompetitive the capital goods sector is (see Aghion and Howitt, 1997, p. 284).

15. Where

$$\lambda \equiv \frac{\int_0^{n_t} (p_{jt} \cdot x_{jt}) \, dj}{Y_t} \,,$$

with $p_{jt} = p_t$ and $x_{jt} = x_t$, $\forall j \in (0; n_t)$.

16. It is outside the scope of this work to discuss the way these four variables (respectively λ, δ, ρ and α) may influence the across-sectors distribution of human capital.

17. See Barro and Sala-I-Martin (1995, p. 184, eq. 5.29). In our case the elasticity of intertemporal substitution equals one.
18. This is the only case considered in Bucci (2003b) where the mark-up rate and the returns to specialization are not disentangled (they both depend exclusively on α in a symmetric, steady state equilibrium).
19. Namely, Aghion and Howitt (1992).

REFERENCES

Aghion, P. and P. Howitt (1992), 'A model of growth through creative destruction', *Econometrica*, **60**(2), 323–51.
Aghion, P. and P. Howitt (1996), 'Research and development in the growth process', *Journal of Economic Growth*, **1**(1), 49–73.
Aghion, P. and P. Howitt (1997), 'A Schumpeterian perspective on growth and competition', in D.M. Kreps and K.F. Wallis (eds), *Advances in Economics and Econometrics: Theory and Applications*, Vol. II, Cambridge, UK: Cambridge University Press, pp. 279–317.
Aghion, P., M. Dewatripont and P. Rey (1997), 'Corporate governance, competition policy and industrial policy', *European Economic Review*, **41**(3–5), 797–805.
Aghion, P., M. Dewatripont and P. Rey (1999), 'Competition, financial discipline, and growth', *Review of Economic Studies*, **66**(4), 825–52.
Aghion, P., C. Harris and J. Vickers (1997), 'Competition and growth with step-by-step innovation: an example', *European Economic Review*, **41**(3–5), 771–82.
Aghion, P., C. Harris, P. Howitt and J. Vickers (2001), 'Competition, imitation and growth with step-by-step innovation', *Review of Economic Studies*, **68**(3), 467–92.
Arnold, L.G. (1998), 'Growth, welfare, and trade in an integrated model of human capital accumulation and R&D', *Journal of Macroeconomics*, **20**(1), 81–105.
Barro, R.J. and X. Sala-I-Martin (1995), *Economic Growth*, New York: McGraw-Hill.
Benassy, J.P. (1998), 'Is there always too little research in endogenous growth with expanding product variety?', *European Economic Review*, **42**(1), 61–9.
Blackburn, K., V.T.Y. Hung and A.F. Pozzolo (2000), 'Research, development and human capital accumulation', *Journal of Macroeconomics*, **22**(2), 189–206.
Blundell, R., R. Griffith and J. Van Reenen (1995), 'Dynamic count data models of technological innovation', *Economic Journal*, **105**, 333–44.
Bucci, A. (2003a), 'Horizontal innovation, market power and growth', *International Economic Journal*, **17**(1), 57–82.
Bucci, A. (2003b), 'When Romer meets Lucas: on human capital, imperfect competition and growth', in N. Salvadori (ed.), *Old and New Growth Theories: An Assessment*, Cheltenham, UK and Northampton, MA, USA: Edward Elgar, pp. 261–85.
Grossman, G.M. and E. Helpman (1991), *Innovation and Growth in the Global Economy*, Cambridge, Mass.: MIT Press.
Lucas, R.E. (1988), 'On the mechanics of economic development', *Journal of Monetary Economics*, **22**(1), 3–42.

Nickell, S.J. (1996), 'Competition and corporate performance', *Journal of Political Economy*, **104**, 724–46.

Nickell, S.J., D. Nicolitsas and N. Dryden (1997), 'What makes firms perform well?', *European Economic Review*, **41**, 783–96.

Rebelo, S. (1991), 'Long-run policy analysis and long-run growth', *Journal of Political Economy*, **99**(3), 500–521.

Smulders, S. and T. van de Klundert (1995), 'Imperfect competition, concentration and growth with firm-specific R&D', *European Economic Review*, **39**(1), 139–60.

Uzawa, H. (1965), 'Optimum technical change in an aggregative model of economic growth', *International Economic Review*, **6**, 18–31.

van de Klundert, T. and S. Smulders (1997), 'Growth, competition and welfare', *Scandinavian Journal of Economics*, **99**(1), 99–118.

2. Scientific research, externalities and economic growth

Maria Rosaria Carillo and Erasmo Papagni

2.1. INTRODUCTION

Study of the causes of economic growth since the industrial revolution has highlighted the importance of technological development. This interpretation of long-period growth has come to the fore in the applied literature, and recently also in the theoretical literature which recasts Schumpeter's theories of the first half of the 20th century. On closer inspection, however, this interpretation is incomplete because it fails to consider the origin of technological advancement, namely the progress of science. Historians and scholars of science, in fact, stress the concomitance between the appearance of important scientific discoveries and the transition from a period of slow productivity growth to that of exponential expansion which led up to the contemporary age.

The alliance between basic research, technology and growth has been particularly close and fruitful since the 19th century. Rosenberg and Birdzell (1986, 1990) argue that the economic miracle of the Western world can be explained by the marked increase in science's ability to investigate the secrets of nature. This greater efficiency of basic research was initially due to important changes in its organization and closer interaction with the rest of society and with the economy.

In this chapter we put forward an analytical approach to economic growth which seeks to capture the essential features of the interaction between the work of the scientific community and long-period economic activity.

The traditional theory of growth, which originated with Solow (1956), considers the academic world to be exogenous with respect to the economy. As in the case of other public goods, the production of knowledge is the task of the state. Exceptions in this theoretical tradition are the works of Karl Shell (1967, 1973) in which the production of knowledge is endogenous. In this model, the state collects resources from the activities of private agents in order to finance basic research, which is the public input to the private sector.

The economic problem analysed by Shell is essentially that of the dynamic allocation of resources between the production of goods and the production of knowledge.

With the advent of 'endogenous growth theory' – the new scientific paradigm for the analysis of growth – innovation has become a central topic of inquiry. The works of Romer (1990), Aghion and Howitt (1992), and Grossman and Helpman (1991) have generated a rich Schumpeterian strand in growth theory which draws heavily on the microeconomic literature on industrial innovation in which innovative firms get a patent that prevents others from profiting from new knowledge. However, these models do not investigate the sector of basic research taking account of the peculiar features that distinguish the world of science with respect to that of technology. This is also the case of growth models with general purpose technology in which radical changes in technologies improve production possibilities in a wide range of sectors. It is quite plausible to admit that these changes should certainly be associated with scientific advances which alter the constraints to which technologies are subject.

The model analysed in this chapter represents the working of an economy which consists of agents who may choose to work either in the goods production sector or in scientific research. These two economic activities are organized according to different objectives and rules. Research is financed by the state out of taxes, and its output is a public good that benefits all firms and improves their productivity. Researchers are engaged in competition with other researchers for a new discovery. The probability of a new finding being made by a researcher is a function of his/her effort, and his/her interactions with other researchers. The latter effect takes account of the strong presence of externalities in the sector of basic research. The real prize for the winner of a race in a scientific field comes from resources collected by the state from real income in the goods sector. This prize lasts until a new discovery appears since scientists who win a race cannot 'rest on their laurels' because science proceeds and new findings may make the previous discovery obsolete.

The model builds upon the analysis of Shell (1967) by considering races among scientists in which effort is endogenously determined and by making researchers' work affected by positive externalities. The model innovates with respect to existing Schumpeterian literature in several respects. First, it shows how instantaneous externalities may make a no-growth trap more likely. Second, consideration of effort distinct from research employment provides a richer picture of innovation and growth since we can show that a no-growth trap may occur in the research sector size but not in effort, and that policy analysis should consider opposite effects of instruments such as more resources and better environment of basic research upon the size of the sector and on effort of scientists, hence on the economy's rate of growth.

The chapter is organized as follows. The second section surveys the theoretical literature on the relationship between science and economic growth. The third section sets out the basic theoretical model. The fourth analyses the model's equilibrium solution. Conclusions follow in Section 2.5.

2.2.   THE RELATED LITERATURE

Arrow's 1962 essay laid the basis for economic analysis of the production of and the demand for knowledge, which was subsequently developed with reference to technological innovation. In the very general terms of Arrow's analysis, the various forms that knowledge can assume are likened to information. According to Arrow, on the supply side, once knowledge has been produced it can be transmitted at a considerably lower cost than that required for its production. On the demand side, information has the characteristic of non-rivalry in its consumption, because its use by one individual does not reduce the quantity available for consumption by another individual. These two features of knowledge make it similar to a public good.

Arrow's article prompted Dasgupta and David (1987) to investigate the fundamental differences between the production of knowledge in the institutions of science and technology. This important essay laid the basis for the modern economic theory of science. The main differences between the worlds of science and technological innovation lie in their organization and goals pursued. The fundamental difference between science and technology concerns the dissemination of results, which is immediate and complete in scientific research, as academic researchers seek to publish their discoveries as soon as possible and obtain, through peer evaluation, recognition by the scientific community of the validity of their results. This is contrary to what happens in technological research where new knowledge is kept secret.

The scientific community on the one hand enjoys the advantage of complete information; on the other, it is concerned to ensure the researcher's property right on the item of new knowledge that s/he has produced. As full disclosure is the optimal solution from the point of view of society's well-being, this social norm adopted in the scientific community serves that purpose. Obviously, full disclosure conflicts strongly with the secrecy necessary to be able to profit from technological innovation. Firms, in fact, obtain a return on investments in R&D in relation to the degree of market power that a patent or the restricted circulation of an innovation may generate for them.

Radically different from this objective is the 'quest for priority' in attribution of the paternity of a discovery that motivates academic researchers. The latter immediately submit the results of their work for publication which will certify their priority in the discovery. From this comes recognition in monetary terms (career advancement, awards, etc.) and in terms of reputation and prestige in the scientific community.

The incentives system that operates in research is characterized by great uncertainty and by the principal's difficulty in monitoring effort. The evolution of state-organized academic research seems to have struck a balance between the private motivations of researchers and the needs of society. Individual scientists take part in contests in which those who obtain an innovative result first receive recognition from the scientific community and the advantages that ensue therefrom. Because the work of those who do not win is valueless, the contest belongs to the category of tournaments in which the winner takes all (Dasgupta, 1989; Lazear, 1997).

Comparison with reality shows that this system efficiently provides academic researchers with incentives, in that they are generally highly motivated and committed to their research. In effect, this result also derives from the assurance of an income, often from teaching duties, which mitigates the effects of the risk in research.

The rules of the academic world favour the spread of forms of collaboration and information-sharing which have important externalities. Work in academic departments is characterized by forms of knowledge sharing and discussion such as in seminars and mimeo circulation and also by several informal externalities in everyday life interactions. The transmission of tacit knowledge takes place in academic departments whose composition is an important factor in the work of individual researchers. This relationship may also hold among researchers belonging to different institutions but who work in the same field and interact with each other to form 'invisible colleges' (David, 1998). Furthermore, scientific work is often carried out by teams of researchers, in that the advantages deriving from obtaining priority are generally indivisible, while the pooling of kindred and specialized skills considerably increases the chances of success (Stephan and Levin, 1992). Data on publications show that collaborations have increased over time.

Externalities in knowledge production have been analysed by Carraro and Siniscalco (2003) in a model that concerns a race between academic researchers and researchers in private firms to a specific discovery with possible commercial use. This paper shows under what conditions the coexistence of Science and Technology institutions can be welfare maximizing.

Finally there are a number of papers that have tried to measure empirically the influence of scientific advances on technological innovation and on the productivity of economic systems. The influence of scientific advances on technological innovation and on the productivity of economic systems, has been the subject of applied inquiry for a number of years. The studies by Mansfield (1991, 1995) are based on surveys of firms' opinions on the importance of scientific advances for innovation in products and processes. The first study was based on a sample of 76 of the largest USA firms and found that in the period 1975–85 around 11 per cent of new products and 9 per cent of new processes could not have been developed without the results of academic research conducted in the previous fifteen years.

An equally direct approach has been used by Adams (1990), who estimates the contribution of scientific knowledge to productivity growth in 18 manufacturing sectors. The main feature of this study is its meticulous construction of an indicator of the stock of scientific knowledge obtained by considering both the number of publications in scientific fields closest to the sector's technology since the 1930s, and the scientific personnel employed in the sector.

Another strand of studies considers the spatial effects of research spillover on the innovative activities of firms. Among the most important of these studies is Jaffe (1989), which considers data on corporate patents in each state of the USA. The estimation of a model of simultaneous equations shows that there are important spillover values for academic research, especially in the cases of pharmaceuticals and chemicals industries.

2.3. THE ECONOMY

A class of growth models that can be used to represent the salient features of the science sector described in the previous sections comprises so-called neo-Schumpeterian models. Here we follow the framework of Aghion and Howitt (1992) in which there is no capital accumulation.

In our economy there is a continuum of individuals, of measure 1, who can find employment in one of two different sectors: one is a competitive consumption good sector, the other is the basic research sector which produces the body of knowledge used in the production process of the final good. Manufacturing firms are owned by all agents in the economy, and labour and capital markets are perfectly competitive. The state owns and organizes the science sector. Time is indexed by t, while the state of knowledge is indexed by k.

The consumption good, which acts as numeraire, is produced using the following technology:

$$Y_{kt} = R_k l_{kt}^{\alpha} Z^{1-\alpha} \qquad (2.1)$$

with $0 < \alpha < 1$, where l_{kt} denotes the number of specialized workers used at time t, R_k is a technological parameter which measures the productivity of the basic knowledge freely disposable in the technological era k, and Z is an input available with fixed supply, that in the following we normalize to 1.

In this economy, innovation consists in the birth of a new body of knowledge, $k + 1$, produced in the science sector, able to increase the productivity of final good workers by a constant parameter $\gamma > 1$. That is to say, as common in Schumpeterian growth models, we assume that:

$$R_k = \gamma^k \qquad (2.2)$$

Consequently k denotes the type of basic knowledge and the technological era that comes to an end with a scientific discovery and the introduction in manufacturing of an innovation. Because the parameters that define the economy, and therefore the choices made by the agents, remain constant during each technological era, henceforth we can simplify the notation by omitting the time index t when it is not indispensable.

Each individual has an infinite life-span and is characterized by one (identical for all agents) intertemporal utility function of consumption and effort required by the job performed. We assume the following instantaneous utility function for scientists:

$$u_{kt}^R = c_{kt} - dx_{kt}^{1+\sigma} R_{kt} \qquad (2.3)$$

with $0 < \sigma < 1$, where c is consumption and x is effort on the job. As a matter of fact, scientists make research essentially applying cognitive resources and effort whose disutility of effort also depends on the extent of knowledge that must be mastered on the job.

However, to simplify the algebra, we assume that workers in manufacturing derive utility from consumption only:

$$u_{kt}^y = c_{kt}$$

The intertemporal preference rate, r, is constant and in equilibrium coincides with the rate of interest at which firms collect savings.

2.3.1. The Science Sector

The science sector in this economy produces the new basic knowledge which is a public good freely available for the production of the final good. Public good production usually involves considerable problems with workers' incentives and effort. In our model, this issue is crucial since new knowledge production – hence economic growth – depends on the effort of scientists.

The main characteristic of academia is the high value attached to the priority of discovery. Due to the norm of 'priority' in scientific discoveries (Merton, 1957) researchers compete in contests to be the first to introduce an innovation and be rewarded by the scientific community. In this 'winner take all' contest the prize consists in a monetary reward, m_{k+1} that is funded by the state and will last until the arrival of a new innovation and a new technological era.

In this model innovation is uncertain and, following the literature on patent races, we assume that the probability that a single researcher obtains an innovation depends on the effort that he devotes to his research, and follows a Poisson stochastic process with an arrival rate given by:

$$\theta(x_k) = \theta x_k + \theta h \bar{x}_k \tag{2.4}$$

where x_k is the effort employed by the scientist in the research activity, $\bar{x}_k$ is the average effort in the research sector, and θ and h are two positive parameters. While, as regards the probability of an innovation occurring in the economy, we have:

$$\theta n_k (x_k + h \bar{x}_k) \tag{2.4a}$$

The role of colleagues is of a paramount importance in science. In fact, good science is produced in communities of scientists where there is close cooperation between colleagues. Scientists talk with other scientists, share ideas, discuss one another's work. This occurs in informal fashion and in formal presentations of seminars and papers. The interchanges that result from such discussions can make spectacular differences in science.

The importance of the group is further enhanced by the rules which govern academia: indeed, the rule of priority induces the exchange of ideas in order to obtain at the earliest opportunity the recognition of others. In other words, the rule of 'full disclosure' works (Dasgupta and David, 1994) that increases the interconnections among researchers and the externality effects.

To capture such important aspects we assumed that the productivity of a single researcher depends not only upon his own effort but also upon the effort put into the research activity by his colleagues, represented by the average effort of the scientists' group. We use average effort since it best represents the intellectual and psychological resources of others to whom scientist may have access, which are substantial not only in quantity but rather in quality.

Given the above hypotheses the total expected benefits of being an innovator are:

$$V_{k+1} = \theta\left(x_k + h\overline{x}_k\right) \int_{t_0}^{\infty} e^{-\left[r+\theta n_{k+1}\left(x_{k+1}+h\overline{x}_{k+1}\right)\right](t-t_0)} m_{k+1} dt \qquad (2.5)$$

Substituting this expression in equations (2.3), (2.4) and (2.4a), and solving the integral, we obtain:

$$V_{k+1} = \frac{\theta\left(x_k + h\overline{x}_k\right)m_{k+1}}{r+\theta n_{k+1}\left(x_{k+1}+h\overline{x}_{k+1}\right)} \qquad (2.6)$$

Hence, the total expected benefits of participating in the research sector are given by the following:

$$U^R_{\;k} = \int_{t_0}^{\infty} e^{-\left[r+\theta n_k\left(x_k+h\overline{x}_k\right)\right](t-t_0)}\left[V_{k+1} - R_k dx_k^{\,1+\sigma}\right] dt \qquad (2.7)$$

2.3.2. The Consumption Good Sector

In the consumption good sector each worker can supply inelastically one unit of labour factor, and there is no disutility connected with work. The expected utility obtainable by workers in this sector is:

$$U^y_{\;k} = \int_{t_0}^{\infty} e^{-\left[r+\theta n_k\left(x_k+h\overline{x}_k\right)\right](t-t_0)} w_k dt \qquad (2.8)$$

where w_k is the wage obtainable in that sector.

The consumption sector receives technology from the research sector at no cost, but it pays taxes that the state uses to fund the research sector. Considering the production function (2.1) and bearing in mind that this sector operates in perfect competition, profit maximization yields the wages in the consumption good sector, as given by:

$$w_k = \alpha R_k l_k^{\alpha-1} \qquad (2.9)$$

2.3.3. The Public Sector

The state levies taxes, $\tau\alpha Y$, on wages in the consumption good sector in order to finance production of knowledge by the research sector:

$$m_k = \tau\alpha Y_k .$$ (2.10)

2.4. EQUILIBRIUM

Equilibrium in this economy is defined by both the optimal level of effort that each scientist puts into research and in the optimal number of scientists that are allocated to the science sector.

The optimal level of effort undertaken by scientists, x_k, maximizes the present net value of the total expected benefits of doing research. We assume that a scientist does not have a strategic behaviour so that she does not consider the effect of her effort on the arrival rate of discoveries in the economy. In this case, maximization of total benefits gives the following first order equilibrium condition:

$$\frac{\theta m_{k+1}}{r + \theta n_{k+1}\left(x_{k+1} + h\bar{x}_{k+1}\right)} - d\left(1+\sigma\right)R_k x_k^\sigma = 0$$ (2.11)

According to equation (2.11), each researcher chooses the optimal amount of effort by equating the expected discounted marginal benefit of one more unit of effort to the marginal disutility that derives from that effort. The optimal choice of effort depends positively on the prize for a discovery and negatively on the likelihood that a new finding will mark the end of the period during which he is the winner of the race. Hence, it depends on how many resources (scientists and effort) the economy will put into research in the next knowledge era $k + 1$.

Since individuals can choose, without sustaining costs, to participate in the labour market either as workers in the consumption sector or as researchers in the science sector, in equilibrium the maximum utility yielded by the two types of activity should be the same. By equations (2.9) and (2.10) we have the following equilibrium condition for the labour market:

$$V_{k+1} - dR_k x_k^{1+\sigma} = \left(1-\tau\right)w_k$$ (2.12)

where effort in research is the optimal value that derives from equation (2.11).

Given that individuals are homogeneous, equilibrium will be symmetric, which implies that $\overline{x}_k = x_k$. Finally, in equilibrium all individuals find employment, then we have:

$$n_k + l_k = 1 \tag{2.13}$$

2.4.1. Dynamics

The analysis of general equilibrium dynamics can be summarized by the last three equilibrium conditions. After substitution of equations (2.11) and (2.13) in equation (2.12) we obtain the following difference equation in the variable n_k in the domain $(0, 1)$:

$$\Psi\left(n_{k+1}\right) = \Omega\left(n_k\right) \tag{2.14}$$

where

$$\Psi\left(n_{k+1}\right) \equiv \frac{\alpha\theta(1+h)\tau\gamma\left(1-n_{k+1}\right)^{\alpha}}{r+\theta(1+h)n_{k+1}D^{1/1+\sigma}\left(1-n_{k+1}\right)^{(\alpha-1)/(1+\sigma)}}, \tag{2.15}$$

with

$$D \equiv \frac{(1-\tau)\alpha}{d(1+\sigma)(1+h)-d};$$

and

$$\Omega(n_k) \equiv \left(1-n_k\right)^{\frac{(\alpha-1)\sigma}{1+\sigma}}\left[dD^{\frac{\sigma}{1+\sigma}} + (1-\tau)\alpha D^{\frac{-1}{1+\sigma}}\right] \tag{2.16}$$

As in Aghion and Howitt's model, equation (2.14) enables us to determine the amount of labour employed in the science sector in era k as a function of the labour employed in the successive technological era. In fact, we are able to characterize the functions $\Psi\left(n_{k+1}\right)$ and $\Omega\left(n_k\right)$.

Given that:

$$\frac{\partial\Omega(n_k)}{n_k} = \frac{(1-\alpha)\sigma}{1+\sigma}\left[dD^{\frac{\sigma}{1+\sigma}} + (1-\tau)\alpha D^{\frac{-1}{1+\sigma}}\right]\left(1-n_k\right)^{\frac{(\alpha-1)\sigma-1-\sigma}{1+\sigma}};$$

and

$$\frac{\partial\Psi\left(n_{k+1}\right)}{\partial n_{k+1}} = -\Psi\left(n_{k+1}\right)^2\left(1-n_{k+1}\right)^{-\alpha-1}\frac{1}{\tau\gamma\alpha} *$$

$$\left[\frac{r\alpha}{\theta(1+h)}+D^{\frac{1}{1+\sigma}}(1-n_{k+1})^{\frac{\sigma+\alpha}{1+\sigma}}+D^{\frac{1}{1+\sigma}}\frac{1-\alpha}{1+\sigma}n_{k+1}(1-n_{k+1})^{\frac{\alpha-1}{1+\sigma}}+\alpha D^{\frac{1}{1+\sigma}}n_{k+1}(1-n_{k+1})^{\frac{\alpha-1}{1+\sigma}}\right]<0$$

we know that $\Omega(n_k)$ is monotone increasing and $\Psi(n_{k+1})$ is monotone decreasing. Furthermore,

$$\lim_{n_{k+1}\to 1}\Psi(n_{k+1})=0;\qquad\qquad \Psi(0)=\frac{\alpha\theta(1+h)\tau\gamma}{r};$$

$$\lim_{n_1\to 1}\Omega(n_k)=\infty;\qquad\qquad \Omega(0)=dD^{\frac{\sigma}{1+\sigma}}+D^{\frac{-1}{1+\sigma}}(1-\tau)\alpha.$$

Hence, an intersection between the functions exists if $\Psi(0)>\Omega(0)$. In this case, we have one steady state of scientists' employment. Given $\Omega_n(n_k)\neq 0$ we can apply the implicit function theorem and define the difference equation that describes the economy's dynamics:

$$n_k=\Gamma(n_{k+1}),\qquad\qquad(2.17)$$

with $\partial\Gamma(n_{k+1})/\partial n_{k+1}<0$.

The study of equilibrium dynamics can proceed as in Aghion and Howitt, (1992). We assume agents have perfect foresight, hence the employment of scientists at each era k is determined according to the forecast of future employment n_{k+1}. Equilibrium dynamics are defined by sequences of scientists' employment that start from the value n_0 and go into the future, and satisfy the difference function $n_k=\Gamma(n_{k+1})$.

A steady state equilibrium is defined as a value of n such that $n=\Gamma(n)$. Monotonicity properties of the functions $\Psi(n)$ and $\Omega(n)$ (see Figure 2.1) ensure that there exists a unique stationary solution to equation (2.17). This steady state $\overline{n}$ is asymptotically stable if:

$$\Psi_n(\overline{n})+\Omega_n(\overline{n})<0\qquad\qquad(2.18)$$

In this case, there are cycles of n_k that converge towards the steady state $\overline{n}$.

Otherwise, when inequality (2.18) is reversed, two different kinds of dynamic equilibrium may exist: one in which employment in basic research converges to a stable two-cycle where it assumes alternatively a low and a high value; another equilibrium in which a stable two-cycle is made by a nil value of employment. This interesting case defines a 'no-growth trap' (see Aghion and Howitt, 1992) and occurs when the economy converges to an equilibrium in which a high forecast of future employment in research causes a nil value today, that will remain the equilibrium outcome of the model dynamics in any time period. Inspection of Figure 2.1 reveals that a no-growth trap may exist when both $\Psi(0)$ and $\Omega(0)$ are high since in this case the equilibrium cycle can be made by a high foreseen value of research employment to which a nil value of n_k corresponds.

Interestingly enough, such a dynamic equilibrium is more likely when the parameter h increases[1] since in this case both $\Psi(0)$ and $\Omega(0)$ increase. The economic meaning of this result could lie in the dependence of externalities on the size of science sector. Instantaneous externalities in the scientific sector may cause nil investment in basic research because they magnify the negative effect of a high foreseen future value of n_{k+1}. Actually, environmental effects and social interactions are an important feature of modern systems of scientific research in the industrialized world. Our result suggests that this phenomenon could be responsible for the fact that many countries – not only the very poor – choose to remain outside the international scientific community After convergence to a dynamic equilibrium, the economy evolves along a balanced growth path. Given the distribution of employment between science and good production, effort in basic research is determined by the equilibrium conditions equations (2.11) and (2.12). Then the rest of endogenous variables derive from general equilibrium of markets.

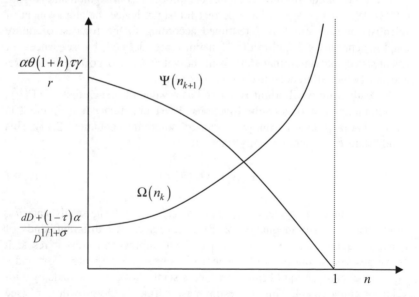

Figure 2.1   The equilibrium dynamics of basic research employment

Even if our analysis of equilibrium dynamics focuses on employment, a similar study can be performed with reference to effort. In fact, equations (2.11), (2.12) and (2.13) can be manipulated to derive a difference equation in effort only. After these steps we are able to derive the equation:

$$\Psi^x(x_{k+1}) = \Omega^x(x_k), \tag{2.19}$$

where:

$$\Psi^x(x_{k+1}) \equiv \frac{\alpha\theta\tau\gamma D^{\alpha/1-\alpha}}{rx_{k+1}^{[(1+\sigma)\alpha]/(1-\alpha)} + \theta(1+h)\left(x_{k+1}^{(1+\sigma\alpha)/(1-\alpha)} - x_{k+1}^{[(\alpha-1)\sigma]/(1-\alpha)}D^{1/1-\alpha}\right)} \tag{2.20}$$

and

$$\Omega^x(x_k) \equiv x_k^\sigma\left[D(1-\tau)\alpha+d\right]. \tag{2.21}$$

In Figure 2.2 we represent the two functions. It is straightforward to verify that $\Omega^x(x_k)$ is concave increasing starting from the origin. In the appendix we prove that $\Psi^x(x_{k+1})$ is monotone decreasing, and

$$\lim_{x_{k+1}\to\underline{x}}\Psi^x(x_{k+1}) = \infty; \qquad \lim_{x_{k+1}\to\infty}\Psi^x(x_{k+1}) = 0$$

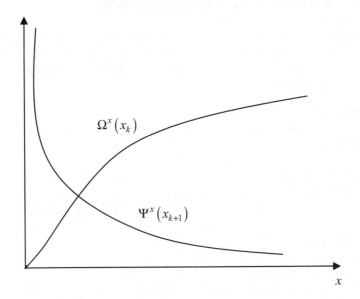

Figure 2.2   The equilibrium dynamics of effort in the science sector

with $\underline{x} > 0$. Hence, equilibrium values of effort always exist, and we can define a difference equation that slopes downward and summarizes the equilibrium dynamics of effort:

$$x_k = \Gamma^x\left(x_{k+1}\right) \tag{2.22}$$

Concerning this function some comments can be drawn similar to those that apply to the dynamics of employment n_k. In this case too, a stationary equilibrium exists that can be stable, and equilibrium cycles of effort should be associated with cycles of n_k. However, inspection of Figure 2.2 rules out the possible existence of a no-growth trap in equilibrium effort dynamics because effort cannot be lower than a positive threshold $\underline{x}$. This means that when forecast employment in basic research in period $k+1$ is so high as to deter any positive investment in research today, effort would be positive and not negative or nil.

With this result we have a picture of the no-growth trap in which people are unwilling to start up scientific businesses even if they were to spend some time at work if engaged as scientists. Hence, this feature of our model makes the definition of a no-growth trap more realistic.

In the following section we will analyse the properties of equilibrium focusing on the stable steady state.

2.4.2. Comparative Statics and Balanced Growth

In order to derive the effects of some relevant parameters on the steady state value of scientist employment, we concentrate on the case of a single steady state and we assume that it is stable. After some algebra we are able to state the following proposition:

Proposition 1

a) Let us consider $\bar{n}$, the stable steady state of the equation $n_k = \Gamma\left(n_{k+1}\right)$, then:
   - $\bar{n}$ increases when τ increases if $\tau < 1 - \tau$;
   - $\bar{n}$ increases when h or γ increases;
   - $\bar{n}$ decreases with the interest rate r.

b) Let us consider $\bar{x}$, the stable steady state of the equation $x_k = \Gamma^x\left(x_{k+1}\right)$, then
   - $\bar{x}$ increases with an increase in γ;
   - $\bar{x}$ decreases with an increase in r;
   - $\bar{x}$ has an ambiguous behaviour when τ increases.
   - $\bar{x}$ has an ambiguous behaviour when h increases.

Proof: in Appendix.

Some interesting comments can be made on the statements of this proposition. Public policies aimed at the enlargement of the science sector can be achieved by collecting more resources from the private sector that will be channelled to higher prizes for scientific discoveries. This kind of policy improves the reward for doing basic research. Major effects on the size of the science sector may derive from the strength of externalities in scientific environments. Indeed, cooperative and collaborative departments may provide an incentive to joining the world of science. This effect accords with both common sense and a large part of the sociological literature dealing with science.

Interesting results derive also from comparative statics of equilibrium effort of researchers. In fact, both the negative effects of externalities and the ambiguous effect of state resources seem to be counterintuitive. The ambiguous effect of state resources can be explained by the fact that when state resources increase there are three effects: there is an increase in the resources devoted to the prize for an innovation, which raises the effort, but there is also an increase in the size of the research sector which increases the probability of an innovation occurring in the economy, thereby reducing the duration of the prize; finally an increase in state resources reduces the wage obtainable in the alternative sector and, given the labour market equilibrium condition, this also reduces the reward of all the specialized workers and consequently their level of effort.

We performed some simulations of the relation between steady state effort and the tax rate. Figure 2.3 reports the graph of such a relation when parameters assume the following values:

$$\theta = 0.1, \ \alpha = 0.3, \ \gamma = 1.03, \ h = 0.6, \ \sigma = 0.8, \ r = 0.03, \ d = 1.$$

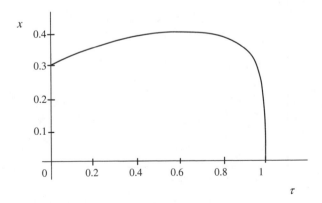

Figure 2.3   Simulation of the effect of τ on steady state effort $\alpha = 0.3$

In this case as τ increases from the origin of axes, $\bar{x}$ increases and, after reaching a maximum, decreases to zero at $\tau = 1$. Hence, there seems to exist a value of the tax rate that produces such a prize for scientists that maximizes their effort. This might happen when positive and negative effects of taxes are balanced. In Figure 2.4 we present the graph of a different simulation in which only α takes a different value: 0.6. This figure shows a decreasing function of effort with respect to the tax rate, and tells us that the negative effects of increasing the size of the science sector might prevail over the positive when the weight of employment in good production is high and a lower number of workers produces less at higher wages.

Concerning the negative effect of externalities, this can be explained by similar considerations. In this case too we have two opposite effects: on the one hand, an increase in externalities increases the probability that a researcher obtains an innovation, but on the other, there is an increase in the probability that an innovation occurs in the economy, which would reduce the duration of the prize.

The ambiguous effects that externalities could produce on size and effort in the science sector provide us with an important motivation for the separate introduction of effort in our model. This effect reminds us that there are limits to collaborative behaviour that should consider the individual incentive to work in science.

In our economy, production of the final good increases only when an innovation occurs, and this is a probabilistic event. The expected average steady state rate of growth of per capita income depends on the number of

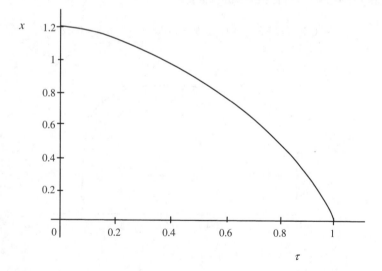

Figure 2.4   Simulation of the effect of τ on steady state effort $\alpha = 0.6$

researchers employed in science, on the productivity of these workers, on the optimal level of effort and on the magnitude of the technological advance brought about by the innovation. In particular we consider the determinants of balanced growth characterized by the steady state values of scientists' employment and effort $\bar{n}$, $\bar{x}$:

$$E(g) = E\left(\ln Y_t - \ln Y_{t-1}\right) = \theta\bar{n}\left(\gamma,\tau,h\right)\bar{x}\left(\gamma,\tau,h\right)\left(1+h\right)\ln\gamma \quad (2.23)$$

Taking into account comparative statics results of Proposition 1, we are able to write the following:

Proposition 2 *In balanced growth equilibrium the expected rate of growth of per capita income increases with an increase in the parameter γ, and with a decrease in the interest rate r. The sign of the effect of the importance of externalities in research – h – and that of the tax rate – τ – are undetermined.*

Proof: it is trivial from Proposition 1.

This proposition paints a picture that highlights the role that the science sector may have in economic growth. It also summarizes some important results of the chapter. In this model two forces drive the production of new knowledge and economic growth. One is the individual choice of scientists who take part in an organization in which knowledge spillovers can be strong. The other is the collective choice made by all agents from which the relative size of the science sector derives. The real incentive to work in basic research has both an individual and an aggregate dimension, since the latter concerns the distribution of physical resources between the two sectors of the economy.

The rate of growth of per capita income is affected in complex ways by the organization of science and by the share of real resources withdrawn to fund it. Our results seem to show that at low values of τ both steady state values of n and x increase with an increase in the tax rate, hence the growth rate of the economy increases too. However it is reasonable to suppose that such positive effects should end at high values of τ and h since the former reduces the size of good production and the second reduces the incentive to effort in science.

2.5.   CONCLUSIONS

This chapter represents an attempt to model basic research and long-run
economic growth along the lines of the work done by Karl Shell in the late
1960s. As commonly occurs in the framework of endogenous growth
models, we provide a formalization of the interactions between the scientific
sector and the rest of the economy which work both ways. Our focus is on
the role of externalities in basic research that affect the probability of success
of each scientist racing for a new finding. The state organizes production of
new knowledge – a public good – with resources taken from the private
sector.

   Scientists compete with each other to get priority over a discovery; such
races are affected by several forms of social interactions. In fact, scientists'
informal interactions give rise to externalities that hasten discoveries. Given
that science is financed by taxes taken from private firms, output growth and
structure of basic research jointly determine the dynamics of the economy.
These dynamics are not trivial as multiple steady state equilibria can derive
from strong effects of social interactions in science.

   Here we set the main lines for analysing such an important issue for long-
run growth that in a future paper we will further develop in order to deal with
welfare issues and public policy.

APPENDIX

2.A1.   Properties of the function $\Psi^x\left(x_{k+1}\right)$

Let us consider the function

$$\Psi^x\left(x_{k+1}\right) \equiv \frac{\alpha\theta\tau\gamma D^{\frac{\alpha}{1-\alpha}}}{rx_{k+1}^{\frac{(1+\sigma)\alpha}{1-\alpha}} + \theta\left(1+h\right)\left(x_{k+1}^{\frac{1+\sigma\alpha}{1-\alpha}} - x_{k+1}^{\frac{(\alpha-1)\sigma}{1-\alpha}} D^{\frac{1}{1-\alpha}}\right)},$$

then

$$\frac{\partial\Psi^x\left(x_{k+1}\right)}{\partial x_{k+1}} \equiv$$

$$\equiv -\alpha\theta\tau\gamma D^{1-\alpha} \frac{r\frac{(1+\sigma)\alpha}{1-\alpha}x_{k+1}^{\frac{(1+\sigma)\alpha}{1-\alpha}-1} + \theta(1+h)\left[x_{k+1}^{\frac{1+\sigma\alpha}{1-\alpha}-1} - x_{k+1}^{\frac{\sigma\alpha-\sigma}{1-\alpha}-1} D^{\frac{1}{1-\alpha}} \frac{\sigma\alpha-\sigma}{1-\alpha}\right]}{\left[rx_{k+1}^{\frac{(1+\sigma)\alpha}{1-\alpha}} + \theta(1+h)\left(x_{k+1}^{\frac{1+\sigma\alpha}{1-\alpha}} - x_{k+1}^{\frac{(\alpha-1)\sigma}{1-\alpha}} D^{\frac{1}{1-\alpha}}\right)\right]^2} < 0$$

We can write $\Psi^x(x_{k+1})$ as:

$$\Psi^x(x_{k+1}) \equiv \frac{\alpha\theta\tau\gamma D^{\frac{\alpha}{1-\alpha}}}{x_{k+1}^{\frac{(1+\sigma)\alpha}{1-\alpha}}\left[rx_{k+1}^{\frac{\alpha}{1-\alpha}} + \theta(1+h)x_{k+1}^{\frac{1}{1-\alpha}} - x_{k+1}^{\frac{-\alpha}{1-\alpha}} D^{\frac{1}{1-\alpha}}\theta(1+h)\right]}$$

This version of the function shows the denominator that is zero when the increasing function $rx_{k+1}^{\alpha/(1-\alpha)} + \theta(1+h)x_{k+1}^{\alpha/(1-\alpha)}$ crosses the decreasing function $x_{k+1}^{-\alpha/(1-\alpha)}D^{1/1-\alpha}\theta(1+h)$. It can be easily seen that this intersection always occurs for a positive value of x_{k+1}, hence we can state that:

$$\lim_{x_{k+1}\to \underline{x}} \Psi^x(x_{k+1}) = \infty; \qquad \lim_{x_{k+1}\to\infty} \Psi^x(x_{k+1}) = 0$$

2.A2. Proof of Proposition 1

Starting from $\Psi(\bar{n}) = \Omega(\bar{n})$ we can write:

$$\frac{r(1-\bar{n})^{\frac{1-\alpha}{1+\sigma}}}{D^{\frac{1}{1+\sigma}}} + \theta(1+h)\bar{n} = \frac{\theta(1+h)\tau\gamma\alpha(1-\bar{n})}{dD + (1-\tau)\alpha} \qquad (2A.1)$$

hence:

$$r(1-\bar{n})^{\frac{-(\alpha+\sigma)}{1+\sigma}} + \theta(1+h)D^{\frac{1}{1+\sigma}}\bar{n}(1-\bar{n})^{-1} - \frac{\theta(1+h)D^{\frac{1}{1+\sigma}}\gamma\tau\alpha}{dD + (1-\tau)\alpha} = 0.$$

Taking the differentials of that equation with respect to $\bar{n}$ and τ we get:

$$\left\{ r\frac{\alpha+\sigma}{1+\sigma}(1-\bar{n})^{\frac{-\alpha-\sigma}{1+\sigma}-1}+\theta(1+h)D^{\frac{1}{1+\sigma}}\left[(1-\bar{n})^{-1}+(1-\bar{n})^{-2}\bar{n}\right]\right\}d\bar{n}+$$

$$-\theta(1+h)(1-\bar{n})^{-1}\bar{n}\frac{D}{(1+\sigma)(1-\tau)}d\tau+$$

$$-\theta(1+h)\gamma\frac{\left(D^{\frac{1}{1+\sigma}}+\frac{\tau}{1+\sigma}D^{\frac{1}{1+\sigma}-1}D_{\tau}\right)\left[dD+(1-\tau)\alpha\right]+\frac{\tau dD^{\frac{1}{1+\sigma}+1}}{1-\tau}+\alpha\tau D^{\frac{1}{1+\sigma}}}{\left[dD+(1-\tau)\alpha\right]^{2}}d\tau=0$$

where $D_{\tau}=-\left\{\alpha/\left[d(1+\sigma)(1+h)-d\right]\right\}$, hence $\partial\bar{n}/\partial\tau>0$ if $\tau<1-\tau$.

From the above equations it can be easily verified that $\partial\bar{n}/\partial\gamma>0$, and $\partial\bar{n}/\partial r<0$.

As regards the effect of externalities on scientist employment, equation (2A.1) can be rearranged in the following way:

$$(1+h)=\frac{r(1-\bar{n})^{\frac{-\alpha-\sigma}{1+\sigma}}}{\theta D^{\frac{1}{1+\sigma}}\left[\frac{\alpha\tau\gamma}{dD+(1-\tau)}-\bar{n}(1-\bar{n})^{-1}\right]}$$

from which $\partial\bar{n}/\partial h>0$ derives.

NOTE

1. It can be easily verified that $\left[\partial\Psi(0)\right]/\partial h>0$; and $\left[\partial\Omega(0)\right]/\partial h>0$.

REFERENCES

Adams, J.D. (1990), 'Fundamental stocks of knowledge and productivity growth', *Journal of Political Economy*, **98**, 673–702.

Aghion, P. and P. Howitt (1992), 'A model of growth through creative destruction', *Econometrica*, **60**, 323–51.

Arrow, K.J. (1962), 'Economic welfare and the allocation of resources for invention', in *The Rate and Direction of Inventive Activity: Economic and Social Factors*, Princeton: Princeton University Press, pp. 609–25.

Carraro, C. and D. Siniscalco (2003), 'Science versus profit in research', *Journal of the European Economic Association*, **1**, 576–90.

Dasgupta, P. (1989), 'Patents, priority and imitation: the economics of races and waiting games', *Economic Journal*, **98**, 66–80.

Dasgupta, P. and P.A. David (1987), 'Information disclosure and the economics of science and technology', in G. Feiwell (ed.), *Arrow and the Ascent of Modern Economic Theory*, London: Macmillan Press, pp. 519–42.

Dasgupta, P. and P.A. David (1994), 'Toward a new economics of science', *Research Policy*, **23**, 487–521.

David, P.A. (1998), 'Communication norms and the collective cognitive performance of "invisible colleges" ', in G. Barba Navaretti, P. Dasgupta, K.-G. Maler and D. Siniscalco (eds), *Creation and Transfer of Knowledge*, Berlin: Springer-Verlag.

Grossman, G.M. and E. Helpman (1991), *Innovation and Growth in the Global Economy*, Cambridge, Mass.: MIT Press.

Jaffe, A.B. (1989), 'Real effects of academic research', *American Economic Review*, **79**, 957–70.

Lazear, E.P. (1997), 'Incentives in basic research', *Journal of Labor Economics*, **15**, S167–S197.

Mansfield, E. (1991), 'Academic research and industrial innovation', *Research Policy*, **20**, 1–12.

Mansfield, E. (1995), 'Academic research underlying industrial innovations: sources, characteristics and financing', *Review of Economics and Statistics*, **77**, 55–65.

Merton, R.K. (1957), 'Priorities in scientific discovery: a chapter in the sociology of science', *American Sociological Review*, **22**, 635–59.

Romer, P.M. (1990), 'Endogenous technological change', *Journal of Political Economy*, **98**, 71–102.

Rosenberg, N. (1990), 'Why firms do basic research (with their own money)?', *Research Policy*, **19**, 165–74.

Rosenberg, N. and L.E. Birdzell (1986), *How the West Grew Rich: The Economic Transformation of the Industrial World*, Basic Books.

Rosenberg N. and L.E. Birdzell (1990), 'Science, technology and the western miracle', *Scientific American*, **263**, 42–54.

Shell K. (1967), 'A model of inventive activity and capital accumulation', in K. Shell (ed.), *Essays on the Theory of Optimal Economic Growth*, Cambridge, Mass.: MIT Press.

Shell K. (1973), 'Inventive activity, industrial organization and economic growth', in J.M. Mirlees and N.H. Stern (eds), *Models of Economic Growth,* London and New York: J. Wiley and Sons, pp. 77–100.

Solow, R.M. (1956), 'A contribution to the theory of economic growth', *Quarterly Journal of Economics*, **70**, 65–94.

Stephan, P.E. (1996), 'The economics of science', *Journal of Economic Literature*, **34**, 1199–235.

Stephan, P.E. and S.G. Levin (1992), 'How science is done; why science is done', in *Striking the Mother Lode in Science: The importance of Age, Place and Time*, New York: Oxford University Press, pp. 11–24.

SECTION TWO

Variety and Quality Innovation

3. Consumption variety and growth*

Mauro Caminati

3.1. INTRODUCTION

This chapter seeks to clarify some channels through which the accumulation of variety may affect long-term growth, through its influence on consumption. In general, it is worth distinguishing between two different ways in which variety may affect the pattern of consumption. The first is consistent with the standard growth-model environment where preferences are exogenously given; the second requires the preliminary exploration of a relatively unknown model environment, which is capable of reconciling the focus on long-term growth with the notion of endogenous preferences.

It may be argued that the growth of variety is consistent with the assumption of exogenous preferences provided that radically new goods respond to previously unmet, but still 'objective', needs. For the sake of interpretation, it is useful to think of consumption goods as inputs to the consumption–service production which is (implicitly) built into the instantaneous utility function featuring in growth models (see Becker, 1965; Lancaster, 1971). New goods convey new service characteristics, or at least a combination of previously unavailable characteristics. For instance, the creation of the internal combustion engine powered automobile offered a new mix of transportation services combining speed with flexibility of use in time and space and lack of animal waste. Such a vector of service characteristics could not be supplied by the competing land-transportation systems of the time based on trains and horses (see Bresnahan and Gordon, 1997). A similar case is offered by the first introduction of domestic refrigerators bringing to previously unimaginable levels the time flexibility of fresh food consumption. Holding to this interpretation, Bresnahan and Gordon (1997) suggest that such innovation examples enable the production of consumption services to meet 'objective (previously) unmet needs' (ibid., p. 11). It may be worth stressing that, insofar as such needs are 'objective', they are not induced by innovations or other endogenous changes in the economy, and can be specified ex-ante, even if 'unmet'.

The assumption of exogenous preferences is unsuited whenever there is a process of learning and preference-formation associated with the creation of new goods which is contingent upon the unpredictable specification of the innovation characteristics and therefore cannot be reduced to the creation of new inputs to an *unchanging process* of well-being production. Instead of, or in addition to, meeting a previously unsatisfied need, a radically new good may open up a host of changes in the sphere of consumption through the creation of new needs, in ways that were unpredictable before the new good came into being. Add to a car sophisticated digital instruments for audio and video communication and the experience of a driver at the wheel will not be the same as before. In this sense, information-communication technology not only creates the home computer, but also modifies the definition of what is a car, a camera, etc. and affects the utility of car driving, picture taking, and the like. The construction-industry product innovation of supplying on a large scale non-luxury suburban dwellings with private gardens not only brought this type of housing within the reach of the middle class, but also greatly changed the nature of services offered by family cars.[1]

The suggested interaction between innovation and preference formation is not devoid of predictive implications that are relevant to a discussion of the growth effects of consumption. The theme will, however, be introduced only in the two final sections of this chapter and in ways that merely intend to fix guideposts for future research.

The following pages will be mostly concerned with the economic environment where preferences are exogenous. It will suffice for our purposes to identify this case with the creation of a new consumption good which is *not a close substitute* of any other existing good[2] and meets a well-defined, objective need. The new good is not subject to the same demand constraints that would fall upon a perfect substitute of a mature good that is consumed in plenty and has an almost 'saturated demand' (low relative marginal utility). We shall assume that the new good in question is produced by a *new industry*.

In principle, the assumption of exogenous preferences may be also suited to handle situations in which the new goods exert complementarity or externality effects on the preferences for pre-existing goods. Insofar as the types of goods that will at any time come into existence can be predicted in advance, also their complementarity effects are predictable. However, for the sake of simplicity, our treatment of exogenous preferences will rule out direct consumption complementarities between any specific pair of goods, to the effect that the marginal benefit from increasing the consumption of good j at t depends only on the quantity $c_{j,t}$ and on the total number of goods n_t that enter the consumption basket at t. Preference for variety ensures that the distribution of the composite consumption flow $C_t = \int_0^{n_t} c_{i,t} dj$ across a larger number of goods makes the consumer better off, provided that C_t / n_t is sufficiently large. In particular, we shall restrict our attention to growth paths where consumption differentiation is only constrained by the available number of goods. Moreover, the availability of a larger number of goods makes a given increase in the total consumption flow C more desirable than would have been the case otherwise.

The now classic reference for the analysis of endogenous growth through expanding consumption variety is Grossman and Helpman (1991, ch. 3). In their framework, differentiated goods can be interpreted either as inputs to the production of a final good, available for consumption, or directly as differentiated consumption goods. In the former case they enter a Dixit–Stiglitz production function, in the latter a Dixit–Stiglitz utility function. The two interpretations are alternative, in that in the economy contemplated by Grossman and Helpman there is no double possibility of using the same type of differentiated good in production and in consumption. Correspondingly, if there is any effect of variety on growth, this may occur through love of variety, or through increasing returns to specialization in production, but not through both simultaneously. The consumption good interpretation of differentiated commodities is considered with some detail in Barro and Sala-I-Martin (1995, ch. 6, section 2, pp. 231–7) where the possibility is discussed that the steady-state number of varieties may grow, thus affecting welfare, in an economy where a given labour supply L produces a quantity Y of total output, which cannot grow by construction, because labour productivity is constant. In this economy the given total output Y can be allocated to R&D expenditure, which increases variety, or to consumption, in the sense that one unit of Y produces one unit of differentiated commodity. Their conclusion is that the number of varieties and the quantity of each differentiated consumption are constant in steady state; hence no steady growth of welfare can possibly occur unless variety positively affects the production side of the economy.

The Dixit–Stiglitz specification adopted by Grossman and Helpman (1991) and Barro and Sala-I-Martin (1995) implies that parametric changes in the monopolistic–competitive mark-up also exert effects either on preference for variety or on returns to specialization, depending on the chosen interpretation. Benassy (1998), partly following Ethier (1982), generalizes the Dixit–Stiglitz specification and shows how the effects of changes in the monopolistic–competitive mark-up can be separated from the other effects referred to above.

Aoki and Yoshikawa (2002) study the growth path generated by the creation and diffusion of varieties in a model environment where innovations are exogenous and preferences, though exogenous, depend on the time interval from when the new goods were first introduced. To emphasize the long-run production response to changes in demand, Aoki and Yoshikawa (2002) assume that all inputs to production are themselves producible. Moreover, differentiated goods are used both as productive inputs in capital production and in family consumption, as it happens in the real-world example of the computer. In their framework, short-run behaviour is affected by the influence of adjustment costs on capital utilization.

This chapter studies some aspects of the relation between consumption innovation and long-run growth in an economy in which, as in Aoki and Yoshikawa (2002), there are no 'fixed factors' of production and differentiated goods are used in production and in consumption.[3] The linear technology of physical production is specified in Section 3.2. In particular, the technology of the competitive firms using differentiated goods as inputs is but a special case of Benassy (1998), with the restriction that returns to specialization are zero. As will emerge, the 'no-fixed-factors' and linear technology assumptions adopted in this chapter crucially modify Barro and Sala-I-Martin's (1995) conclusion concerning the steady-growth effects of consumption variety in situations where the productivity of inputs is constant. Since technology is ultimately of the AK type, there is a source of endogenous growth in the production side of the economy, notwithstanding the constant productivity of inputs. In this way, love of variety may affect steady growth by inducing a persistent increase in the savings ratio.

Preference assumptions and the family inter-temporal plan are considered in Section 3.3. Our analysis is focused on symmetric equilibria in which the steady-state distribution of consumption is uniform across the growing number of varieties.[4] The main results can be summarized as follows. When innovations are exogenous (Section 3.4) and, correspondingly, all markets are competitive, the interest rate is fixed by the linearity of the technology; in this case a stronger preference for variety causes a faster long-run growth. The unambiguous result is ultimately explained by the inter-temporal substitution of future for present consumption. The same incentive to postpone consumption to dates in which the infinite-life agent will be able to benefit from the wider variety of goods available may not guarantee the same result when innovations are endogenous (Section 3.5). In this case the markets for the differentiated goods are non-competitive, the steady-state interest rate comes to depend upon preferences and a demand externality creates the possibility of multiple equilibria. Section 3.6 contains some remarks on the problems posed by the growth of consumption variety in a more general framework in which well-being depends also upon leisure. Speculations on the analytical and conceptual difficulties of introducing endogenous preferences into the analysis of long-term growth are offered in Section 3.7. It is argued that salient features of the model economy which is relevant to the modified environment are the close link between knowledge accumulation and preference formation and the information asymmetry concerning the characteristics of innovations. This requires a heterogeneous-agents framework. Section 3.8 concludes.

3.2. TECHNOLOGY OF PHYSICAL PRODUCTION

In the economy at time t there are n_t differentiated goods and one capital good. A differentiated good can be either consumed, or it can be used as intermediate input in capital good production. c_{jt} is the quantity of the differentiated good j consumed at t, x_{jt} is the quantity of the same good used as intermediate input at t. This feature of the model is designed so as to construct a model environment which lends itself to the planned integration between the twofold dimensions of new good introduction: consumption variety and specialization in production. In this chapter only the former is discussed.

Capital good output at t is produced by perfectly competitive firms according to the constant returns to scale production function:

$$\dot{K}_t = n_t^{\frac{\alpha-1}{\alpha}} \left[\int_0^{n_t} x_{j,t}^\alpha \, dj \right]^{\frac{1}{\alpha}} \tag{3.1}$$

where $0 < \alpha < 1$. Consistent with the specific focus of the chapter on the growth effects of variety that take place through consumption demand only, an important property of the specification (3.1) is that the productivity effects of specialization are sterilized.[5]

To emphasize the response of the production system to changes in demand, it is assumed that all the inputs to production are themselves producible. There are not 'fixed factors' in the economy.

The functional form of (3.1) and competition imply that the price p_j of the intermediate input j and the price p_K of one unit of the capital good are as follows:

$$p_{j,t} = n_t^{\alpha-1} \dot{K}_t^{1-\alpha} p_{K,t} x_{j,t}^{\alpha-1} \tag{3.2a}$$

$$p_{K,t} = n_t^{\frac{1-\alpha}{\alpha}} \left[\int_0^{n_t} p_{j,t}^{1-\varepsilon} \, dj \right]^{\frac{1}{1-\varepsilon}} \tag{3.2b}$$

where $1 - \varepsilon = -\alpha/(1-\alpha)$. It is worth observing that (3.2a) implies that the demand for the intermediate input j by competitive firms has elasticity

$-\varepsilon = -1/(1-\alpha)$ with respect to p_j. A lower α entails a less elastic demand curve of the differentiated good j, *qua intermediate input*. Since the demand curve of the differentiated good j, *qua consumption good*, will turn out to have price elasticity -1, a lower α is unambiguously related to a higher market power of the local monopolist producing good j.

Capital is the single physical input to differentiated-good production. Capital embodying a larger variety of ideas is not more productive. One unit of capital, if assisted by the appropriate blueprint of ideas, and no matter what the number of intermediate-good varieties embodied therein, produces A units of differentiated goods, whatever their kind.

$$AK_{J,t} = \int_0^{n_t} x_{j,t} dj + \int_0^{n_t} c_{j,t} dj \tag{3.3}$$

where K_J is capital invested in differentiated-goods production.

It is a consequence of (3.1) that in a symmetric equilibrium where $x_{j,t} = x_t$, $j \in [0, n_t]$, the capital output flow $\dot{K}_t$ obtained from the given total intermediate-input flow $X_t = \int_0^{n_t} x_{j,t} dj$ is independent of n_t, provided that X_t stays constant.

Taken together, (3.1) and (3.3) imply that variety does not affect productivity.

Final output at t is

$$Y_t = \dot{K}_t p_{K,t} + \int_0^{n_t} c_{j,t} p_{j,t} dj$$

For the sake of later reference we observe that in a symmetric equilibrium where $p_{j,t} = p_t$, $x_{j,t} = x_t$, and $c_{j,t} = c_t$, $j \in [0, n_t]$, from (3.1) and (3.3) we obtain:

$$\dot{K}_t = n_t x_t \tag{3.4}$$

$$p_{K,t} = p_t \tag{3.5}$$

$$Y_t = p_t(\dot{K}_t + n_t c_t) \tag{3.6}$$

$$AK_{J,t} = n_t(c_t + x_t) \tag{3.7}$$

Equation (3.6) reveals that steady state investment and total-consumption expenditures grow at the rate:

$$g = \frac{\dot{n}}{n} + \frac{\dot{p}}{p} + \frac{\dot{c}}{c} \tag{3.8}$$

3.3. PREFERENCE FOR VARIETY AND THE REPRESENTATIVE FAMILY INTER-TEMPORAL PLAN

At time t the representative family holds a stock of assets a_t which, in symmetric equilibrium, consists of the value $K_t p_{K,t}$ of the shares representative of physical capital plus the value $V_t n_t$ of the patent stock. V_t is the symmetric-equilibrium value of one patent. The family maximizes lifetime utility[6]

$$\max \int_0^\infty u_t e^{-\rho t} dt \qquad (3.9)$$

subject to the flow budget constraint that asset accumulation $\dot{a}$ is constrained by current income less consumption expenditure:

$$\dot{a}_t = r_t a_t - \int_0^{n_t} c_{j,t} p_{j,t} dj \ .$$

In this expression asset price is implicitly normalized to 1 throughout and p_j can be interpreted as the price of good j relative to asset price.

The results of the chapter crucially depend on the functional form for instantaneous utility. This intends to capture the basic idea that consumers have a preference for variety, to the effect that they increase their satisfaction by differentiating a given total consumption expenditure $E = \int_{j=0}^{n} c_j p_j dj$ across the highest possible number of goods consistent with the attained variety level n provided that E/n is not too small. In particular, it is assumed:

$$u_t = n_t^{-\theta} \int_0^{n_t} \log c_{j,t} dj \ ; \qquad (3.10)$$

$$n_0 = 1; 0 < \theta < 1.$$

where $(1-\theta)$ measures the intensity of preference for variety. We may notice that in a symmetric equilibrium where the composite consumption flow C is uniformly distributed across n goods, a larger number of goods is desirable,[7] as long as $C/n > e^{1/(1-\theta)}$.

The reasons for deviating from the representation of preference for variety afforded by the more conventional, and to some extent realistic, Dixit–Stiglitz utility function (Grossman and Helpman, 1991, ch. 3) are twofold. The first is a quest for simplicity. As already observed, the model aims at preparing the ground for the treatment of product innovations that are used both as consumption goods (inputs to the household production of consumption services) and as inputs to the factory production of some final good (capital, in our case) by competitive firms. The much debated case of the personal computer offers a relevant example of this double possibility of use. The specification (3.10) will greatly simplify the treatment of differentiated-good demand for consumption purposes. The second, but not independent reason is that, unlike the Dixit–Stiglitz utility function, the representation (3.10) will enable the effects of a parametric change in the preference for variety to be separated from those of a parametric change in monopoly market power.

Expression (3.10) fully abstracts from the features, realistic as they may be, that make the contribution to instantaneous utility from consumption of a differentiated good depend on the time interval elapsed since the good in question was first introduced.[8] Such features are inessential to the argument made in this chapter.

Let μ_t and λ_t be the discounted and undiscounted shadow price of the state variable a_t in the present-value and current-value Hamiltonian (respectively) associated to (3.9): $\lambda_t = e^{\rho t}\mu_t$. Necessary conditions for an interior optimum[9] are:

$$n_t^{-\theta}\lambda_t^{-1} = c_{j,t}p_{j,t} \tag{3.11}$$

$$\dot{\mu}_t = -\mu_t r_t \tag{3.12}$$

$$\lim_{t\to\infty}\mu_t a_t = 0 \tag{3.13}$$

Equation (3.11) implies that consumption expenditure is uniform across varieties and total consumption expenditure at t is:

$$E_t = \frac{1}{\lambda_t}n_t^{1-\theta} \tag{3.14}$$

Equations (3.11) and (3.12) yield the consumption growth equation:

$$\frac{\dot{c}_{j,t}}{c_{j,t}} = r_t - \rho - \theta\frac{\dot{n}_t}{n_t} - \frac{\dot{p}_{j,t}}{p_{j,t}} \tag{3.15}$$

In symmetric equilibrium with $p_{j,t} = 1, j \geq 0, t \geq 0$, (3.15) boils down to

$$\frac{\dot{c}_t}{c_t} = r_t - \rho - \theta\frac{\dot{n}_t}{n_t} \tag{3.16}$$

3.4. INTERTEMPORAL EQUILIBRIUM WITH EXOGENOUS INNOVATIONS

In this section we consider some qualitative results, recently stressed in Aoki and Yoshikawa (2002), which refer to the model economy where, on the simplifying premise that innovations are costless and exogenous, markets are assumed perfectly competitive. For the sake of simplicity we fully abstract from adjustment costs and their influence on capital utilization.[10]

In this economy varieties grow at the exogenous rate g_n and the interest rate, as well as asset depreciation (see (3.12) above), is fixed by technology:

$$r_t = \frac{\dot{\mu}_t}{\mu_t} = r = A \qquad (3.17)$$

In the symmetric equilibrium where $p_t = 1$, $t \geq 0$, we have $p_{K,t} = 1, t \geq 0$ and $\dot{K}_t = \dot{a}_t$. Holding to this restriction, the transversality condition (3.13), together with (3.7), (3.16) and (3.17), implies the steady-state restriction:

$$\frac{\dot{a}}{a} = \frac{\dot{c}}{c} + g_n = A - \rho + (1-\theta)g_n < A \qquad (3.18)$$

that is,

$$(1-\theta)g_n < \rho \qquad (3.19)$$

In this economy all capital is invested in differentiated-good production ($K_J = K$). Thus, for $s \equiv c/x$, (3.4) and (3.7) reveal that

$$\frac{\dot{K}_t}{K_t} = \frac{A}{(s_t + 1)}$$

where $1/A$ and $1/(s+1)$ can be interpreted as 'capital–output ratio' and 'savings propensity', respectively.

A discrete once-and-for-all increase in innovation growth at time t, if consistent with (3.19), has the effect that consumers seek to increase their future consumption at a faster rate. They substitute future for present consumption. This requires a higher flow of saving and investment which in a symmetric equilibrium is instantaneously achieved through a discrete rise of μ_t and a corresponding discrete fall in c_t. The economy instantaneously attains the higher steady-state (symmetric) equilibrium growth rate $A - \rho + (1-\theta)g_n$.

Likewise, a once-and-for-all increase in the preference for variety $(1-\theta)$ does not interfere with the technologically determined interest rate A and, if consistent with (3.19), instantaneously brings the economy to a higher steady-state growth rate.

As stated in the introduction, the above growth-enhancing effect of preference for variety is at odds with the results in Barro and Sala-I-Martin (1995, ch. 6, section 6.2). In their framework, the constant productivity of inputs implies that there is no source of endogenous growth in the production side of the economy, such that preferences do not affect the rate of steady growth. In our framework, technology is ultimately of the *AK* type. The existence of a source of endogenous growth in the production side of our model economy explains the difference in results.

3.5. INTERTEMPORAL EQUILIBRIUM WITH ENDOGENOUS INNOVATIONS

In this section it is shown that the growth-enhancing effects of preference for variety considered above may not hold if the new goods result from a purposeful and costly innovation effort and do not affect productivity. For the sake of simplicity, technology of the R&D sector is described by the deterministic equation

$$\dot{n}_t = \delta K_{n,t} = \delta z_{n,t} K_t \qquad (3.20)$$

Where $K_{n,t}$ is the capital stock invested in R&D and $z_n \equiv K_n / K$. Since $0 \leq z_n \leq 1$, equation (3.20) implies the steady-state restriction:[11]

$$g_n = g_K \qquad (3.21)$$

Using (3.21), from (3.4) and (3.7) we derive the further steady-state restriction:

$$g_x = g_c = 0 \qquad (3.22)$$

Equations (3.21), (3.22) and (3.16) yield the symmetric equilibrium, steady-state growth rate:

$$g_n = g_K = \frac{r - \rho}{\theta} \qquad (3.23)$$

We are left with the task of studying the endogenous determination of the interest rate in this economy and its relation with the savings propensity and the allocation of capital between physical-output production and ideas production. We shall consider both steady-state and transitional equilibrium paths.

The right to produce the differentiated good j comes from the acquisition of the corresponding infinite-life patent, which has market value $V_{j,t}$ at time t. Patent acquisition represents a fixed cost for the producer of the differentiated good j, which is the local monopolist j. His flow profit $\pi_{j,t}$ is determined by current revenue $p_{j,t}(x_{j,t} + c_{j,t})$ minus flow-cost $[(x_{j,t} + c_{j,t})/A] p_{K,t} r_t$. At any date in a symmetric equilibrium such that $0 < s_t < \infty$ and

$$p_{j,t} = p_t = 1, \ 0 \le j \le n_t, \ 0 \le t \tag{3.24}$$

we have:

$$\pi_{j,t} = x_t(1 + s_t)\left(1 - \frac{r_t}{A}\right) \tag{3.25}$$

Equation (3.11) implies that the price elasticity of consumption demand for the differentiated good j is -1. Using this property, and the demand for the intermediate good j implied by (3.2a), in symmetric equilibrium[12] the first order condition for monopoly-profit maximization yields:

$$r_t = \frac{\alpha A}{(1 - \alpha)s_t + 1}$$

since $0 < \alpha < 1$, and $s_t > 0$, $r_t < \alpha A$. Conversely, in symmetric equilibrium:

$$s_t = \frac{\alpha A - r_t}{r_t(1 - \alpha)} \equiv s(r_t) \tag{3.26}$$

It is worth recalling that in equilibrium the fraction of income which is not consumed can be written as $1/(s_t + 1)$; thus the equilibrium propensity to save is fully determined by the rate of interest and we are informed by (3.26) that there is a positive relation between the two variables. In other words, the local monopolists' maximizing behaviour fixes the relation $1/[s(r_t) + 1]$ between the interest rate at t and the equilibrium composition of output between investment and consumption at the same date. Preferences can be interpreted as affecting the equilibrium composition of output through their effect on the interest rate.

Innovation value at t is

$$V_{j,t} = \int_t^\infty \pi_{j,\tau} \exp\left(-\int_t^\tau r_u du\right) d\tau \ .$$

In a steady-state symmetric equilibrium, $x_{j,t} = x, 0 \le j, 0 \le t$; steady-state innovation value can be written as:

$$V_{j,t} = V = x(1+s)\left(\frac{A-r}{Ar}\right) \tag{3.27}$$

Capital is instantaneously transferable across sectors. Free entry in R&D implies that at any date t the rate of return on capital invested in R&D is equal to the rate of interest:

$$\frac{\dot{n}_t V_t}{K_{n,t} p_{K,t}} = r_t = \delta V_t \tag{3.28}$$

This yields the steady-state symmetric equilibrium restriction $\delta V = r$ or, using (3.27):

$$\delta x(1+s)\left(\frac{A-r}{Ar}\right) = r \tag{3.29}$$

Recalling that $K_t(1 - z_{n,t}) = K_{J,t}$, from (3.4), (3.7), (3.20), (3.23) and (3.29) we obtain the steady-state conditions:

$$1 - z_n = \frac{(r-\rho)\alpha(A-r)}{A\theta r(1-\alpha)} \tag{3.30}$$

$$1 = \theta\frac{z_n}{(1-z_n)}\frac{r}{(A-r)} + \frac{\rho}{r} \equiv F(r) \tag{3.31}$$

$$\frac{K_t}{n_t} = \frac{r-\rho}{\theta\delta z_n} \tag{3.32}$$

The expressions from (3.25) to (3.32) are well defined for $\alpha A > r > \rho$. The restriction is justified by the following proposition.

Proposition 1: *An economically acceptable steady-state solution r to (3.31) is such that $\alpha A > r > \rho; 1 > z_n(r) > 0$.*

Proof: From (3.26), $r > \alpha A$ is inconsistent with $s \geq 0$, and $r = \alpha A$ would produce $s = 0$, which is inconsistent with consumers plans (3.11), (3.12), (3.13) at finite prices. $r < \rho$ yields $z_n(r) > 1$, and $r = \rho$ is not acceptable because it is inconsistent with equilibrium: $g_n = g_K = 0$ for $r = \rho$, hence $x = 0$ and capital is entirely required to produce consumption goods. Since capital good production is zero, the equality (3.5) ceases to hold and the local monopolist producing good j would set p_j at infinity, leaving his revenue unchanged but minimizing his cost. We conclude that at $r = \rho$ there is an excess supply of capital.

Proposition 2: *Let r_1 and r_2 be the real values of the interest rate that satisfy $1 - z_n = 1$ in equation (3.30). The following inequality holds:*

$$0 < \rho < r_1 < r_2 < A(1-H),$$

where $H \equiv \theta(1-\alpha)/\alpha$. Further,

$$\lim_{H \to 0} r_1 = \rho \qquad \lim_{H \to 0} r_2 = A.$$

If $r_1 < \alpha A$, there exist r^*, $\rho < r^* < r_1$, that satisfies (3.31). Moreover, if $r_2 < \alpha A$ and $F(\alpha A) > 1$, there exists also $r^{**}, r_2 < r^{**} < \alpha A$, that satisfies (3.31). Since the solution r^* is relatively close to ρ, it meets the transversality condition (3.13) for a 'large' set of parameter values. The same transversality condition (3.13) will impose much stronger restrictions on parameters at r^{**}.

Proof: see Appendix.

It is a direct implication of Proposition 2 that the same point in parameter space, in particular, the same state in the preference for variety and R&D technology, may be consistent with a 'low' or a 'high' value of the interest and growth rates. The same proposition suggests that there is a non-negligible set of parameter values such that the 'high-growth' regime may not exist.[13]

The possibility that there are multiple equilibria in the model has the following suggested interpretation. Since technology in the R&D and the differentiated goods sectors is linear in the unique input capital, transfers of capital between these sectors do not directly influence the rate of return through changes in physical productivity. The influence in question takes place only through the general equilibrium relation between z_n and monopoly profits, which is crucially affected by the demand for differentiated goods. It is a demand externality in the model that gives rise to the multiplicity of equilibrium. A high (low) interest rate makes capital accumulation and therefore the intermediate-input demand for each differentiated good large (small). Correspondingly, monopoly profits and innovation value V_t are high (low), so that the free-entry equilibrium relation $V_t = \delta r_t$ can obtain.

Proposition 3: *(Transitional dynamics): Let r be a steady-state interest rate identified in Proposition 2 and consider the corresponding steady-state path of the economy. At the initial date $t = 0$ the stocks K_0 and n_0 are pre-determined and fix a transitional-equilibrium path converging to steady-state, with the following properties:*

$$r_t = r, \ t \geq 0; \ V_t = r/\delta, t \geq 0$$

$$z_{n,t} = 1 - \frac{r^2}{(A-r)\delta} \frac{n_t}{K_t}$$

$$\frac{\dot{n}_t}{n_t} = \delta \frac{K_t}{n_t} - \frac{r^2}{A-r}$$

$$\frac{\dot{K}_t}{K_t} = \frac{A}{(1+s)} - \frac{r^2}{(A-r)\delta} \frac{n_t}{K_t}$$

$$\frac{\dot{c}_t}{c_t} = r - \rho - \theta \left(\delta \frac{K_t}{n_t} - \frac{r^2}{A-r} \right)$$

Proof: see Appendix.

Proposition 3 implies that the ratio between the stocks of physical capital and ideas, from any arbitrarily given initial condition, converges monotonically to its steady-state value determined by (3.32). On the assumption that the initial value of this ratio is higher than at steady state, then the growth rate of physical capital $g_{K,t}$ converges to $g = (r - \rho)/\theta$ from below and the growth rate of ideas $g_{n,t}$ converges to $g = (r - \rho)/\theta$ from above. During the transition, the share of resources invested in R&D is larger than at steady state. In other words, this share converges to its steady-state value from above.

Proposition 2 points to the possibility of multiple steady-state equilibria. The next proposition reveals that the local comparative-statics properties of the model, at the low interest rate equilibrium r^*, may not confirm the growth-sustaining effect of a parametric increase in the preference for variety that was found in the previous section.

Proposition 4: *(Comparative-statics effects of a change in the preference for variety): Fix a given point* $\mathbf{q} = (A, \alpha, \delta, \theta, \rho)$ *in parameter space, such that* r^* *defined in Proposition 2 exists and meets the transversality condition. For the small parameter change* $\mathbf{q}' - \mathbf{q} = (0, 0, 0, \theta' - \theta, 0)$, *with* $\theta' - \theta < 0$, *consider the effects on the steady-state interest rates* r^* *and* r^{**}. *We obtain:*

$$r^*(\mathbf{q}') < r^*(\mathbf{q})$$

$$g^*(\mathbf{q}') = \frac{r^*(\mathbf{q}') - \rho}{\theta'} \geq or \leq \frac{r^*(\mathbf{q}) - \rho}{\theta} = g^*(\mathbf{q})$$

Moreover, if r^{**} defined in Proposition 2 exists at $\mathbf{q}$ and it meets the transversality condition, then we also obtain the following comparative-static result:

$$r^{**}(\mathbf{q}') > r^{**}(\mathbf{q})$$

$$g^{**}(\mathbf{q}') = \frac{r^{**}(\mathbf{q}') - \rho}{\theta'} > \frac{r^{**}(\mathbf{q}) - \rho}{\theta} = g^{**}(\mathbf{q})$$

Proof: see Appendix.

The possibility that $g^{*}(\mathbf{q}') < g^{*}(\mathbf{q})$ is shown in the following.

Example: *Let* $\mathbf{q} = (2, 0.8, 1, 0.5, 0.02)$, $\mathbf{q}' = (2, 0.8, 1, 0.4, 0.02)$. *This yields:*

$$r^{*}(\mathbf{q}') = 0.0203757, \quad r^{*}(\mathbf{q}) = 0.0204729,$$

$$g^{*}(\mathbf{q}') = 0.00093925, \quad g^{*}(\mathbf{q}) = 0.0009458.$$

In this example r^{**} does not meet transversality.

The implications of Proposition 4 concerning the local steady-state effects of changes in the preference for variety at the low interest rate regime r^{*} are worth emphasizing, because we are informed by Propositions 2 and 4 that there is a non-negligible set of parameter values such that r^{*} is the only steady-state solution to the model.

Proposition 5: *(Comparative-statics effects of a change in the productivity of R&D): Fix a given point* $\mathbf{q} = (A, \alpha, \delta, \theta, \rho)$ *in parameter space and consider the steady-state effects of the parameter change* $\mathbf{q}^{\circ} - \mathbf{q} = (0, 0, \delta^{\circ} - \delta, 0, 0)$, $\delta^{\circ} - \delta > 0$. *A small increase in the productivity of R&D leaves the steady-state interest rate locally unaffected and causes a fall in the steady-state ratio* K_{t}/n_{t}.

Proof: Direct inspection of (3.30), (3.31) and (3.32) yields the stated results.

Proposition 6: *(Comparative-statics effects of a change in market power): Fix a given point* $\mathbf{q} = (A, \alpha, \delta, \theta, \rho)$ *in parameter space, such that r^{*} defined in Proposition 2 exists and meets transversality. Consider the local steady-state effect on r^{*} of the parameter change* $\mathbf{q}^{\S} - \mathbf{q} = \left(0, \alpha^{\S} - \alpha, 0, 0, 0\right)$, *where* $\alpha^{\S} - \alpha < 0$. *We obtain:*

$$r^*(\mathbf{q}^{\S}) > r^*(\mathbf{q})$$

Moreover, if r^{**} defined in Proposition 2 exists at $\mathbf{q}$ and it meets the transversality condition, then we also obtain the following comparative-static result:

$$r^{**}(\mathbf{q}^{\S}) < r^{**}(\mathbf{q})$$

Proof: see Appendix.

3.6. REMARKS ON VARIETY AND LEISURE

Two special features of the model outlined in Sections 3.3, 3.4 and 3.5 lie in the fact that leisure does not enter the utility function and capital is the only input to production in both the R&D and the differentiated goods sectors. As already observed, since differentiated goods are used partly as consumption goods, partly as intermediate inputs in capital production, it is as if capital were the only input in the economy. The special features mould the stated effects of preference for variety in various ways, but two in particular are worth emphasizing here.

The first implication is that the intra-temporal substitution effects of preference for variety are confined to a set of consumption goods existing at the same date and are for this reason separable from the inter-temporal substitution effects. If, however, well-being depends also on leisure, preference for variety would generally affect the rate at which agents are prepared to substitute at any given date the current consumption of goods for the current consumption of leisure. With labour entering the physical-output and R&D production technologies, this intra-temporal substitution effect would also have inter-temporal repercussions. The above separability between intra-temporal and inter-temporal substitution effects would no longer be at hand.

The second implication is concerned with the conditions enabling the existence of a steady state. With leisure entering the utility function, the existence of a steady state may require further restrictions on the technology of consumption activities and on the rate at which agents are prepared to substitute goods for leisure.

Indeed, preference for leisure may be approached on the plausible hypothesis that well-being depends not only on the physical amounts of goods actually consumed, but also on the 'ease' with which the corresponding activity is performed, where such ease depends on the fraction of time invested in it. Insofar as the agent consuming a given quantity of good *j* in a smaller fraction of time is more hurried, she is worse off. But there may be an upper bound on the time that may be rewardingly invested in a consumption activity. Likewise, having more time at one's disposal may be only boring, if there is no way of investing the extra time in some activity. This is a way of saying that leisure consumption and goods consumption are complements and the specific complementarity relation depends upon the technology of the corresponding activities.

These quite obvious remarks bring to the fore the very restrictive nature of the conditions enabling the existence of a steady state with growing per-capita consumption.

The first restriction is that the fraction of time *necessary* to consume any given quantity is not bounded away from zero by a separate time constraint on consumption activities.[14] In fact, since the fraction of time devoted to consumption activities must be constant in steady state, the expanding per-capita consumption resulting from variety growth will hardly be plausible, unless more varieties $c_j, ..., c_i, ..., c_h, ...$ can be jointly and simultaneously consumed, in that they add up to a more sophisticated composite good. Think of driving a car while listening to the music reproduced by a CD driver and stereo equipment. Alternatively, it must be assumed that consumers like having more and more goods at their disposal, however small the fraction of time they can invest in the specific consumption activity corresponding to any of them. Think again of driving a car equipped with several audio, video, computational and information-communication digital devices, but using only one device at one time.

The second restriction is that the elasticity of substitution between consumption and leisure is constant.[15]

3.7. SPECULATIONS ON ENDOGENOUS PREFERENCES IN A LONG-TERM GROWTH PERSPECTIVE

The crucial characteristic of preference for variety, as outlined in Section 3.3, is that it is a well-defined preference ordering over a time-varying choice set, which is known *ex ante*. The approach, as further examined in Sections 3.4 and 3.5, brings to the fore the following implications for equilibrium growth:

At any given interest rate r_t and growth rate of varieties $g_{n,t}$ a higher preference for variety (lower θ) causes a higher desired growth rate of consumption (3.16) of each differentiated good, and a corresponding higher savings flow at *t*, because the optimizing agent prefers to postpone consumption to dates in which she will be able to benefit from the opportunity of a wider choice set. The particular model structure separates the above inter-temporal substitution effect from other intra-temporal substitution effects that arise when leisure affects well-being and labour is an input to technology (see Section 3.6).

In the full-fledged general equilibrium model with complete markets, constant returns to the endogenous factor capital and no labour input, the steady state is unique if variety growth is exogenous. In this case, higher preference for variety, or faster arrival of new goods, are unambiguously associated to faster growth of per-capita output, even if the productivity-enhancing effects of greater differentiation are ruled out ex hypothesis. When the creation of new goods is again unrelated to productivity, but is the outcome of a purposeful and costly innovation effort, the above results cannot be taken for granted. The chapter builds a model example where the possibility arises that the same state of preference for variety maps to two steady growth (and interest rate) regimes: a slow growth and a fast growth regime. In the slow growth regime a higher preference for variety is locally conducive (in a comparative-statics sense) to a lower interest rate and may also cause slower growth. It is only in the fast growth regime, *if one exists*, that a stronger preference for variety invariably causes faster growth.

For the sake of interpretation, a stronger preference for differentiation in consumption, corresponding to a lower level of the parameter θ, can be thought of as resulting from more radical qualitative differences between goods, hence from a higher and perfectly foreseen novelty content of the innovation flow. Surprise, learning and endogenous preference formation, that are so characteristic of consumption innovation, are ruled out by definition from the above representation. In this sense we are inclined to interpret the effects *(i)* and *(ii)* as related to the *perfectly foreseen component* of variety growth, based on the given-preference approach. In a long-term framework innovation phenomena become part of a normal state of affairs and to some extent their effects can be predicted.

Other phenomena beyond those considered in *(i)* or *(ii)* above can be brought under the umbrella of the given-preference approach. In particular, the preference assumptions of Sections 3.3, 3.4 and 3.5 above can be extended to include the possibility that there is a hierarchy of needs, with older goods satisfying more basic needs, to the effect that the distribution of consumption is not uniform across goods, but there are long-term, regular changes in the pattern of consumer expenditure. As per-capita income grows, the family can afford to satisfy less basic needs, through the consumption of new goods, which characteristically come to have an initially high, but subsequently declining, income-elasticity of demand. The sequel of the chapter will entirely abstract from these extensions, which have already been the focus of recent literature;[16] instead, it will briefly consider the problems brought to the analysis of long-term growth by consumption innovation as a carrier of true novelty and the existence of a large *unforeseen component* of variety growth.

The formation of preferences for truly new goods entails learning and knowledge acquisition processes that mostly occur in the course of consumption activities (Bianchi, 1998a; Loasby, 1998; Swann, 1999; Witt, 2001b) or of interactions with other heterogeneous consumers (Dosi et al., 1999) and in any case not before the relevant information or reinforcement signals are released. Preference for variety is often the outcome of an experience-based discovery of consumption complementarities (Bianchi, 1998b, 2002). To this extent, consumers mostly become aware of their preference for variety only after the new goods are marketed. Self-perception of preference for variety may entail surprise[17] and its effects cannot be thoroughly recounted within the straitjacket of an equilibrium framework where, paradoxically, novelty is fully anticipated.

The argument above suggests that the demand effects of a variety-innovation flow will largely depend upon the prevailing foreseen or unforeseen nature of the flow. Unforeseen substitution effects are triggered by the diffusion within the population of agents of the knowledge about the consumption opportunities disclosed by innovations that have already taken place. The consumers newly reached by the diffusion process have both motives and knowledge for formulating a new inter-temporal consumption plan, conditional on their current information set, and on the awareness that further surprises may arrive in the future.

If a representation of the consumer's choice problem truly concerned with the emergence of novelty and the necessary updating of plans and expectations cannot but refer to bounded rationality, a bounded rationality approach encounters problems when faced with the task of considering the *persistent growth effects* of endogenous preference formation. A compromise solution open to future research may come from avoiding unfulfilled expectations, while at the same time avoiding infinite planning horizons.

Moreover, the emphasis on knowledge creation and its influence on preference formation brings to the fore the relevance to the present discussion of the *information distribution* concerning the characteristics of the new goods. In this respect, the representative agent framework of Sections 3.3, 3.4, 3.5 is particularly defective. In this framework we could disregard the asymmetric position held on the demand side by the consumer and the innovator. It seems to be more plausible to posit that the latter is the primary holder of the information concerning the nature and service characteristics of the new goods to be marketed. For this reason, he is normally[18] in a better position to correctly predict the demand for the variety which he is about to introduce. Information distribution is relevant to endogenous preference formation, and non-uniform knowledge distribution requires agents' heterogeneity.

Bringing the preceding remarks together, the concluding section of this chapter suggests a departure from the approach followed in Sections 3.4, 3.4 and 3.5 to the long-term-growth effects of consumption innovation and variety. The alternative approach, while more consistent with endogenous preference formation and non-uniform knowledge distribution across agents, seeks to avoid a fully-fledged bounded-rationality approach to consumption knowledge, because of its undesirable consequences on the determination of a long-term growth path.

3.8. CONCLUSIONS

A possible approach to analysing the *long-term growth* effects of consumption variety is to proceed on the bold assumption that the innovation effort is sustained by the innovators' self-fulfilling anticipation of consumer preferences for the new set of goods that the innovation itself is about to deliver. On an equilibrium growth path innovators' expectations are fulfilled and consumer preferences are endogenous. An equilibrium innovation flow will be one based on the correct understanding of endogenous preference formation. Here the emphasis shifts from the effects flowing from the choice and the once-and-for-all changes of the parameters representing a given state of preferences, to the processes of knowledge accumulation, preference formation and the structural factors behind them. The processes in question select the properties of the equilibrium innovation flow.

It is here conjectured that an overlapping generations framework may offer a minimal model environment capable of reconciling endogenous preference formation, fulfilled innovators' expectations and the further requirement of a non-uniform knowledge distribution across agents. In particular, while exerting their R&D effort and human capital accumulation when young, agents accumulate knowledge consumption and more general kinds of knowledge and in so doing, they shape their preferences when old. Emphasis is then laid on the fact that the formation of preferences for the new goods is part and parcel of knowledge and human capital accumulation, hence of the decisions that economic agents take with the prospect of raising productivity. Simultaneously, doing away with the infinite-lived representative agent would also presumably downplay the effect that preference for variety exerts through inter-temporal substitution *in consumption*.[19]

In a more general setting, however, inclusion of the labour input and of leisure would bring new forms of intra-temporal and inter-temporal substitution. In particular, consumption variety would affect lifestyles, the stringency of income and time constraints on consumption activities

(Metcalfe, 2001) and the arbitraging between the benefits from goods and leisure consumption on the one hand, and between leisure and labour effort on the other.

APPENDIX

Proof of Proposition 2: r_1 and r_2 are the real solutions to the equation $(r - \rho)\alpha(A - r) = 0$. It is easily seen that they meet the stated restrictions. The function $F(r)$ defined by (3.31) is continuous in the intervals (ρ, r_1) and $(r_2, \alpha A)$. Moreover, we have: $F(\rho) = +\infty$ and $F(r_1) < 1$; $F(r_2) < 1$. □

Proof of Proposition 3: Using

$$\dot{K}_t + n_t c_t = A(1 - z_{n,t})K_t$$

together with the equilibrium equality between income $(K_t + n_t V_t)r_t$ and expenditure $\dot{K}_t + n_t c_t + \dot{n}_t V_t$ and (28) we obtain:

$$(1 - z_{n,t}) = \frac{n_t}{K_t} \frac{r_t^2}{\delta(A - r_t)} = \frac{\dot{K}_t}{K_t} \frac{(1 + s_t)}{A} \quad (3.33)$$

Using the above results and (3.25) we obtain that at any date t in symmetric equilibrium:

$$\pi_{j,t} = \frac{r_t^2}{\delta} \quad (3.34)$$

Substituting from (3.34) into the asset equation $\dot{V}_t = -\pi_{j,t} + r_t V_t$ yields that at any date t in symmetric equilibrium:

$$\dot{r}_t = 0; \dot{V}_t = 0; \dot{s}_t = 0 \quad (3.35)$$

n_t and K_t are predetermined at any date t. Thus, using (3.33) and (3.35) we derive the transition paths for $z_{n,t}$, n_t, and K_t:

$$z_{n,t} = 1 - \frac{r}{A - r} \frac{1}{\delta} \frac{n_t}{K_t}$$

$$\frac{\dot{n}_t}{n_t} = \delta \frac{K_t}{n_t} - \frac{r}{A - r}$$

$$\frac{\dot{K}_t}{K_t} = \frac{A}{(1+s)} \frac{r^2}{(A-r)} \frac{1}{\delta} \frac{n_t}{K_t}$$

This completes the proof.

Proof of Proposition 4: Let us compute the derivative:

$$\frac{d\left[z_n(r)/1 - z_n(r)\right]}{dr} = \alpha(1-\alpha)A\theta(r^2 - A\rho)\left[(r-\rho)\alpha(A-r)\right]^{-2}.$$

r_1 and r_2 are the only real solutions to $z_n(r) = 0$. By inspection of the above derivative, continuity, $z_n(r^*) > 0$ and $\rho < r^* < r_1 < r_2$ imply that $z_n(r)$ is decreasing in r in the interval (ρ, r_1). Similarly, inspection of $F(r)$, continuity and the fact that $F(r)$ is necessarily decreasing in r at some point $r', r^* < r' < r_1$, can be used to prove that $F(r)$ is (*a fortiori*) decreasing in r at every point in $(\rho, r_1]$. By a similar argument, on the assumption that the solution r^{**} exists and meets transversality, $z_n(r)$ is increasing in r at every point in $(r_2, \alpha A)$. Moreover, there exists r'', $r_2 < r'' < r^{**}$ such that $F(r)$ is increasing in r at every point in $[r'', \alpha A]$.

Inspection of (3.30) shows that a parametric fall of θ causes a fall of $z_n(r)$ and $F(r)$ at given r. This proves the proposition. $\square$

Proof of Proposition 6: (3.30) implies that a *ceteris paribus* parametric fall of α causes a discrete rise of $z_n(r)$ at given r, that is, $z_n(\mathbf{q}^\S, r) > z_n(\mathbf{q}, r)$ at given r. The proposition follows from the above inequality, using the local properties of the functions $z_n(r)$ and $F(r)$ discussed in the proof of Proposition 4.

NOTES

*   I wish to thank Alberto Bucci, Massimo De Francesco and Reto Föllmi for their useful comments and criticism. The usual caveats apply.

1.   Obviously enough, there are also examples of negative complementarities or externalities that may come to mind. The pleasure from shopping at the nearby grocery or from having half a pint of lager at one's favourite pub may largely depend on the relations of acquaintance, friendship, solidarity with the clients usually met in that place; these relations, or the very possibility of meeting the 'regulars', may be destroyed by the diffusion of 'lifestyles' associated with the emergence of the new goods.

2.   There are of course innovations that produce close substitutes of existing consumption goods. We shall not be concerned with these innovations, in that they are less interesting in terms of the long-term relation between variety, consumption and growth.

3.   The double use possibility for differentiated goods ensures that the model environment lends itself to an integrated analysis of the growth effects that variety may exert not only through

consumption demand, as is specifically considered in this chapter, but also through specialization in production. This extension will be the subject of future research.

4. We shall therefore abstract from possible differences between the new and old goods concerning their income-elasticity of demand. Such differences, at least in the form which has been the focus of recent research (see for instance Föllmi and Zweimüller, 2002), are justified on the grounds that older goods satisfy more basic needs. A stimulating result of this literature is that it generalizes upon the notion of a steady state. It is however easy to think of examples in which radically new goods create new forms of satisfying very basic needs.

5. After this chapter was completed I realized that the production function (3.1) is but a special case of that specified in Benassy (1998, p. 5), namely,

$$Y = n_t^{v+\frac{\alpha-1}{\alpha}} \left[\int_0^{n_t} x_{j,t}^\alpha \, dj \right]^{\frac{1}{\alpha}} ,$$

which was assumed by the author, following Ethier (1982) with the purpose of *separating* the effects of the returns to specialization v from those of the monopolistically competitive mark-up $1/\alpha - 1$. The reason for assuming $v = 0$ here is to *sterilize* the effects of specialization on productivity. I thank Alberto Bucci for bringing Benassy's paper to my attention.

6. Here and elsewhere in the chapter, e is understood to be the base of natural logarithms.

7. Massimo De Francesco pointed out to me the need to qualify the statement that, according to the preferences (3.10), a larger differentiation of consumption is desirable.

8. These features are responsible for the logistic diffusion curves that are observed empirically and are explicitly introduced in Aoki and Yoshikawa (2002). As argued in Section 3.8, a more thorough and satisfactory analysis of such features can be obtained only at the cost of removing the assumption of exogenous preferences, to consider the relation between novelty, preference for variety and the accumulation of consumption knowledge.

9. Here and in what follows, attention is focused on those growth paths where the optimal differentiated consumption flow $c_{j,t}$ is bounded away from zero for all j in $[0, n_t]$ and all dates $t \geq 0$.

10. The influence of adjustment cost is instead prominent in Aoki and Yoshikawa (2002).

11. Variables without the time subscript will henceforth indicate steady-state magnitudes.

12. Symmetric equilibrium is henceforth understood to be an equilibrium such that (3.24) holds.

13. A sufficient condition for $r_2 < \alpha A$ is $A - H \leq \alpha A$, that is, $\theta \geq \alpha$.

14. On the effects on consumer choice flowing from the introduction of a separate time constraint, in addition to the conventional budget constraint, see Steedman (2000) and Metcalfe (2001).

15. Ortigueira and Santos (1997) discuss problems related to instantaneous utility depending on leisure in a Lucas-type endogenous-growth model.

16. See Föllmi and Zweimüller (2002), Kongsamut, Rebelo and Xie (2001) and Laitner (2000). Applied studies include Bils and Klenow (2001a, 2001b). These contributions partly draw upon an older tradition of studies on growth, structural change and technological progress as a source of non-linear Engel curves. See Kuznets (1953), Pasinetti (1981).

17. A consumer who is truly and favourably surprised at time t_0 by the acquired consumption knowledge on the number and service characteristics of the new goods available, and who is not expecting further favourable surprises, may wish to do more than simply modify the planned composition of her consumption basket (partly substituting the new goods for the old ones). She would wish at time t_0 to increase her consumption at dates close to t_0 over and

above what she had planned to do on the basis of the misperception that such broad and attractive consumption differentiation would be available only in a more distant future.

18. The qualification is needed to account for cases in which innovating firms were quite blind to the consumer-demand opportunities open to their innovations. The radio and the telephone are cases in point (see Metcalfe, 2001, p. 47 and the references cited therein).

19. For instance, it would not be far from realistic to have an overlapping generations model in which consumption when young is decided by the old parent.

REFERENCES

Aoki, M. and H. Yoshikawa (2002), 'Demand saturation-creation and economic growth', *Journal of Economic Behaviour and Organization*, **48**, 127–54.

Barro, R.J. and X. Sala-I-Martin (1995), *Economic Growth*, New York: McGraw Hill.

Becker, G. (1965), 'A theory of the allocation of time', *Economic Journal*, **75**, 493–517.

Benassy, J.P. (1998), 'Is there always too little research in endogenous growth with expanding product variety?', *European Economic Review*, **42**, 61–9.

Bianchi, M. (ed.) (1998a), *The Active Consumer*, London: Routledge.

Bianchi, M. (1998b), 'Taste for novelty and novel tastes: the role of human agency in consumption', in Bianchi (1998a), pp. 64–86.

Bianchi, M. (2002), 'Novelty, preferences, and fashion: when goods are unsettling', *Journal of Economic Behaviour and Organization,* **47**, 1–18.

Bils, M. and P.J. Klenow (2001a), 'Quantifying quality growth', *American Economic Review*, **91**(4), 1006–30.

Bils, M. and P.J. Klenow (2001b), 'The acceleration in variety growth', *American Economic Review*, **91**(2), 274–80.

Bresnahan, T.F. and R. Gordon (eds) (1997), *The Economics of New Goods*, Chicago: The University of Chicago Press.

Dosi, G., G. Fagiolo, R. Aversi, M. Meacci and C. Olivetti (1999), 'Cognitive processes, social adaptation and innovation in consumption patterns: from stylised facts to demand theory', in Dow and Earl (1999), pp. 139–72.

Dow, S.C. and P.E. Earl (eds) (1999), *Economic Organization and Economic Knowledge*, Cheltenham, UK and Northampton, MAm USA: Edward Elgar.

Ethier, W.J. (1982), 'National and international returns to scale in the modern theory of international trade', *American Economic Review*, **72**, 389–405.

Föllmi, R. and J. Zweimüller (2002), 'Structural change and the Kaldor facts of economic growth', CEPR Discussion Paper no. 3300, April.

Grossman, G.M. and E. Helpman (1991), *Innovation and Growth in the Global Economy*, Cambridge, Mass.: MIT Press.

Kongsamut, P., S. Rebelo and D. Xie (2001), 'Beyond balanced growth', *Review of Economic Studies*, **68**, 869–82.

Kuznets, S. (1953), *Economic Change*, New York: Norton.

Lancaster, K. (1971), *Consumer Demand: A New Approach*, New York: Columbia University Press.

Laitner, J. (2000), 'Structural change and economic growth', *Review of Economic Studies*, **67**, 545–61.

Loasby, B.J. (1998), 'Cognition and innovation', in Bianchi (1998a), pp. 89–106.

Metcalfe, J.S. (2001), 'Consumption, preferences, and the evolutionary agenda', in Witt (2001a), pp. 43–64.

Ortigueira, S. and M.S. Santos (1997), 'On the speed of convergence in endogenous growth models', *American Economic Review*, **87**, 383–99.

Pasinetti, L.L. (1981), *Structural Change and Economic Growth*, Cambridge, UK: Cambridge University Press.

Schumpeter, J.A. (1928), 'The instability of capitalism', *Economic Journal*, **38**, 361–86.

Steedman, I. (2000), *Consumption and Time*, The Graz Schumpeter Lectures, London: Routledge.

Swann, G.M.P. (1999), 'Marshall's consumer as an innovator', in Dow and Earl (1999), pp. 98–118.

Witt, U. (ed.) (2001a), *Escaping Satiation*, Berlin: Springer-Verlag.

Witt, U. (2001b), 'Learning to consume. A theory of wants and the growth of demand', in Witt (2001a), pp. 29–42.

4. Consumption composition: growth and distribution

Davide Gualerzi

4.1. INTRODUCTION

The main objective of this chapter is to begin to articulate the relationship between consumption composition and growth in the long run. In this attempt a central position is occupied by new products and innovative investment, ultimately refocusing the analysis of growth on effective demand. In fact, it is the lack of an elaboration of the theory of effective demand in the long run that can explain why the issue of composition has become so elusive to theoretical analysis and even to the recent literature on variety in consumption.

Though a prominent issue in the macro literature, consumption spending is mostly treated in aggregate terms. When wages and employment are set, that is, when income distribution is determined, consumption follows. Moreover, it is widely assumed that supply will dominate in the long run, leaving room for demand only in the short run. The exception is the model of growth and structural change of Pasinetti (1981, 1993), which establishes a bridge between the effects of technological change and demand and, because of that, it must consider its structure as an essential aspect of the growth process.[1]

The questions raised by Pasinetti's comprehensive study of structural dynamics indicate several possible directions of investigation. For one thing the model lays the ground for a dynamic theory of consumption. New products play an important role in it, but it is mostly hinted at, rather than developed, given the more general purposes of the study (see Gualerzi, 1996). They are nevertheless a key issue for the question of consumption composition and its relationship with growth and distribution. Thus, while the second section examines how the analysis of composition develops out of the foundation laid by the Harrod Domar and Pasinetti model, the third section outlines the main approaches to the question of new products, and examines the revamping interest in new commodities and variety in consumption one finds in the literature. As becomes clear from the discussion of new products, the mechanism by which in the long run consumption interacts and determines growth needs a dynamic theory of consumption, or at least a sketch of it. The fundamental notions and relationships of such a theory are presented in Section 4.4. Section 4.5 discusses instead the substantive development of a theory in which changes in the structure of consumption are an essential aspect of growth. The challenge for a demand-oriented approach to growth is to construct an independent account of consumption evolution and its feedback on the growth mechanism.

Though this mechanism concerns a long-run process, the actual structural dynamics is specific to each cycle of expansion. The last sections of the chapter analyse the structural dynamics of the two expansive cycles of the 1980s and 1990s in the US economy, illustrating how the theoretical model can shed light on the similarities and differences in the pattern of growth. They also discuss the effects of the growth pattern on distribution. Not only are they an important part of the transformation, but they also show interesting complementarities with the trends of structural transformation, although this aspect is not part of the analytical approach.

4.2. GROWTH AND CONSUMPTION COMPOSITION

4.2.1. Effective Demand in the Long Run

Starting the analysis of consumption composition from the Keynesian principle of effective demand appears at first rather peculiar. Keynes's aggregate analysis pays no attention to consumption composition, since the main purpose is that of analysing income and employment levels in the short run. It is precisely the attempt to extend to the long run Keynes's principle of effective demand of the Harrod–Domar model that poses the problem of composition in the process of growth. In fact, we have first to undo the drastic separation between income determination and the question of consumption composition to uncover its relationship to growth and distribution.

If we add to the short-run condition $I = S$ the long-run condition $Y_c = Y_d$, where Y_c is output, that is productive capacity, and Y_d is aggregate demand, then the warranted path of growth requires that $Y_c = K/v = I/s = Y_d$, where s is the marginal propensity to save and v is the capital output ratio. Moving to the long run requires full appreciation of the capacity creating effect of investment, previously considered only for its capacity to determine income.

Still, early Keynesian growth theory focuses on aggregate growth in its long-run analysis. This is very 'Keynesian' in spirit, given the stress laid by Keynes on income determination and the level of economic activity. It appears indeed reasonable in the short run to take productive capacity, and its composition, as given. Similarly, the role of consumption as a purely income determined variable of expenditure appears justified by the fact that autonomous investment is considered only in its capacity to determine income and employment. However, in the long run these explanations no longer apply. Maintaining the attention on the aggregates permits us to focus sharply on the inherent instability of the growth path and the relationship between growth and employment, but overshadows the question of output composition, though the latter becomes, quite obviously, a proper topic of investigation in a long-run perspective. While it is of little damage to the short-run perspective of Keynes, this obscures the many implications of the principle of effective demand for the theory of growth. In particular, the fact that the growth rate of aggregate demand must be such as to absorb the output of the new installed capacity suggests that the proportions between industries and expenditure components may remain constant and the structure of demand adjusts to that of supply. Thus, the theory of output ends up concerning only its level.[2]

These remarks do not call into question the central role of investment and of the multiplier in determining output and employment. They simply call attention to the structural aspect of the growth process, and especially changes in the volume of spending in new areas of consumption. If we follow the lead of Keynes's principle of effective demand and search in the demand side the key to the pace and direction of accumulation, the question of demand composition immediately arises and poses the problem of a theory on the level and composition of output.

4.2.2. Structural Dynamics and Demand Composition

A growing economic system in which the proportions between industries and the demand structure are unchanged is typical of most growth theory. This is precisely what Pasinetti calls 'pseudo-dynamics'. It assumes that consumption will adjust to supply. Therefore, no independent account of consumption is needed. The main novelty of Pasinetti's model (1981, 1993) is to consider together changes in the structure of production *and* in the structure of final demand. The starting point is the recognition that technical progress proceeds at a different pace in different sectors and productivity growth is uneven between sectors. It is precisely uneven productivity growth that makes it difficult to accept the notion of an unchanging structure of consumption. That would require demand to grow proportionally to absorb any increase in sectoral outputs resulting from technical progress. Alternatively, it requires a theory of its evolution, that is a dynamic theory of consumption.

One thing we know about demand, argues Pasinetti: 'it does not expand proportionally'. A path of different growth rates of sectoral demands can be anchored to the Engel law. Pasinetti's theory of consumption is therefore based on an endogenously generated and income-driven rule of non-proportional expansion. Limits to the expansion of expenditure on certain products are set by saturation levels at which the growth rate of demand decelerates and then flattens out.

There is an obvious overlap between the (changing) composition of consumption expenditure and new products and/or product variety. The non-proportional rule of expansion of expenditure, however, cannot say much about the specific, commodity-based forms of satisfaction of such broad categories of needs as those considered in the structure of consumption expenditure. These are specific to a social and production structure in a certain stage of development of the economy. Especially, they reflect firms' investment and marketing strategies. Pasinetti makes reference to new products several times in the analysis. He acknowledges that they are an essential aspect of technical progress and in the few passages he speaks of product innovation as a way to promote demand. He also seems to attribute to them some autonomous role in determining consumption patterns. 'The variation in the composition of consumption may well occur independently of the increase in income and of the changes in prices, as a consequence of the appearance on the market of newly invented goods and services' (1981, p. 40). This line of reasoning implies that a lot of attention should be given to product innovation.

This is more so because the fundamental force underlying Pasinetti structural dynamics is the learning principle, which operates both on the production side, that is technical change, and the demand side, through consumer learning. According to Pasinetti the limits set by saturation (of certain needs) imposes a periodical speeding up of consumer learning. Learning their new preferences would allow consumers to redirect spending to new areas of consumption. Learning these new preferences appears, however, from the logic of the argument inextricably than linked to product innovation. Indeed, the notion of learning is better suited to an approach to consumer choice in which, rather than being discovered, new preferences are developed within an adaptive, socially conditioned process, where contact with products, and especially new products, as well as the social rules of consumption, are essential aspects. Furthermore, this appears to be particularly true when what is involved is the development of needs that may cause a deep repositioning of consumption spending. Thus, learning new preferences at least implicitly suggests an analysis of consumption focusing on the relationship between product innovation, endogenous taste formation and the development of the structure of needs.

4.3. PRODUCT INNOVATION

4.3.1. Theoretical Perspectives on New Products

New products have been approached in rather different theoretical perspectives. They are an important theme of the literature on industrial organization, based on the work of E. Mansfield and F. Scherer, for example. The question seems to originate in the work of Chamberlain and J. Robinson on monopolistic and imperfect competition and in the theory of the firm of E. Penrose. Especially the famous expression of Mansfield, 'the frost on the cake', suggests a rather narrow focus on differentiation as a key element of marketing strategies with rather minimal technological innovation.

At the opposite end of the spectrum we can put the fundamental role that new products have, when treated as a basic innovation, in the analysis of the Neo-Schumpeterian literature.[3] The notion of 'technological systems' (Clark, Freeman and Soete, 1982) is specifically designed to explain the macroeconomic, long-term effects of basic innovations. Here the relationship to growth is straightforward: new products are part of the technology-push driving autonomous investment and the long wave of development. New products are therefore a central issue because of the association with technology development and investment.

In this respect it is of great interest to observe that product innovation plays a fundamental role also in some of the New Growth Theory models, in particular the Schumpeterian models *à la* Aghion–Howitt. Reference to the same roots, however, only emphasizes the fundamental difference in the perspectives. Neo-Schumpeterian theory, as stressed by Freeman, is sympathetic of the notion of animal spirits, and therefore to the stress laid by Keynes on the role of demand.[4] In New Growth Theory models the transmission mechanism of the effects of innovation and variety on growth rests on savings and is therefore supply determined.

While in agreement with the stress laid on the close relationship between technology advances and investment, which indeed is the basis for the notion of innovative investment introduced below, the problem of Neo-Schumpeterian theory is the scant attention given to the demand side, at least in its earlier formulation. This might largely stem from the fact that the issue of new products from the demand side has been elaborated mostly within consumer theory. While opening up the consumer problem to product innovation (Lancaster, 1966, 1971) and indicating ways in which new commodities can shape consumption patterns (Ironmonger, 1972), the refinements of consumer theory could not overcome the framework of static consumer choice. Lancaster's main motivation was indeed to enable traditional consumer theory to cope with product innovation and differentiation. Thus, though addressing the problem of new items of choice, he was not concerned with their impact on consumption expenditure or growth.

The problem has been addressed in more recent evolutionary theory, specifically directed to build up the demand side of economic growth (Witt, 2001). In an evolutionary framework the relationship between new products and demand patterns shows all its relevance for the analysis of growth. A review of the advances and shortcomings of these contributions with respect to demand-led approaches and the particular view of effective demand put forward here, is certainly an interesting theme, but cannot be pursued here. Two contributions can be mentioned since they explicitly take Pasinetti's analysis of structural dynamics as the starting point.[5] Following Schumpeter's insight Saviotti (2001) notes that 'producers must play a very large role in the creation of demand for new products, the more so the greater the degree of novelty of the new product...' (p. 129). He then develops a theory of demand evolution. The 'replicator dynamics model of demand evolution' deals with the factors determining entry and exit from the consumer population, taking into account agents' heterogeneity. This allows for formal treatment of the conditions under which output variety will growth. Since 'the development of demand is a necessary condition for economic development' (p. 135), the replicator model establishes a link between variety and growth. It can be said that this link is rather tenuous since it does not address the actual process by which new goods come into being and support growth. Still, full appreciation of the problem posed by Pasinetti leads us to address the relationship between variety and growth.

In yet another development of Pasinetti's ideas Andersen (2001) elaborates on the notion of satiation observing that 'in a model with multiple levels of income, different firms and consumers will meet the satiation constraint at different points of time' (p. 162). This would add a new element to the determination of innovative investment and consumption innovation.

Finally, one should note that the issue of structural change is addressed by two recent articles. In one of them the change in the composition of consumption expenditure plays an important role. Laitner (2000) argues that the average saving propensity may rise as a result of industrialization, in a model in which structural change depends on the operation of the Engel law, thus on changes in the composition of consumption. Structural change in the form of reallocation of labour from agriculture to manufacturing is also the theme of Kongsamut, Rebelo and Xie (2001). The authors present a model that reconciles the 'Kaldor facts', which they associate with balanced growth, with the empirical evidence on structural change, what they call the 'Kuznet facts'.

4.3.2.   Quality and Variety

The question of product innovation and consumption composition has resurfaced in the recent literature under the heading of quality improvement and variety growth. The revamping interest for the issue of new goods (Bresnahan and Gordon, 1997; Boskin Commission, 1996) stems mainly from a specific problem, that is whether quality improvements are correctly taken into account by prices. The particular issue at stake is to measure quality improvement so as to have a better measure of inflation (hedonic pricing), and therefore of growth. Typically the expectation is that some of the price increases should be netted off to take quality into account, thereby decreasing the rate of price inflation so that 'real growth' appears underestimated.

Bils and Klenow (2001b) observe that 'the hedonic techniques ... have been applied to only a limited number of goods'. The problem is that the measurement of quality requires very detailed knowledge obtainable only for specific goods. In fact, even the estimates of the Boskin Commission are based on a limited number of good-by-good studies.[6] The main purpose of their work is then to devise a method that can overcome this limitation, which they use to estimate 'the rate of unmeasured quality growth for 66 durable consumer goods that constitute over 80 percent of U.S, spending on consumer durables' (p. 1006). Their focus is on quality upgrading, which partially overlaps with a second theme, that of variety, which is of more direct concern here.[7]

In a previous article (Bils and Klenow, 2001a) they had developed a model to estimate the effects of variety, and in particular the acceleration in variety growth, on consumption spending. As opposed to the central role played by the growth of variety in theoretical growth models, they argue, there is no empirical evidence on this point. The difficulty consists in estimating consumer surplus 'from the myriad of new models and features that are continually introduced.' Their 'indirect approach' consists of inferring the importance of variety from the relative growth rates of consumption expenditure in dynamic goods, those for which variety is growing. In a few cases of 'dramatic product innovations' (cable television, VCR and movie rentals, personal computers, cell phones), there is a clear positive effect on spending.[8] A more exhaustive test is then conducted on a set of dynamic goods, considering the sub-periods 1959–79 and 1979–99.

To isolate the effects of variety growth, that is product innovation, they estimate Engel curves for 106 categories of spending in order to net off income and price effects on spending. This confirms a shift of expenditure away from static goods and a sizable residual growth rate. They then relate 'changes in the spending shares for 1980–96 to the rate of item substitution within each category, as recorded by the BLS for 1997' (p. 277) [9] to find out that item substitution rates predict shifts in spending even after controlling for income, price and demographic effects. This further confirms that product innovation is an important determinant of spending.

It must be observed that item substitutions rates are an indicator of rapid innovation, but also of new products replacing old ones. This is why Bils and Klenow (2001a, p. 277) focus 'on those item substitutions that the BLS judges to be noncomparable, meaning no closely similar model exists or appears on the outlet'. This better represents their interest in 'important new varieties'. However, the problem remains somewhat unresolved, as they themselves point out. This is confirmed by the persistent difficulty in distinguishing between quality improvement and novelty. This does not greatly affect their main conclusion: variety sustains spending and this is confirmed by the shifts in expenditure shares as variety growth accelerated very considerably in the second sub-period 1979–99. Therefore, there is 'an important role for quality growth in consumption growth' (2001b, p. 1007). They further suggest viewing that in parallel with the growth of patents since the mid 1980s. It remains unclear, however, how spending driven by variety and/or quality affects income growth. Indeed, in their conclusions Bils and Klenow simply argue: 'We find that spending shares have shifted dramatically, with these shifts poorly anticipated by relative Engel-curve or price effects ... new products have played an important role in the substantial shifts in spending' (2001a, p. 279). There is no clear way in which this links up to issues of aggregate spending and growth, unless we fall back on the issue of unmeasured growth, which pops up again in some of the literature they discuss in connection with the measurement of variety.

4.4.   INNOVATION IN CONSUMPTION

The study of variety and quality growth, while indicating the importance of the relationship between consumption spending and product innovation, and the difficulties involved, leaves open the question of whether and how consumption composition and its change can drive growth. Quite clearly this approach re-proposes the issue of a dynamic theory of consumption beyond the regularities of the Engel curve. The issue eluded the traditional theory of consumer choice, inherently static, but also the effort to introduce technological change and new commodities in that framework. To move in that direction it is first necessary to overcome the contrast between exogenous preferences and product innovation. A possible solution is to partially internalize the process of innovation in consumption into the consumer choice problem. It requires active participation of consumers in defining viable new alternatives of consumption. This makes it possible to consider the role of product innovation in determining consumption composition and develop, in a second step, the analysis of consumption patterns as part of the growth process.

The problem is that when we consider new commodities shaping the ways of satisfying needs there seems to be no more room for consumer choice. If indeed, as Schumpeter suggests, consumers are 'educated' by producers, then the issue seems to disappear and the entire question of composition seems to be entrusted to the product innovation strategies of firms. An alternative approach should, first of all, focus precisely on novelty and change in consumption. This lies at the root of the problem, but also indicates the way out. On the one hand, it makes it difficult to define the optimizing problem of the consumer, on the other it opens the way to an active role of consumers beyond the notion of consumer choice. When the problem is closely examined, it can be concluded that what matters is the contribution of consumers to establishing a way of satisfying needs as the norm of consumption, that is, a socially acceptable and desirable alternative. Consumers then have a role precisely in the process of change. The subjective element is better captured by some notion of personal development than by exogenous preferences. Thus, there is no contrast between endogenous preferences and subjectivity to the extent that locating taste formation within the economic process does not exclude and actually finally gives full recognition to the agency of individuals as consumers. The third element of this approach to consumer choice is then to partially internalize individuals' drive to self-realization, based on the development of personal identity, into *an interactive process of innovation in consumption*.

The notion of innovation in consumption is presented here in fairly general, theoretical terms, to indicate how it can contribute to a dynamic theory of consumption and the fundamental role it plays in the transmission mechanism connecting consumption to growth.[10]

It is largely consistent with empirical studies of innovation and historical examples, which illustrate the forms taken by the interaction between consumers and product innovation. Citing a few examples taken from the journal *Technology and Culture*, Metcalfe (2001) notes that, in most cases, the establishment of mass-produced products owes something important to product innovation aiming at shaping consumer taste. In the case of automobiles, product development implied the shifting emphasis from technical aspects to their image and prestige-creating characteristics. In the case of electrical appliances a fundamental role in their diffusion was the continued evolution of design. Even more to the point he observes the role played by a specialist group – the young listening to radio broadcasting of rock and roll – in establishing the miniature radio as a mass consumption good, therefore the 'significance of communities of latent users to act as a vehicle to identify and publicise unmet needs' (p. 46). Frenken and Windrum (2002) stress the importance of user heterogeneity and design complementarities in the successive cycles of innovation in mature industries. They point out the role of single lens reflex camera and 126 film cartridge in catering to distinct groups of users and therefore the development of the camera industry. Similarly, the four main cycles of innovation that mark the development of the computer industry – the mainframe, the integrated circuit, the microprocessor, the diffusion of the Internet – were combined with the emergence of distinct needs and groups of users.

With respect to the literature the distinguishing element of the approach to consumption innovation outlined here is the elaboration of the role of consumers based on the self-realization of individuals and needs development. The subjective element in the interactive process of consumption innovation consists in the fact that individuals pursue the realization of personal identity facing a constantly changing world of commodities and the evolution of consumption alternatives which that entails. Individuals strive to be people within the economic process and social structure, bending towards their private aims the system of commodities that grows larger and more sophisticated because of product innovation. They behave as interactive social agents responding to this process of change and 'inventing' the consumption practices and use systems that validate the final specification of commodities and the selection of technologies of production and distribution.

A socially moulded individuality then contributes to determine change in consumption. It does so by interacting with the major source of innovation, that is, the dynamism of the production system. Thus, change need not be identified purely with the supply side and the development of technology. It is a broader process than the introduction of new products, in which consumption practices and the definition of use systems determine the success of new items of consumption and their diffusion paths. This, as much as technical change, can explain the concrete forms taken by the efforts of consumers to satisfy their needs. The interactive process of consumption innovation fully redefines the consumer choice problem. It does so by focusing on the active participation of consumers in defining viable new alternatives of consumption. In this perspective taste formation is the self-realization of individuals, which may well be articulated according to social rules and values, as much as it is the development of the needs structure realized in a specific pattern of consumption.[11] This is a crucial element, since it follows from the establishment of a new product within the previous structure of consumption. In this way consumption innovation validates the investment in this product. In turn, it allows for analysis of technical change and new products that departs from the straitjacket in which consumption composition has been approached, for instance in the literature on variety, and makes its relationship to growth explicit.

4.5. THE COMPOSITION EFFECT: NEW PRODUCTS AND EXPANSION

Indeed new products, and innovation in general, do not fall from the sky, they are the outcome of firms' development strategies. More specifically, they represent the effort of firms to enlarge and structure the market for the purposes of expansion. The tool for that purpose is investment (see Gualerzi, 2001, ch. 4).[12] Consumers validating new products as a viable innovation in consumption contribute to the success of a particular strategy of investment of the firm. It follows that: a) new products contribute to innovation by their insertion in the current pattern of consumption, which they contribute to transform, and b) new products matter for growth in aggregate because they are the result of investment.

Thus, within a changing structure of consumption as in the Pasinetti model, product innovation acquires its full relevance for the study of growth. The composition effect is therefore the result of interaction between a changing consumption composition and investment strategies.

A specific pattern of consumption, that is, a structure of expenditure *and* commodity-based forms of needs satisfaction, affects growth, creating the stimulus for new commodities and validating net investment in these commodities.

4.5.1. Basic Relationships

This is what we can call the composition effect. It unfolds as part of the growth process, which concerns the creation of capacity, but also its changing composition. Approaching growth as a process, while reminding us of Joan Robinson, blurs to a large extent the distinction between the long and short run. At the centre of this process is a growth mechanism that has a long-term time perspective, like that found in the analysis of accumulation of Classical Theory. But the forms it might take, for example the characteristics of product innovation or the sectors where innovative investment is stronger, are specific to particular cycles of expansion. The mechanism is then realized in specific episodes of growth that can be analysed empirically.

The mechanism accounting for expansion in essence says that the aggregate rate of growth depends on aggregate net investment through structural change, realized in a particular consumption composition. Admittedly, this is a very simplified rendering of the process of transformation, almost provocatively simple. To better indicate the kind of causation imbedded in this approach the mechanism can be broken down into a set of functional relationships, reflecting the structural determination originating in the process of innovation and learning that permeates structural dynamics.

We can interpret these relationships as operating at one moment in time, but they are in fact ongoing relationships, as the mechanism they describe is realized through time. It must be stressed that the point here is not to develop a model of the process, that might require distinguishing between a short-run model, a business cycle model or a long-run equilibrium path. Instead the focus has to be on some significant relationships and their interdependence. Together they show the forces involved in determining consumption composition, an issue that has not been satisfactorily addressed. In particular, the point is to take investment seriously for what it does in the actual process of transformation of the economy.

Aggregate net investment depends on variables such as the trend of sales and the level of utilization of capacity (Z), which are determined as averages of distinct sectoral dynamics. But the dynamic element is what we can call *innovative investment*, that is, investment directed to innovation, aimed at exploiting the potential implicit in the established structure of need and the current pattern of consumption, proxied by current consumption composition (C_c). Innovative investment should be understood in a broad sense, beyond the introduction of new physical capital goods, to include product development, market research and product testing.

1) Aggregate net investment = $I = f_1$ (Sales trend, Z, I_i)

Here it is necessary to keep in mind that innovative investment includes both product development, associated with the first phase of the product cycle, and the creation of productive capacity, associated with subsequent phases of the product cycle, that is, the steep part of the product cycle curve. Thus, while innovative investment of the first kind will lead to changes in consumption composition, via product innovation, innovative investment of the second kind will respond to this change, once product innovation is established in a niche market. Causality goes in both directions, that is, the mechanism of expansion rests on a positive feedback.

Innovative investment, on the other hand, will depend on technology development and respond to the degree of market saturation. The former can be proxied by some technological index (T), the latter by the ratio of current sales over potential sales, estimated by marketing methods. The relationship between innovative investment and the degree of market saturation is a direct one, to the extent that product development counters the negative effects of saturation on sales.[13]

2) Innovative investment $= I_i = f_2$ (T, Sales ratio, dC_c)

3) Changes in consumption composition $= dC_c = f_3$ (I_i, NP)

The focus on investment clarifies that changes in consumption composition, that is, the transformation of consumption patterns, is expansionary.[14] An increase in the level of effective demand, due to innovative investment, is the first mover of expansion, which will then be sustained by the validation of the investment strategies in innovation, captured by changes in consumption composition (dC_c). In turn, the change in consumption composition depends itself on innovative investment resulting in product innovation, with the addition of a variable taking into account the appearance of new products (NP), that is, products fundamentally affecting the structure of consumption. Innovation in consumption, while endogenously determining taste formation, will affect consumption patterns. This will result in the growth of sales of certain products that signals a successful investment in innovation. Depending on the phase of the diffusion process – and the position in the sigmoid representing the expenditure in that particular category of consumption expenditure (Pasinetti, 1981) – growth of sales may signal either market expansion or barely holding down the market share, that is, countering the effects of saturation.

These behavioural relationships, therefore, spell out the mechanism by which the composition effect, rooted in the structure of consumption, affects the pattern of growth and contributes to determine it. In this respect the set of relationships can be completed with an additional relationship concerning new products, which would otherwise be exogenous, though they are obviously at the centre of the endogenous dynamic of change.

4) $NP = f_4$ (I_i, T) makes it explicit that new products depend on innovative investment and the level of technological development.

Here again it must be observed that the functional relationships, while a possible basis for building a model, are not primarily designed for that purpose.[15] They are used instead to focus more sharply on the forces determining consumption composition and their interdependence. In fact, the methodological point that this approach underscores is that conceptual relationships are useful to think about the problem as a necessary preliminary to model building.

4.5.2. Composition Effect: Discussion

This approach can clarify a number of issues that eluded other treatments of consumption composition. In particular, the mechanism described above can accommodate different kinds of product innovation, and therefore distinct firm strategies and the impacts on growth, that have the same root. They are in fact variations of the same fundamental logic governing the relationship between investment, product innovation and consumption composition, and ultimately determining the strength of expansion.

The reference to new preferences and the promotion of demand suggests that product innovation may work to sustain spending in products that are in the maturity phase of the product cycle and/or approach the saturation levels set up by the non-proportional growth of demand in specific markets. From the firms' standpoint such a strategy of investment in product innovation aims at maintaining market share. This is where the traditional notion of differentiation, or minimal innovation of the literature on industrial organization more clearly applies. It can be associated also with the search for novelty, assimilated into the marketing strategies of new models and new designs typical of large-scale consumers' markets. In this case the expansionary effect of new products may still be small and consumption composition changes might be not very significant. However, the diffusion process is also the typical milieu in which incremental innovation, quality improvement and variety may uncover new potential for consumption innovation, therefore establishing the condition for additional investment.

The fundamental point is that the structure of needs realized in a specific pattern of consumption has implicit potential for development, which is uncovered precisely by innovation. New products may substitute old products in the consumption basket, because they are variations or improvements on old ones, or because they satisfy the same need in a different form. We need not conclude that it is a zero sum game. Additional investment must in any case take place to develop and establish the new product. The successful introduction of a new product sets up the conditions for a diffusion process that drives additional investment. Finally, consumption innovation and diffusion uncover new complementarities and interdependencies. Ultimately, it is the structure of needs that is affected and therefore the possibility to face further development of that structure.[16] On the other hand, new ways displacing old ways of satisfying needs imply that the system is bound to a pattern of development that will not explode. Net investment flows creating new industries will come at the expense of net decreases in declining industries and the rate of growth associated with that, though undetermined, will be bounded as well.

The effects on growth will be greater when considering new products that more fundamentally affect the forms of needs satisfaction and hence the pattern of consumption. Not only might innovative investment be much larger, but its induced effects much stronger. Innovation in this case would affect needs development more greatly, channelling spending into new areas of consumption. Changes in consumption composition would then be associated with stronger expansionary effects of a changing pattern of growth.[17]

In sum, the notion of new products can then be clarified rigorously in relation to the role they play in accumulation, that is, for the amount of (autonomous) investment they set in motion. Accordingly, there are three expansive effects of a changing composition. The first is innovative investment, in the phase of product introduction. We assume that most radical innovation, that is, new products that determine a significant process of consumption innovation, will require larger investment spending. A differentiated product, although it may be a non-perfect substitute, or have additional attributes, will mobilize less resources than a new product, which we assume to be a non-perfect substitute. The second expansive effect concerns the establishment of the new product as a viable way of satisfying a certain need. The diffusion process will have a significant impact on product development and induced investment. A third expansive effect concerns complementarities and interdependencies. They may open up prospects for more innovation in consumption, thereby reinforcing investment spending and creating the conditions for another round of investment. Ultimately the intensity of the investment drive will depend on the extent to which the pattern of consumption is transformed, recreating the conditions for innovative investment.

4.5.3. Needs Development and Collective Goods

The heuristic model based on an articulation of the principle of effective demand in the long run outlined above is designed to capture the inherent dynamism of changes in consumption composition. This crucially depends on the relationship between product innovation, consumption composition and the development of the structure of need. This is ultimately the reason why changes in composition are expansionary.

Without elaborating on the implications for the analysis of growth we can introduce the distinction between private and collective goods (Nell, 2002) to further clarify how the structure of need is an inherently dynamic concept.[18]

We need first to reconsider the fact that the needs structure reflects a hierarchy and the rate of growth of expenditure decreases as a result of the saturation of certain needs. Basic needs, those at the bottom of that hierarchy, such as food, clothing and shelter, are satisfied by 'private goods', goods that provide satisfaction to the single consumer and are consumed in isolation, without externalities. As income grows, other needs begin to be satisfied and the corresponding expenditure categories become more important in household budgets. Communication, entertainment and education are typically collective goods; they are rarely consumed in isolation. Indeed, they are useful only if combined with personal interaction, and the more people consume them the better they work.

The point about needs development is that it is precisely this collective aspect, and the externality it implies, which is the most dynamic component of product innovation and consumption expenditure. Indeed, it is becoming increasingly important even for private goods. Product innovation, and the ensuing consumption innovation, in food, clothing and shelter, may improve quality and variety, but it mostly enhances this collective aspect of private goods. Sustaining expenditure, thus forestalling satiation, it is increasingly a matter of defining food not simply as a life-sustaining product, and not even a product of better quality and presence. Instead, innovation will enhance the notion of eating together and of the physical and social ambience, where this collective consumption takes place. Fashion is an even clearer example: identification is based on the collective aspect of clothing, which implies status and social recognition. Therefore, needs development may concern also basic needs, to the extent that changing the social practices of consumption will realize more fully their collective aspect.

It appears that this is at least part of the story of the glamorous consumption of the 1980s, discussed below. It might be particularly relevant in the absence of radically new products and when income distribution is more uneven.

4.6. AN EMPIRICAL ILLUSTRATION: TWO DECADES OF DEVELOPMENT OF THE US ECONOMY

The two following sections examine the structural dynamics of the 1980s and 1990s in the US economy. The reference to specific cycles of expansion has the main purpose of illustrating, with the support of the evidence on a case study, the mechanism of growth outlined in general in the sections above, rather than being an empirical test of the composition effect. The relationship between product innovation, consumption composition and aggregate growth is the main focus of the illustration, as it is assumed that it can shed light on the structural dynamics of the two periods. The latter is consistently contrasted with the aggregate performance.

The two decades of development of the US economy considered highlight similarities and differences in the growth pattern that can be comprised within the theoretical model. Such variations contribute to further clarify its internal dynamic. To this extent the illustration can complement theoretical analysis.

4.6.1.   The Recovering 1980s and the Booming 1990s

As regards the cyclical pattern of the US economy in the post-war period[19] it can first be noticed that, though hailed as a strong recovery after the years of stagflation and despite seven years of positive growth rates, the average growth rate over the cycle 1979–89 was modest by post-war standards (2.6 per cent), indeed in line with that of the 1970s.[20] The second peculiarity for a strong upturn is relatively weak investment spending.[21] Gross Private Domestic Investment grew rapidly after a dramatic collapse in 1982, but by 1985 it had already stabilized, with no indication of further growth. Gross investment in producers' durable equipment had a similar pattern, though somewhat more vigorous. Other available measures of investment tend to confirm relatively weak investment spending.[22] At the same time there is evidence of a consumption-fuelled recovery, combined with deep changes in the consumption structure and in the income distribution.

In contrast with the 1980s cycle, which began with the most severe recession since 1950, followed by a dramatic rebound and a progressively lower growth rate, the 1990s cycle set in after a brief and less severe downturn in 1990 and 1991.[23] Here again, though often described as one of the longest and strongest expansions of the post-war period, comparison with the previous decades considerably lowers these claims. In fact, annual growth rates remained substantially in line with the 1980s average until 1995, except for a peak in 1994, to accelerate considerably from 1996.[24] Even so, the average is not close to that of the 1960s (see Table 4.1). Nevertheless, both the growth rate after 1996 and the role played by investment suggest stronger expansion than in the previous cycle.

There is evidence that investment had a much bigger role and underlay the growth acceleration in the late 1990s. Gross private fixed investment recovered in 1992 and shows a steady growth till 2000. A pivotal role was played by investment in the ICT (Information and Communication Technologies) sector, which experienced what can be called a real boom.[25]

So while the distinction between the two cycles should not be overstated, because of the rather brief downturn in the early 1990s and the strong expansion only in the last five years of the two decades, there are important differences confirmed by the structural dynamics sustaining the expansion in the two periods. Indeed, it is precisely the relationship between investment and consumption composition, mediated by product innovation, which highlights distinct growth patterns.

Table 4.1   Macroeconomic indicators

Average Annual rate %	60–70	70–80	80–90	90–00	96–00
Δ GNP	4.4	3.3	3.1	3.1	4.3
Δ Labour Productivity	2.9	1.0	1.4	1.9	2.6
Δ Employment	1.9	2.4	1.7	1.3	1.8
Unemployment	4.8	6.2	7.3	5.8	4.5
Inflation	2.3	7.1	5.6	3.0	2.0
Δ Real return S&P 500	6.6	–0.5	12.9	15.9	26.4

Sources: Lossani, 2001; Bank of St. Louis, 2000; IMF 2000; BLS, 2000

It was noted above that in the 1980s relative weak growth was combined with significant changes in the structure of consumption, as a result of the expansion of some categories of consumption expenditure. In particular, three categories show an unequivocal pattern of expansion above that predicted by an income-led model: personal business, which includes financial services, medical and recreation expenditures (see Gualerzi, 2001, ch. 8). This is an indication of the areas of need most affected by innovation in consumption, in fact modifying quite significantly consumption composition. This is mirrored by the rapid growth and transformation of the industries serving these markets. The 1980s were indeed the decade of the rise of finance and the spread of financial services into the consumption basket of households. This entailed the rapid industrialization of the provision of such services, an instance of a more general process of industrialization of consumer services. This applies to a large extent also to the other two industries, medical and entertainment services, but also to tourism and travel.

Innovative investment certainly had a role in establishing these industries but, due to the characteristics of industrial restructuring and expansion and possibly its concentration in a handful of industries, it did not drive the expansion, as confirmed by the relatively modest part played by investment in the recovery. This is also consistent with a relatively weak process of consumption innovation. The point is precisely the form taken by consumption innovation outside the new consumer services industries and its relationship to investment and technology development.

The benchmarks of a new epoch, in the fields of information technology, telecommunications, biotechnology and a few other areas of scientific and technological research, represent new long-term trends of technological development. During the 1980s they reach a new level of maturity. And yet, looking in retrospect, they appear at an early stage of development. Though important for process innovation and industrial restructuring, they were unable to sustain an investment wave, nor the creation of radically, or at least significantly, new consumer durables. This contrasts with the effects of technological development in the 1990s. It was pointed out above that the ICT (Information and Communication Technologies) sector had a fundamental role in shaping the 1990s cycle, especially with respect to the rapid growth of output and productivity in the late 1990s. The studies on productivity, despite differences in estimates and interpretations (see Lossani, 2001; Gualerzi, 2004), all agree on three points: the growing importance of ICT products as investment goods in the productive process; the rapid growth of productivity *within* the ICT sector and the central role played by the efficiency gains in the semiconductor industry; the existence of a spill-over affecting productivity growth of the economy, though opinions diverge on the importance of this spill-over, ranging from the notion of a new long-term trend of productivity growth, at times associated with the term 'new economy', to an improvement restricted to the ICT sector, affecting, at least to some extent, the manufacturing of durables (Gordon, 2000).[26] In general the link between productivity growth and the ICT sector appears to stem, on the one hand, from the spread of computers and communications equipment as part of the productive equipment, on the other, from the efficiency gains in the production of ICT products resulting in falling prices and improvements in their capabilities.

The other side of this investment drive in ICT products is of course their impact on consumption composition. From this point of view the development of new ICT products and of the Internet is prepared by a first wave of innovative investment. The rapid diffusion of these products validated the investment strategy and sustained an investment boom, with innovation in consumption reinforcing product innovation and technological development. So, while there is evidence that investment played more of a role than in the 1980s, it appears that innovative investment in the ICT sector not only sustained the acceleration of growth in the second part of the decade, but also had strong effects on consumption and a significant impact on the structural dynamics of growth.

4.6.2. Glamorous Consumption

We can conclude that some phenomena, which were in their early stages in the 1980s, more fully displayed their potential for growth and transformation during the 1990s. Instead, in the 1980s, since there are no major technological developments acting as instruments of innovative investment, or new consumer durables setting up a generalized process of consumption innovation, the process of product innovation focuses on the one hand on the introduction of a new generation of improved consumer durables, and on the other on the restructuring of consumer markets around two distinct patterns of innovation.

The list of what we can call 'a second generation' of consumer durables is rather long. However, the VCR, the microwave oven, the new TV sets, to mention the most important, are hardly new products in the way electrical appliances were in the 1960s, rather a further step in an evolving path. They introduce new dynamism into consumption patterns, but do not sustain a comparable process of transformation of consumption patterns.

To counter the effects of saturation, lacking real alternatives in terms of new products, what emerges is indeed a *divergent pattern of product innovation*. On the one hand, we have novelty and high quality standards, associated with the consumption and lifestyles of the wealthy and emerging social strata; on the other, a process of imitation, based on the industrialization of the same novelty at the lower end of the market, exploiting scale economies, cheap inputs and standardized design.

For consumer durables, such as automobiles, appliances and consumer electronics, but also for non-durables, like clothing and food, this translates into a strategy of introduction of new lines of products with higher standards of performance, which define the up-to-date level of quality for specific areas of consumption spending. A good example may be the fashion industry. New lines of products embody most recent technologies. Typically this takes the form of substitution of mechanical and electrical devices with electronic components in durables, increasing sophistication of the technology of materials, components and ingredients mix for non-durables, and the diffusion of computer-based design and manufacturing for both. As a result of the new technology desirable characteristics of the product are more fully realized and new ones are made possible. Thus, in a competitive environment dominated by saturation and low growth rates in the markets that represent the bulk of consumption expenditure, the effort to gain a competitive edge depends on updating the performance and perception of consumer goods by means of technological improvement.

In the case of durables and non-durables, product innovation not only propels newness and high quality but also sustains imitation. The fundamental difference with the traditional notion of market segmentation and product differentiation is that novelty does not generalize to the rest of the market in the way predicted by the traditional pattern of diffusion, with new products spreading throughout the basket of consumption of all consumers. Imitation of course implies that cheaper counterparts of the high-quality durables and non-durables as well as the items previously restricted to relatively small elites find their way into the basket of consumption and lifestyles of less affluent consumers. But they are not the same commodities, and do not contribute to the same lifestyle, to the extent that they have lost the high-quality attribute and the glamour of status and distinctive prestige consumption that sustains spending by affluent consumers. Thus, we can identify a tenuous but clear line separating the imitation effect from the diffusion pattern of consumer durables in the 1960s and 1970s.

Rather than simply diffusing, product innovation aims from the beginning at a different market. Products are designed, produced and marketed for two distinct consumer markets. Thus, though sustained by industrialization, imitation is qualitatively different from the diffusion and generalization of novelty. We observe instead a transformation leading to a *macro segmentation* of consumption markets (Gualerzi, 2001, ch. 11), which determines the specifics of product and consumption innovation.

Product innovation not only establishes distinctive characteristics of the same kind of products. It leads to a fundamental rupture, rather than continuity, in diffusion patterns. Above all, it sustains a *polarized pattern of consumption*, distinguishing between high-quality, luxurious, status-creating goods and 'standardized', cheaper counterparts. This segmentation corresponds to distinct pricing policies. Product innovation aimed at high quality and elevated standards of performance is combined with a distinction between highly-priced, high quality, 'new' (up-to-date) products and low-priced, standardized, 'old' products. The marketing effort is directed to establish new, high-quality products as the standard of cutting edge consumption, distinguishing them from old counterparts and products, catering to less affluent consumers. Thus, contrary to the claim that technology and new products were the foundation of a strong recovery, innovative investment and innovation in consumption were mainly aimed at industrial restructuring and the reshaping of consumption patterns. The transformation rests on a subtle and pervasive mechanism which stresses consumption spending by identifying it with the quality standards of the 'glamorous' consumption of the new wealthy classes. Indeed, this pattern of consumption innovation, while unable to reverse the tendency of modest growth rates, is consistent with and supported by income dynamics and a new hierarchy of wealth.

4.6.3.   Innovation in Consumption: Access and Communication

Interestingly, the glamorous consumption and associated macro-segmentation of the market emerging in the 1980s has marked a permanent change in consumer markets. The transformation seems to be the redefinition of the market in two layers, each of which has distinct market development strategies. The cover story of *Business Week* (March 17, 1997) focuses on 'two-tier marketing' as the fundamental market strategy of companies now 'tailoring their products and pitches to two different Americas'. The distinction between 'upscale' and 'downscale' products runs through most items of consumption and includes the distinction between used and new cars and used and new clothing. More in general it suggests a now stabilized split between the pattern of consumption of the wealthy and that of less affluent consumers. Within each, new phenomena emerge, fuelled by technological change, product variety and differentiation of restructuring of distribution and communication channels.

The main difference in the 1990s was, however, the rise of innovation in consumption due to new products. The investment drive, focused mainly in the ICT sector, combined with the rapid diffusion of new ICT-related products. New home electronic goods, cell phones and computer networks – including hardware and software for network access – are the most identifiable items of this new wave of consumption goods, defining a new standard of consumption in a certain critical area of needs, that of communication and access. Superimposed on the 'two-tier market' is therefore the spread of new ICT products, as well as the rise of services and products available on the Internet.[27] Just as computerization was a phenomenon changing the organization of production, the rapid diffusion of ICT products affected consumer markets, determining a major process of innovation in consumption and needs development.

The impact of ICT products is greater and more complex as we move from home electronics to the Internet. However, they share a characteristic, that is, rapid diffusion combined with constant technical improvements adding new features. Rapid innovation in consumption has transformed these new products from status symbols and/or attributes of technology freaks into generalized items of consumption, following a diffusion path similar to that of mass consumption.

Penetration rates provide evidence for the pace of diffusion of these new products. Factory sales of cell phones, including analogue, dual band and PCS types, soared from 1,830,000 units in 1990, with a household penetration rate of 5 per cent, to 57,000,000 units in 2000, with a penetration rate of 60 per cent. Factory sales of computers, including monitors, keyboards, mice and other peripherals, went from 4,000,000 units in 1990 to

16,400,000 in 2000, with a penetration rate up from 22 per cent to 58 per cent (see EBrain Market Research Report, 2003).

Focusing on the effects on needs development, the consumer electronics sector has ushered in a new standard of consumption in certain areas of needs, that of home entertainment, for example, with the increasing use of digital signals for video and music and the spread of video games. Cell phones and Internet access are more important because they more fully realize an aspect of needs development crucial to an understanding of modern society, that of communication and access.[28] Cell phones appear at first as an addition and an improvement of the telephone, not a new product in itself. However, cell phones substantially extend the possibility of being in contact and make communication virtually available at any time and in any place. As such, they build on a parent's need to be in touch with their offspring in whatever situation as well as making it simple to make decisions and set up appointments. They have become part of the mobile office, which is indeed another new product made possible by the combination of processing capabilities with advanced telecommunication. Cell phones have not only fulfilled the need for communication more completely, but have also generated additional communication needs and the transfer to increasingly sophisticated information such as that contained in images. An important aspect of lifestyles has been modified, together with the consumption practices associated with communication. Similarly, the Internet has made possible a substantially different use of the computing capacity installed in computers. Here again is the issue of access and communication that lies at the core of the new development. However, it has had an even greater impact and created greater prospects for further development. Indeed, the pivotal role played by ICT in structural dynamics cannot be appreciated without attaching full importance to the possibilities created by advanced telecommunications and the growth of networks.

The point, as was stressed above, is how a new product becomes part of the consumption structure. Its position within the system of needs, realized in a specific composition of consumption, and the characteristics of consumption innovation determine the size of the induced effects, both in terms of further development of needs and stimuli to more investment. Information processing capabilities are now interconnected in a network, with two main results: on the one hand the development of network externalities, on the other, the possibility of reorganizing productive processes, the transactions of goods and services, and in the end the supply of new products and services.

The Internet has created the condition for unprecedented development of what was a rather narrow notion of distributed data processing and information services. Through the development of the network, rapidly growing computing capabilities have led to the rise of new products and services and thus of consumption innovation. This is the basis for a *composition effect* rooted in the increased sophistication of the ICT sector. In turn, this suggests that ICT-driven development is crucial not only for productivity growth, but also for structural transformation (Gualerzi, 2004).

Furthermore, the growth prospects of a larger, far-reaching process of innovation in consumption failed to materialize and the enormous expectations created by the development of ICT were the first reason for its folding back with the end of the expansion in 2000. This opens a host of questions that cannot be addressed here. At the same time it suggests that the theoretical model based on innovative investment and consumption composition can be useful to explain also the end of the boom: they both share the fundamental characteristic of effective demand, that of operating in both directions, namely expansion and contraction.

4.7. TRENDS IN STRUCTURAL CHANGE

From the analysis of the 1990s cycle it can be concluded that the ICT sector sustained an acceleration of growth lasting a few years and set in motion a process of transformation which, however, was unable to lead the economy into a long term of steady expansion. Nevertheless, the strong upturn in the latter part of the 1990s suggests that information technologies reached a new level of dominance in the economy and within business. Whether this signals a long-term growth trend is open to discussion. What is debatable is whether the kind of transformation centred on ICT will be capable of sustaining a long-term growth pattern, as other 'general purpose technologies' appear to have done in the past.

Drawing on a parallel between the computer and the dynamo, Paul David has argued (1990) that 'a general purpose engine' may need time and appropriate conditions to fully realize its potential for productivity growth, as indeed the history of electrification indicates. Therefore

> from the perspective afforded by the economic history of the large technical systems characteristic of network industries ... many features of so-called productivity paradox will be found to be neither so unprecedented nor so puzzling as they might otherwise appear (ibid., p. 355).

David's argument is based on the similarities with the process of electrification that he describes in some critical moments explaining the pace of diffusion. This is the 'diffusion lag' argument. His second argument concerns deficiency in the existing productivity measures, which are problematic with regard to new products and process applications. Even more so for computers which, as he says, are *not* dynamos:

> The nature of man-machine interactions and the technical problems of designing efficient interfaces for humans and computers are enormously more subtle and complex than those that arose in the implementation of electric lighting and power technology (ibid., p. 360).

Indeed some of the problems arising during full realization of ICT potential pertain to these general issues.

Paul David writes in 1990, drawing on an earlier 1989 paper. His comments seem to confirm that the 1980s did not indeed mark the infancy of the ICT industry but certainly a moment when its effects were still at an initial stage. By the same token, the spurt of productivity in the late 1990s, which is so much part of the story of the boom, appears to be a moment in which these effects were felt more massively. Whether they have reached the peak or just a new stage of development preparing for another one is part of the question raised above. I would argue that indeed one of the problems has been that the structural transformation associated with the 1990s expansion, though very significant, was not sufficient, and a more radical process is necessary to sustain ICT-driven development. But this is highly speculative.

What appears much less speculative is that, in line with the argument made around the computer and the dynamo, the boom in the ICT sector must be seen as a result of long-term phenomena such as advances in basic electronics and computer science along the associated technological trajectory. Moreover, there is evidence of a long-term trend in at least two core industries of the sector. Based on an analysis of growth rates of 3-digit manufacturing industries in the post-war period it can also be said that such industries as Office and Computing Machines (SIC 357) and Electronic Components and Accessories (SIC 367) are in the small group of industries (seventeen out of 143) whose growth rate of output has been consistently above the manufacturing average since 1958 (Gualerzi, 2001, ch. 7).

Views on the long-term transformation centred on the rise of new industries in the hi-tech sector presented above are largely consistent with the findings of two recent studies of US economic development in the last twenty years that have a somewhat different, but largely complementary, focus. Simonazzi (2003) clarifies the conditions that led to the rise of the high-tech sector, and ICT in particular, in the US. This is part of the explanation for the dismal employment performance in Europe vs. the US in the 1980s and 1990s. The latter, she argues, depends not so much on labour market rigidities,[29] but rather on the role played by demand factors in the process of industrial restructuring and new industry development.[30] The rapid diffusion of ICT-based innovations – in both consumption and investment – sustained the US high-tech manufacturing industry when the government demand weakened in the late 1980s due to cuts in spending on defence, space and energy (p. 657). On the other hand, the deregulation of financial services, which in general had 'mixed results', was 'facilitating the financing of investment in new industries and sustaining consumption' (p. 661). Most relevant is that the effects of IT go well beyond cost reduction, to affect structural change, transmitting through this channel the effects of innovation to old industries (see Gualerzi, 2004).

Testing the correlation between investment and productivity, widely believed to be positive and strong in the literature, Bonifati (2002) finds it instead relatively weak.[31] His explanation is that the relationship overlooks the fact that increasing returns are generated by technological development and the use and creation of new knowledge, which are not captured by the growth of physical capital.[32] Hence the increase in output requires less labour, but also less capital, therefore less investment per unit of output. However, the non-uniform growth of labour productivity is positively correlated with compensation and the price of investment goods. This positive correlation crucially depends on the adoption of technology whose price, adjusted for quality improvements, falls with respect to labour, as is the case with Information Technologies. Thus, the experience of the US strongly suggests that the process of structural change depends on the development of new industries.

4.8. STRUCTURAL DYNAMICS AND DISTRIBUTION

4.8.1. Income Distribution and Social Polarization

In this last section the structural dynamics examined above are contrasted with a few stylized facts about income distribution, to highlight the most important aspects of their relationship. They suggest a number of theoretical points that should be taken up by further research.

It was pointed out above that the other side of the macro-segmentation of consumption markets in the 1980s is a clear pricing policy. Firms' market development strategies typically result in high prices for new, cutting edge products and low prices for old, standardized products. Indeed, the pattern of consumption innovation outlined above was consistent with and sustained by quite clear distribution dynamics, dominated by a substantial stagnation of wages and a less than exceptional growth of profits. In particular, the recovery did not reverse the decline of workers' compensation occurring at the end of the 1970s, which remained through the 1980s at the level it was at the end of the 1958–66 cycle.[33] Data on profits do not give a clear cut picture. Corporate Profits after Taxes peak in 1979, come down sharply and recover after 1983. An unambiguous indication of profits growth can be drawn from a more complex business indicator, the Composite Index of Profitability.[34]

The deterioration of the relative position of lower income earners is confirmed by the percentage of aggregate income going to the top fifth of the population, which increased almost two points from 1981 to 1987 (Consumer Income Series, p. 60, Bureau of Census) and by the median annual family income, which grew notably only for the top two-fifths and especially for the highest fifth of the population (Bureau of Census).

The distribution dynamics can be explained largely by labour market dynamics. In fact, polarization in consumption is reinforced by a differentiation developing within the social structure between the losers and winners in the changing competitive environment. This is reflected in a growing segmentation of the labour market between well-paid and low-paid jobs. The reference here is to the tri-partition of the labour market indicated by Reich (1992), which defines a compensation structure centred on a large minority of well-paid jobs and a majority of low-wage workers. The profile of the 'symbolic analyst' is typical of that part of the labour force whose opportunities grow and is therefore the backbone of glamorous consumption. Low-paid jobs are typical of workers in the service industries, with blue-collar workers' compensation somewhat in between.

4.8.2. Financial Markets and Income Distribution

These fundamental traits of income distribution dynamics in the 1980s do not change in the 1990s. However, the booming stock market that accompanied the transformation centred on the ICT sector is a key element in the explanation of income distribution of the decade.

Even the boom has not changed a dynamic unfavourable to wages. Profits are widely confirmed to be at a post-war peak, while real wages grew at a rate lower than that of productivity in the entire period 1990–2000 (see Gualerzi, 2004). It can be concluded that most of the productivity gains have been passed on to capital owners. On the other hand, returning to Table 4.1 which outlines the growth performance of the US economy in the post-war period, it can be noted that the single indicator showing an exceptional performance is the real returns in financial markets, as measured by the S&P 500 index.

One may ask why in a boom with fairly low unemployment there has been little pressure to increase wages. There are in fact a number of reasons that might explain the lack of an explicit distributive conflict. The literature has focused on a new argument, maintaining that there was no distributive conflict over the level of wages because wages are only one part of workers' income. This might be so given the large number of workers that have their saving invested in the stock market, directly or through some mutual funds, or receive compensations based on their company performance, and/or own shares of the company where they are employed.

Assuming that most US families have invested their savings on the stock market, the performance of the stock market becomes one of the main determinants of their incomes. The spread of the *worker-capitalist* combined with the exceptional performance of the financial markets in the 1990s, would then explain why a distribution of income increasingly skewed towards profits has not fuelled a strong distributive conflict. Indeed, *shared capitalism* seems capable of reconciling the stylized facts of income distribution with the centrality of financial market performance and the lack of wage, and therefore inflation, pressures arising from a distributive conflict (see Table 4.1).

One should, however, treat this interpretation with caution. While the existence of workers' revenues originating in invested savings and a changing structure of workers' income appear reasonable assumptions, the importance of workers' capital income might be poorly overstated.[35] The weaknesses of the argument suggest we should consider other, in fact complementary, explanations.[36] In particular, one may wonder whether the labour demand generated by the ICT industries has followed the same lines as those which led in the 1980s to increased labour market segmentation, associated with different levels and dynamics of wages. If indeed the ICT industries reflect and reinforce a demand for labour split between highly-paid jobs for a minority and low-paid jobs for the majority, we would then have a depressive effect on the level of wages.

4.9. CONCLUDING REMARKS

One of the main conclusions that can be drawn from the last twenty years of development of the US economy is that our analysis should tackle both theoretically and empirically the role of new products and new industries in the long-term growth of advanced market economies. This chapter contributes a heuristic model to this research, focusing on the interaction between innovative investment and consumption composition. It has argued that, in the perspective of an extension to the long run of the principle of effective demand, the question of consumption composition becomes a fundamental issue and that it requires a dynamic theory of consumption open to the relationship between composition and growth.

Bils and Klenow inquire whether variety can account for shifts in consumption spending shares, beyond income and price effects. Their empirical analysis shows that variety is important to determine the growth of spending. They say little about the relationship between variety and income creation. The relationship with growth remains unexplored except when variety includes quality improvement, since the latter affects the level of real output via a decline in the price level.

In the approach presented here, consumption composition affects growth through investment in new products that act as a stimulus for consumption innovation. The latter builds on the possibility of developing needs that is inherent to a system of market relations. An approach based on effective demand can therefore explain what remains otherwise quite hidden even in new generation growth models. In this framework the reference to product innovation reaches out where the analysis of consumption spending is insufficient and makes explicit the mechanics of growth implicit in the process of change in consumption composition. However, focusing on the sectors where innovation is stronger and on the induced effects of the rise of new industries is the key, in turn, to the demand for factors, which affects income distribution.

In the 1980s we witness a composition effect determined by the rise of the new service industries, while consumers' goods markets are increasingly structured around a new pattern. Product innovation for high quality and the high segment of the market, directed to affluent consumers, led innovation in consumption. The relatively weak effects of the transformation can be distinguished from the rapid diffusion of new ICT products that characterizes consumption innovation in the 1990s, affecting in more fundamental way the structure of need. In the 1990s large and steady investment flows determined a new stage of development in the long-term technological trajectory of the ICT sector. In particular, computer networks and cell phones enlarged the access of firms and the general public to communication and information, a new area of needs development.

While the glamorous consumption of the 1980s was associated with an increasingly uneven income distribution, the income distribution dynamics of the 1990s confirms stagnation wages, at least to the extent that the benefits of growing productivity overwhelmingly went to capital owners. This forces attention on the stock market as one of the determinants of income distribution. The second conclusion of the chapter is therefore that the rise of new industries and the composition effects associated with specific cycles of expansion is the starting point to examine the dynamics of distribution via labour market segmentation.

NOTES

1. The other exception is Transformational Growth (Nell, 1998), where the analysis of structural dynamics is combined with institutional change and historical trends of transformation.
2. Hidden in Keynesian growth theory is then, as pointed out by Joan Robinson, a steady state path of growth, with constant proportions within sectors.
3. For a recent review of the Neo-Schumpeterian theory see Verspagen (2002).
4. 'Disappointingly, he [Keynes] did not investigate the role of innovations in generating the revival of animal spirits and raising the level of expectations for future profits. But the aphrodisiac effect of a new wave of investment opportunities based on a cluster of innovation is quite consistent with his general approach to expectations and investment behavior' (Freeman, 1986, p. 28).
5. Both have been published in the *Journal of Evolutionary Economics*. Quotes are from that source.
6. 'The Boskin Commission Report (Boskin Commission, 1996) cites only an handful of studies in arriving at its estimate that unmeasured quality change biases U.S. Consumer Price Index (CPI) inflation upward by 0.6 percent per year' (p. 1006).
7. Similarly, the Boskin Commission considers studies on both new goods and higher quality goods.
8. For example cable television has increased spending on television as a share of the expenditure in recreation.
9. 'Item-substitution rates measure how often the BLS replaces an item in the pricing basket with another model because the former has disappeared from the sample outlet' (p. 274).
10. The full specification of the approach based on the notion of the active, albeit not sovereign, consumer is in Gualerzi (1998).
11. There is an element of subjectivity in the interactive process of consumption innovation. It concerns the self realization of individuals through consumption. The fundamental difference from the traditional approach to consumer choice, and also other approaches sensitive to social determinations of taste, is that the individual we are referring to is a social construct, not in any general sense of being social, but insofar as needs development reflects the development of individuality as a social phenomenon. We therefore do not have any abstract individual making choices, nor is the issue one of recognizing that they are influenced socially. The point is that individuals do not exist except in relationship to other individuals and within society. Consequently the development of needs is a social phenomenon in which subjectivity and social determination are not counter-posed or added to one another, they are the same thing. Individuals become what they are in connection with their consumption practices and new products.
12. 'Investment is the activity of building the structure of expansion. But the peculiarity of capital is to be found in the fact that the building of the structure is also the purpose of the structure' (Levine, 1981, Vol. II, p. 184).
13. We have an inverse relationship if we focus on innovative investment as capacity creation, since the diffusion prospects for a product already established in a market niche, will stimulate entrepreneurs to invest to take advantage of a rapid growth in demand. However, the notion of market saturation appears to be associated mainly with the negative prospects for sales determined by a high sales ratio as defined above.
14. We might add that this expansionary effect rests on the assumption of a secular positive trend of productivity growth resulting in conditions for rising income, such that product innovation can enter the consumption basket without necessarily displacing established products.

15. A dynamic model would then require us to model the introduction and development of new products. It is also conceivable to try to endogenize preference formation, though the task may be excessively demanding, given the interaction between new products and taste formation that depends on the development of need and innovative investment. On the other hand, an empirical test will have to take into account the construction of proxies and consider a structure of lags, given data availability. It may also involve some sectoral desegregation, though not necessarily a full multisectoral approach.

16. 'What is really new about an innovation can only be known when experience of the social practice associated with its use uncovers its real potential. The starting point must be the unity of old and new; the movement into the unknown world of a new structure of needs starts out by masquerading as a part of the prevailing structure' (Levine, 1981, vol. 2, pp. 141–2).

17. To this extent there is an analogy with the role of basic innovation in Neo-Schumpeterian theory. Incidentally, one may note that this would temper its technological determinism.

18. This distinction has important consequences for the development of a dynamic theory of demand married with transformational growth (Nell, 1998).

19. The analysis is based on four 'peak to peak' cycles: 1958–66, 1966–73, 1973–79, 1979–89 (see Gualerzi, 2001, ch. 7). This choice stresses the relevance attributed to the 1960s cycle, the last cycle of strong expansion in comparison with the sluggish growth of the 1970s.

20. The severe depression at the beginning of the cycle lowers the average growth rate of GNP over the cycle, contributing to give a worse growth scenario than it may otherwise be. However, the point of taking peak to peak intervals is precisely that of making possible comparisons between different cycle.

21. Other disturbing peculiarities of the 'strong recovery' are the growth of debt, accumulated by both households and firms, slow productivity growth, relatively high unemployment (see Table 4.1) and low level of utilization of productive capacity.

22. Gross and net investment as a percentage of GNP rebound in 1983 and 1984, declining in 1985 and 1986 and then remaining stable, with net figures weaker than gross figures. Another indicator, business expenditure in new plant and equipment as a percentage of GNP, shows a modest rebound in one year, 1984, followed by two years of decline and a new modest surge. A first desegregation shows that business expenditure in new plant and equipment in manufacturing grows very little after 1983, while in commerce it continues a long-term expansive trend.

23. The last two quarters of 1990 and the first of 1991 show negative growth rates, but only 1991 has a negative annual rate. This compares with the negative growth rates in 1980 and 1982.

24. Bureau of Economic Analysis, GDP per cent change based on chained 1996 dollars.

25. 'The growth rate of gross private fixed investment remained high in the following years, registering an annual average of 9% for the period 1993–2000. The increase was particularly high for machinery, equipment and software ... which registered average yearly growth of 13.5% ...' (Maffeo, 2001, p. 8). It can be noted that the proportion of investment in this sector accounted for by data processing equipment and programs rose from 45.5 per cent in 1991 to 72.5 per cent in 2000.

26. Most recently Robert J. Gordon addressed the possibility of sustained growth of productivity, discussing a scenario in which the GDP grows at 4 per cent (Gordon, 2003).

27. This would lead us to elaborate on the fact that the pattern of intensive market growth (see Gualerzi, 2001, ch. 11) was modified, though not fundamentally disrupted.

28. Jeremy Rifkin has captured this aspect (*The Age of Access*, 2000), though referring to a more general trend in which, in the net economy, access substitutes property.

29. Maffeo (2001) argues along similar lines that the focus on labour market rigidities is misplaced.
30. 'The American performance can be explained in terms of the interaction of supply/technology factors with demand factors. The features of the US institutional context have allowed the US economy to exploit the growth potentialities of the information and communication technology (ICT) revolution and to consolidate its comparative advantage in those industries ... the exploitation of dynamic comparative advantages require(s) dynamic demand in order to activate the virtuous circle of growth' (p. 650). 'Given the macroeconomic policies adopted since the inception of the EMS, the disappointing EU growth and employment performance is hardly surprising' (p. 652).
31. The test concerns the desegregated US manufacturing industry over the period 1960–94.
32. We note that this is instead captured by the notion of innovative investment, though there may be a serious problem in its measurement.
33. Gross Hourly Earnings of Non-Agricultural Production Workers, 1982 constant dollars. Another indicator, Average Hourly Earning Index in constant 1977 dollars, confirms the stagnation of wages, showing only a modest improvement and earnings remained well below the level reached in the 1970s.
34. The index grows rapidly from 1982, reaching a peak which is well above that of the 1960s and 1970s.
35. Just to give a hint of the problem involved, Lester Thurow has argued that 90 per cent of the gains in the stock market was pocketed by the 10 per cent of the wealthiest families, while 60 per cent of the families had no stock shares. ('The Boom That Wasn't', *The New York Times*, p. A19, January, 18, 1999). Simonazzi (2003) recalls 'the highly skewed distribution of stock ownership' as a reason for arguing against strong direct wealth effects in the explanation of the surge of consumption spending in the 1990s.
36. It must be noted that the stock market explanation of income distribution also emphasizes spending, sustained by the wealth effect generating a booming stock market, as the main reason for the expansion, downplaying the role of fixed investments.

REFERENCES

Andersen, E.S. (2001), 'Satiation in an evolutionary model of structural economic dynamics', *Journal of Evolutionary Economics*, **11**(1).

Bils, M. and P.J. Klenow (2001a), 'The acceleration of variety growth', *American Economic Review*, May.

Bils, M. and P.J. Klenow (2001b), 'Quantifying quality growth', *American Economic Review*, September.

Bonifati, G. (2002), 'Produzione, investimenti e produttività. Rendimenti crescenti e cambiamento strutturale nell'industria manifatturiera americana (1960–1994)', *Moneta e Credito*, n. 217, March.

Boskin Commission (1996), *Towards a More Accurate Measure of the Cost of Living*, Final Report to the Senate Finance Committee from the Advisory Commission To Study the Consumer Price Index, Washington, DC: Senate Finance Committee.

Bresnahan, T.F. and R.J. Gordon (eds) (1997), *The Economics of New Goods*, Chicago: The University of Chicago Press

Business Week, March 17, 1997.

Clark, J., C. Freeman and L. Soete (1982), *Unemployment and Technical Innovation*, Westport, CT: Greenwood Press.

David, P. (1990), 'The dynamo and the computer: an historical perspective on the productivity paradox', *American Economic Review*, May.

EBrain Market Research Report (2003), *Consumer Electronics Ownership and Market Potential*, March.

Freeman, C. (ed.) (1986), *Design, Innovation and Long Cycles in Economic Development*, New York: St. Martin's Press.

Frenken, K. and P. Windrum (2002), 'Successive cycles of innovation: the importance of user heterogeneity and design complementarities for radical product innovations in the camera and computer industries', mimeo.

Gordon, R. (2000), 'Does the "new economy" measure up to the great inventions of the past', *Journal of Economic Perspectives*, **14**(4), Fall.

Gordon, R. (2003), 'Exploding productivity growth: context, causes and implications', *Brookings Papers on Economic Activity*, September.

Gualerzi, D. (1996), 'Natural dynamics, endogenous structural change and the theory of demand: a comment on Pasinetti', *Structural Change and Economic Dynamics*, **7**(2), June.

Gualerzi, D. (1998), 'Economic change, choice and innovation in consumption', in M. Bianchi (ed.), *The Active Consumer: Novelty and Surprise in Consumer Choice*, London: Routledge.

Gualerzi, D. (2001), *Consumption and Growth: Recovery and Structural Change in the U.S. Economy*, Cheltenham, UK and Northampton, MA, USA: Edward Elgar.

Gualerzi, D. (2004), *The distribution effects of ICT-driven (Information and Communication technology) development*, Paper presented at the Conference 'Growth and Income Distribution', Lucca, Italy, June 16–17.

Ironmonger, D.S. (1972), *New Commodities and Consumer Behaviour*, Cambridge: Cambridge University Press.

Kongsamut, P., S. Rebelo and D. Xie (2001), 'Beyond balanced growth', *Review of Economic Studies*, **68**(237).

Laitner, J. (2000) 'Structural change and economic growth', *Review of Economic Studies*, **67**(237).

Lancaster, K.J. (1966), 'A new approach to consumer theory', *Journal of Political Economy*, **74**, 132–57.

Lancaster, K.J. (1971), *Consumer Demand: A New Approach*, New York: Columbia University Press.

Levine, D.P. (1981), *Economic Theory*, Vol. I and II, London: Routledge & Kegan Paul.

Lossani, M. (2001), 'Old wine in the new economy bottle', ITEMQ, Università Cattolica, Milano, published in G. Nardozzi (ed.), *I rapporti tra finanza e distribuzione del reddito*, Rome: LUISS edizioni, 2002.

Maffeo, V. (2001), 'Effective demand versus wage flexibility: some notes on the causes of the growth of employment in the USA in the nineties', *Contributions to Political Economy*, **20**.

Metcalfe, J.S. (2001), 'Consumption, preferences, and the evolutionary agenda', in U. Witt (ed.), *Escaping Satiation*, Berlin: Springer Verlag.

Nell, E.J. (1998), *The General Theory of Transformational Growth*, Cambridge: Cambridge University Press.

Nell, E.J. (2002), 'Notes on the transformational growth of demand', in M. Setterfield (ed.), *The Economics of Demand-Led Growth. Challenging the Supply Side Vision of the Long-Run*, Cheltenham, UK, and Northampton, MA, USA: Edward Elgar.

Pasinetti, L.L. (1981), *Structural Change and Economic Growth*, Cambridge: Cambridge University Press.

Pasinetti, L.L. (1993), *Structural Economic Dynamics*, Cambridge: Cambridge University Press.

Reich, R. (1992), *The Work of Nations*, New York: Vintage Book.

Rifkin, J. (2000), *The Age of Access*, London: Penguin Books.

Saviotti, P.P. (2001), 'Variety, growth and demand', *Journal of Evolutionary Economics*, **11**(1).

Simonazzi, A. (2003), 'Innovation and growth: supply and demand factors in the US expansion', *The Cambridge Journal of Economics*, **27**(5), September.

Verspagen, B. (2002), 'Structural change and technology. A long view', Working paper 02.13.

Witt, U. (ed.) (2001), *Escaping Satiation*, Berlin: Springer Verlag.

5. Partial imitation, inequality and growth: the role of the courts' interpretation of patent law[*]

Carmelo Pierpaolo Parello and Luca Spinesi

5.1. INTRODUCTION

According to Lanjouw and Schankerman (2001), patent litigation has grown dramatically during the period 1978–99. Combining data from the LitAlert database with other information collected by the U.S. Patent and Trademark Office, they report that the number of patents rose by almost tenfold, with much of this increase concentrated during the 1990s. Lerner (1995) and Lanjouw and Lerner (2002) provide empirical evidence that even if parties can settle their patent disputes without resorting to suits, the effective threat of litigation influences the incentive to undertake R&D by preventing small firms entering those R&D areas where the threat of litigation from larger firms is high. Lanjouw and Schankerman (2001) find that the mean filing rates vary substantially across technology fields and that the plaintiff's probability of winning the patent suit does not depend on the characteristics of patents and their owners among patent disputes.[1] On such concerns, they state that:

> From a policy perspective, this is good news because it means that enforcement of patent rights relies on the effective threat of court actions (suits) more than on extensive post-suit, legal proceedings that consume court resources (Lanjouw and Schankerman, 2001, p. 26)

In this chapter we study the implication for R&D of the determinants of patent infringement and declaratory judgement suits. In particular, can court decisions represent the guidelines for interpreting and applying the patent law? By fixing a bound to the incumbent's power to invalidate more recent claims made by others, do courts affect both the firm's freedom in setting price, the incentive of doing innovative R&D, and income distribution? The importance of patent protection for R&D-intensive sectors has been widely highlighted by the R&D-based growth literature. In the 'Neo-Schumpeterian' endogenous growth theory, as exemplified by Romer (1990), Grossman and Helpman (1991) and Aghion and Howitt (1992, 1998), patent protection – or more generically, intellectual property (IP) rights protection – plays a primary role in the process of economic development.

By granting patents, firms establish a product's virtual everlasting monopoly, which allows entrepreneurs to recoup the enormous amounts of cash spent in the R&D process. When a new groundbreaking invention improves the existing stock of technological knowledge, the discoverer of the new method, good, or production process, must preserve its discovery from any possible attempt of being copied or imitated.

In a sense, IP rights are a sort of compromise between preserving the incentive to create knowledge and the desirability of disseminating knowledge at little or no cost, and constitutes a second best solution to a failure in the markets for knowledge and information.[2]

On the other hand, patents may be thought of as strategic tools. In many industries – in particular in the pharmaceutical sector – firms use their original priority date to obtain several patent applications, each of which protects a different aspect of the same technology.

The aim is to establish patent-blocking around the new product or process, and to keep a patent application filing always alive, so that when a competitor enters the innovation marketplace, firms have the opportunity to analyse the competitor's product and file new patent claim language to block its commercialization.

The question of patent infringement refers to different aspects of IP rights protection of an idea and then of the patented product. A concept which is often used, but quite vague, as the most basic test for infringement, is the issue of the 'use of a technology'. If a product uses a technology covered by the claims of a patent, then the product infringes the patent. However, as O'Donoghue (1998) maintains, 'the use of technology is a vague concept, so the court has a lot of discretion in how to interpret it' (p. 657). Since the meaning of the 'use of a technology' is quite vague, a number of different doctrines have arisen that address the question of infringement. Our work focuses on the doctrine of disclosure and enablement, which addresses the validity of the patent. The core of such a theory maintains that if a product falls within the claims of a patent, then the product infringes the patent. However, for the claims to be valid, the patent must contain information not in the prior art that is required to make the product, and thus the patent must contain enough information to make the product without significant experimentation.

The doctrine of disclosure and enablement concerns the so-called patent breadth, which specifies a set of products that no other firm can produce without permission from the patentholder, often in the form of a licence agreement. The doctrine of disclosure and enablement concerns in particular the lagging breadth question, that is the set of inferior products (that is, products that require no further innovation) that would infringe a patent.[3] As O'Donoghue (1998) maintains 'the strength of lagging breadth is determined by the interpretation of the doctrines of disclosure and enablement' (p. 658).

It is worth noting that the term 'breadth' covers both products horizontally and/or vertically removed from the patented product.[4] The standard 'Neo-Schumpeterian' endogenous growth theory (for example, Grossman and Helpman, 1991; Aghion and Howitt, 1992, 1998) has often used the notion 'patent scope', 'patent protection', in order to mean leading or lagging breadth.[5] Protection against imitators is granted by a perfectly enforceable patent law by 'assuming that the patent law protects indefinitely a firm's exclusive right to sell the goods it invents' (Grossman and Helpman, 1991, p. 89).[6]

Because of intrinsic characteristics, institutional issues are very slippery to handle for economic theory. The standard 'Neo-Schumpeterian' endogenous growth theory envisages stationary patent policies; that is, policies under which all generations are treated identically. Moreover it envisages complete lagging breadth, which means that any patentable innovation receives sufficient lagging breadth to protect the entire quality increase facilitated by the innovation. In this work we address the concern of whether institutional setting may affect both the long-term economic performance and income distribution by relaxing the current literature's assumption of a complete lagging breadth protection. We assume that patent law cannot definitively determine the effective protection of a patented product against imitators, since there exists the possibility to interpret the same patent law by courts. In doing so, we relax complete lagging breadth protection of patents by considering the possibility that courts allow firms to enter the market with a partial imitation of the top quality product.[7]

In the US, for instance, it was both the Federal Circuit Judges and the Supreme Court who decided how to interpret and apply the patent law. In an ever-evolving society, such as that of incremental innovations and cumulative improvements, courts adapt the effective patent protection to the changing environment, which increasingly creates new cases and situations. All these matters, we believe, are important concerns for economic growth.

The chapter is organized as follows. In Section 5.2 we construct a modified version of the quality-ladder R&D-based endogenous growth model of Grossman and Helpman (1991, ch. 4) by introducing the partial imitation. In Section 5.3 we sketch the dynamic properties of the general equilibrium and discuss the main findings of the chapter in Section 5.4. Finally, Section 5.5 concludes.

5.2. THE MODEL

In this section we discuss a modified version of a scale-invariant quality-ladder endogenous growth model. Although we use the general equilibrium framework of Grossman and Helpman (1991, ch. 4) as a building block, the model is substantially different from the current literature because it brings to the forefront the roles of the institutional setting and patent litigation.

5.2.1. Preferences

Let us consider a closed economy with a continuum of L_t identical individuals living at time $t > 0$. Individuals are infinitely lived and are endowed with one unit of labour. The demographic dynamics are such that population grows over time at a constant rate $n > 0$. As in Grossman and Helpman (1991, ch. 4), individuals choose their consumption from a continuum of goods indexed by $j \in [0, 1]$, which differ in their quality level, m. By definition, new vintages are better than old, in the sense that consuming a new vintage of good provides more services than consuming goods of the previous vintage. In particular, all goods start at time $t = 0$ at a quality level $m = 0$; the starting quality level is $q_0(j) = 1$. Assuming a quality jump, $\lambda > 1$, exogenous, constant and common to all industries, the quality of the mth vintage of a good in industry j will be $q_m(j) = \lambda^m$. The representative consumer has additively separable intertemporal preferences of logarithmic type given by the following intertemporal felicity function

$$U_0 = \int_0^\infty L_0 e^{-(\rho-n)\tau} \log u_\tau d\tau \qquad (5.1)$$

Its intertemporal optimization problem is to maximize (5.1) subject to the following

$$\log u_t \equiv \int_0^1 \log\left[\Sigma_m q_m(j) x_{t,m}(j)\right] dj \qquad (5.2)$$

$$E_t \equiv \int_0^1 \left[\Sigma_m p_{t,m}(j) x_{t,m}(j)\right] dj \qquad (5.3)$$

$$W_t + A_t \equiv \int_t^\infty E_\tau e^{n\tau} e^{-R(t)(\tau - t)} d\tau \qquad (5.4)$$

Equation (5.2) is the Dixit–Stiglitz consumption index specification for the extent of the 'love of quality' preferences, where $x_{t,m}(j)$ denotes the consumption of the vintage m of the jth brand at time t. Equation (5.3) is the static budget constraint where E_t is the per capita consumption expenditure, with $p_{t,m}(j)$ denoting the price of the vintage m of the jth brand at time t. Finally, equation (5.4) is the intertemporal budget constraint, where W_t is the present value of the aggregate labour income at time t, A_t is the aggregate value of asset holdings at time t, and $R_t \equiv \int_0^t r(s) ds$ is the cumulative interest rate from time t to 0.

Because of the separability of equation (5.1), the representative consumer's maximization problem can be solved in three steps: (i) solving the within-industry static maximization problem (ii) solving the across-industry static maximization problem in such a way as to allocate the instant expenditure across existing brands $j \in [0, 1]$ – for example, choosing the composition of each instantaneous level of spending that maximizes equation (5.2) subject to the static budget constraint (5.3); (iii) solving the dynamic optimization problem in such a way as to determine the optimal allocation of lifetime wealth over time – for example, determining the optimal time path of spending, E_t, that maximizes intertemporal utility (5.1) subject to the budget constraint (5.4).

In the first subproblem, consumers choose to only buy the product with the lowest quality-adjusted price $p_{t,m}(j)/\lambda^m$. For the sake of simplicity, in the analytical procedure we assume that when two products of the same brand have the same quality-adjusted price, consumers only buy the higher quality product.

In the second subproblem, individuals maximize static utility by allocating expenditure across existing product lines and by purchasing the single brand $\widetilde{m}(j)$ in each line offering the lower quality-adjusted price, where the tilde denotes the top quality of each brand (for example, the last vintage of each brand). Solving this static optimization problem yields the representative consumer's static demand function

$$x_{t,m}(j) = \frac{E_t}{p_{t,m}(j)} \qquad (5.5)$$

where $\widetilde{m}(j) = m$.

The individual's demand function (5.5) features unitary price and expenditure elasticities, and takes the following form for the aggregate spending

$$X_t(j) = \frac{E_t L_t}{p_t(j)}$$

where we drop the subscript m since in equilibrium only the top quality is produced and consumed.

In the third subproblem, consumers maximizes discounted utility (5.1) given (5.2), (5.5) subject to the intertemporal budget constraint (5.4). The solution to this optimal control problem leads to the following well-known intertemporal saving rule or Euler equation for the case of logarithmic preferences

$$\frac{\dot{E}_t}{E_t} = r_t - \rho \tag{5.6}$$

This condition holds for every individual and also for the aggregate spending. Following Grossman and Helpman (1991), we impose a normalization of prices that makes nominal spending constant through time and equal to 1. that is, $E_t = 1$. Hence the Euler equation (5.6) determines the usual condition $r_t = \rho$ which must hold over time.

5.2.2. Production

As usual in the neo-Schumpeterian growth models, we assume that once a new good has been invented in the research lab, the producers with the requisite know-how can manufacture it with a constant returns to scale technology. Labour is the only production factor, so that we can choose units in such a way that one unit of any good requires one unit of labour input. This makes the marginal cost of every brand of consumption good $j \in [0, 1]$ equal to the wage rate w_t.

We rule out the existence of multiple producers of the same state-of-the-art product, by assuming that the patent law indefinitely protects the firm's exclusive right to sell the good that it invents. In such an environment, and assuming non-drastic innovations, Bertrand competition between producers in the same industry line implies that the quality leader will set a limit price equal to the quality jump over the marginal production cost, that is, $p_t = \lambda w_t$. This limit pricing allows the quality leader to capture the whole consumption demand and eventually to exclude the producers of the preceding vintage of the same brand.[8]

Let us now assume that patent law perfectly protects the patentholders against those imitations that perfectly replicate the state-of-the-art technology embodied in the latest vintages. At the same time, let us depart from the current literature and assume that patents are not perfectly enforceable when a new competitor enters the market by producing a partial imitation of lower quality than the existing state of the art, but of higher quality than the previous incumbent producer. Then, between two given quality-rungs (say, m and $m+1$), a firm is able to produce a lagged-quality good which may infringe the claim of a patent based on lagging breadth.[9] Patent law is defined by legislative sector, but since it is also defined and effectively applied by courts, we suppose that the courts can determine the effective degree of protection against partial imitations by applying the doctrine of disclosure and enablement.

The potential threat that a new competitor may enter the market and sell an 'imperfect imitation' of the latest vintage without resulting with certainty in a legal infringement, will induce the quality leader to lower the limit price in order to serve the whole market. This also holds even in the event that the patent infringement could be recognized by the courts. Indeed, the mere existence for the leader of a positive probability $(1-q)>0$ of losing the patent suit when it is imperfectly imitated, will induce it to lower the limit price. Assuming rational expectations, the leader will adopt the following Bertrand–Nash equilibrium limit pricing:

$$p_t = \begin{cases} \lambda w_t \cdots with \cdot prob \cdot q \\ \dfrac{\lambda}{\varepsilon} w_t \cdots with \cdot prob \cdot 1-q \end{cases} \tag{5.7}$$

where $q>0$ is the plaintiff's probability of winning the legal fight against imperfect imitators, $(1-q)>0$ is the probability of losing the legal fight against an imperfect imitator, and $\varepsilon \in (1,\lambda)$ is a parameter that proxies the degree of tolerance by which Courts judge patent suits concerning lagging breadth infringement.

Our interpretation of the parameter ε stems from the use of the doctrine of disclosure and enablement. The parameter ε represents a sort of degree of tolerance whereby courts rule in patent litigation in which lagging breadth infringement is involved. When $\varepsilon = 1$, partial imitation coincides with the preceding vintage, whereas when $\varepsilon = \lambda$, partial imitation consists in a perfect imitation that perfectly replicates the top quality of a brand. In the remaining parts of the chapter, we will exclude the extreme of the imitation interval $(1, \lambda)$ and we will concentrate to the extent in which partial imitations constitute an inferior version of the top quality.

Denoting the expected price by p_t^e, one can write

$$p_t^e = \left[q + \frac{1}{\varepsilon}(1-q) \right] \lambda w_t$$

Since the Arrow effect is at work even in such an economy, no industry leader undertakes research in the general equilibrium and all the innovations are carried out by outsider firms. Once innovations occur, the succeeding firms will find themselves one step ahead of the former leaders that they have displaced. Given the limit pricing (5.7) and the aggregate demand (5.5), the profit flow of each industry leader at time t will be

$$\pi_t(j) = \begin{cases} \left(1 - \dfrac{1}{\lambda}\right)L_t \cdots with \cdot prob \cdot q \\[2ex] \left(1 - \dfrac{\varepsilon}{\lambda}\right)L_t \cdots with \cdot prob \cdot 1 - q \end{cases} \qquad (5.8)$$

which can be solved in terms of the expected profit yielding

$$\pi_t^e(j) = \left(1 - \frac{1}{\lambda}\right)L_t q + \left(1 - \frac{\varepsilon}{\lambda}\right)L_t(1-q) \equiv (1-\eta)L_t \qquad (5.9)$$

where, to simplify the formula, we define $\eta \equiv \left[(1-\varepsilon)q + \varepsilon\right]/\lambda$.[10]

The higher (lower) the probability for the plaintiff of winning the litigation against the producer of the partial imitation, q, the higher (lower) is the expected profit flow of the leader. These two effects are easily explained. For a given ε, an increase in the plaintiff's probability of winning the litigation against the producer of the partial imitation reduces the risk of being partially imitated and induces the leader to set a higher limit price. Note that the mere existence of the threat that a partial imitation may erode the monopoly rent, on the one hand, reduces the leader's market power in fixing price, on the other it raises consumer demand for every existing brand.

These two opposite forces testify that the negative effects on the flow of profit deriving from an increase in the opponent's probability of winning the patent suit and of the court's degree of tolerance, as measured by an increase in both the probability $(1-q)$ and parameter $\varepsilon \in (1, \lambda)$, operates through an increase in the leader's production costs.

5.2.3. R&D Sector

Innovation is a risky venture which requires firms to invest resources in laboratory research. The premium consumers are willing to pay for higher quality products is the incentive inducing agents to invest resources in improving the existing quality levels. As in the bulk of the R&D-based endogenous growth literature, we model the process of innovation as a continuum memoryless Poisson process and assume constant returns to scale in research effort. To achieve an R&D intensity of ι a firm must invest $a\chi_t$

units of labour per unit of time and incur a cost of $a\chi_t w_t$, where χ_t denotes the difficulty of conducting R&D. We specify χ_t in such a way as to avoid explosive growth and scale effect. In particular, in this model we adopt the PEG specification (or dilution specification) developed by Dinopoulos and Thompson (1998), which captures the idea that difficulty in conducting R&D is proportional to the size of the total market

$$\chi_t = \delta L_t$$

where $\delta > 0$ is exogenously given.[11]

Each firm that invests resources in R&D at intensity ι for a time interval of length dt, will succeed in creating a new generation of a product with probability ιdt, and will fail with probability $(1 - \iota dt)$.

As mentioned above, in this model we relax the perfect enforcement hypothesis of lagged-quality products, by allowing competitors to grant a patent to cover innovations with a quality jump λ / ε. This implies that the value of an innovation depends on the probability that a new competitor (with an imperfect copy of the top quality of an existing brand) has to win the lawsuit in the event that the incumbent incurs a legal reprisal against its decision to enter the market. Such a probability, $(1 - q)$, affects the present value of all the innovating firms, in the sense that each incumbent has to take into account the possibility of competing with a hypothetical producer of a worse copy of its product.

For the sake of simplicity, we assume that q does not vary among industries, so that jurisdictional institutions do not affect the stock market evaluation of any research firm.[12] In other words we are assuming that the courts' degree of tolerance regards all the existing industry lines in the same manner. Free entry into innovation implies that the expected present value of the representative research firm, v_t^e, must be no higher than the cost of R&D, and equal to it when R&D is actually taking place

$$v_t^e \leq a\chi_t w_t \tag{5.10}$$

with equality for $\iota > 0$.

Free entry condition (5.10) prevents firms from earning excess returns and also denotes the scale of aggregate research effort that, due to constant returns to scale technology, proves indeterminate.

As usual in the R&D-based endogenous growth model, stock-market evaluation of profit-maximizing research firm is such that a no-arbitrage condition relates the expected equity returns to a yield on a riskless bond. Moreover, we assume that the capital market is Walrasian, such that equity holders expect that gains or losses must match the change in the expected value of the research firm. Because the flow of profit does not vary among industries, the research firms will be indifferent as to the target of their innovation efforts if and only if the expected monopoly duration does not vary among industry. Of course, this is the case when we assume q identical to $j \in [0, 1]$, so that investors can offset the risk of capital loss by just diversifying their asset portfolio. Over a time interval dt, the shareholder receives an expected dividend $\pi_t^e dt$, and the value of the monopolist appreciates by $v_t^e dt$ in each industry. Because each quality leader is targeted by other firms that conduct R&D to discover the next higher quality product, the shareholder suffers a loss of v_t^e if further innovation occurs.

This event occurs with probability ιdt, whereas no innovation occurs with probability $(1 - \iota dt)$. Thus, perfect-foresight equilibrium in the capital market requires that the expected rate of return from holding a stock of a quality leader is equal to the riskless rate of return $r_t dt$. Taking limits as dt approaches zero, we obtain the following no-arbitrage

$$\frac{\dot{v}_t^e}{v_t^e} + \frac{\pi_t^e}{v_t^e} = r_t + \iota \qquad (5.11)$$

Note that in the steady-state equilibrium $r_t = \rho$, and free entry condition (5.10) implies that $\dot{v}^e / \dot{v}^e = \dot{\chi} / \chi = n$. Equation (5.11) can thus be solved for the expected present value of the firm yielding

$$v_t^e = \frac{1 - \eta}{\rho + \iota - n} L_t \qquad (5.12)$$

where we used (5.9) for the expected profit π_t^e.

5.2.4. The Dynamic Equilibrium System

In the rest of the chapter, we will focus on a rational-expectations equilibrium where a positive long-run rate of innovation coexists with market-clearing in all markets. Because any individual firm will achieve a flow of sales that depends on the plaintiff's probability of winning q, the expected employment in manufacturing will be

$$x^e = \frac{L_t}{p} q + \frac{L_t}{p'} (1 - q) = \eta \frac{L_t}{w}$$

With a symmetrical R&D intensity ι, a unit measure of industries, and a labour productivity parameter a, employment in R&D will be $a\iota\chi_t$. In this light, the labour market-clearing condition requires that

$$L_t = a\iota\chi_t + \eta\frac{L_t}{w_t} \tag{5.13}$$

According to (5.13), it is easy to verify that our model predicts an interior solution, that is, an equilibrium where the labour market-clearing condition proves compatible with a positive rate of innovation $\iota > 0$ – if the equilibrium wage is such that the following inequality holds[13]

$$w_t > \eta \tag{5.14}$$

Thus, since free entry in the R&D sector states that $\iota > 0$ implies $v_t^e \geq a\chi_t w_t$ and full employment in the labour market imposes $w_t > \eta$, an internal solution with a positive long-run rate of innovation implies that the expected flow of profit respects the inequality $v_t^e > a\eta\chi_t$.

Accordingly, plugging free entry condition (5.10) into (5.13) yields

$$\frac{L_t}{a} = \iota\chi_t + \eta\frac{L_t}{v_t^e}\chi_t \tag{5.15}$$

Equation (5.15) represents the side condition of the model, which implicitly relates the long-run rate of innovation, ι, to the equilibrium expected value of an innovation. To close the model, we plug the profit function (5.9) into the no-arbitrage equation (5.11) yielding

$$\frac{\dot{v}_t^e}{v_t^e} = \rho + \iota - (1-\eta)\frac{L_t}{v_t^e} \tag{5.16}$$

Equations (5.15) and (5.16) form the equilibrium system of the model. For the sake of simplicity, in the remainder of the chapter we define $V_t^e \equiv 1/v_t^e$ as the inverse of the expected aggregate stock market valuation of the quality leader, such that the equilibrium system can be reduced to the following two-dimensional system:

$$\frac{\dot{V}_t^e}{V_t^e} = \rho + \iota - (1-\eta)L_t V_t^e \tag{5.17}$$

$$\frac{1}{a\delta} = \iota + \eta L_t V_t^e \tag{5.18}$$

where in calculating (5.18) we considered the extent to which the population-adjusted difficulty index χ_t / L_t is constant and equal to δ.

5.2.5.   The Steady-State Equilibrium

Let us now focus on the case of a steady-state equilibrium. A steady-state consists in all those pairs of (V^e, ι) such that the long-run rate of innovation ι, and the inverse of the expected aggregate value of the stock market V^e, are constant, and where labour market clears at any moment in time.

Because we reduced the model in a system of one differential equation (5.17) and a side condition (5.17), imposing the steady-state condition $\dot{V}^e / V^e = -n$, we can solve equation (5.18) for the steady-state rate of product development ι, yielding

$$\iota = (1-\eta)LV^e - (\rho + n) \qquad (5.19)$$

Because $(1-\eta) > 0$, ι is an increasing function of higher rates of product development ι, must be matched with lower expected aggregate values of the stock market v^e. The intersection of equations (5.19) and (5.18) – see point A in Figure 5.1 – gives us the steady-state pair (V^e, ι) in which market-clearing conditions hold in each market and where the economy grows at a growth rate proportional to the constant rate of innovation ι. Since (5.18) slopes downward and (5.19) slopes upward, there exists an internal solution for the steady-state system since $1/a\delta > -(\rho + n)$ always holds.

As we will demonstrate in the next section, the dynamics of the model is such that the economy jumps immediately to the steady state (point A in Figure 5.1), and the long-run rate of innovation will be equal to

$$\iota = (1-\eta)\frac{1}{a\delta} - \eta(\rho + n) \qquad (5.20)$$

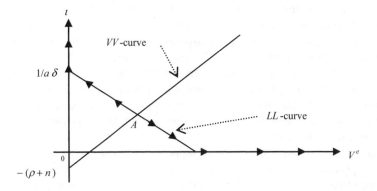

Figure 5.1   Phase diagram

With a population growing at a constant rate n and the dilution specification of the R&D-complexity index χ, equation (5.20) is the scale-invariant long-run rate of innovation of the economy. Note that for both ε and q approaching one, η approaches $1/\lambda$ and the rate of innovation, ι, is the same as in Grossman and Helpman (1991, ch. 4, p. 96). Due to the presence of η in equation (5.20), the expected rate of innovation will depend on the plaintiff's probability of winning q and on the courts' degree of tolerance ε.

5.3   THE DYNAMICS OF THE MODEL

In describing the dynamic property of the model we keep in track with Grossman and Helpman (1991) and follow a diagrammatical approach. In carrying out the analysis we will suppose an invariant probability of success for the leader q, by addressing the comparative statics analysis in the next section.

Let us first define $X \equiv \int_0^1 X(j)dj$ as the economy-wide manufacturing employment. In the phase diagram (Figure 5.1) the *LL*-curve represents the resources constraint of the economy (equation (5.18)) and the *VV*-curve represents the steady-state solution of the no-arbitrage condition (equation (5.17)). Rational-expectations equilibrium implies that the labour market clears at every moment in time. Along the *LL*, a higher rate of innovation implies a larger share of the labour force employed in the R&D sector and a smaller amount of labour for manufacturing activity. This means, in turn, that the supply of goods must be lower and prices must be higher; in spite of a decline in sales, higher prices imply a higher expected aggregate stock market valuation (or, alternatively, a lower value of the inverse of the expected aggregate stock market valuation).

As stated above, from the steady-state solution of the no-arbitrage equation (5.17) we know that a smaller expected aggregate value of the stock market, v^e (a greater value of the inverse of the expected aggregate value of the stock market, V^e) must be matched with a faster innovation rate. Thus, equation (5.20) is the only possible equilibrium trajectory since any other trajectory violates rational expectations because of an inconsistency in the stock market valuation of firms.

To see this in greater detail, let us suppose that the initial expectations of future aggregate stock market value, v^e (an inverse of the aggregate stock market value, V^e) are smaller (greater) than that associated with point A. In the long run the dynamics of the model are such that investors would expect ever less research and an ever smaller (greater) aggregate stock market value (inverse of the aggregate stock market value). This means that investors would expect the long-run rate of innovation and the expected aggregate stock market value v^e (inverse of the expected aggregate stock market value, V^e) to approach zero (infinity). But even in the event of total absence of leapfrogging, that is, $\iota = 0$, each incumbent must have an expected value

$$\frac{\pi^e}{\rho - n} = \frac{(1-\eta)L_t}{\rho - n}$$

which contradicts investor expectations.

Similarly, for the trajectories lying below the *VV*-curve, along which the initial expectations of future aggregate stock market value, v^e (an inverse of the aggregate value of the stock market, V^e) are greater (smaller) than that associated with point *A*, in the long run investors would expect ever more research so that the aggregate stock market value (inverse of the aggregate stock market value) would be ever smaller (greater) over time until the rate of innovation, ι, reached its maximum $1/a\delta$. Then, in the long run investors would expect the aggregate stock market value (inverse of the expected aggregate stock market value) to tend to infinity (zero) so that, again, rational expectations must be violated.

Thus, expectations can be fulfilled only if the economy jumps immediately to the steady-state point *A* and stays there until an exogenous shock, for instance a change in q, makes the rest point *A* change and sets the adjustment dynamics in motion.

5.4. DISCUSSION OF THE MODEL

In the preceding sections we studied a scale-invariant R&D-based endogenous growth model and its dynamic properties. The long-run rate of innovation we obtained negatively depends on the parameter η. Due to the existence of a negative relationship between the parameter η and the expected profit flow of the monopolist, equation (5.20) is a downward-sloping curve that can be taken as a sort of policy function (see Figure 5.2).

According to (5.20), the long-term economic performance of the economy is affected by the plaintiff's probability of winning, q, and by the degree of the court's tolerance ε. Indeed, having defined $\eta \equiv [(1-\varepsilon)q + \varepsilon]/\lambda$, it is easy to ascertain that the long-run rate of innovation of the economy depends on the institutional setting represented by the pair ε and q. In particular, any increase in the incumbent's probability of winning the lawsuit against the imperfect imitator (that is, any increase in the parameter q) positively affects both the patentholder's expected flow of profit and the long-run rate of innovation of the economy.

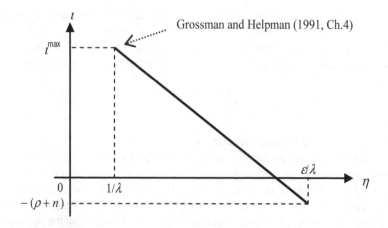

Figure 5.2   Policy function

Indeed, as shown by equation (5.9), the existence of a negative relationship between η and the firm's expected flow of profit π^e, is such that for a given ε, any increase in the probability of winning a patent dispute against the producer of a partial imitation q, raises the expected mark-up and spurs the long-run innovation process through a rise in v^e.

For ι converging to its steady-state value (5.20), it may be easily verified that the steady-state wage rate converges to the value

$$w=\frac{1-\eta}{a\delta\left[\rho-(\rho+n)\eta-n\right]+(1-\eta)} \qquad (5.21)$$

which is a strictly increasing function of η.

Since equation (5.21) also depends on the institutional setting represented by the pair (ε,q), any increase in the court's degree of tolerance, ε, or in the opponent's probability of winning the suit, $(1-q)$, also raises the steady-state wage rate, w. Therefore, whenever a partial imitation is involved in patent litigation, there is a trade-off between inequality and growth, and the use of the enablement and disclosure doctrine – hence the interpretation of the claims of the patent with respect to partial imitations – can contribute to determine both the long-run prospects of economic growth and income inequality of a country.

5.5. CONCLUSIONS

In this chapter we address the concern of the long-run implication of institutional setting on both the rate of innovation and income inequality. To this goal, a scale-invariant quality-ladder endogenous growth model in the spirit of Grossman and Helpman (1991) has been constructed.

There exist different routes for intellectual protection. By following the seminal work by O'Donoghue (1998), one route consists to protect the patentholder against partial imitations. In our chapter, this happens through the use of the doctrine of disclosure and enablement interpretation whereby infringement of the lagging breadth are at the core of the disputes. Empirical evidence shows that there is the possibility for outsiders to create and market an imperfect imitation of the state of the art.

We show that the mere existence of such a threat forces the patentholder to reduce the monopolistic limit price by lowering both the mark-up and the expected value of a patent. Courts' interpretation of patent law also affects the long-run innovation rate of the economy and income distribution.

We show that when court decisions tend to favour the patentholder against potential newcomers, the model generates a positive effect on the expected markup such as to increase the expected profit flow. This, in turn, will spur more R&D effort and will enhance the long-run rate of innovation of the economy. However, higher protection of the patentholder reduces the long-run wage rate. This means that there is a negative relationship between inequality and growth and that courts' behaviour may be reconsidered from a policy perspective.

NOTES

*   We are indebted to Guido Cozzi for helpful comments and suggestions and for his kind assistance during our PhD at the University of Rome 'La Sapienza'. We thank the University of Rome 'La Sapienza' and the Italian Ministry of Higher Education for financial support for this project; Davide Gualerzi, Louise C. Keely and Stafano Staffolani for comments, and all seminar participants at University of Catania and at the Lucca International Conference.
1. In theoretical studies of patent litigation (for example, P'ng, 1983; Bebchnuk, 1984; Waldfogel, 1998), the plaintiff win rate at trials considerably differs across models depending on whether information is asymmetric or whether there are divergent expectations among parties.
2. Although IP rights are important to encourage domestic innovation also as effective mechanisms to disseminate information, it has been widely shown that appropriate policy toward IP rights are not independent either of the level of development or of the overall institutional setting (see Maskus, 2000a, 2000b). In Europe and the US, for instance, a democratic IP system has been crucial to ensure that returns to individual investments in

creativity accrue to society as a whole. The setup of an efficient IP rights regime has been assessed in a broader institutional context including trade and antitrust policies, with a different level of protection which took into account intersectoral differences as part of a more general industrial policy. Indeed, while the US patent system undoubtedly contributed to economic growth, its effects varied widely between different industries especially from the mid 19th century onwards (Khan, 2002).

3. Patent breadth also specifies the set of superior products – that is the products that require further innovation – that would infringe the patent. The literature and the law refer to such cases as leading breadth of a patent.

4. Klemperer (1990) suggests using breadth for horizontal infringement, and height for vertical infringement.

5. For a more detailed analysis of how the patent policies may impact R&D in the endogenous growth framework, see O'Donoghue and Zweimuller (2004).

6. The standard neo-Schumpeterian endogenous growth literature rules out the possibility of multiple producers under Bertrand competition considering costly imitation.

7. By partial imitation we mean a product of lower quality than existing state-of-the-art products, but with a quality level higher than the previous incumbent producer. Note that our definition of partial imitation coincides with what O'Donogue (1998) and O'Donogue and Zweimuller (2004) call inferior product.

8. The mark-up over the marginal cost equals the quality jump $\lambda > 1$ since with an elasticity of substitution between any two brands equal to one we are automatically treating the case of a model with non-drastic innovation. Li (2003) further generalized this framework by allowing the model for elasticity of substitution between any two brands greater than one. However, our main conclusions do not vary by adding drastic innovation in the model.

9. Since as in Grossman and Helpman (1991) there is a perfect intertemporal knowledge spillover in the same industry line, we assume that once it is known how to produce the best quality product, each firm will be able to produce a 'worse' product in the same industry line. That is, we assume that the imitating firm, which produces a product of lower quality than the state of the art, only incurs production labour costs.

10. Note that η crucially depends on the probability q. For q approaching 1, η approaches $1/\lambda$ (the standard case of Grossman and Helpman, 1991, ch. 4), while for q approaching zero, η approaches ε/λ.

11. The addition of this variable is the direct consequence of Jones's (1995) critique of scale effect. An alternative way to avoid scale effects on per capita output growth would be to consider that as the economy grows, χ_t increases over time, and innovating becomes more difficult. This approach, introduced by Segerstrom (1998), assumes that R&D starts off being equally difficult in all industries and that R&D difficulty grows in each industry as firms do more R&D (that is $\dot{\chi}_t / \chi_t = \mu_t$ with $\mu > 0$). By considering this alternative specification we do not alter the results of the model.

12. Since we will focus our attention on a symmetric equilibrium, the plaintiff probability rate of winning, q, does not vary across industries. An interesting extension of our research would be to reconsider the model with a different industrial organizational setup generating heterogeneous quality improvements.

13. Notice that whenever $w = 1/\eta$, the whole labour force is employed in the manufacturing sector leaving no resource to R&D. To this effect, R&D does not take place and long-run rational expectations equilibrium will present a rate of innovation equals to zero.

REFERENCES

Aghion, P. and P. Howitt (1992), 'A model of growth through creative destruction', *Econometrica*, **60**, 323–51.

Aghion, P. and P. Howitt (1998), *Endogenous Growth Theory*, Cambridge, Mass.: MIT Press.

Bebchuk, L. (1984), 'Litigation and settlement under imperfect information', *RAND Journal of Economics*, **15**(3), 404–15.

Dinopoulos, E. and P. Thompson (1998), 'Schumpeterian growth without scale effects', *Journal of Economic Growth*, **3**, 313–35.

Grossman, G. and E. Helpman (1991), *Innovation and Growth in the Global Economy*, Cambridge, Mass.: MIT Press.

Klemperer, P. (1990), 'How broad should the scope of patent protection be?', *RAND Journal of Economics*, **21**(1), 113–30.

Khan, Z. (2002), 'Intellectual property and economic development: lessons from American and European history', CIPR Working Paper No. 22, London.

Jones, C. (1995), 'Time series tests of endogenous growth models', *The Quarterly Journal of Economics*, **110**, Issue 2.

Lanjouw, J.O. and J. Lerner (2002), 'Preliminary injunctive relief: theory and evidence from patent litigation', *Journal of Law and Economics*, **40**, 463–96.

Lanjouw, J.O. and M. Schankerman (2001), 'Enforcing intellectual property rights', NBER Working Paper No. 8656.

Lerner, J. (1995), 'Patenting in the shadow of competitors', *Journal of Law and Economics*, **38**, 463–96.

Li, C. (2003) 'Endogenous growth without scale effects: A comment', *American Economic Review*, 93(3), 1009–17.

O'Donoghue, T. (1998), 'A patentability requirement for sequential innovation,' *RAND Journal of Economics*, **29**(4), 654–79.

O'Donoghue, T. and J. Zweimuller (2004), 'Patents in a model of endogenous growth', *Journal of Economic Growth*, **81**(9), 81–123.

Maskus, K.E. (2000a), 'Regulatory standards in the WTO: comparing intellectual property rights with competition policy, environmental protection, and core labor standards', Working Paper No. 23 , World Bank.

Maskus, K.E. (2000b), *Intellectual Property Rights in the Global Economy*, Washington, DC: Institute for International Economics.

P'ng, IFFP.L. (1983), 'The strategic behavior in suit, settlement and trial', *Bell Journal of Economics*, **14**, 539–50.

Romer, P. M. (1990), 'Endogenous technological change', *Journal of Political Economy*, **98**(5), 71–102.

Segerstrom, P. (1998), 'Endogenous growth without scale effects', *American Economic Review*, **88**, 1290–310.

Waldfogel, J. (1998), 'Reconciling asymmetric information and divergent expectations theories of litigation', *Journal of Law and Economics*, **41**, 451–76.

SECTION THREE

Employment and Inequality

6. Bargaining, distribution and growth

Renato Balducci and Stefano Staffolani

6.1. INTRODUCTION

During the 1950s and 60s, the complex relationship between income distribution and economic growth was extensively studied. This issue was debated, amongst others, by Kaldor (1956), Pasinetti (1962, 1969) and Samuelson and Modigliani (1966). Attention focused mainly on the different propensities to save of the social classes comprising workers and capitalists, and on the change in the average rate of saving brought about by variations in the proportions of total income accruing to one or other class. Our aim is to re-examine bargaining, functional distribution of income and endogenous growth, following a two-stage model which combines the long-run optimality of the economic system, as seen by a 'social planner', with the short-run potentially myopic behaviour of collective agents, that is, trade unions and firms. In particular, we consider: (1) the role played by profits in explaining the investment rate through capital market imperfections. Real profits (internal funds) enable firms to combat liquidity constraints when access to capital markets is not perfect, as described by Stiglitz and Weiss (1981), Greenwald and Stiglitz (1987), Chirinko (1987), and Fazzari et al. (1988). Because of transaction costs in the financial market, the capital share is partially or, if the Modigliani–Miller theorem holds, totally reinvested in physical capital, whereas the labour share is optimally allocated between consumption and investment in human capital.[1] We obtain that long-run optimality is dependent on factor shares; (2) the role of trade unions and firms (whose objective function may not take into account long run-optimality), who bargain efficiently (McDonald and Solow, 1981) at a decentralized level over wages and employment. The exogenous bargaining power of unions sets the employment level, the wage rate and the short-run labour share.

We obtain the result that, in steady state, the optimal wage rate must be such that the last unit invested in physical capital and in human capital generates the same increase in the current value of the utility deriving from consumption. Furthermore, the optimal labour share, depending on preferences, technological parameters and capital market imperfections alone, must be higher than that arising from perfect competition on the labour market (the α parameter of the production function): hence, trade unions are needed to attain optimality in the economic system.

In Section 6.2 we present a short survey of growth models in the unionized labour market. In Section 6.3 we define an endogenous growth model where firms invest a part of their profits in physical capital while workers optimally allocate their earnings between consumption and investment in human capital. Section 6.4 deals with the behaviour of trade unions and firms in the short run. In Section 6.5 we analyse the relationship between short-run behaviour and long-run optimality. Finally, we propose some concluding remarks.

6.2. A SHORT SURVEY OF GROWTH IN UNIONIZED MARKETS

It has long been recognized that trade unions are able to influence capital accumulation through their involvement in the fixing of wage and employment levels. In a competitive firm, higher wages lead to the substitution of labour by capital and to a fall-off in production. The overall effect on the capital stock is therefore ambiguous. When companies and unions bargain over both wages and employment, in the absence of binding agreements between the parties it is likely that the incentive to invest will diminish (Grout, 1984; Van der Ploeg, 1987; Duranton, 2000): a larger capital stock and greater labour productivity will induce the unions to demand higher wages, thereby eroding the expected return on capital. When firms see the shortfall in their expected return, they will have less incentive to invest.

Daveri and Tabellini (1997), using an overlapping generation model, consider the effect of taxation of labour income on firms' labour costs. When government taxes labour income the share of the tax which is incurred by the firm increases when unions exist. Therefore, unions increase labour costs. Higher labour costs (with respect to the case of a competitive labour market) increase unemployment and induce firms to substitute capital for labour, thereby reducing the marginal productivity of capital and so the incentive to accumulate. Unions lead the economic system to a reduced employment rate and a lower growth rate.

Using a similar model (growth driven by externalities, overlapping generation model), Irmen and Wigger (2001) show that the negative effect of the lower employment rate on accumulation may be overstated by a positive effect which arises from the higher revenue young people receive due to trade-union activity. The higher saving rate of the young generation increases accumulation and growth. Which of the two effects prevails depends on the characteristics of the aggregate production function and on the importance that unions give to employment level in their objective function. Therefore, unions may be growth-enhancing.

Agell and Lommerud (1993) present a two-sector model where the availability of resources in the modern sector (which uses capital-intensive technologies) is the engine of growth. Unions reduce wage disparities between the two sectors, which induces firms operating in the traditional sector to reduce their number of employees and firms operating in the modern sector to increase it. In this way, unions, unless wage disparities are reduced 'too much', increase the growth rate. However, the employment rate should be reduced by the unions' actions.

A paper presented by Lingens (2002) bases endogenous growth on *R&D* and considers three productive sectors. Unions bargain on wages in the intermediate sector in accordance with the right-to-manage hypothesis. The research-sector labour market is competitive. In the intermediate sector, wages are above the competitive level because of union bargaining. These hypotheses lead to two consequences: on the one hand, unemployment rises and, consequently, the growth rate falls; on the other, the relative wage in the research sector diminishes so that employment rises in the sector that is the engine of growth. According to Lingens' hypothesis on production and utility functions, the former effect always prevails; therefore an increase in union bargaining power reduces the economy's growth rate.

Parreño and Sánchez-Losada (2002) assume an overlapping generation model where individual actions may depend on altruistic action towards the future generation. Given a final sector and an educational sector, these authors assume both that trade unions operate in both sectors and solely in one of the two. The results of the paper show that the relationship between growth and trade-union power may assume both a positive and negative sign, because 'fathers' have an interest in investing in their children's education only if altruism exists but is not too strong; in this case, trade unions enhance growth because, by raising the wage rate, they increase investments in education. This positive relationship is more likely to exist if unions operate in the final sector, thereby reducing the relative wage in the educational sector and hence the relative cost of education.

'Wait unemployment' is the engine of the De Groot (2001) model. Two sectors coexist in the economy: a high-tech monopolistic sector, where unions operate, and a traditional competitive sector. Unions increase the relative wage in the high-tech sector so that unemployed people (the new entrants, or those fired by the high-tech sector) find it more worthwhile to search for a job in the unionized sector than to accept job offers in the competitive sector. Search unemployment increases, and the employment rate in the high-tech sector decreases. These two effects give rise to a negative correlation between union bargaining power and growth.[2]

Wapler (2001) introduces heterogeneity in the labour market, considering skilled and unskilled workers. The former have greater human capital and are paid more by firms (skill premium). Unions seek to increase the relative wage of unskilled workers, so that the unskilled alone are supporters of unions. Higher union bargaining power leads to a reduction in the amount of unskilled employment; depending on the complementarity between the two kinds of workers, the number of skilled employed and their productivity may move in either direction; the same holds for the growth rate of the economy as a whole.

The models briefly presented above show that the results concerning the relationship between union power and economic growth are diverse and that the paths to these results are also diverse. This suggests that there is no consensus on the effects of labour unions on endogenous growth. We intend to highlight this relationship by considering a growth model based on human capital.

6.3.   ENDOGENOUS GROWTH AND OPTIMAL FACTOR SHARE

We consider the behaviour of a 'benevolent social planner', who is interested in the long-run optimality of the economic system.[3]

The technology is described by the following Cobb–Douglas constant return to scale production function:

$$y(h,k) = h(t)^{\alpha} k(t)^{1-\alpha} \tag{6.1}$$

where $h(t)$ is human capital, $k(t)$ is physical capital, both expressed in per capita terms. The labour force is supposed to be constant and normalized to one.

We assume a CRRA utility function:

$$U(t) = \frac{1}{1-\sigma} c(t)^{1-\sigma} \tag{6.2}$$

We assume that a given share of profits, ϕ, is always invested in physical capital, $\dot{k}(t)$, whereas the share $1-\phi$ is distributed to households as dividends. Total household income is optimally allocated between consumption, $c(t)$, and investment in human capital, $\dot{h}(t)$. Therefore:

$$\dot{k}(t)=\phi(1-q)y[h(t),k(t)] \qquad (6.3)$$

$$\dot{h}(t)=[1-\phi(1-q)]y[h(t),k(t)]-c(t) \qquad (6.4)$$

where q is the labour share. In this economic system, there exist two choice variables: the first is $m \equiv \phi(1-q)$ which defines the investment in physical capital; the second is consumption level, $c(t)$, which residually determines the accumulation of human capital.

The Hamiltonian for the problem is:[4]

$$\Lambda(c,q,h,k,\lambda,\mu)=e^{-\rho t}\frac{1}{1-\sigma}c^{1-\sigma}+\lambda\left[(1-m)y(h,k)-c\right]+\mu m y(h,k)$$

The first order conditions are:

$$\Lambda'_c = e^{-\rho t}c^{-\sigma}-\lambda=0 \qquad (6.5)$$

$$\Lambda'_q = \phi y(h,k)(\lambda-\mu)=0 \qquad (6.6)$$

$$-\Lambda'_h = \dot{\lambda} = -\{\lambda(1-m)+\mu m\}\alpha\frac{y(h,k)}{h} \qquad (6.7)$$

$$-\Lambda'_k = \dot{\mu} = -\{\lambda(1-m)+\mu m\}(1-\alpha)\frac{y(h,k)}{k} \qquad (6.8)$$

and transversality conditions are:

$$\lim_{t\to\infty}\lambda(t)h(t)=0 \qquad \lim_{t\to\infty}\mu(t)k(t)=0 \qquad (6.9)$$

Given that $m \neq 0$ and $y(t) \neq 0$, equation (6.6) implies $\lambda(t)=\mu(t)\forall t$, which, in turn, implies $\dot{\lambda}/\lambda=\dot{\mu}/\mu\forall t$.

The dynamic laws of equations (6.7) and (6.8) become, respectively:

$$-\frac{\dot{\lambda}}{\lambda}=\alpha\frac{y}{h} \qquad (6.10)$$

$$-\frac{\dot{\mu}}{\mu}=(1-\alpha)\frac{y}{k}$$

Hence:

$$k = \frac{1-\alpha}{\alpha} h \qquad (6.11)$$

Therefore, along the optimal growth path, physical and human capital must grow at the same rate, so that the production function of equation (6.1) can be written as:

$$y(k) = \frac{\alpha}{1-\alpha} k \qquad (6.12)$$

and:

$$y(h) = \frac{a}{\alpha} h \qquad (6.13)$$

where $a = \alpha^{\alpha}(1-\alpha)^{1-\alpha}$ represents the marginal productivity of the total (human and physical) capital stock in the steady state equilibrium.

Substituting equation (6.12) in equation (6.3), we obtain:

$$\frac{\dot{k}}{k} \equiv g_k = m\frac{a}{1-\alpha} \qquad (6.14)$$

Equation (6.10) becomes:

$$-\frac{\dot{\lambda}}{\lambda} = a \qquad (6.15)$$

Substituting equation (6.13) in equation (6.4), we obtain the human capital growth rate:

$$\frac{\dot{h}}{h} \equiv g_h = \frac{a}{\alpha}(1-m) - \frac{c}{h}$$

Substituting equations (6.12) and (6.13) in equations (6.3) and (6.4) and equalizing the growth rates of human and physical capital, we obtain:

$$\frac{c}{h} = \frac{a}{\alpha}\left(1 - \frac{m}{1-\alpha}\right) \qquad (6.16)$$

Substituting equation (6.13) in equation (6.16), we obtain the marginal propensity to consume:

$$\frac{c}{y} = 1 - \frac{m}{1-\alpha} \qquad (6.17)$$

which is positive if $m < 1 - \alpha$.

Differentiating equation (6.5) with respect to time and substituting in equation (6.15) we obtain the consumption growth rate:

$$\frac{\dot{c}}{c} \equiv g^* = \frac{a - \rho}{\sigma} \tag{6.18}$$

The growth rate of consumption[5] is equal to that of human capital because of equation (6.16) and because of the constancy of the labour share; and, given equation (6.11), it must also be equal to the growth rate of physical capital. The per capita production function (equation (6.1)) shows that the optimal economy growth rate (g^*) coincides with the per capita consumption growth rate.[6]

Note that the optimal growth rate does not depend on the parameter ϕ; in fact we obtain the same result as the Modigliani–Miller theorem: for firms, the way in which investment is financed (through dividends – our ϕ – or credit) is irrelevant.

Equations (6.18) and (6.14) give the following definition for the optimal share of investment in physical capital:

$$m^* \equiv \phi(1 - q) = (1 - \alpha)\frac{g^*}{a}$$

such that m depends on the fundamentals, that is, technology and preferences. Note that the product between the capital share $(1 - q)$ and the parameter α must be constant in steady state; that is, the higher α is, the lower must be the capital share.

Therefore, the optimal labour share is:

$$q^* = 1 - (1 - \alpha)\frac{g^*}{a\phi} \tag{6.19}$$

in other words, greater than α if g^* is lower than ϕa. For $\phi = 1$, it is easy to show that q^* is always greater than α if the per capita consumption is positive and the transversality conditions (equation (6.9)) hold.[7]

6.4.   SHORT-RUN BARGAINING

In the short run trade unions and firms, whose objective functions do not take into account long-run optimality, bargain over wages and employment.

We assume decentralized efficient bargaining, in the sense that each firm and each trade union bargain jointly on wage and employment (McDonald and Solow, 1981).

The trade union in firm j maximizes the following union utility function:

$$W_j = L_j(w_j - v)^z$$

where v represents the outside options (the last bargained wage, or the wage of some foreign 'reference' country, or unemployment benefits augmented by the utility deriving from greater leisure, and so on) for union members not employed, which we assume to be invariant across firms. Risk-neutral firms maximize profits:

$$\Pi_j = AL_j^\alpha - w_j L_j$$

where, in the short-run production function $Y(L) = AL^\alpha$, we define $A = H^\alpha K^{1-\alpha}$ where H and K are respectively the stock of human and physical capital, given in each bargaining round.

The Nash bargaining solution is given by maximizing the weighted product of agents payoffs net of the outside options (which we assume are equal to v for unions and to 0 for firms) with respect to the employment level and wage level. The function to be maximized is

$$\left[L_j w_j + (1-L_j)v - v\right]^\eta \left[AL_j^\alpha - w_j L_j\right]^{1-\eta},$$

where $0 \le \eta \le 1$ is the trade unions' bargaining power. From the first order conditions we obtain the set of tangency points between trade unions' iso-utility and firms' iso-profit curves[8] in the space w_j, L_j so that $\left(W_{L_j}/W_{w_j}\right) = \left(\Pi_{L_j}/\Pi_{w_j}\right)$ which can be solved for the employment level and can be aggregated across firms (with a mass equal to equation (6.1)) in order to obtain the aggregate contract curve:

$$L(w) = \left(\alpha \frac{A}{v}\right)^{\frac{1}{1-\alpha}} \tag{6.20}$$

We obtain a vertical contract curve, such that the employment level is now independent of the bargained wage. Substituting this result in the first FOC, we obtain the bargained wage rate (w), which takes the form:

$$w = \left[(1-\eta) + \frac{\eta}{\alpha}\right]v$$

The labour share may be written as follows:

$$q = \frac{wL^*}{Y(L^*)} = \alpha \frac{w}{v} = \alpha + \eta(1-\alpha) \tag{6.21}$$

Hence, $q(\eta)$ is increasing in union bargaining power.

In steady state the labour share is constant if (see equation (6.21)) $\dot{w}/w = \dot{v}/v$ and, from equation (6.20), the employment rate is constant if: $\dot{L}/L = (\dot{A}/A) - (\dot{v}/v)$ which, given the definition of A, implies $\dot{v}/v = g^*$. The three equations above imply that the wage rate grows at the same rate as the whole economy.

6.5. TRADE UNIONS AND OPTIMALITY

Henceforth, we consider the relationship between short-run equilibrium and long-run optimality, and we assume, alongside the classical tradition, that the whole capital share is reinvested in physical capital, such that our parameter ϕ equals unity.

We have no guarantee that bargaining between firms and unions, as described in equation (6.21), leads the economy to the optimal equilibrium of equation (6.19). To reach the optimal growth path, the bargained wage level should be such that the two equations mentioned are equal, so that:

$$\frac{w^*}{v} = \frac{q^*(\rho,\sigma)}{\alpha} \tag{6.22}$$

where $q^*(\rho,\sigma)$ is defined in equation (6.19).

Are there factors which make equation (6.22) respected? Let us conceive of the economy described as a sequence of short-run equilibria, where the trade unions determine the wage rate:

- considering the existence of a wage rate which maximizes household utility (rational behaviour);
- according to their goals, completely ignoring the existence of an optimal wage rate (myopic behaviour).

In the first hypothesis (rational trade unions) the dynamic behaviour of the wage rate is completely determined by considering the optimal wage rate defined in equation (6.22). Unions operate in order to maximize the expected utility of individuals.

With efficient bargaining, the short-run labour share, as defined in equation (6.21) and the optimal labour share, $q^*(\rho,\sigma)$, as defined in equation (6.19) are equal if:

$$\eta^* = 1 - \frac{g^*}{\alpha} = 1 - \frac{a-\rho}{\sigma\alpha} \tag{6.23}$$

which is increasing in σ and ρ, has a maximum for $\alpha = 0.50$ and is always positive because of the transversality condition.

Therefore, there exists a level of trade-union bargaining power that is 'optimal' for the economic system. Consider that the unions' bargaining power η equals the average propensity to consume. In fact, from equation (6.17), for $\phi = 1$, substituting $m = 1 - q = (1-a)g^*/\alpha$, we obtain:

$$\frac{c}{y} = 1 - \frac{g^*}{a} = \eta$$

Obviously, on *a priori* grounds there is no reason to believe that trade union power is exactly that described in equation (6.23). Suppose that bargaining power, and hence wages and the labour share, are less than optimality: in this case, employment is higher. Even if this situation is a stable steady state, because equation (6.22) is respected, such that the labour share and the employment rate are constants, the growth rate of human capital is lower than optimality. This is a situation of human capital shortage. Households consume less output, and at a reduced growth rate. On the contrary, if $\eta > \eta^*$, then $q(\eta) > q^*(\rho, \sigma)$; therefore profits and investment in physical capital are lower and the propensity to consumption higher than optimality.

Are there endogenous mechanisms able to lead the bargaining power to the optimal level? Obviously, trade union bargaining power is influenced by various factors, like the unemployment level, the general public's perception that the trade unions are doing the 'right thing' in bargaining, the relative level of wages and profits. But, at least in our model, there are no evident factors which can lead the parameter η to the optimal value of equation (6.23).

Hence, even if unions are indeed useful for economic growth (by raising the wage rate above the competitive one), they should incorporate household optimal behaviour in their objective function.

6.6. CONCLUSION

In this chapter we have revisited the relationship between the functional distribution of income and growth envisaged by the Ricardian tradition. In an endogenous growth model based on human capital, we have assumed that the functional distribution of income influences investment in accumulable factors.

In the long run, the capital share accruing to firms defines the growth path of physical capital, whereas the labour share accruing to households is optimally split between human capital investment and consumption. In the short run, efficient bargaining between the firms and unions determines the employment level and the labour share as a function of the wage rate.

We have thus obtained analytical results for long-run optimal growth (as the outcome of the social planner intertemporal maximization) and for short-run equilibrium (as the outcome of bargaining between firms and unions).

Our main result is that there exists a given labour share depending on preferences and technology alone which maximizes expected household utility. This labour share is greater than the 'traditional' one, requiring a functional distribution of income which is more favourable to workers than that in a competitive market $(q > \alpha)$.

This result depends on the hypothesis of an imperfect capital market which induces firms to partly invest their profit in physical capital due to liquidity constraints and leaves the financing of human capital to households alone.

The optimal labour share may be achieved thanks to the trade unions. In fact, our results show that trade unions are required to allow the economic system to reach optimality, but also that their presence, albeit necessary, is not sufficient. The effective behaviour of trade unions gives rise to the optimal labour share only if the unions are able to internalize the effect of their behaviour on growth (the 'rational' trade unions). Otherwise, in the case of 'myopic' unions, there is a given positive union bargaining power (coinciding with the propensity to consume) which maximizes the economy's growth rate. A still unresolved question concerns the economic mechanism which may eventually lead trade union bargaining power towards optimality.

APPENDIX: HUMAN CAPITAL AS AN EXTERNALITY

We assume that the government behaves in order to maximize the expected utility of the representative household. It therefore withdraws taxes from households and uses the amount it obtains to finance the general education system, which must be attended by every individual. It is thus able to solve the coordination problem among individuals raised by the externality generated by education.

Given the production function (equation (6.1)) and the utility function (equation (6.2)) presented in the text, we must now change the dynamic constraint of equation (6.4) (in what follows, we consider the case where the capital share is completely reinvested in physical capital, such that $\phi = 1$):

$$\dot{h} = \tau q y \left[h(t), k(t) \right]$$

where τ is the tax rate, whereas constraint (6.3) remains unchanged.

Per capita consumption is simply given by:

$$c(t) = (1-\tau)qy\big[h(t),k(t)\big]$$

Now, households choose the labour share whereas the government chooses the rate of taxation. Consequently, first order conditions (6.5) and (6.6) become, respectively:

$$\Lambda_\tau = \left\{-e^{-\rho t}\big[(1-\tau)qy\big]^{-\sigma} + \mu\right\}qy = 0$$

$$\Lambda_q = \left\{-e^{-\rho t}\big[(1-\tau)qy\big]^{-\sigma}(1-\tau) - \lambda + \mu\tau\right\}y = 0$$

Combining the two first order conditions yields $\lambda(t) = \mu(t)\forall t$. Given this result, all the other optimality conditions are completely equal to that in the text referring to the decentralized solution.

Therefore, with the same procedure as shown in the text, we obtain the following results:

- the transversality condition $q > \alpha$ holds;
- the optimal economic growth rate is the same as that shown in equation (6.18);
- the optimal labour share is the same as that in equation (6.19); it defines the optimal tax rate:

$$\tau^* = \frac{\alpha}{1-\alpha}\frac{1-q^*(\rho,\sigma)}{q^*(\rho,\sigma)}$$

which is lower than unity only if $q^*(r,s) < a$, that is, if consumption is positive;

- all the other results presented in the text hold.

NOTES

1. Investment in human capital is usually measured by school enrolment, financed partly by the general taxation system and partly by households directly. Hence, the cost of schooling is mainly transferred to households. For a recent survey of empirical measures of human capital see Wößmann (2003); Le, Gibson and Oxley (2003); Zagler and Dürneker (2003).
2. Other channels which confirm the negative relationship are analysed by De Groot.
3. The same result would apply if we had assumed that human capital is specific to each worker, such that each household is interested in investing in it or if human capital were supposed to increase welfare only through externalities in the production process, even if in the latter case every household could not be interested in investing in education since the traditional free rider problem arises in the presence of an externality. In the Appendix we analyse this case, assuming that the government, through optimal taxation on labour

earnings, induces households to invest the optimal amount of revenue in education. We will obtain the same results shown here.

4. In what follows, we do not write the time index unless it is necessary.
5. Transversality conditions of equation (6.9) are fulfilled if $a > \rho > a(1-\sigma)$.
6. In order to investigate the role played by our hypotheses of equality between capital share and investment in physical capital let us remove, assuming that the whole income accrues to households who decide how to allocate it in consumption, investment in physical capital and investment in human capital. Following the same steps shown above, in the simplified case of $\phi = 0$, we obtain the 'non-constrained' growth rate $\overset{\centerdot}{g}_{NC}$:

$$\overset{\centerdot}{g}_{NC} = \frac{1}{\alpha + \sigma}[a - \rho] = \frac{\sigma}{\alpha + \sigma} g *$$

which is lower than that obtained in equation (6.18): $\overset{\centerdot}{g}_{NC} < g^*$. As might be expected, if profits have to be invested, the economy grows further. Therefore, when capital market imperfections exist, the optimal growth rate of the whole economy is higher than the optimal one of the 'perfectly competitive' economy, but at the expense of a lower per capita consumption.
7. For $\phi < 1$, then $q > \alpha$ if $\rho > a(1 - \phi\sigma) > a(1 - \sigma)$, where the last term represents the transversality condition.
8. From the definition of the union utility function and firm profit function, we obtain the slope of the iso-utility curve, that is $dw_j / dL_j = -[(w_j - v)/L_j]$ and the slope of the iso-profits curve $dw_j / dL_j = -[(Y'_{L_j} - w_j)/(-L_j)]$

REFERENCES

Agell, J. and K.E. Lommerud (1993), 'Egalitarianism and growth', *Scandinavian Journal of Economics*, **95**, 559–79.

Chirinko, R. (1987), 'Tobin's Q and financial policy', *Journal of Monetary Economics*, **19**, 69–87.

Daveri, F. and G. Tabellini (1997), 'Unemployment, growth and taxation in industrial countries', CEPR Discussion Paper No. 1681.

De Groot H.L.F. (2001), 'Unemployment, growth and trade unions', *Growth and Change*, **32**, 69–91.

Duranton G. (2000), 'Growth and imperfect competition on factor markets: increasing returns and distribution', *European Economic Review*, **44**(2), 255–80.

Fazzari S.M., R.G. Hubbard and B.C. Petersen (1988), 'Financing constraints and corporate investment', *Brookings Papers on Economic Activity*, **1**, 141–95.

Greenwald, B.C. and J.E. Stiglitz (1987), 'Imperfect information, credit markets and unemployment', *European Economic Review*, **31**, 444–56.

Grout, P.A. (1984), 'Investment and wages in the absence of binding contracts: a Nash bargaining approach', *Econometrica*, **52**(2), 449–60.

Irmen, A. and B. Wigger (1991), 'Trade union objectives and economic growth', CEPR Discussion Paper No. 3027

Kaldor, N. (1956), 'A model of economic growth', *Economic Journal*, **23**, 94–100.

Le, T., J. Gibson and L. Oxley (2003), 'Cost- and income-based measures of human capital', *Journal of Economic Surveys*, **17**(3), 271–307.

Lingens, J. (2002), 'The effects of unions in a simple endogenous growth model', Working Paper University of Kassel, February.

Lucas, R.E. (1988), 'On the mechanism of economic development', *Journal of Monetary Economics*, **22**, 3–42.

McDonald, I.M. and R.M. Solow (1981), 'Wage bargaining and employment', *American Economic Review*, **71**, 896–908.

Parreño, J.M.R. and F. Sánchez-Losado (1999), 'The role of unions in an endogenous growth model with human capital', Universitat de Barcelona, Divisio de Ciencies Juridiques, Economiques i Socials, Documents de Treball 57.

Pasinetti, L. (1962), 'Rate of profit and income distribution in relation to the rate of economic growth', *Review of Economic Studies*, **29**, 267–69.

Pasinetti, L. (1969), 'Switches of techniques and the rate of return in capital theory', *Economic Journal*, **79**, 508–37.

Samuelson, P.A. and F. Modigliani (1966), 'The Pasinetti paradox in neoclassic and more general models', *Review of Economic Studies*, **33**, 269–301.

Stiglitz, J.E. and A. Weiss (1981), 'Credit rationing in markets with imperfect information', *American Economic Review*, **71**(3), 393–410.

Van der Ploeg, F. (1987), 'Trade unions, investment and unemployment. a non-cooperative approach', *European Economic Review*, **31**, 1465–92.

Wapler, R. (2001), 'Unions, growth and unemployment', University of Tübingen, Discussion Paper No. 206.

Wößmann, L. (2003), 'Specifying human capital', *Journal of Economic Surveys*, **17**(3), 241–70.

Zagler, M. and G. Dürneker (2003), 'Fiscal policy and economic growth', *Journal of Economic Surveys*, **17**(3), 397–418.

7. Job contact networks, inequality and aggregate output[*]

Andrea Mario Lavezzi and Nicola Meccheri

7.1. INTRODUCTION

The importance of social networks in labour markets is well documented in the sociological literature (for example, Granovetter, 1974) which highlights the importance of social links, like friends, relatives and acquaintances, as sources of information on jobs. A number of empirical studies report that approximately between 40 per cent and 60 per cent of employed workers found their jobs through social networks although, in general, these proportions vary with sex, occupations, skills, and workers' socio-economic background.[1]

Another line of empirical research shows that observable individual characteristics (for example, education, skill level, abilities, family, etc.) account for only about 50 per cent of wage inequality (see Arrow and Borzekowski, 2003, for references). The fact that workers have different social ties or links can play a role in explaining such evidence. In particular, all other variables held constant, workers with different networks will on average have different wages and employment opportunities. Furthermore, as remarked by Calvó-Armengol and Jackson (2004), variables such as workers' location or race may capture network effects, and therefore they can interact with other workers' individual characteristics in explaining wage outcomes and inequality.

Joining a growing economic literature, we model social networks in labour markets in order to investigate their role in explaining wage inequality among workers, as well as aggregate production. In particular, we consider a simplified version of the model by Calvó-Armengol and Jackson (2003), in which information about heterogeneous jobs arrives at heterogeneous agents randomly. We study the case of two types of jobs (good/bad) and two types of workers (skilled/unskilled). Unemployed workers accept any offer while employed workers accept it only if the job is more attractive (in terms of pay) than the current one. If this is not the case, they pass the information about the vacancy to a worker in their network.

We find that, in general, the geometry of the network affects aggregate production and inequality. In particular, we show that: i) increasing the number of links in a network increases output and reduces inequality; ii) for a given number of social links connecting all agents, output increases if the average distance among workers decreases; iii) for a given number of social links, output increases and inequality decreases when all agents have some links, given that the productivity of skilled workers in good jobs is sufficiently low.

The rest of the chapter is structured as follows: in Section 7.2, we offer a brief overview of the related literature; in Section 7.3, the basic model is introduced and described; in Section 7.4, we present and analyse some simple examples; in Section 7.5, results of simulations are reported and discussed; in Section 7.6 we derive some policy implications; Section 7.7 concludes.

7.2.   RELATED LITERATURE

A fundamental contribution in economics on the role of social networks in labour markets is the seminal work of Montgomery (1991), who presents an adverse selection model in which job referrals improve the quality of firm-worker matches, when firms cannot perfectly observe workers' ability before hiring. In this model, an increase in the density of social ties increases wage inequality. The reason is that social ties convey to firms more information on workers' quality; this increases the gap between the (higher) wage paid to referred workers, and the market wage paid to those who find a job through other channels.

Montgomery (1994) also analyses the role of 'weak ties', that is relationships with non-frequent social interactions (or transitory relations), and shows that they are positively related to the aggregate employment rate. Furthermore, weak ties reduce inequality, measured by the distribution of employment which obtains with social interactions, relative to a case of absence of a social network, in which individuals are randomly allocated to jobs.

In our model, inequality does not depend on adverse selection,[2] but on the network structure. Furthermore, unlike Montgomery (1994), we do not consider inequality only in terms of employment opportunities but also in terms of wage differentials.

Arrow and Borzekowski (2003) propose a static model which focuses on wage inequality caused by differences in the number of connections of workers to firms, in an imperfect information framework where firms have more information on workers connected to them. In this environment, workers with a different number of connections have on average different incomes. In particular, they find that about 13–15 per cent of the variation in log wages is attributable to the variation in the number of workers' connections.

Firms are imperfectly informed on workers' productivity also in the dynamic model of Krauth (2004). In this model employed workers may provide information on the skills of their unemployed friends, and the number of connections is positively related to employment (both for individual workers and in aggregate).[3]

In our framework, the mechanism through which social networks affect employment, productivity and wages in the economy is quite different from that emphasized in Arrow and Borzekowski (2003) and Krauth (2004). In particular, here the social network is the channel by which workers increase their probability of finding a (better) job, rather than the channel by which firms acquire more information on workers' productivity.

Our chapter is closely related to Calvó-Armengol and Jackson (2003, 2004), who present a framework in which exogenous social networks[4] facilitate the transmission of information on job vacancies among workers. Calvó-Armengol and Jackson (2003) show that wages for workers in the same network are positively correlated, without studying the role of network geometry. This aspect is analysed in Calvó-Armengol and Jackson (2004), but only for the case of homogeneous workers and jobs. In this chapter we extend the analysis of network geometry to the case of heterogeneous workers and jobs. In addition, we study the dynamics of inequality, aggregate output and their correlation over time.

7.3. A MODEL OF THE LABOUR MARKET WITH SOCIAL NETWORKS

7.3.1. Production, Wages and Turnover

We present a model of the labour market which derives from Calvó-Armengol and Jackson (2003). In particular we study the case with two types of jobs and two types of workers. Time is discrete and indexed by $t = 0, 1, 2...$ The economy is populated by a number of risk-neutral, infinitely-lived agents (workers) indexed by $i \in \{1, 2, ..., N\}$. In each period a worker can be either employed or unemployed. Indicating with θ the employment status of the worker, $\theta \in \{n$ (unemployed), b (employed in a bad job), g (employed in a good job)$\}$ and with λ her type, $\lambda \in \{u$

(unskilled), s (skilled)}, then each agent in any period can be in one of the following states:

$$
s_{it}^{\lambda\theta} = \begin{cases}
s^{ub} & \text{if unskilled and employed in a bad job} \\
s^{ug} & \text{if unskilled and employed in a good job} \\
s^{sg} & \text{if skilled and employed in a good job} \\
s^{sb} & \text{if skilled and employed in a bad job} \\
s^{un} & \text{if unskilled and unemployed} \\
s^{sn} & \text{if skilled and unemployed}
\end{cases}
$$

On the production side, we consider one-to-one employment relationships and assume a very simple form of production function, in which productivity depends on the type of match between the worker and the job (firm). In particular, we denote with $y_{it}^{\lambda\theta}$ the output of a firm employing worker i, at time t, for a match $\lambda\theta$ or, in other words, the surplus generated by a match $\lambda\theta$ (output price is normalized to one).

We simply assume that a skilled worker is more productive than an unskilled worker, and that a good job is more productive than a bad job, for instance because it is a hi-tech job. According to these assumptions, the parameter $y^{\lambda\theta}$, indexing the productivity of a match, follows the rule:

$$
y^{sg} > y^{ug} = y^{sb} > y^{ub} > 0 \ (= y^{un} = y^{sn}).
$$

In other words we assume that the highest (lowest) productivity is obtained when a skilled (unskilled) worker has a good (bad) job. Other cases fall in between, and for simplicity are assumed to give the same product.[5]

Wages are a fraction of match surplus, and are denoted by $w^{\lambda\theta} = \beta y^{\lambda\theta}$ with $\beta \in (0,1)$.[6] This produces an ordering of wages obtainable in a given match, which follows the ordering of outputs. Obviously, unemployed workers earn zero wages, and we normalize their reservation utility to zero.

The labour market is subject to the following turnover. Initially, all workers are unemployed. Every period (from $t = 0$ onwards) has two phases: at the beginning of the period each worker receives an offer of a job of type f, with $f \in \{b,g\}$, with arrival probability $a_f \in (0,1)$.[7] Parameter a_f captures all the information on vacancies which is not transmitted through the network, that is information from firms, agencies, newspapers, etc. (say, from the market as a whole). When an agent receives an offer and she is already employed and not interested in the offer, in the sense that the offered job has a lower wage, she passes the information to a friend/relative/acquaintance who is unemployed or employed but receiving a lower wage than that paid for the offered job. At the end of the period every employed worker loses her job with breakdown probability $d \in (0,1)$.

7.3.2. Social Links and Job Information Transmission

Social networks in the economy may be conveniently represented by a graph G which summarizes the links of all agents, where $G_{ij} = 1$ if i and j know each other, and $G_{ij} = 0$ otherwise. It is assumed that $G_{ij} = G_{ji}$, meaning that the acquaintance relationship is reciprocal. Given the assumptions on wages and arrival probabilities, the probability of the joint event that agent i learns about a job and this job ends up in agent's j hands, is described by $p_{ij}(.)$:

$$
p_{ij}(s_{it}^{\lambda\theta}, f) =
\begin{cases}
a_b & \text{if } f = b \ \vee \ j = i \vee s_i = s^{\lambda n} \\
a_g & \text{if } f = g \ \vee \ j = i \vee \left(s_i = s^{\lambda n} \wedge s_i = s^{\lambda b}\right) \\
a_b \dfrac{G_{ij}}{\sum_{k:s_k=s^{\lambda n}} G_{ik}} & \text{if } f = b \vee \theta \in \{b,g\} \vee s_i = s^{\lambda\theta} \vee s_j = s^{\lambda n} \\
a_g \dfrac{G_{ij}}{\sum_{k:s_k=s^{\lambda\theta(\theta\neq g)}} G_{ik}} & \text{if } f = g \ \vee \theta \in \{b,n\} \vee s_i = s^{\lambda g} \vee s_j = s^{\lambda\theta} \\
0 & \text{otherwise}
\end{cases}
$$

In the first two cases, worker i receives an offer with probability a_f and takes the offer for herself. This holds if she is either unemployed or employed in a bad job and receives an offer for a good job. In the third case, worker i is employed and receives with probability a_b an offer for a bad job that she passes only to an unemployed worker $j \neq i$. We assume that among all unemployed workers connected with i by a social link, worker i chooses worker j randomly. Hence, the probability that worker j receives the information from worker i is equal to $G_{ij}/\sum_{k:s_k=s^{\lambda n}} G_{ik}$, that is zero if j is not connected with i ($G_{ij} = 0$) or one over the sum of unemployed workers connected with worker $i(\sum_{k:s_k=s^{\lambda n}} G_{ik})$, otherwise ($G_{ij} = 1$). In the fourth case, worker i receives with probability a_g an offer for a good job when she is already employed in a good job. Hence she passes the offer (with probability $G_{ij}/\sum_{k:s_k=s^{\lambda\theta(\theta\neq g)}} G_{ik}$) to a worker connected with her who is unemployed or employed in a bad job. Clearly, $p_{ij} = 0$ in all remaining cases.

To sum up, a worker who receives an offer makes direct use of it if the new job opportunity increases her wage. Otherwise, she passes the information to someone who is connected with her. The choice of the worker to whom to pass the information is 'selective', in the sense that the information is never passed to someone who does not need it,[8] but it is random with respect to the subset of the connected workers who improve their condition (wage) by exploiting such information (for example, a worker receiving a good job offer is indifferent to pass it to an unemployed contact or a contact employed in a bad job[9]). Finally, we exclude that job information may be transmitted to more than one (connected) worker.[10]

Figure 7.1 shows the timing of the events for a generic period t (for convenience, the period has been represented as composed by four different successive sub-periods, with sub-periods $t.1$, $t.2$ and $t.4$ of negligible length).

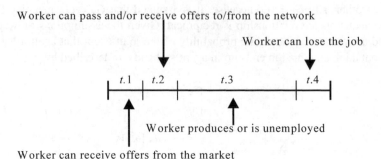

Figure 7.1   Timing of events

7.4.   SOME SIMPLE EXAMPLES

We begin by presenting some examples. First, we consider the role of social ties on the expected wage of a worker. Second, we illustrate the potential effects of changing the network geometry on wage inequality and aggregate output. Although these examples are very simple, they are useful to introduce the effects of social networks on wages and output as well as other relevant aspects that we will investigate afterwards in more detail by providing a number of simulations results.

7.4.1.   Social Links and Expected Wages

Consider an unemployed worker i in period t, that is a worker who entered the period unemployed and did not receive any offer in that period. Her state at the end of period t is $s^{\lambda n}$. Her expected wage in period $t + 1$, when the expectation is formulated in period t, is strictly dependent on the network to which she belongs. As examples, we consider now three simple cases with three agents, i, j and z, and we concentrate our attention on agent i's expected wage in the different situations.

Example 1. Figure 7.2 represents the case in which worker *i* has no links.

Figure 7.2   No links

In this case, the expected wage in $t + 1$ for worker *i* depends only on the exogenous probabilities that she directly receives some job offer at the beginning of that period. In this case, since worker *i* accepts an offer for a bad job only if she does not receive an offer for a good job, her expected wage in the next period is equal to:

$$Ew_{i,t+1} = a_g w^{\lambda g} + a_b (1 - a_g) w^{\lambda b}$$

Example 2. Figure 7.3 represents the case in which worker *i* has a link with worker *j* (who has no links other than with *i*).

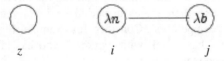

Figure 7.3   One link with a worker in a bad job

Now worker *i* can also find a job, not only when she directly receives some offer, but also when worker *j* transmits some job information. Of course, being employed in a bad job, worker *j* passes to worker *i* only information about a bad job and keeps a good job offer for herself. In particular, worker *j* passes an offer for a bad job to worker *i* if the former does not lose her job (with probability $(1 - b)$) at the end of period *t*, and receives an offer for such a job (with probability a_b) at the beginning of time $t + 1$, or if she loses her job (with probability *b*) at the end of time *t* and receives both an offer for a good and a bad job (with probability $a_b a_g$) at the beginning of time $t + 1$. Thus, in this context, worker *i*'s expected wage in $t + 1$ is given by:

$$Ew_{i,t+1} = \underbrace{a_g w^{\lambda g}}_{\text{i receives an offer for a good job}} + \underbrace{a_b(1-a_g)w^{\lambda b}}_{\text{i receives an offer only for a bad job}} +$$

$$+ \underbrace{a_b(1-d)(1-a_g)(1-a_b)w^{\lambda b}}_{\text{j does not lose her job and receives an offer for a bad job; i receives no offers}} +$$

$$+ \underbrace{a_b a_g d(1-a_g)(1-a_b)w^{\lambda b}}_{\text{j loses her job and receives both an offer for a good and bad job; i receives no offers}} =$$

$$= a_g w^{\lambda g} + a_b(1-a_g)\left[1+(1-d)(1-a_b)+a_g d(1-a_b)\right]w^{\lambda b}$$

Since the expression in square brackets is greater than 1, the expected wage for worker i in $t+1$ is now higher than in Example 1, that is, the social link with worker j has a strictly positive effect (on average) for worker i.

Obviously, when an unemployed worker is linked to a worker employed in a good job, the latter may transmit offers for both types of jobs (conditional on keeping her job at the end of period t). This increases the expected wage in period $t+1$ for worker i.[11]

Example 3. More complicated cases can arise, for instance, when two unemployed workers 'compete' for information, that is when they are both linked to an employed worker who may transmit the information only to one of them. In this case, their wages in period $t+1$ are negatively correlated because they are 'competitors'. Consider, for example, Figure 7.4 in which, at time t, worker i has a link with worker j who has in turn a link with another unemployed worker, worker z.

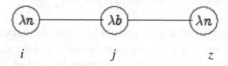

$$\;\;\;\; i \qquad\qquad\qquad j \qquad\qquad\qquad z$$

Figure 7.4   One link with a worker in a bad job with another link

In such a case, worker j passes only with probability of a half a (bad) job offer to worker i. For such a reason, worker i's expected wage in $t+1$ is equal to:

$$Ew_{i,t+1} = a_g w^{\lambda g} + (1-a_g)\left[1 + \frac{(1-b)(1-a_b)+a_g b(1-a_b)}{2}\right]w^{\lambda b}$$

Since in this case the expression in square brackets is lower than the corresponding one in Example 2, the expected wage for worker i in $t+1$ is now lower than in the previous example. Hence one may conjecture that, *ceteris paribus*, a worker (weakly) prefers to be linked to workers with no other links. However, as stressed by Calvó-Armengol and Jackson (2003), this holds in the short run (that is in a one-period perspective), but in a longer run perspective it should be carefully reconsidered. Indeed, referring to the above case, the presence of a 'competitor', worker z, proves useful for worker i since the former helps to improve the wage status of the common connection, worker j, and this, in the longer run, increases the probability that she passes more information to worker i. This aspect outweighs the local (conditional) negative correlation, due to the 'competitive effect', and induces a long-run positive correlation between wages of workers i and z (see Calvó-Armengol and Jackson, 2003).

Given our assumptions, what was stated for expected wages holds true for expected outputs. In Section 7.5 we focus directly on output, while wages are examined in terms of inequality among workers. In particular we study the long-run dynamics by means of simulations.

7.4.2. Changing the Network Geometry: Inequality and Aggregate Output

Before presenting the simulations, we describe in a simple form another example which introduces the consequences of a change in the network geometry on inequality and aggregate output, for a given structure of the population and the same size of the network, that is, the same number of links.

Example 4. Consider the network structures of Figure 7.5, G_1 and G_2, and states of four workers in a generic period t.

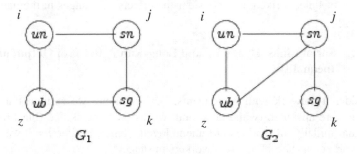

Figure 7.5   Networks G_1 and G_2

In both cases we have two unemployed workers and two employed workers, in one of the possible jobs, and two workers per type. Obviously, output, wages and inequality at time t are equal in the two different networks, but they might differ in $t + 1$ due to different network geometry. For both networks we compute the following expected values for period $t + 1$: i) average output; ii) wages for each worker; iii) wage inequality, measured by the Gini index of (expected) wages.[12]

Table 7.1   Output, wages and inequality

Network	Output	Wages [i, j, z, k]	Inequality
G_1	2.632	0.550; 1.310; 0.750; 1.600	0.220
G_2	2.655	0.550; 1.500; 0.600; 1.600	0.238

We observe that in network G_1 output has increased by 0.8 per cent, as well as inequality, which shows a relatively higher increase of 8 per cent. Output increases as the improvement in the expected output of worker j, who has more links in G_2, outweighs the worsening of the situation of worker z, who in G_1 has one link less with a worker in a good job. This is reflected in the changes in expected wages, which are simply proportional to expected output in our framework.[13]

7.5.   SIMULATIONS

In this section we present the results of the simulations.[14] Our aim is to assess how the presence and structure of social networks affect the dynamics of output and wage inequality in the long run. We begin by considering the effects of the number of social ties. Then we study two cases in which the number of links is fixed, and consider the effects of changes in the network topology.

7.5.1.   Social Links, Dynamics and Long-Run Patterns of Output and Inequality

Consider a network with four agents. For simplicity we assume that two workers are unskilled (white dots) and two workers are skilled (black dots), and that initially all workers are unemployed. Hence, at time $t = 0$ we have two workers in state s^{un} and two workers in state s^{sn}.

We analyse six possible network configurations (see Figure 7.6): an empty network G_A, that is a situation in which no social tie exists; a network with one link between unskilled agents (G_B); a network with one link between skilled agents (G_C); a network with one link between agents with different skill levels (G_D). The last two networks represent more complex 'social environments'. In particular, G_E is a 'path-connected' network, that is a network in which all agents are linked to the two agents on their side, thus with four social ties all agents are (directly and indirectly) connected to each other. Instead, G_F is a complete network in which each agent is directly connected with each other, making a total of six links.

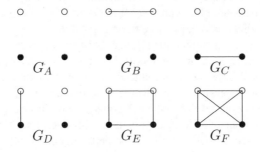

Figure 7.6   *Networks $G_A - G_F$*

We study the relation between the structure of the network and average production in the network, as well as the degree of inequality. In particular, we simulate the economy for 500,000 periods using these parameters: $y^{ub} = 1$; $y^{ug} = y^{sb} = 2$; $y^{sg} = 4$; $a_b = 0.15$; $a_g = 0.10$; $d = 0.015$; $\beta = 0.4$.[15] Results of simulations are reported in Table 7.2: we present the average output per worker and average inequality, measured by the Gini index (both averages are computed over the 500,000 periods of the simulations). Also, we report the correlation of output and inequality over time. Importantly, we are not interested in the effects of an increase of social links on output *per se*, given that from our hypotheses these are unambiguously positive, but on the dynamic relation between output and inequality, which is not *ex ante* so obvious.

Starting from the situation with no social ties, even moving to just a single link (as in G_B, G_C and G_D) we see that (average) output increases and inequality decreases.[16] However, some qualifications are needed according to whether the single link is between low-skill or between high-skill workers. If the link is between agents of the same type, note that with respect to G_A, in G_B the increase in output is less pronounced (+1.45 per cent against +2.84 per cent in G_C) while reduction in inequality is stronger (−7.07 per cent in G_B and −4.24 per cent in G_C).

Clearly, these results make sense. Having a link with another worker increases the probability of getting a (better) job. This increases the average output during time. Furthermore, since high-skill workers are more productive when hired in a good job, and having a link increases the probability of getting that job, output is greater in G_C. At the same time, since wages are in proportion of output, inequality is greater too (even if it is lower than in the 'no links' case) since high-skill workers, with potential higher wages, are the only agents taking advantage of the social tie.[17]

For reasons that should now be clear, the case of G_D, in which the only link is between agents of different type, is intermediate between G_B and G_C: maintaining the same number of social links (one), output and inequality have an intermediate value with respect to G_B and G_C. In this case, therefore, we have the indication of a possible trade-off: 'mixing' the population, that is allowing agents of different type to be connected, decreases output with respect to the case in which two skilled workers are linked, as the flow of good jobs to skilled workers is reduced (in other words more 'mismatches' may occur). However, inequality decreases as one unskilled worker has more opportunities to obtain a job, whether good or bad. Of course, the converse holds if we compare the 'mixed' situation with one in which two low-skill agents are connected. This result can be better qualified with networks with more agents (see Section 7.5.3).

As we see from Table 7.2, adding more links further increases output and decreases inequality. In particular, in a comparison between the two networks in which all agents are connected, we note that in network G_F output is increased by 6.83 per cent with respect to G_A, and inequality is decreased by 16.51 per cent, while in network G_E output has increased by 6.03 per cent and inequality has decreased by 14.62 per cent. Hence, in this framework an increase in the number of links is unambiguously associated with an increase in average output and a decrease in inequality.[18]

Table 7.2   Output and inequality in networks G_A – G_F

G	Output	Inequality	Correlation
G_A	2.751	0.212	−0.773
G_B	2.791	0.197	−0.748
G_C	2.829	0.203	−0.777
G_D	2.810	0.201	−0.785
G_E	2.917	0.181	−0.762
G_F	2.939	0.177	−0.738

In Figure 7.7 we take a closer look at output and inequality dynamics, by considering the first five hundred periods of the simulations.

First note that, in a comparison between the empty network G_A and the complete network G_F, average output (see top of the figures) in the complete network is not only higher, but also more stable over time. Clearly, with all links activated the individual probabilities of being unemployed and unproductive are drastically reduced with respect to the empty network. Hence, the persistence in a state of unemployment is affected by the structure of the network.

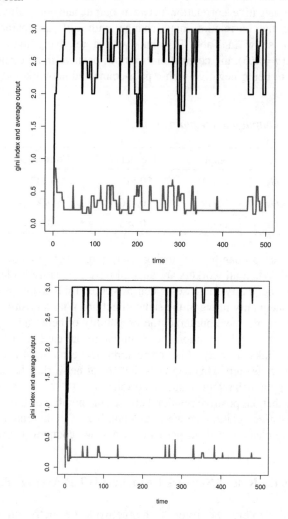

Figure 7.7   Output and inequality: empty network vs. complete network

In both networks, the strong negative correlation between output and inequality is clear. In addition, we note that the (in)stability of output is mirrored in the behaviour of the Gini index over time (see bottom of the figures). The negative correlation depends in general on the parameters. In particular, with a very low breakdown probability with respect to the probabilities of job arrival, the economy is almost always in full employment, corresponding to the maximum per worker output (equal to 3) and to a certain degree of inequality. In this case, inequality increases when a worker loses her job, which corresponds to a drop in average output. This explains the negative correlation between output and inequality. However, the sign of the correlation may change with different parameters. For example we show in Table 7.3 that, with a relatively high breakdown probability ($d = 0.5$), the correlation becomes positive in an empty network, and reverts to being negative with a path-connected network and a complete network.

Table 7.3   *Output and inequality with d = 0.5*

G	Output	Inequality	Correlation
G_A	0.843	0.517	0.142
G_E	0.959	0.486	–0.009
G_F	0.961	0.486	–0.015

With a higher probability of losing their jobs, workers are more often unemployed. When all workers are unemployed, inequality is clearly absent. In this case inequality increases when a worker finds a job, and therefore output and inequality move in the same direction. With a positive number of links, the network may counteract the probability of being unemployed, and in practice makes this situation more similar to the case with low d. Once again, social links strongly affect correlation between output and inequality, even changing its sign. This confirms that social networks play a major role in explaining the behaviour of such a correlation.

We note that the positive relation between the number of links and output, and the negative relation between the number of links and inequality is robust to the change in d, in particular when we compare G_A with G_E and G_F.[19]

7.5.2.   On the Role of Network Geometry: I) The Average Path Length

In order to explore the role of the network geometry on output and inequality, we also consider two networks with the same number and type of agents, and the same number of links, reproducing an example of Calvó-Armengol and Jackson (2004) (see Figure 7.8).

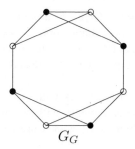 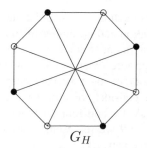

G_G G_H

Figure 7.8   Networks G_G – G_H

In G_G all agents have three links (two neighbours and a neighbour of one of her neighbours) while in G_H they still have three links but one of them is further away. These two networks have different *average path lengths*.

In the terminology of the theory of networks (for example, Albert and Barabasi, 2002), the average path length is the average minimum number of steps to connect any pair of nodes (workers, in our case). In particular, in G_G the average path length is 1.786, while in network G_H it is 1.571. Running simulations[20] for these two different networks, we obtain that inequality is approximately identical (0.178), while average output is slightly higher in G_H than in G_G: 2.943 *vs* 2.940.

Network G_H is a simple way to introduce a typical characteristic of real social network, which are referred to as having the 'small world' property. The small world property in simple terms refers to the fact that despite the network's size (often large for real world networks), it is possible to find a relatively short path between any two nodes.[21]

In our example, the underlying intuition might be explained by the fact that 'long-range' links facilitate the circulation of information. In particular, for an agent, having a link with another worker on the 'other side' of the network permits her to benefit from the presence of the latter's neighbours. This is because they pass information to the connected worker, increasing the probability that she obtains a higher wage and, as a consequence, the probability that she passes more job offers to the former connected agent. Of course, the presence of other distant agents cannot be exploited (if not marginally) with no link to an agent placed among them.

7.5.3.   On the Role of Network Geometry: II) Network Composition and Exclusion

In this section we consider the following issue. Given a structure of the population and a number of links, which network composition is associated to maximum output and minimum inequality? Are there trade-offs? Furthermore, what effects on output and inequality are produced by the exclusion of some workers from the network?

We consider some possible configurations of a network with eight agents (four skilled and four unskilled, all initially unemployed), with six links. In Figure 7.9 we represent various cases in which some agents are excluded from the network.

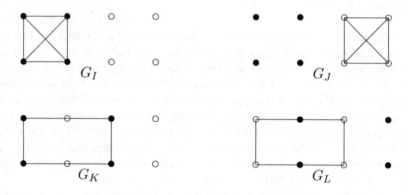

Figure 7.9   Networks $G_I - G_L$

In Figure 7.10, instead, we represent a case with no exclusion, that is in which each agent has at least one link.

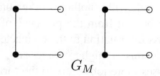

Figure 7.10   Network G_M

Table 7.4 summarizes the results of simulations, with the usual parameters.

Table 7.4   Output and inequality in networks G_I – G_M

G	Output	Inequality	Correlation
G_I	2.876	0.201	–0.868
G_J	2.813	0.194	–0.816
G_K	2.890	0.193	–0.851
G_L	2.862	0.190	–0.830
G_M	2.902	0.188	–0.840

In network G_I all unskilled workers are excluded while all skilled workers are connected with each other. This represents a situation with two social groups: the first enjoys a high level of social interaction, while the second is formed by isolated individuals. This situation, associated with the fact that highly connected workers are also the most productive, results in a high level of output but also a high level of inequality. Network G_J represents the polar case: in this situation output and inequality are lower than in network G_I.[22]

In networks G_K and G_L exclusion is partially removed. These networks represent cases in which the population is more mixed, in the sense that agents of different kinds share social links. In particular, in G_K two unskilled while in G_L two skilled workers are excluded. With respect to G_I, the inclusion of two unskilled agents in the network, associated with the consequent reduction in the density of links among skilled workers, produces an increase in output and a marked decrease in inequality (the average Gini index drops from 0.201 to 0.193). In a comparison with G_L, instead, output in G_K is higher and inequality is practically the same. Network G_L shows a further decrease in inequality, since all unskilled workers have social links and the excluded workers are skilled. However, as expected, this reduces average output.

These results confirm once again that the composition and geometry of the network play a major role in explaining aggregate results, and also that workers with identical observable characteristics have different wage profiles over time according to their social links (for example, in G_I the average wages of skilled and unskilled workers are, respectively, 1.568 and 0.733, while in G_M these values are 1.556 and 0.767).

Network G_M in which no worker is excluded merits special attention. The configuration of this network represents the minimal admissible structure with only six links and no worker excluded. The result is particularly interesting: output is the highest and inequality is the lowest. This result confirms that social integration can be beneficial in terms of efficiency and equality, given that there is no trade-off in moving from a segregated society (like that depicted by G_I and G_J) to a more integrated one.[23]

This result is dependent on the assumption concerning the productivity of different matches ('productivity dispersion'). In particular, it holds if the productivity dispersion, that is the difference in productivities among different matches, is not too high. Indeed, when moving from G_I to G_M, skilled workers are penalized while unskilled workers take advantage from the rewiring of links. The case represented in Table 7.4 is one in which the second effect dominates the first. Clearly, if the productivity of skilled workers in good jobs is sufficiently high, the result is reversed.

In Table 7.5 we present the results when $y^{sg} = 20$ for a comparison between G_I and G_M. We see that in G_M output decreases and inequality is basically constant.[24] In this example, therefore, to increase the efficiency of the system in terms of production, all advantages of exchanging information on jobs should be reserved to skilled workers. In the next section we examine the above findings in order to derive some policy implications.

Table 7.5   Output and inequality with $y^{sg} = 20$

G	Output	Inequality	Correlation
G_I	10.619	0.429	−0.932
G_M	10.563	0.428	−0.959

7.6.   DISCUSSION AND POLICY IMPLICATIONS

Our results indicate that network effects are relevant in the labour market since they strongly influence employment prospects, output and wage inequality as well as correlation between them. In our framework, the most striking indication is that the number of social links produces positive effects both on aggregate production and wage dispersion: when the number of links increases for a given population of workers and given parameters, indicating that members of a society are more interconnected, output generally increases and inequality decreases. For a given number of links, output may also increase when the average distance among workers is reduced.

This result does not often emerge from the literature which, in the presence of social network effects, has often pointed out the existence of a general trade-off between production performance and degree of inequality among workers (for example, Montgomery, 1991). This is due to the fact that in the literature social networks are primarily a tool for conveying information about workers' type or productivity to firms. With such a channel of information, firms become more able to discriminate in hiring and paying among workers, which increases their productivity but also wage dispersion. In our framework, instead, as in Calvó-Armengol and Jackson (2003), social ties permit the transmission of information about job vacancies to workers and this produces clear benefits: output increases, since there is a higher probability that workers are employed and are effectively producing, and wage inequality may decrease, since employment prospects (potentially) improve for all workers.

The most obvious lesson to be learnt from this result is that social ties, or more generally any channel which fosters the transmission of information about job opportunities among workers, should be expanded. Clearly, this depends, at least partially, on our assumptions. For example, firms are totally passive entities in our framework. A natural alternative assumption is that firms 'prefer' to allocate good jobs to skilled workers, and therefore are more willing to dismiss unskilled workers in good jobs. The simplest way to consider this aspect would consist in assuming different values of d for different worker–job matches. This could cause more inequality, as unskilled workers would be at a greater disadvantage than skilled. This, and other extensions, are left for future work.

Another significant result lies in the effects produced by network composition. In other terms, given a population and a *fixed* number of social ties, which network composition produces better welfare results? In the literature on stratification, wage inequality and economic growth (for example, Benabou, 1996a), while stratification is always detrimental for inequality, whether sorting or mixing individuals is growth-enhancing depends on the interplay of two effects. In particular, stratification produces better results if the degree of 'complementarity' between individuals of the same type is sufficiently higher in *local* interactions (that is among individuals of the same type) than in *global* interactions. This appears, for instance, when disparities in knowledge at the local (or community) level entail greater losses (that is, over the education process) than at the global level (that is, over the production process). Moreover, in these models (see also Benabou, 1996b and Durlauf, 1996) the feedback mechanism from the (local) social environment to individual outcomes is related to the local education finance. Our results have also provided some indications in this direction, but the mechanism underlying them is quite different since the social environment is represented by its role in the job search activity.[25] In particular, in our setting, given some technological requirements, networks with links among heterogeneous agents can produce better economic outcomes than networks with links among workers of the same type. Namely, this occurs when the productivity of skilled workers in good jobs is sufficiently low with respect to the productivity in other matches.[26] It may then be possible that, given a case in which the most productive agents derive the maximum benefit from the social network, allowing some of the less productive agents to have some links more than compensates for the loss of output due to the reduction in the number of links among the most productive agents.

The policy implications may range from residential policies to the organization of the school system. Social networks depend heavily on the interaction among individuals and, obviously, neighbourhoods and schools are key determinants of the degree of social interaction. In this case, the indication is that more mixed neighbourhoods and schools which prevent the exclusion of members of some social group, unskilled in our case but in general any ethnic, religious or cultural group, can be beneficial to society in terms of higher production and lower inequality.

7.7. CONCLUSION

We have proposed a simple model of transmission of information on jobs in a labour market. Workers who share a social relation may exchange information. We have shown that an increase in the number of links is generally associated with an increase in the average level of production and perhaps with a decrease in inequality.

In addition, we have studied the effects on output and inequality of the geometry of the network and its composition. We have shown that, for a given number of links, a network without social exclusion and with a more mixed population sharing social connections can produce a higher level of output and be less unequal if the difference in productivity between the most productive matches and the others is sufficiently low.

NOTES

* We are grateful to A. Calvó-Armengol, S. Capasso, M.R. Carillo, T. Kornienko and seminar participants in Padua, Lucca, Amsterdam (CEF 2004), Salerno (NEW 2004), Modena (AIEL 2004), Bologna (SIE 2004), Turin (Wild@Ace 2004) for helpful comments and suggestions. The usual disclaimer applies.

1. See Montgomery (1991) for further discussion and references. Other works on this field are Holzer (1987), Green et al. (1999) and Topa (2001). Pistaferri (1999) is a study on Italian data.
2. Another paper that studies the effects of social networks on inequality in an adverse selection framework is Finneran and Kelly (2003).

3. Krauth (2004) also shows that average employment is positively related to the fraction of weak ties for a given number of connections.

4. For models in which the formation of the network is endogenous, see Jackson and Wolinsky (1996), Bala and Goyal (2000) and Calvó-Armengol (2004).

5. Note that we are assuming that skills have a certain degree of transferability across jobs, since y^{ug} and y^{sb} are strictly positive. In other words, skills are partially general (see Becker (1964) for the distinction between general and specific skills).

6. For instance β may represent the bargaining power of workers when wages are set by Nash bargaining, as is usual in search models. Clearly, profits are $(1-\beta)y^{\lambda\theta}$.

7. That is, each agent can receive both an offer for a good and a bad job.

8. If none of the worker's acquaintances need the job information, then it is simply lost.

9. Hence, these agents are 'competitors' for the information on such a vacancy (see below).

10. Calvó-Armengol and Jackson (2003) provide various extensions on the process of transmission of job information.

11. These aspects are fully analysed in Calvó-Armengol and Jackson (2003). They show that increasing the wage of any of an agent's connections leads to an increase (in the sense of stochastic dominance) in the probability that the agent will be employed and the agent's expected wages.

12. Parameters in this simple example are the following: $a_b = 0.5$, $a_g = 0.5$, $d = 0$, $y^{ub} = 1$, $y^{ug} = y^{sb} = 2$, $y^{ug} = 4$; $\beta = 0.4$. The choice of $d = 0$ is just for simplification and it does not affect the qualitative result that we introduce here.

13. The fact that the expected wage of worker j increases while that of worker z decreases is an application of Lemma 2 in Calvó-Armengol and Jackson (2003). This states that an agent's probability of being employed, expected number of offers and wages all increase (in the sense of stochastic dominance) if the agent's probability of hearing job information through contacts network improves and *vice versa*.

14. All simulations were programmed in R (http://www.r-project.org/). The codes are available upon request from the authors.

15. Values for a_g and d are taken from Calvó-Armengol and Jackson (2004), who consider only one type of job. We have chosen the value of a_b on the assumption that it is more difficult to get a good than a bad job.

16. We are assuming that creating links has no costs. If resources were needed to create links, this in principle could affect welfare as the cost of forming links should be detracted from the benefits of increased output.

17. Even if skilled workers are favoured in G_C with respect to G_A, inequality is lower. With the chosen parameters, in G_C the reduction in inequality among skilled workers outweighs the increase in inequality among workers of different type; this is captured by the Gini index.

18. Individual average wages over the period have a predictable pattern: in G_A unskilled workers' average wage is 0.733, and skilled workers' wage is 1.47; in G_F these values are respectively 0.784 and 1.568. This, as noted, shows that identical workers may earn (on average) different wages according to their social links.

19. The relation may well be non-monotonic, as inequality in G_E and G_F is the same. We have also tried a very high level of production and wage for the match sg ($y^{sg} = 20$ and $y^{sg} = 100$), in order to increase wage differentials, without obtaining significant changes in the results. Increasing the number of links still increases output and reduces inequality; the correlation remains negative. With high $y^{sg} = 20$ and $d = 0.5$, we obtain a positive correlation with an empty network. With a complete network the correlation is still positive, but lower in absolute value. This confirms that increasing the number of links reduces the degree of linear correlation, but in the case of high y^{sg} and d, the correlation is not sufficiently reduced as to become negative.

20. Parameters are the same as in Section 7.5.1.
21. To be exact, in addition to a short average path length, small world networks are also characterized by a high *clustering coefficient* (see Watts, 1999), meaning that agents create dense highly interconnected subgroups (in other words, friends of an agent in turn know each other).
22. Note that networks G_I and G_J may also represent a particular way to represent the 'inbreeding bias' issue (that is, the tendency of individuals to be linked with others like themselves). In this perspective, we can also analyse to some extent the way in which inbreeding bias affects the correlation between output and inequality.
23. A network similar to G_M in which the pairs of unskilled agents are connected produces a similar result.
24. In simulations with $y^{sg} = 100$, we find that in G_M output and inequality are higher. The result on inequality appears to be dependent on the chosen inequality index, as the distribution improves in the lower percentile and worsens in the highest, but the latter effect dominates. Examination of the dependence of our results on the chosen inequality index is left for future research.
25. A recent paper which studies in detail interplaying mechanisms among human capital accumulation, socio-economic stratification, intergenerational mobility and job contact networks is Anderberg and Andersson (2003).
26. Our examples are sufficient to highlight this result. A more detailed analysis of the relationship between productivities in various matches and the dynamics of output and inequality is left for further research.

REFERENCES

Albert, R. and A.-L. Barabasi (2002), 'Statistical mechanics of complex networks', *Review of Modern Physics*, **74**.

Anderberg, D. and F. Andersson (2003), 'Stratification, social networks in the labour market, and intergenerational mobility', mimeo.

Arrow, K.J. and R. Borzekowski (2003), 'Limited network connections and the distribution of wages', mimeo.

Bala, V. and S. Goyal (2000), 'A noncooperative model of network formation', *Econometrica*, **68**, 1181–230.

Becker, G. (1964), *Human Capital: a Theoretical and Empirical Analysis with Special Reference to Education*, Chicago: The University of Chicago Press.

Benabou, R. (1996a), 'Heterogeneity, stratification, and growth: macroeconomic implications of community structure and school finance', *American Economic Review*, **86**, 584–609.

Benabou, R. (1996b), 'Equity and efficiency in human capital investment: the local connection', *Review of Economic Studies*, **63**, 237–64.

Calvó-Armengol, A. (2004), 'Job contact networks', *Journal of Economic Theory*, **115**, 191–206.

Calvó-Armengol, A. and M. Jackson (2003), 'Networks in labor markets: wage and employment dynamics and inequality', mimeo.

Calvó-Armengol, A. and M. Jackson (2004), 'The effects of social networks on employment and inequality', *American Economic Review*, **94**, 426–55.

Durlauf, S.N. (1996), 'A theory of persistent inequality', *Journal of Economic Growth*, 1, 75–93.

Finneran, L. and M. Kelly (2003), 'Social network and inequality', *Journal of Urban Economics*, **53**, 282–99.

Granovetter, M.S. (1974), *Getting a Job: A Study of Contacts and Careers*, Cambridge, Mass.: Harvard University Press.

Green, G.P., L.M. Tigges and D. Diaz (1999), 'Racial and ethnic differences in job-search strategies in Atlanta, Boston and Los Angeles', *Social Science Quarterly*, **80**, 263–78.

Jackson, M.O. and A. Wolinsky (1996) 'A strategic model of social and economic networks', *Journal of Economic Theory*, **71**, 44–74.

Krauth, B.V. (2004), 'A dynamic model of job networking and social influences on employment', *Journal of Economic Dynamics and Control*, **28**, 1185–204.

Holzer, H.J. (1987), 'Informal job search and black youth unemployment', *American Economic Review*, **77**, 446–52.

Montgomery, J.D. (1991), 'Social networks and labor market outcomes: toward an economic analysis', *American Economic Review*, **81**, 1408–18.

Montgomery, J.D. (1994), 'Weak ties, employment, and inequality: an equilibrium analysis', *American Journal of Sociology*, **99**, 1212–36.

Pistaferri, L. (1999), 'Informal networks in the Italian labor market', *Giornale Italiano degli Economisti e Annali di Economia*, **58**, 355–75.

Topa, G. (2001), 'Social interaction, local spillovers, and unemployment', *Review of Economic Studies*, **68**, 261–95.

Watts, D.J. (1999), *Small Worlds: The Dynamics of Networks between Order and Randomness*, Princeton, New Jersey: Princeton University Press.

8. Crime, inequality and economic growth

Salvatore Capasso

8.1. INTRODUCTION

The idea that the level of criminal activity in a society is strictly related to the degree of economic development, and to the distribution of wealth among individuals and classes of individuals, is certainly not new, neither it is really counterintuitive. Despite this consideration, only very recently have economists started to study in complex macroeconomic models the channels of interaction between crime, the incentives to commit crime and economic development and growth. Indeed, in comparison to the wealth of microeconomic literature studying the optimal choice of agents in the presence of incentives to commit criminal offences and rent-seeking behaviour (Glaeser, Sacerdote and Sheinkman, 1996; Fender, 1999; Burdet, Lagos and Randal, 2001; Huang, Laing and Wang, 1999; Lochner, 1999; Gould, Mustard and Weinberg, 2002 among others), the macroeconomic literature on the issue is very thin (Mehhulm, Moene and Torvik, 2001, 2003; Lloyd-Ellis and Marceau, 2003; Josten, 2003). However, only within a general equilibrium macroeconomic framework is it possible to fully grasp the extent to which the crime rate can affect the growth performance of an economic system.

One can guess various possible links between the diffusion of criminal activities and economic growth. On the one hand, for example, a low level of economic development entails a higher degree of poverty and, to the extent that poverty is often a major cause of crime, a high level of criminal activity. Moreover, as empirical evidence shows, economic stagnation can further increase the crime rate if it increases inequality in income distribution. On the other hand, crime can negatively affect economic growth by affecting return on investments and business profitability. The idea is that a high diffusion of criminal offences, such as extortion, affects the riskiness of investments and the return on legal activities.

Obviously, a key factor in driving investment decisions is the possibility of securing the return on the investment itself. If property rights are insecure, or investors run a high risk of being defrauded of their legitimate profits, the decision to invest is hindered. In this perspective, as Lloyd-Ellis and Marceau (2003) argue, this insecurity can be very detrimental to growth. For these authors, among the many factors influencing the level of insecurity in the economy, the level of crime plays a crucial role. An increase in the crime rate translates into an increase in the level of insecurity and a decrease in the rate of capital accumulation and growth. Moreover, income distribution can affect the level of crime. The idea is that if individuals need to borrow, and there is uncertainty concerning the repayment (for example because the borrower might be robbed of his income before repaying the loan), the rate of interest charged by lenders – the lower the probability of repayment, the higher the rate of interest – can decrease when borrowers can pay for protection against theft. As a consequence, poorer individuals who cannot afford to pay for protection might be charged a higher rate of interest on their loan and forced out of the market. These individuals will ultimately turn into criminals themselves.

Following very similar arguments, Josten (2003) shows that crime can hamper growth since it can discourage investments and capital accumulation. Once again, the reason is that the level of criminal activity can affect the security of property rights and therefore it can discourage investments. In Josten, inequality in income distribution is the key factor which creates the incentive to crime and illegal activities.

This chapter offers an alternative interpretation of the causal relationship between the degree of criminal activity, income distribution and economic growth. The key proposition is that the level of criminal activity in the economy can not only influence the return on private investment, as already argued, but also the efficiency and the return on public investments. In fact, a high level of criminality forces the government to allocate a higher proportion of public resources towards investments in security and measures to ensure public order, like the financing of police, the system of justice and prisons. This misallocation of resources, which are diverted from investments in more productive activities like investments in education and research, undoubtedly has a detrimental impact on growth. In addition, this chapter investigates the effects of crime on the level of economic activity through its effects on the magnitude of the labour supply. Indeed, many people who undertake criminal activities end up in prison and are unable to supply labour in the market. The reduction in labour supply has an impact on labour productivity and, ultimately, on the level of production in the economy. This effect is far from negligible given that the number of people ending up in jail is relatively high in many countries and that such people are mainly males of working age.

The story goes specifically as follows. In a two-period overlapping generation economy, heterogeneous agents are born with different endowments of skills and labour productivity. In this framework, agents who are endowed with a low level of education also have a lower expected level of wage income, and since the wage forgone is the main alternative cost for being imprisoned after committing a crime, these agents also have a greater incentive to commit criminal offences. This would explain why for low levels of capital accumulation, when the wage rate is low, and income inequality might be particularly severe, the economy might experience high crime rates. The role of government, in this framework, is not only to directly redistribute resources through taxation, but also to supply the necessary infrastructure and services, like public education and schooling, in order to increase individuals' labour productivity and wage income. Such a role is hindered in the presence of a large number of individuals who do not participate in the legal process of output and income production – for example because they are in jail. Indeed, in such circumstances, not only are government revenues particularly low due to a lower actual amount of taxable resources, but also because a large portion of such resources are diverted from productive investments, such as in education, to unproductive investments, such as in defence and safety measures. This would explain the negative impact of crime on the process of capital accumulation and growth.

It is worth stressing that our point is not arguing that only poor people are inclined to crime. Unarguably, the motives for crime can be different and complex; some have a 'monetary' content, others do not. It is extremely difficult and, to a large extent, misleading to try to take into account all these in a single framework. In this perspective, the chapter focuses on a particular motive for crime which is income level and poverty, and the consequences of this on economic growth.

When the level of capital accumulated in the economy is particularly low, the incentives for crime are stronger, and with an unequal distribution of income, they are stronger for poorer people. The high level of criminal activity forces the government to invest more in security and less in more productive investment, such as education. This, in turn, lowers labour productivity and income, and hence increases the incentive to commit crime. As capital accumulates this vicious circle might break and the economy might be set on a dynamic path characterized by a decreasing crime rate and increasing wealth. All the same, this might not happen under well-specified parameter restrictions with the economy being trapped in a state of high crime and low growth.

The chapter is structured as follows. Section 8.2 describes the economy. The role of each type of agent, the productive system and the role of government are all described in this section. Section 8.3 studies the optimal behaviour of agents and the rationale behind the choice to commit crime. Section 8.4 describes the equilibrium in the economy while Section 8.5 studies the capital accumulation path. The last section, Section 8.6, contains some concluding remarks.

8.2. THE ECONOMY

The economy is inhabited by an infinite sequence of two-period lived overlapping generations of agents divided at birth into firms and workers. The population of each generation is constant and normalized to 2, half of which are firms and half households (or workers). Workers can be born either with an initial low endowment of labour productivity: *l-type* workers (fraction μ of workers population), or with a high endowment of labour productivity: *h-type* workers (fraction $1-\mu$ of workers population). By borrowing a commonly used terminology in this literature, we will refer to the first group of workers as *predators*, and to the latter as *prey*. These terms signal what the optimal behaviour of each group of agents might be in equilibrium.

As a matter of fact, in this economy, low-labour productivity agents – that is agents with a relatively lower income endowment – might have the incentive to undertake a predatory activity against the other group of agents. We assume that all agents are risk neutral and strictly prefer to consume only in the second period of their life, when old. This last assumption allows us to bypass problems of consumption-saving choices without losing in generality. A single good which can be either used for consumption, or employed as capital in the production process, is manufactured by competitive firms. Time is discrete and indexed by 1, 2, ... We now turn to a more detailed description of agents' endowments in order to determine their optimal behaviour in this environment.

8.2.1. Households

All households are endowed with one unit of labour in each period of their life which they supply inelastically to old firms in exchange for the competitive wage rate. In spite of equal labour endowment, labour productivity is not the same for all workers. As a direct consequence of birth differences, one group of agents is more skilful than another and, ultimately, we assume that workers will either display a high degree of labour productivity or a low degree of labour productivity. We denote with a_l the efficiency in production of low-labour productivity agents – the predators – and with a_h the efficiency in production of high-labour productivity agents –

the prey – with $a_l < a_h$. Under the assumption of perfectly competitive markets, in which each production factor is paid its productivity, and in the absence of bequests, these differences reflect differences in income for the two types of households: the low-labour productivity agents are able to obtain from their labour services a lower income than high-labour productivity agents. Thus, in this framework, the assumption of heterogeneity among agents in the innate amount of skill level is essentially required to explain the existence of agents with differences in the initial income endowments. Birth differences in productivity and incomes can be justified in different ways. One can think of these differences in labour productivity as generated by the advantage, in the learning process, which the newborn in rich or more educated families might have with respect to the newborn in poorer families. The idea is that children who grow up in a better family environment have more stimuli and more resources available for the learning process. It is worth stressing that this assumption of only two income classes of individuals only aims to simplify how the model actually works. Adding a thicker distribution of income across agents would not alter the main results or the implications of the model.

Besides working, each young household inhabiting the economy has the possibility of committing criminal actions. The idea is that each young agent is endowed with a given amount, $\bar{\theta} > 0$, of non tradable extra time, or energy, which can be either employed as leisure time or diverted towards predatory and illegal activities.[1] In order to simplify the matter, we focus on the simplest predatory activity: theft. At a given point in time, each young household can approach another agent in the economy with the criminal intent of stealing some of her resources. The amount of resources, $\sigma(\theta)$, each agent can steal is a direct function of the amount of extra-time, $0 < \theta < \bar{\theta}$, employed in the criminal action, that is $\sigma'(\theta) > 0$. If apprehended, the young agent is put in jail where he will spend the second period of his life. The disutility of going to jail is exogenously given and denoted by $J < 0$. Under the assumption that the penalty for committing a crime is the same whatever the amount stolen, each young agent who decides to commit a criminal offence will steal as much as possible for a given amount of extra-time endowment, that is $\sigma(\theta) = \sigma(\bar{\theta}) = \bar{\sigma}$. In other words, once the agent has decided to steal, he will employ all his extra time in the criminal activity and steal as much as possible.

When old, agents who have not committed any criminal offence in their youth, and those who have done so but have not been apprehended by the police, supply their labour endowment in the market for the current wage. Soon after this, they consume whatever they have saved in the first period and earned in the second, and die.

8.2.2.   Firms

In the first period of their life firms are inactive and produce output only in the second period by employing physical capital, k_t, in conjunction with either low productivity labour, x_{lt}, or high productivity labour, x_{ht}, or a combination of both. Output production involves a Romer type technology of the following kind:

$$y_{t+1} = A(e_{t+1})(a_l x_{lt+1}^{\alpha} + a_h x_{ht+1}^{\alpha})k_{t+1}^{1-\alpha}K_{t+1}^{\alpha}, \quad 0 < \alpha < 1 \tag{8.1}$$

where K_t denotes the aggregate level of capital at time t. The technology specification implies not only a positive externality in the accumulable factor – physical capital – but also a positive externality of government expenditure in the non-accumulable factor – labour services. Indeed, the technology factor, $A(e_t)$, is endogenously determined and is a positive function of the expenditure in education/output ratio, $E_t/Y_t = e_t$. As in Barro (1990), government expenditure can positively influence the process of capital accumulation and economic growth. However, we do not consider total government expenditure, and only focus on the positive effect of expenditure in education on the marginal productivity of accumulable and non-accumulable factors such as labour services in production.[2] In the specification of (8.1), government expenditure in education has a positive, $A'(e_t) > 0$, but decreasing, $A''(e_t) < 0$, impact on the marginal productivity of labour and capital. Moreover, we set $A(0) = B > 0$. The idea is that public investment in education can increase the aggregate skill level in the economy and the efficiency in production of labour services. One can think, for example, of the beneficial effects on the average level of human capital in the economy streaming from a better and more accessible education system. The underlying idea is that more public funding channelled into education can both improve the efficiency of the system and increase the volume of services that this can provide. In turn, the increase in the aggregate skill level in the economy entails higher labour productivity with a beneficial impact on output. In particular, as for the formulation in (8.1), the efficiency in labour production is determined by the combination of innate abilities, a_l and a_h, and the improvement in the skill level by means of public supplied services in education, $A(e_t)$. Moreover, it is reasonable to think that the effects of public expenditure in the economy depend on the size of the latter. Specifically, we assume that congestion effects lead to a lower efficiency of public services in education as the size of the economy – measured by the aggregate output, Y_t – increases.

In equilibrium each firm will employ in production the same amount of capital. Therefore, recalling that the total number of firms is 1, per firm capital stock will be equal to the aggregate level of capital, $k_t = K_t$. This result, together with the assumption of perfectly competitive markets, in which each factor of production is paid its marginal productivity, allows us to write the wage rates for low productivity workers, w_{lt}, and for high productivity workers, w_{ht}, as follows

$$w_{lt} = \alpha A(e_t) a_l x_{lt}^{\alpha-1} k_t ,$$ (8.2)

$$w_{ht} = \alpha A(e_t) a_h x_{ht}^{\alpha-1} k_t .$$ (8.3)

Under the same assumptions the rate of interest is

$$r_t = (1-\alpha) A(e_t)(a_l x_{lt}^{\alpha} + a_h x_{ht}^{\alpha}).$$ (8.4)

Given factor prices in (8.2), (8.3) and (8.4), each firm's labour and capital demand will be determined by profit maximization:

$$\Pi_t = y_t - w_{lt} x_{lt} - w_{ht} x_{ht} - r_t k_t .$$

8.2.3. Government

Government finances a balanced budget through taxation. We assume that only income from labour services is taxed and that the government imposes different tax rates on *l-type* workers and on *h-type* workers. A progressive tax system requires *h-type* workers to pay a higher proportion, τ^h, of their labour income than *l-type*, τ^l, that is $\tau^h > \tau^l$. In order to simplify the matter, we also set $\tau^l = 0$ and assume that each agent receives the wage income already net of taxation. In other words, as often happens in reality, employers pay taxes on behalf of employees and transfer the wage income to workers already net of taxation.

Assuming a balanced budget deficit and recalling that at each point in time only *h-type* agents (old and young) pay taxes in the economy ($\tau^l = 0$), the volume of government expenditure, G_t, that can be financed will consist of

$$G_t = \tau^h w_{ht} 2(1-\mu),$$ (8.5)

where $2(1-\mu)$ is the total number of *h-type* agents (young and old both in the number of $1-\mu$), at time t, in the economy.

Government can allocate public expenditure towards two competitive alternatives: investment in education, E_t, and investment in security services and public order maintenance, S_t. Therefore, government budget deficit reads very simply $G_t = E_t + S_t$. The possible presence in the economy of individuals who can break the law by committing criminal actions requires the government to finance police forces to prevent crimes, and to capture the culprits, as well as to build and sustain a prison system. It is plausible to think that investments in security and public order are an increasing function of the number of individuals that commit criminal offences and, in general, of the level of criminal activity in the economy, for now generically denoted with ζ. We can therefore write $S_t = S(\zeta)$, where $S'(\zeta) > 0$.

8.3. SOMETIMES CRIME PAYS: INCENTIVES TO COMMIT CRIME

Young agents, as already stressed, have the chance to commit criminal offences (here generically represented by theft). Soon after supplying their labour in the market, young households can approach another agent and steal part of her wage. Given the extra amount of energy they are endowed with, θ, and the fixed punishment for committing crime, if agents find it optimal to break the law and commit theft, they will steal as much as possible, $\bar{\sigma}$, from their victim. An agent, born at time t, who has committed a criminal offence in his youth, will remain free to supply labour in the market only if not apprehended by the police, which happens with probability π.[3] If the thief is captured by the police, he is put in jail and derives a disutility of J. We have now enough elements to determine the payoffs attached to each possible action of the two types of agents in the economy, and the consequent optimal behaviour. Let us first consider the low-skilled workers. Given the above, the expected lifetime utility of a young *l-type* agent breaking the law and committing theft can be written in the following way

$$\tilde{U}_l = w_{lt}(1 + r_{t+1})(1 - \tau^l) + \bar{\sigma} + w_{lt+1}(1 - \tau^l)(1 - \pi) + \pi J , \qquad (8.6)$$

As already stressed, agents can capitalize on their savings by lending these resources to firms. The return on savings is the next period interest rate, r_{t+1}, which is the return on capital. Given that agents are risk neutral, and have a discount rate equal to 1, they strictly prefer to consume all income in old age. In order to avoid complications of non-use, we assume that the resources, $\bar{\sigma}$, agents have stolen in their youth cannot be capitalized through official channels. In other words, the loot from theft does not earn any interest. This assumption can be justified in various ways, the most immediate of which is the following. It is reasonable to argue that the government can very easily observe agents' savings, and therefore it can immediately detect whether an agent has committed a crime when extra resources of questionable origin are discovered. As a direct consequence of this assumption, agents might find it optimal either to consume immediately such resources or simply, if they can, they will hide and store these resources without earning any interest. Actually, if one thinks of what happens in reality, the easiest way for the police to trace stolen funds is through the study of movements in bank accounts and savings. Better for thieves to keep stolen money under the bed.

If, alternatively, a young *l-type* agent decides not to commit a criminal offence, the expected lifetime utility is simply the sum of his capitalized wage income in youth and his second period net wage income,

$$\hat{U}_l = w_{lt}(1-\tau^l)(1+r_{t+1}) + w_{lt+1}(1-\tau^l). \tag{8.7}$$

Clearly, an agent who does not commit any crime will have the opportunity to supply his labour services in old age with probability 1 since he does not run the risk of ending up in jail.

It is now possible to determine the optimal behaviour of an *l-type* agent. A simple comparison between the expected lifetime utility under the two options reveals that a sufficient condition for predators not to steal is

$$\hat{U}_l > \tilde{U}_l \iff w_{lt+1} > \frac{\bar{\sigma} + \pi J}{(1-\tau^l)\pi}. \tag{8.8}$$

The latter shows that the key variable in the choice between criminal and legal behaviour is the expected wage rate. For a given level of disutility of going to prison, a given tax rate, a given probability of being apprehended and a given utility derived from stolen goods, the higher the wage income in old age, the higher is the cost of theft. The forgone second period wage rate is the alternative cost agents sustain for committing a crime. If the second period wage rate, as determined by (8.2), is low enough, they will have the incentive to commit the criminal offence. A predator will decide whether or not to steal according to the following:

$$\hat{U}_l \gtrless \tilde{U}_l \iff \alpha A(e_{t+1})a_l x_{lt+1}^{\alpha-1} k_{t+1} \begin{matrix} > \\ < \end{matrix} \frac{\bar{\sigma} + \pi J}{\pi} \equiv \Theta, \tag{8.9}$$

where we assume $\bar{\sigma} + \pi J > 0$. It is important to stress that since agents are homogeneous within the same type, for a given wage rate, when one action rather than the other is optimal for an individual, then the same action is optimal for all other individuals of the same type. So, if it is optimal for a single predator to commit a crime, then crime is the optimal choice for all predators. A similar argument, in the opposite direction, applies when the condition holds with a reversed sign of inequality. However, it is worth adding that since the wage rate is not exogenous, but depends on agents' choices, what is optimal at individual level might not be consistent with the macroeconomic equilibrium. We will discuss this in detail in the next section. At this stage, as a corollary to the previous conclusions, we can argue that if the crime condition holds with strict equality, then predators must be indifferent between the two options, committing a crime or remaining in legality. This implies that in the economy there must be a fraction of predators choosing to remain legal and a fraction committing theft. We will denote with $\gamma_t \in [0,1]$ the fraction of young predators who decide to steal at time t.

It has been argued that if an individual decides to steal, he will steal the maximum amount of resources, that is $\bar{\sigma}$. Since at each point in time each predator can approach only one victim, it will be sufficient to assume that $w_{ht} > \bar{\sigma} > w_{lt}$ $\forall t$ to conclude that no *l-type* agent will ever steal from another predator.[4] In other words, poor do not steal from poor. For the similar but opposite argument, *h-type* agents run the risk of being robbed.

We now turn to the description of *h-type* agents' opportunities. Potential victims of predators are only *h-type* agents whose expected lifetime utility under the assumption they abide by the law is

$$U_h = w_{ht}(1-\tau^h)(1+r_{t+1}) + (1-p_t)w_{ht+1}(1-\tau^h) + p_t[w_{ht+1}(1-\tau^h) - \bar{\sigma}], \quad (8.10)$$

where p_t is the probability of being robbed. We implicitly assume that predators can steal only from old prey and do not rob young prey. This can be reasonably justified, for example, by arguing that young prey have the energy and the resources to defend themselves, which is not the case for old prey. While this assumption simplifies the matter, it does not substantially alter the results.

The probability of each prey being robbed depends both on the number of predators that decide at each point in time to opt for crime and, of course, on the total number of prey that can be robbed in the economy. Clearly, this probability is increasing in the number of predators committing crime and decreasing in the number of old prey. More specifically we can write $p_t = (\mu \gamma_t)/(1-\mu)$ where $p_t \in [0, \mu/(1-\mu)]$. For obvious reasons of feasibility, we will assume that $1-\mu > \mu$, that is the number of prey in the economy is large enough to allow for an equilibrium in which all predators might decide to steal.

Similar to what happens to *l-type* agents, *h-type* agents have the opportunity to commit crime. If they do so, they derive an expected lifetime utility of

$$\hat{U}_h = w_{ht}(1-\tau^h)(1+r_{t+1})+\bar{\sigma}+$$
$$+\left\{(1-p_t)w_{ht+1}(1-\tau^h)+p_t[w_{ht+1}(1-\tau^h)-\bar{\sigma}]\right\}(1-\pi)+\pi J. \tag{8.11}$$

Hence, following the same arguments developed above, a sufficiently high wage rate for the *h-type* agents ensures that they will always abide by the law and do not commit crimes. For the sake of exposition and clarity of the results, we will henceforth assume that the expected utility in (8.10) dominates the expected utility in (8.11), that is we will assume $w_{ht+1} > [(1+\pi p_t)\bar{\sigma}+\pi J]/[(1-\tau^h)\pi]$, $\forall$ w_{ht+1}. Under this restriction no *h-type* agent will ever commit any crime. Of course, we do not intend to argue that in reality no rich individual ever commits a crime, and this assumption should not be interpreted in a strict sense. There are many motivations behind crime and some rich people might be more inclined to crime than poorer ones. However, here we are focusing on a particular motive for crime, which is the loss in future earnings, and it is reasonable to think that under this specific perspective, individuals with higher expected income sustain a higher cost when committing a crime. If this is the case, one can simplify to a great extent the understanding of the results by imposing a condition for which only one group of agents – the poorer – might find it optimal to commit crimes.

8.4. THE EQUILIBRIUM

As one can intuitively understand, labour supply in the economy, at each point in time, is an endogenous variable and depends on the level of criminal activity. Indeed, as already discussed, predators who have committed a criminal offence when young might be apprehended by the police when old, and put in jail. If this is the case, they are unable to supply labour in the market. As a result, the higher the level of criminal activity in the economy, the lower is *l-type* agents' labour supply. In general, total labour supply at time t will be $2-\pi\mu\gamma_{t-1}$, which is given by the labour supply of young and old agents (prey and predators) minus the labour supply of predators who have been jailed. Importantly, the action chosen by predators at time t will only influence labour supply in the next period, at time $t + 1$. Since labour services have distinct deployment in production technology, we will distinguish between high productivity and low productivity labour supply. At time t, total labour supply from old and young predators will be

$$x_{lt} = 2\mu - \pi\gamma_{t-1}\mu,$$

which, clearly, depends negatively on the fraction of old predators who have committed a criminal offence when young. On the other hand, under the restriction that no prey ever finds stealing optimal, *h-type* workers' labour supply at any point in time will be constant and equal to

$$x_{ht} = 2(1-\mu).$$

Given the above labour supply, the wage rates of predators and prey can be respectively written as

$$w_{lt} = \alpha A(e_t)a_l(2 - \pi\gamma_{t-1})^{\alpha-1}\mu^{\alpha-1}k_t, \tag{8.12}$$

$$w_{ht} = \alpha A(e_t)a_h[2(1-\mu)]^{\alpha-1}k_t, \tag{8.13}$$

Government, as already outlined, collects taxes, and, with these resources, finances expenditures in education, E_t, and maintaining public safety and order, $S_t = S(\zeta)$, which is thought to be a generic function of the level of criminal activity in the economy, ζ. In our economy, in which all crime takes the form of simple theft, and in which only predators commit criminal actions, it seems plausible to assume that expenditure on security is a linear function of the number of predators who decide optimally to commit a criminal offence. More specifically, we will assume

$$S_t = \beta\gamma_{t-1}G_t.$$

Hence

$$E_t = (1 - \beta\gamma_{t-1})\, G_t.$$

Substituting for the wage rate as determined by (8.12) and (8.13), and recalling that a balanced budget deficit implies $G_t = \tau^h w_{ht}2(1-\mu)$, we can write the ratio of education expenditure to total output as

$$e_t(\gamma_{t-1}) = \frac{E_t}{Y_t} = (1 - \beta\gamma_{t-1})\frac{\alpha\tau^h a_h[2(1-\mu)]^\alpha}{a_l(2 - \pi\gamma_{t-1})^\alpha \mu^\alpha + a_h[2(1-\mu)]^\alpha}. \tag{8.14}$$

Therefore, as extensively argued, government expenditure in education is a function of the number of predators who find it optimal to commit crime. Indeed, γ_t not only directly influences government expenditure on education by forcing the government to increase the share of public expenditure on security, but also indirectly, since it affects the aggregate labour supply of *l-type* agents and hence aggregate output, Y_t. It is easy to show that under the specified assumptions of the model, and the restriction on the parameters, the share of government expenditure in education is a decreasing function of γ_{t-1}, that is $e'(\gamma_{t-1}) < 0 \ \forall \gamma_{t-1} \in [0,1]$. Appendix 8.1 provides a formal proof of this result. We now have all the ingredients to study the equilibrium conditions.

Essentially, the economic system can display three possible equilibria: the first is the equilibrium in which all predators find it optimal to opt for crime; the second is the equilibrium in which no predator will choose to commit a criminal action; the third is the equilibrium in which only a fraction of predators decides to commit crimes. We will refer to the first equilibrium as the *crime equilibrium*, to the second as the *no crime equilibrium* and to the third as the *mixed equilibrium*. Let us analyse each of these in detail.

1. *Crime equilibrium*

If all predators in the economy opt for crime, then we must have $\gamma_{t-1} = \gamma_t = 1$. However, this option is consistent with the macroeconomic equilibrium if, for this value of $\gamma = 1$, the condition in (8.9) is such that each predator finds it optimal to opt for crime, that is:

$$\alpha A(\underline{e}) a_l (2-\pi)^{\alpha-1} \mu^{\alpha-1} k_{t+1} < \Theta \tag{8.15}$$

where $e_t = \underline{e} = (1-\beta) \dfrac{\alpha \tau^h a_h [2(1-\mu)]^\alpha}{a_l (2-\pi)^\alpha \mu^\alpha + a_h [2(1-\mu)]^\alpha}$.

2. *No crime equilibrium*

By contrast, if all predators in the economy choose not to commit any crime, we must have $\gamma_{t-1} = \gamma_t = 0$. Again, this choice is consistent with the equilibrium if, for this value of $\gamma = 0$, the condition in (8.9) is such that no predator finds it optimal to steal:

$$\alpha A(\overline{e}) a_l (2\mu)^{\alpha-1} k_{t+1} > \Theta \tag{8.16}$$

where $e_t = \overline{e} = \left\{ \alpha \tau^h a_h [2(1-\mu)]^\alpha \right\} \big/ \left\{ a_l (2\mu)^\alpha + a_h [2(1-\mu)]^\alpha \right\}$.

It is clear that from $e'(\gamma_{t-1}) < 0$, it follows that $\underline{e} < \overline{e}$ and hence $A(\underline{e}) < A(\overline{e})$.

3. *Mixed equilibrium*

In the mixed equilibrium case, only a fraction of predators will optimally choose to steal, while the other fraction will not commit any crime. More formally, we will have $\gamma_{t-1}, \gamma_t \in]0,1[$. If this is the case, the crime condition in (8.9) must hold with equality:

$$\alpha A(e_{t+1})a_l(2 - \pi\gamma_t)^{\alpha-1*}\mu^{\alpha-1}k_{t+1} = \Theta, \qquad (8.17)$$

where e_{t+1} is given by (8.14). That is, for the optimal choice at individual level to be consistent with the macroeconomic equilibrium, each predator must be indifferent between the two options, and the equilibrium fraction of predators choosing to steal must be such that equation (8.17) is satisfied.

A rapid analysis of the condition determining agents' optimal choices, equation (8.9), shows that, other things being equal, the variable that determines the nature of the regime – equilibrium with crime, no crime equilibrium and mixed equilibrium – is the stock of accumulated capital. Indeed, capital accumulation can influence the wage rate and, consequently, the incentive that predators have to undertake unlawful activities. However, it is also true that agents' choice can influence the rate of capital accumulation. In fact, as already seen, the level of crime in the economy can influence the allocation and size of government expenditures and hence the return to the accumulable factor and economic growth. We now turn to the study of the dynamics of the economic system.

8.5. CAPITAL ACCUMULATION

Capital accumulation is ultimately a function of the degree of criminal activity in the economy. Indeed, predator choice and the nature of the realized equilibrium will influence, through different channels, the amount of resources channelled to investments.

Since in this economy investments depend exclusively on the amount of savings, and therefore on young agents' net income wage, capital accumulation, at any point in time, will simply be governed by the following dynamics

$$k_{t+1} = w_{lt}\mu + (1 - \tau^h)w_{ht}(1 - \mu)$$

$$= \alpha A(e_t)[a_l(2 - \pi\gamma_{t-1})^{\alpha-1}\mu^\alpha + a_h(1 - \tau^h)2^{\alpha-1}(1 - \mu)^\alpha]k_t, \qquad (8.18)$$

in which we have substituted for the wage rates the expressions in (8.12) and (8.13), while e_t is given by (8.14). In order to ensure stability in the system we will require the variables and the parameters to satisfy the following restriction

$$\alpha A(e_t)[a_l(2-\pi\gamma_{t-1})^{\alpha-1}\mu^\alpha +$$
$$+a_h(1-\tau^h)2^{\alpha-1}(1-\mu)^\alpha] \geq 1 \quad \forall \gamma_t \in [0,1] \qquad (8.19)$$

It is clear that capital accumulation, as determined by (8.18), is influenced by the fraction of predators in the economy and, ultimately, by predators' optimal choice. In an environment in which each and every predator finds it optimal to steal, the rate of growth will be given by the following expression

$$g^c \equiv k_{t+1}/k_t = \alpha A(\underline{e})[a_l(2-\pi)^{\alpha-1}\mu^\alpha + a_h(1-\tau^h)2^{\alpha-1}(1-\mu)^\alpha]. \qquad (8.20)$$

In this case, which involves the maximum degree of criminal activity, government channels the minimum amount of resources towards education, $e_t = \underline{e}$, the wage rate is very low and the condition governing *l-type* agents' behaviour holds with strict inequality, as in (8.15). This regime, as one can immediately verify by analysing the crime condition (8.15), is likely to occur at low levels of capital accumulation.

With similar arguments, but in the opposite direction, it may be argued that for very high levels of capital accumulation, the condition governing agents' choice is likely to hold with reversed sign, as in (8.16). In this case the wage rate is particularly high and no predator has any incentive to commit a criminal action, $\gamma_t = 0$. The growth rate of the economy with no criminal activity will be given by:

$$g^n \equiv k_{t+1}/k_t = \alpha A(\overline{e})[a_l 2^{\alpha-1}\mu^\alpha + a_h(1-\tau^h)2^{\alpha-1}(1-\mu)^\alpha] \qquad (8.21)$$

It is easy to prove that the system in both these cases, summarized by (8.20) and (8.21), displays constant growth rates. Most importantly, one can easily prove that if the impact of government expenditure in education on the labour productivity is relatively large, the growth rate under no crime equilibrium is higher than the growth rate in crime equilibrium. A sufficient condition for this to happen is[5]

$$A(\overline{e}) > \left(\frac{2}{2-\pi}\right)^{1-\alpha} A(\underline{e}). \qquad (8.22)$$

In order to understand the nature of this result, it must be noted that crime displays two opposite effects on capital accumulation and growth. On the one hand, a decrease in crime can harm growth since it increases the low productivity labour supply (fewer people end up in prison) and thus reduces the wage rate, the amount of savings and hence the rate of growth. On the other hand, a decrease in the crime rate can boost capital accumulation and growth since it allows the government to reallocate more resources towards education. The rise in investments in education increases labour productivity (both of high skilled and low skilled workers) and hence the wage rate, savings and the rate of growth.

The dynamics of capital is much more difficult to determine in the mixed equilibrium framework, in which $\gamma_t \in]0,1[$. In this case, the capital accumulation path is represented by equation 8.18 and, hence, the rate of growth is simply

$$g^m \equiv \frac{k_{t+1}}{k_t} = \alpha A(e_t)\left[a_l(2-\pi\gamma_{t-1})^{\alpha-1}\mu^\alpha + a_h(1-\tau^h)2^{\alpha-1}(1-\mu)^\alpha\right] \quad (8.23)$$

Even though the dynamics of the system, in this case, is apparently similar to the dynamics governing the economy in the previous two cases, g^c and g^n, it is in reality more complex since it is jointly determined by two difference equations, (8.17) and (8.23). Indeed, while the level of capital in (8.23), at each point in time, depends on the values of γ; the level of γ, which keeps the system in equilibrium, and predators indifferent between choosing crime and no crime, depends, in turn, on the level of capital accumulated in the economy, as expressed in equation (8.17).

Leaving aside a full study of such dynamics, which despite its complexity might not add substantial insight to the story, the following considerations can be made. Under the restriction in (8.19), for every value of γ, capital is either always increasing – when this condition is holding with strict inequality – or it is stationary – if this condition is holding with equality for a value of $\gamma_t \in]0,1[$. What we can rule out by assumption is a decreasing capital stock.

Let us first consider the case of a continuously increasing capital stock. The economy will develop through the following stages. Initially, when the level of capital accumulation is particularly low, and so is the wage rate, the crime rate will be at its maximum, $\gamma = 1$, and the growth rate of the economy will be given by g^c, equation (8.20). The condition governing agents' behaviour will be given by (8.15). As capital grows, the economy will start displaying a lower crime rate with $\gamma_t \in]0,1[$. During this stage only a fraction of *l-type* agents choose to commit crimes: predators are indifferent between the two alternatives and equation (8.17) is in place. During this stage, γ_t is no longer constant and changes with k_t. In these circumstances the mixed equilibrium prevails and the rate of growth is given by g^m, equation (8.23). Since capital by assumption is increasing for whatever value of γ_t, sooner or later the condition governing agents' behaviour will hold with strict inequality. This is the final stage when no predator finds it optimal to commit crime, as expressed by equation (8.16). The new rate of growth will be g^n as in equation (8.21) and there will be no crime.

Let us now consider the other case which entails the economy ending up in a growth trap with zero growth and a positive and non-decreasing level of crime. As in the previous case, starting with a sufficiently low initial capital stock the prevailing regime is that with maximum crime. The rate of growth, at this initial stage, is g^c and the crime rate is at its maximum, $\gamma = 1$. As capital grows, the economy will migrate towards the mixed equilibrium in which the level of crime decreases and only a fraction of predators decides to commit criminal acts, $\gamma_t \in]0,1[$. At this stage the economy keeps growing (recall that by (8.19) capital is increasing) until the value of $\gamma_t = \gamma_{t+1} = \gamma \in]0,1[$ which satisfies the system of equations

$$\alpha A(e)[a_l(2-\pi\gamma)^{\alpha-1}\mu^{\alpha} + a_h(1-\tau^h)2^{\alpha-1}(1-\mu)^{\alpha}] = 1$$

$$\alpha A(e)a_l(2-\pi\gamma)^{\alpha-1}\mu^{\alpha-1}k = \Theta$$

is reached and $k_t = k_{t+1} = k$. Under this circumstance, the system enters a growth trap characterized by a high level of criminality and a stagnating economy.

8.6. CONCLUSIONS

It is commonly accepted that the level of criminal activity in the economy has a great impact on the level of production and economic activity. Yet one can think of different channels through which crime can affect real variables, investment decisions and growth. Some economists have recently focused on the negative impact crime can have on private investment profitability in order to explain the long-run role played by criminal activity in resource allocation.

Approaching from a different perspective, we explore another line of research and analyse the impact of crime on public investments. Our main argument is that in the presence of crime, government cannot allocate enough resources to productive activities, such as investments in education or research, and is, instead, forced to spend resources to ensure security and public order in the economy.

This chapter provides the 'classical' argument according to which crime mainly finds its roots in the unequal income distribution among agents. The analysis is based on the idea that if the highest alternative cost of crime is the probability of going to prison, and not being able to work, then people with lower expected incomes will have a higher incentive to commit crimes. Of course, this is only part of the story. Other factors, such as reputation issues, cultural factors or, simply, people's consciences may play a decisive role in shaping attitudes to crime. Indeed, the analysis of these elements may open up very interesting avenues for further research.

The working of the model is quite simple. In the presence of severe asymmetric income distribution, poorer agents might have a higher propensity towards predatory and criminal activities. This state of affairs is likely to occur at low levels of capital accumulation when the economy is relatively poor. In turn, when the level of criminal activity is high, a higher proportion of public investment is diverted towards low-return investments such as those ensuring public security and order rather than investments with higher returns such as investment in research and education. This misallocation of resources lowers the rate of capital accumulation and growth with a positive impact on the level of criminal activity. This mechanism accounts for a two-way causal relationship between growth and crime, and is able to explain the co-existence of high crime rates and low levels of economic development observed in many economies.

APPENDIX 8.1

Differentiating (8.14), we obtain

$$\frac{\partial e_t(\gamma_{t-1})}{\partial \gamma_{t-1}} = \frac{\alpha \tau^h R}{M + R} \left\{ (1 - \beta \gamma_{t-1}) \frac{\alpha a_l (2\mu - \pi \gamma_{t-1}\mu)^{\alpha-1} \pi\mu}{M + R} - 1 \right\}$$

where

$$M = a_l (2 - \pi \gamma_{t-1})^\alpha \mu^\alpha \quad \text{and} \quad R = a_h [2(1 - \mu)]^\alpha.$$

A simple analysis of the derivative shows that

$$\frac{\partial e_t(\gamma_{t-1})}{\partial \gamma_{t-1}} < 0$$

requires

$$(1 - \beta \gamma_{t-1}) \frac{\alpha a_l (2\mu - \pi \gamma_{t-1}\mu)^{\alpha-1} \pi\mu}{M + R} < \beta.$$

Rearranging the latter, we obtain

$$\left[\frac{(1 - \beta \gamma_{t-1})\alpha\pi}{2 - \pi \gamma_{t-1}} - \beta \right] a_l (2\mu - \pi \gamma_{t-1}\mu)^\alpha < a_h [2(1 - \mu)]^\alpha.$$

A sufficient condition for the latter to be satisfied is

$$\beta > \frac{\alpha\pi}{2-(1-\alpha)\pi\gamma_{t-1}}$$

which recalling that $\gamma_{t-1} \in [0,1]$ is always satisfied if

$$\beta > \frac{\alpha\pi}{2-(1-\alpha)\pi}.$$

In other words, a sufficiently large β ensures

$$\frac{\partial e_t(\gamma_{t-1})}{\partial \gamma_{t-1}} < 0.$$

Note that for $\beta = 1$ this is always satisfied given that $(1-\alpha)\gamma_{t-1}\pi < 1$ and $\alpha\pi < 1$.

APPENDIX 8.2

$g^n > g^c$ requires

$$A(\bar{e})[a_l 2^{\alpha-1}\mu^\alpha + a_h(1-\tau^h)2^{\alpha-1}(1-\mu)^\alpha] >$$

$$A(\underline{e})[a_l(2-\pi)^{\alpha-1}\mu^\alpha + a_h(1-\tau^h)2^{\alpha-1}(1-\mu)^\alpha].$$

Rearranging the latter we obtain

$$[A(\bar{e})-A(\underline{e})]a_h(1-\tau^h)2^{\alpha-1}(1-\mu)^\alpha + a_l\mu^\alpha[A(\bar{e})2^{\alpha-1}-A(\underline{e})(2-\pi)^{\alpha-1}]>0.$$

A sufficient condition for the latter to be satisfied is

$$A(\bar{e})2^{\alpha-1}-A(\underline{e})(2-\pi)^{\alpha-1}>0.$$

NOTES

1. One can think of this time as night-time. Young agents, unlike old ones, can employ this time in a criminal activity instead, for example, of resting in bed. However, it is worth stressing that they cannot employ this time working.

2. Actually, $A(\cdot)$ could represent any kind of externality of public spending in production, capturing, for example, the impact of financial services, infrastructure provision, public services etc. on both labour and physical capital productivity. Our objective, however, is to highlight only the role of those public expenditures which bring about an increase in labour productivity. In this perspective, even though we do not model an educational process explicitly, the production function implicitly entails the effects of education on labour productivity. To see this, let us consider the production function $y_{t+1} = [\tilde{A}(\cdot)\tilde{a}_l x_{lt+1}]^{\alpha} + [\tilde{A}(\cdot)\tilde{a}_h x_{ht+1}]^{\alpha} k_{t+1}^{1-\alpha} K_{t+1}^{\alpha}$ where $\tilde{A}(\cdot)\tilde{a}_i$, $i = l,h$, is the efficiency of one unit of labour as determined by a fixed component, a_i, and by the factor $A(\cdot)$, which captures the endogenous increase in labour productivity and lets us set $\tilde{A}(\cdot)^{\alpha} = A(\cdot)$ and $\tilde{a}_i^{\alpha} = a_i$.

3. This probability is here taken as given in order to simplify the framework. It is possible to imagine a more complex economy in which the government, here a passive player, could actively choose the optimal level of π.

4   Since wage rates depend on capital as well as labour-specific productivity parameters (see equations (8.2) and (8.3)), this condition is easily satisfied for a sufficiently high a_h and/or a sufficiently low a_l.

5. See Appendix 8.2.

REFERENCES

Barro, R. (1990), 'Government spending in a simple model of endogenous growth', *Journal of Political Economy*, **98**(5), part II, S103–25.

Burdett, K., R. Lagos and Randall Wright (2003), 'Crime, inequality, and unemployment', *American Economic Review*, **93**(5), 1764–77.

Fender, J. (1999) 'A general equilibrium model of crime and punishment', *Journal of Economic Behaviour & Organisation*, 437–53.

Glaeser, E.L., B. Sacerdote and A. Scheinkman (1996), 'Crime and social interactions', *Quarterly Journal of Economics*, **111**, 507–48.

Gould, E., D. Mustard and B. Weinberg (2002), 'Crime rates and local labor market opportunities in the United States, 1979–97', *Review of Economics and Statistics*, **84**, 45–61.

Huang, C.-C., D. Laing and P. Wang (1999), 'Crime and poverty: a search theoretic analysis', Working Paper, The Pennsylvania State University.

Josten, S.D. (2003), 'Inequality, crime and economic growth. A classical argument for distributional equality', *International Tax and Public Finance*, **10**, 435–52.

Lloyd-Ellis, H. and N. Marceau (2003), 'Endogenous insecurity and economic development', *Journal of Economic Development*, **72**, 1–29.

Lochner, L. (1999), 'Education, work and crime: theory and evidence', Working Paper, University of Rochester, Rochester, NY.

Mehhulm, H., K. Moene and R. Torvik (2001), 'A crime induced poverty trap', University of Oslo Discussion Paper.

Mehhulm, H., K. Moene and R. Torvik (2003), 'Predator or prey? Parasitic enterprises in economic development', *European Economic Review*, **47**, 275–94.

9. Redistributing opportunities in a job search model: the role of self-confidence and social norms[*]

Francesco Drago

9.1. INTRODUCTION

Search theories in the labour market have recently been used to analyse empirical regularities such as worker flows and wage dispersion. In particular one of the most important results from this strand of literature shows how pure wage dispersion among identical workers arises as an equilibrium outcome in a general equilibrium model characterized by search frictions (Burdett and Mortensen, 1998). In this respect the standard job search model offers an explanation of why identical workers that search for better jobs receive offers that differ in wage rates, and contributes to explain inequality in the labour market.

Another compelling explanation of why identical workers are paid differently concerns the theory of the behavioural determinants of earnings. Robust empirical evidence shows that behavioural traits, such as some aspects of personality, may be considered to some extent as determinants of earnings (see, for example, Bowles, Gintis and Osborne, 2001 and Cawley, Heckman and Vytlacil, 2001). Social networks, patience, perseverance and self-confidence among others may then explain part of the inequality that is not explained by the (neoclassical) standard wage equation (Bowles, Gintis and Osborne, 2001). All these traits explain part of earnings differences, as well as different (upward) mobility rates, although they are not productive skills, that is, they do not contribute to production as they do not enter the production function.

In this chapter we seek to study some key factors that result in inequality and individual labour market success (for example, earnings, employment–unemployment status, time experienced to find a better job). In particular we are interested in the job arrival rates of better jobs for employed workers that are identically productive. We do so by taking into account the two strands of literature outlined above. Indeed a prime concern of this chapter is to bring together the behavioural determinants of individual labour success and search theories. We focus on self-confidence (self-esteem) and on workers' search effort for better jobs.[1] Our modelling implies that heterogeneity in the broad innate behavioural trait of self-esteem generates heterogeneity in job arrival rates. More precisely, different levels of self-esteem lead workers to supply different levels of search effort and then to experience different job arrival rates. To the best of our knowledge this is one of the first attempts to include self-esteem and motivation theory in a job search model. Dubra (2004) analyses the implications of optimism in a search model where the distribution of wages is unknown and agents may become under-confident or over-confident. Our perspective is different as we focus on innate behavioural traits and assume that imperfect information does not concern wage distribution.

In our model employed workers search for better jobs. Workers differ only with respect to their level of confidence in their own ability.[2] For each wage rate at which they are employed, their job arrival rate is the product between a given search efficiency parameter and the costly search effort that they supply. The former parameter is determined by the search intensity of the vacant employers and is faced by all the workers in the same way.[3] Our model is characterized by imperfect information as workers (wrongly) believe that they can modify the search efficiency parameter they face. In particular workers believe that they can increase this parameter by signalling their ability. Showing the level of self-confidence is a device to signal their ability where signalling is costly. We interpret signalling as an investment in forms of social capital concerned with a worker's image and reputation. It will be shown that those who invest in signalling their ability experience greater job arrival rates. Paradoxically this result is achieved not as a consequence of signalling (since employers do not observe the ability in our model), rather because workers who signal will provide higher optimal search effort. This is due to the fact that search effort and self-confidence turn out to be complements, provided that self-confidence is signalled.

In Section 9.2 we account for the main assumptions of the model following the studies on individual investment in social capital (Alesina and LaFerrara, 2000; DiPasquale and Glaeser, 1999, and Glaeser, Laibson and Sacerdote, 2002) and the studies on self-image and task choice (Köszegi, 2004 and Bénabou and Tirole, 2002). A crucial assumption for our results is that the cost of such an investment is equal for all the workers and proportional to the wage rate they earn. What varies is the expected return to this investment measured by the perceived increment in the search efficiency parameter after investment. Indeed such an increment is believed to be proportional to the level of self-confidence. We detect the threshold level of self-confidence according to which workers invest in their image (signal their ability) if and only if their level of self-confidence exceeds the threshold value. Interestingly the threshold value varies with the worker's current wage level (it is state dependent). As will be shown, this is important because it implies that those who invest are less likely to invest again once they have found a job. In other words, it is as if workers learned the true gain function of their search, or as if they learned that the employer does not observe ability. We emphasize that this mechanism results without assuming any kind of learning.

The second aim of the chapter is to show how the effectiveness of a redistributive policy that attenuates job arrival rate differentials may crucially depend on social norms. Insofar as job arrival rate differentials are driven by different degrees of self-esteem, that in a certain sense are beyond the individual control, voters may be concerned to redistribute the opportunities that workers have to move to better jobs.[4] In our chapter we impose a tax rate on those workers who invest and therefore experience higher arrival rates and a subsidy rate on those who do not invest. We term this policy 'redistributing opportunities' in that identically productive individuals, who differ only in their level of self-esteem, may experience more similar job arrival rates. We analyse this redistributive policy in the presence of social norms. A social norm is intended as a shared rule in a society. The main feature of social norms is that disobeying (deviating from) norms results in social disapproval that creates (emotional) disutility and that this disutility depends on situations, that is, it is endogenous. We mainly follow Lindbeck, Nyberg and Weibull (1999) where interactions between the welfare state and social norms are studied. They analyse the binary choice of work or living off transfers in the presence of a social norm 'against living off other people and a corresponding normative pressure to earn one's income from work'. In our case the choice is whether or not to invest and the social norm is that workers prefer to self-help, which thus implies a disutility (for example, guilt) for those who receive a subsidy.

Would the social norm be relevant for the effectiveness of the redistributive policy? Yes, if, as in Lindbeck, Nyberg and Weibull (1999), we assume that such a disutility is decreasing with the share of population that receives the subsidy. In this case people face a strategic environment, the decision to invest also depends on the share of the population who invest (and thus that are not recipients), and it is shown that we may obtain multiple equilibria with different degrees of effectiveness of the redistributive policy.

The analysis in the first part of the chapter is relevant to income distribution dynamics as the importance of on-the-job search is widely recognized as one of the main factors determining individual wage growth.

The second part of our chapter also highlights the fact that the effectiveness of a redistributive policy may also depend on social norms.

The chapter is structured as follows. In the next section we introduce the basic assumptions and the related literature. In the third section we introduce the basic framework. In the fourth section we provide the model. Then we analyse the redistributive policy. Finally we draw our conclusions.

9.2. RELATED LITERATURE AND BASIC ASSUMPTIONS

Searching for a (better) job is a task that is best performed if, beyond exerting effort, an individual has a high degree of self-confidence in his abilities. This may hold for at least two reasons. Workers who appear more self-confident may be more attractive for an employer who is recruiting. Furthermore, self-esteem may enhance motivation of individuals to perform search activities. In the theories relating self-esteem and performance the first reason is termed as the signalling one and the second as the motivational (Bénabou and Tirole, 2002). In our model the reason why more self-confident workers experience better search performances is the second, although the workers' belief in the effectiveness of the first plays a crucial role.

We based our analysis on some psychological evidence. Camerer (1997) lists some studies documenting that people in general tend to overrate the chance of good events because they are self-confident. Self-confidence is captured by the 'above median effect' according to which people tend to believe to be better than the median of the population in some major respects (Fang and Moscarini, 2005). For example in Meyer (1975), less than 5 per cent of employees rated themselves below the median. Other studies that give psychological evidence on self-confidence are reported by Svenson (1981) and Larwood and Whittaker (1977).[5] Recently self-confidence has been taken into account by economists attempting to model agents' incentives to 'think positive' about themselves, that is to maintain and enhance a high degree of self-esteem, to have rosy views about the probability of success of the projects they are involved in, not to consider bad signals and the like. For example Köszegi (2004) argues that these incentives stem, among other factors, from the fact that people care about their self-image and to this extent they derive 'ego-utility'. This of course affects many economically important decisions. However, to model this attitude and its consequences it is necessary to assume that people have imperfect information about the real process that governs the probability of success of the projects they are involved in.

Incorporating this issue in our arguments we denote the expected payoff from search λsE, where λ is the given search efficiency parameter, that all the workers face, s is the search effort that involves a cost and E is the gain from moving to a better job.[6] In our model workers differ only with respect to what extent they believe they are above the median and they believe that by signalling their ability they increase the search efficiency parameter they face. In addition workers believe that until they show their ability, they face a parameter equal to λ. Indeed workers consider λ a parameter that reflects the ability of the median of the population. Accordingly, if they signal their level of self-esteem, they think they are facing $\hat{\lambda} > \lambda$, with $\hat{\lambda}$ increasing in each worker's level of self-esteem. Then when they have to choose the search effort, given the search cost, workers maximize their welfare taking account of $\hat{\lambda}$; it is simple to show that this induces them to choose a higher search effort than that they would choose if they thought they were facing λ. Therefore the mistake (they actually face λ) leads them to experience greater arrival rates (see Section 9.4). We posit that the mechanism through which workers signal their ability is a costly investment in some forms of social capital.[7]

Our analysis concerns the studies of behavioural economics on motivation and self-confidence (Bénabou and Tirole 2002 and Köszegi, 2004). Our approach differs in two respects. First, in our context the nature of the problem is different in that people who overrate their own ability need to invest in social capital to signal their degree of self-confidence. Second, we do not allow the worker to learn about his own ability. In our chapter this is not a strong assumption as the positive impact of self-confidence on the choice of effort depends on whether or not the investment is made. As we anticipated in the introduction, the structure of the model implies that workers do not make systematic mistakes: those who invest are less likely to invest again once they find a job.

The formation of social capital resulting from individual investments is analysed by Alesina and LaFerrara (2000), DiPasquale and Glaeser (1999) and Glaeser, Laibson and Sacerdote (2002). In particular the latter paper includes in the individual component of social capital all the personal characteristics that are useful to individuals in order to reap market and non-market returns from interactions with others. This investment implies a cost that is equal to a fraction of the wage rate.[8] The fact that the (perceived) return from social capital is equal to $(\hat{\lambda} - \lambda)sE$, where $\hat{\lambda}$ is proportional to the initial level of self-esteem, is consistent with the notion of individual social capital.[9]

9.3. PRELIMINARIES OF THE MODEL

In this section we present the maximization problem of the worker in a standard job search model. We consider a continuous and infinite time horizon model. We take into account just one type of economic agent: workers. Workers are identical and the measure of workers is normalized to one. Workers are assumed to search for a job both when employed and unemployed, they choose a search effort that increases the rate at which job offers are sampled given the search cost they incur. All the agents discount the future at the rate r. Workers search by drawing a sequential random wage sample from a cumulative distribution function $F(w)$. Assume $F(w)$ to be continuous on $[-\infty, +\infty]$. Assume an interval $[b, \overline{w}]$ such that $F(b) = 0$ and $\lim_{w \to \overline{w}} F(w) = 1$, and $F(w)$ is twice differentiable on the interval $[b, \overline{w}]$, with the first derivative strictly positive on $[b, \overline{w}]$.[10] Note that $1 - F(w)$ is the probability that a wage offer is at least as great as w, and $F(w)$ is the probability that a wage offer is less than w. Every time an offer arrives, the worker decides whether or not to accept the job offer. There is no recall. For employed and unemployed workers job offers arrive at the rate λs where λ is the so-called search efficiency parameter and s the endogenous search effort. Workers incur the search cost $c(s)$, with $c'(s) > 0$, $c''(s) > 0$ and $c(0) = c'(0) = 0$ and receive unemployment benefit b when they are unemployed. Moreover jobs are destroyed at the exogenous Poisson rate δ. The value of being employed at wage w_i and of unemployment, denoted by V and $W(w_i)$, respectively, solve the following Bellman equations:

$$rV = b - c(s) + \lambda s \int \max[W(w) - V, 0] dF(w), \qquad (9.1)$$

$$rW(w_i) = w_i - c(s) + \lambda s \int_{w_i}^{\overline{w}} [W(w) - W(w_i)] dF(w) + \delta[V - W(w_i)]. \qquad (9.2)$$

Expression (9.1) states that at each instant the value of unemployment yields a net return equal to the unemployment benefit minus the search cost plus the expected gain from receiving an acceptable job offer. Expression (9.2) states that the value of being employed yields at each instant a net return equal to the wage rate, minus the search cost, plus the expected return of finding a better job, minus the expected loss of being unemployed. Workers accept employment if the wage offer is greater than the reservation wage defined as wage R such that $W(R) = V$. Moreover as the derivative of the value of employment is

$$W'(w_i) = \frac{1}{r + \delta + \lambda s[1 - F(w_i)]} > 0 \qquad (9.3)$$

by the envelope theorem and the Leibniz rule, an employed worker quits to another job if and only if it pays a higher wage (see Mortensen, 2003). The search effort s maximizes the difference between the revenue from searching and the search cost, and it depends on the current wage:

$$s^* = \arg\max_{s \geq 0} \left\{ -c(s) + \lambda s \int_{w_i}^{\overline{w}} [W(w) - W(w_i)] dF(w) \right\} \qquad (9.4)$$

Optimality requires the marginal search cost to be equal to the marginal revenue of searching:

$$c'(s) = \lambda \int_{w_i}^{\overline{w}} [W(w) - W(w_i)] dF(w). \qquad (9.5)$$

The theorem of implicit function assures that the optimal level of effort is monotone decreasing in w_i and monotone increasing in λ. For a worker employed at wage w_i the instantaneous rate at which he finds a job with a wage rate greater than w_i is:

$$H(w_i) = \lambda s^* [1 - F(w_i)], \qquad (9.6)$$

where s^* is implicitly defined by (9.5), and $1/H(w_i)$ is the expected waiting time to find a better job. Equation (9.1), (9.2) and the fact that the reservation wage R solves $W(R) = U$, together imply that the search intensity of an unemployed worker is the same as that of a worker employed at the reservation wage. Hence we obtain the result that $R = b$ (see Mortensen, 2003 and Mortensen and Pissarides, 1999).

In the standard job search model it is important to distinguish between the distribution of wages offered to job seekers, denoted by $F(w)$, and the distribution of wages received by workers who are currently employed, that is, the earnings distribution that we denote by $G(w)$, that in general may differ from $F(w)$. If u is the fraction of workers currently employed, in equilibrium the flow into unemployment must be equal to the flow into employment:[11]

$$\delta(1 - u) = \lambda s(R)u. \qquad (9.7)$$

Moreover in equilibrium the flow of workers into jobs that pay w or less must be equal to the outflow of workers from this job. The outflow is the sum of workers who become unemployed because of destruction plus the flow of workers that find a better job offer. The flow into these jobs is equal to the unemployed workers who find a job paying w or less:

$$(1-u)\left\{\delta G(w)+\lambda[1-F(w)]\int_R^w s(w_i)dG(w_i)\right\}=\lambda s(R)F(w)u. \quad (9.8)$$

In general the efficiency parameter λ depends on the recruiting effort of employers and is derived from the matching function that governs contacts between workers and firms. In what follows we take into account the framework above and we consider the steady state of the economy under which λ is constant.

9.4. THE MODEL

All the formalization in this section regarding self-confidence and investment in social capital is based on the assumptions and on the discussion in Section 9.2. We take into account only employed workers and we set up a simple model where self-confidence is an innate attribute partially defined by the comparative evaluation that the single worker makes about himself with respect to other workers. We assume that each worker is characterized by the following parameter:

$$\sigma=\frac{self-esteem}{luck}=\frac{x}{y}. \quad (9.9)$$

where $0<x\le 1$ is a measure of to what extent the worker believes he/she possesses abilities above the median. The denominator $0<y<1$ is an attribute that denotes to what extent the worker believes that luck is important for individual labour market success, for example, $y\cong 1$ means that according to the worker, individual labour success is almost completely determined by factors that are beyond the individual's control, that is, luck.[12] The parameter σ is distributed in the population according to the c.d.f. $\Phi(\sigma)$, continuous and differentiable, with $\Phi(\sigma)'>0$ and support defined on the interval $[\underline{\sigma},\overline{\sigma}]$.

According to the assumption in Section 9.2 workers overrate their ability proportionally to the attribute σ. We assume that when workers invest in their image to signal their ability they believe they are facing a parameter $\lambda+\varepsilon\sigma$, where ε is a constant less than one, instead of the true parameter λ. We denote η the fraction of the wage rate to be paid for the investment. Then the lifetime utility to be employed at wage rate w_i for a worker who invests now solves the following equation:

$$rW(w_i) = (1-\eta)w_i - c(s) +$$

$$+(\lambda + \varepsilon\sigma)s \int_{w_i}^{\overline{w}} [W(w) - W(w_i)] dF(w) + \delta[V - W(w_i)]. \tag{9.10}$$

The cost of investment is equal for all the workers and is proportional to the wage rate, whereas the perceived benefits vary from individual to individual according to the parameter σ, defined above. Equation (9.10) is easily interpretable: the more self-confident the worker, the more effective he thinks he is in the search process, provided that he signals his ability by investing in his image. However given the cost of the investment not all workers will find it convenient to pay ηw.

Proposition 1: *For each wage rate w there exists a threshold level $\sigma^*(w)$ such that for any worker with $\sigma(w) \geq \sigma^*(w)$ it is optimal to pay ηw. The critical level $\sigma^*(w)$ is an increasing function of the wage rate.*

At any wage rate, we term the worker with $\sigma(w) = \sigma^*(w)$ as the marginal participant.[13] Proposition 1 states that there exists a threshold level of σ that defines the participation constraint to the investment and that this level depends positively on the wage rate currently earned. Intuitively while the perceived benefit from investment, that is $\varepsilon\sigma s \int_{w_i}^{\overline{w}} [W(w) - W(w_i)] dF(w)$, is decreasing with respect to the wage rate currently earned, the cost of the investment is increasing with respect to the wage rate, which is why the higher the wage, the higher is $\sigma^*(w)$.

As a consequence of Proposition 1, for the share of workers with $\sigma(w_i) \geq \sigma^*(w_i)$ the lifetime utility of being employed at wage rate w_i solves equation (9.10), while for the share with $\sigma(w_i) < \sigma^*(w_i)$ the lifetime utility solves equation (9.2). Employed workers with $\sigma(w_i) < \sigma^*(w_i)$ still overrate their ability but do not find it convenient to show their degree of self-confidence. Therefore in the absence of any investment, this share believes it faces λ, which it is considered an average parameter that reflects the ability of the median of the labour force. This formalization is interesting for two reasons. First, it makes the efficacy of the parameter σ distributed in the labour force state-dependent. Whether σ is active also depends on the situations that the workers face and the (perceived) efficacy of self-confidence is endogenous to the model.[14] Second, this formulation divides the employed workers into two shares: one consisting of workers who appear, to different degrees, optimistic (self-confident) in their own efficacy with respect to others, believing they are dealing with an efficiency parameter equal to $\lambda + \varepsilon\sigma$ (for those with $\sigma(w_i) \geq \sigma^*(w_i)$); the other consists of workers who, although overrating their ability, do not invest and then (correctly) believe they are facing a parameter equal to λ.

However despite the fact that workers with $\sigma(w_i) \geq \sigma^*(w_i)$ are mistaken in believing that they are up against a search efficiency parameter greater that λ, they experience higher job arrival rates.

Proposition 2: *For any wage rate w, the job offer arrival rate for workers with* $\sigma(w_j) \geq \sigma^*(w_i)$ *is relatively higher than that of workers with* $\sigma(w_i) < \sigma^*(w_i)$.

Workers with $\sigma < \sigma^*$ think they are facing $\lambda + \varepsilon\sigma$, which makes them supply more effort and finally experience a greater job arrival rate than that of those who (correctly) believe they are facing the true parameter λ. [15] In this respect beliefs in one's ability and effort are complementary. This in turn can justify why some workers are willing to pay the fraction η of the wage rate.

We did not specify learning dynamics about the beliefs in one's ability (x and y are fixed innate components); however note that in this context the results we would expect from learning are consistent with those we in effect obtain here. Indeed, while the expected waiting time to find a better job for a worker with $\sigma(w) \geq \sigma^*(w)$ is $1 \backslash (\lambda + \varepsilon\sigma) s^{**}[1 - F(w)]$, on average he will experience $1 \backslash \lambda s^{**}[1 - F(w)]$, where s^{**} is the solution in program of the Bellman equation (9.10). If we allowed for learning about x, this would induce workers to decrease their degree of self-confidence. On the other hand, workers with $\sigma(w) \geq \sigma^*(w)$ may observe that the average amount of time to find a better job for workers with $\sigma(w) < \sigma^*(w)$, $1 \backslash \lambda s^*[1 - F(w)]$, where $s^* < s^{**}$ is the solution in program of (9.2), is discretely higher than their average waiting time (by Proposition 2). By the same token, if we allowed for learning about x, this would induce them to increase their degree of self-esteem, in particular x in expression (9.9). [16] In our model it is as if the former effect prevailed. Taking into account an individual who invests, let $p[\sigma(w)] \in [0,1)$ be the probability that such an individual will invest once he has found a new job.

Proposition 3: *For the marginal participant* $p[\sigma(w)] = 0$. *For the worker with* $\sigma(w) > \sigma^*(w)$, $p[\sigma(w)]$ *is monotone decreasing with respect to the wage currently earned.*

9.5.   REDISTRIBUTIVE POLICY

According to the results derived from the basic model above, for those who pay the fraction η of their wage rate (those with $\sigma(w) \geq \sigma^*(w)$) the offer arrival rate is discretely higher than those embedded with $\sigma(w) < \sigma^*(w)$. In this framework we analyse the implementation and the effects of a redistributive policy of opportunities. We use this term to mean a policy that aims to compress the distribution of the expected job arrival rates for the population at any wage rate. For the sake of clarity, let us take into account two individuals 1 and 2 employed at the same wage rate w_i; with $\sigma_1(w) < \sigma^*(w) < \sigma_2(w)$, the redistributing policy aims to reduce the differences in the job arrival rate between workers 1 and 2. The policy we implement imposes a linear tax rate on search effort for the (over)confident worker (the one who invests), that is, worker 2, and delivers a linear subsidy on search effort to worker 1. While search subsidies are quite common in literature, a linear tax on search activity may appear somewhat unrealistic at first glance.[17] However, in this context it will be clear that such a linear tax is formally equivalent to a tax on job mobility and that its effect consists in a reduction of the return to search activity.[18]

Assume a linear tax on search effort on those who pay the fraction η of their wage rate and a subsidy rate on search effort on those who do not invest. Let the tax rate and the subsidy rate be ρ and γ respectively. To this framework we add the presence of a social norm with regard to the social stigma suffered by those who receive benefits from the welfare state. Note that in our case those who do not invest evaluate, to a lesser extent, their ability above the median but do not find it worth investing. Therefore besides social stigma they can suffer guilt for being subsidized. In general it is widely documented that there exists a social disutility for being recipients on a welfare program. The most striking evidence is in the US where only 40–70 per cent of the individuals eligible for welfare programs (for example, subsidies, transfers) finally takes part in them (see Lindbeck, Nyberg and Weibull, 1999). We denote such a disutility as μ that enters the lifetime utility of the recipients with a minus sign. In this situation lifetime utilities to be employed at wage rate w_i solve the following:

$$rW(w_i) = (1-\eta)w_i - c(s) +$$

$$+ s \left\{ (\lambda + \varepsilon\sigma) \int_{w_i}^{\overline{w}} [W(w) - W(w_i)] dF(w) - \rho \right\} + \delta[V - W(w_i)],$$

if $\sigma(w_i) \geq \sigma^*(w_i)$. $\qquad\qquad$ (9.11)

$$rW(w_i) = w_i - c(s) + s \left\{ \lambda \int_{w_i}^{\bar{w}} [W(w) - W(w_i)] dF(w) + \gamma \right\} + \delta [V - W(w_i)] - \mu$$

if $\sigma(w_i) < \sigma^*(w_i)$. (9.12)

Taxes and subsidies make the decision to invest more costly; in other words with taxes and subsidies σ^* increases for all the wage rates. However this effect is attenuated by the social stigma μ and we assume that ρ and λ are fixed in a way that the effect of μ on the critical level of σ (to lower it) does not dominate over the effect of ρ and λ.[19] The critical level of $\sigma^*(w)$ that defines the participation constraint must be written as $\sigma^*(w, \rho, \sigma, \mu)$, increasing in the first, the second and the third argument and decreasing in the last. In aggregate it is clear why such a policy reduces job arrival rate differentials: with this scheme, a share of workers will search more, namely those who previously had $\sigma(w) < \sigma^*(w)$, and a fraction of workers will search less.

For any level of ρ, λ and μ, denote with $z = \Phi[\sigma^*(w, \rho, \sigma, \mu)]$ the share of recipients, that is obviously decreasing in μ and increasing in ρ and λ.[20] Following Lindbeck, Nyberg and Weibull (1999 and 2002) we assume that μ is a decreasing function of z. More precisely, we define $\mu = g(z)$, where $g : [0,1] \to R_+$, continuously differentiable with $g'(z) < 0$.

This simple formalization brings about a set of interesting results. In this way the critical level $\sigma^*(w)$ now depends also on the share of recipients z (substitute $\mu = g(z)$ in the expression of z), that is, both $\sigma^*(w)$ and the intensity of μ are endogenous to the model. Now the share of recipient is $z = \Phi\{\sigma^*[w, \rho, \sigma, g(z)]\}$ and for $z = 0$ this share is equal to zero as there are no recipients, that is, all the workers invest and $\sigma^*(w, \rho, \sigma, \mu) = \underline{\sigma}$ (the lower support of the distribution of σ). In this context individuals face a strategic environment as the payoff of worker's behaviour depends on the behaviour of the other workers. As is customary, a profile of individual choice, given ρ and λ, and for each level of the wage rate, is a Nash equilibrium if and only if z satisfies the following fixed point equation:

$$z = Q(z), \tag{9.13}$$

where Q is a function that maps the unit interval into itself: $Q : [0,1] \to [0,1]$ and z is defined above to be equal to $z = \Phi\{\sigma^*[w, \rho, \sigma, g(z)]\}$, where ρ and λ are taken as given. In equation (9.13), $Q(z)$ is an increasing function of the endogenous variable z.[21]

The function $Q(z)$ is continuous in the unit interval. Thus, given ρ and λ, there exists at least one fixed point, denoting the Nash equilibrium. Note that if the disutility μ were a constant then there would be exactly one fixed point. However as μ is a decreasing function of the share of the recipients, depending on the functional form of $g(z)$, we can obtain more than one fixed point, that is, multiple equilibria. This is a result commonly found in the literature on social norms, just as social norms are studied in the context of welfare state.[22] It is possible to show with the usual arguments that if we posit that at each instant the prediction of each worker about the share z may not be correct, then in the case of three equilibria, given the feedback effect above, the only stable equilibria are the extreme ones (see Lindbeck, Nyberg and Weibull, 1999).

In case of multiple equilibria the usual critique is that reported by Lindbeck, Nyberg and Weibull (1999) that 'anything can happen' and therefore the indeterminacy of equilibrium reveals the futility of the theory. But as Lindbeck et al. (1999) point out this is not the case, and even if it were this would not justify the 'exclusion of social norms from our models'. Provided that the strength of social stigma is very high, or, to put it another way, provided that $g(z)$ is very sensitive to changes in z, to relate the result of the last section to those obtained by Lindbeck et al. (1999), if we have three fixed points resulting from (9.13), as the interior equilibrium is unstable, we may basically have two results. Suppose that the linear tax and subsidy rates are fixed. In the first case (that we term A) we have a majority of tax payers mirrored by a high share of investors in social capital. For the same tax and subsidy rates, in the second (that we term B) we have a majority of subsidized mirrored by a low share of investors. Indeed in A (B) the disutility from being a recipient is very high (low), implying a low (high) value of σ^* for all wage rates. With regard to the redistribution, the effect of the policy brings about more equal opportunities in both cases A and B regarding the situation in Section 9.3. However the policy is more effective in case B, in that being σ^* very high, the job arrival rate differential is lower than that in case A where σ^* is lower for all wage rates.

In what follows we restrict our analysis to balanced policies, that is policies that satisfy the budget constraint according to which the total revenue from taxes has to be equal to the total amount of subsidies delivered. Denote with T and S the total revenue and the total amount of subsidies, respectively:

$$T = (1-u)\left\{1 - \Phi\left[\sigma^*(w,\rho,\gamma,\mu)\right]\right\} \int_R^{\bar{w}} \rho s(w)dG(w), \qquad (9.14)$$

$$S = (1-u)\Phi\left[\sigma^*(w,\rho,\gamma,\mu)\right] \int_R^{\bar{w}} \gamma s(w)dG(w) \qquad (9.15)$$

We call a balanced equilibrium the equilibrium such that equation (9.13) and $T = S$ are simultaneously satisfied. We end up with the following proposition that closes the model.[23]

Proposition 4: *For each share of recipients z there is exactly one balanced policy such that T = S and for any balanced policy there exists at most one share of recipient z that satisfies fixed point equation (9.13).*

9.6. CONCLUSION

In this chapter we introduced in a very simple fashion the behavioural trait of self-confidence in the standard job search model. We modelled and explored the effects of self-confidence and we found some interesting results in line with the theory according to which behavioural traits may be important for individual labour market success. In our case self-confidence affects the rate at which wage offers are sampled as well as the expected time to find a better job. Self-esteem and effort are complementary, and rewards (for finding a new job) are most likely to be negative reinforcers for the subsequent decisions to invest in image. This is important because it means that in the absence of any learning structure workers do not actually make systematic mistakes in our model. We explored the effects of a simple redistributing policy that attenuates the job arrival rate differential. We introduced into the analysis the presence of social norms, namely social stigma and guilt deriving from being subsidized. The presence of the social norm is relevant when we assume that the extent to which it affects individual decision is endogenous to the model. In this case we found equilibrium conditions and optimal strategies and we show how we can obtain multiple equilibria and the implications of the model. Future research will concern in-depth analysis of the interaction of social norms and of the behavioural traits presented in Section 9.4, as well as the introduction of evolutionary game theory for analysing conventions in such a framework.

APPENDIX

Proof of Proposition 1: Denote $\int_{w_i}^{\bar{w}}[W(w)-W(w_i)]dF(w)$ with E. For the worker it is optimal to pay ηw_i if and only if the resulting lifetime utility is greater than that resulting from not paying ηw_i, that is:

$$c(s^*)-\lambda s^* E-c(s^{**})+\lambda s^{**} E > \eta w_i - \varepsilon\sigma s^{**} E , \tag{9.16}$$

where s^* is given by (9.4),

$$s^{**} = \underset{s\geq 0}{\arg\max}\left\{-c(s)+(\lambda+\varepsilon\sigma)s\int_{w_i}^{\bar{w}}[W(w)-W(w_i)]dF(w)\right\}$$

and then $s^{**} > s^*$. Note that the LHS of equation (9.16) is strictly negative. Indeed s^* is the arg max of $[-c(s) + \lambda sE]$, whereas $s^{**} > s^*$ is not. Then a necessary condition for (9.16) to hold is $\varepsilon \sigma s^{**} E - \eta w_i > 0$. Inequality (9.16) is satisfied as an equality for a unique σ denoted in the text as σ^*. If we derive the explicit value of σ^* from (916), then σ^* is the σ that satisfies $c(s^*) - \lambda s^* E - c(s^{**}) + \lambda s^{**} E + \varepsilon \sigma s^{**} E - \eta w_i = 0$. If we totally differentiate the last expression with respect to wage rate w_i, using the envelope theorem, we obtain $-\lambda s^* E' + \lambda s^{**} E' + \varepsilon (d\sigma / dw_i) s^{**} E + \varepsilon \sigma s^{**} E' - \eta = 0$, where E' is the derivative of E respect to w_i. From the last expression $d\sigma / dw_i$ is positive. Proposition 2 derives from equation (9.5) (see also note 15) and Proposition 3 from the proof of Proposition 1. For a proof of Proposition 4 see Lindbeck et al. (1999, pp. 11–12).

NOTES

*   I am indebted to Dora Kadar for encouragement, suggestions, and comments on this chapter. I would also like to thank Marianna Belloc, Federico Bozzanca, Maria Rosaria Carillo, Filippo Caruso, and Gioacchino Miligi for useful comments and suggestions on preliminary drafts. All the errors are mine.
1.   In this section and in the next we will use the terms self-confidence and self-esteem interchangeably. We give a precise definition of self-confidence in Section 9.4.
2.   We give evidence for this assumption in the next section.
3.   Therefore, for each wage rate, the only source of heterogeneity in the job arrival rate may derive from heterogeneity in the search effort.
4.   Recently many studies have shown that demand for redistribution is higher in societies where rewards are believed to depend on factors that people cannot control, for example, luck or behavioural traits (see Fong, 2001).
5.   This evidence is taken from Fang and Moscarini (2005).
6.   Note that the job arrival rate is λs.
7.   The social capital we consider in this context has to do with all the 'social skills' useful to reap market interaction, in our case with all the capabilities a worker can exploit to look self-confident, with higher ability and the like.
8.   In our framework, an alternative and psychological interpretation of the cost proportional to the wage rate goes as follows. Whenever workers show their degree of self-confidence to other people they may at the same time be afraid of discovering that their optimistic view about themselves is unjustified, for example due to failure of a project. This fear, which in this interpretation is expressed in monetary terms, increases with the wage rate because the higher the individual's position in the wage ladder, the higher is the reputation of that individual and then the higher is the cost of being embarrassed by failure after investment in image.
9.   The return to the individual component of social capital can be decomposed into an innate attribute (in our case the innate level of self-esteem) and into skills that an individual can acquire (in our case components useful to enhance his image), see, for example, Glaeser, Laibson and Sacerdote (2002).
10. Rather than an assumption, $F(b) = 1$ is derived in the version of the general equilibrium search model, where b is the unemployment benefit that, as will be clear, is equal to the

reservation wage. For a simple derivation of the market equilibrium see, for example, Mortensen (2003).

11. As customary, we assume in what follows that the resulting share of the population equals the expected one. Since the population is a continuum, this implies that, for example, the resulting share of population employed at a wage less than or equal to w that enters the unemployment pool is $\delta(1-u)G(w)$.

12. The attribute x captures the 'above average effect' mentioned in Section 9.2, whereas the attribute y is similar to that often referred to as the 'fundamental attribution error' (Aronson, 1994).

13. For notational concerns, $\sigma(w)$ denotes the specific attribute of a worker employed at wage rate w.

14. In particular given the stationarity of the wage distribution, workers who are already at the top of the distribution have little to gain from searching and as a consequence they do not find it worth showing their degree of self-confidence, that is, to pay ηw.

15. Formally the search intensity of self-confident workers is

$$s^{**} = \arg\max_{s \geq 0} \left\{ -c(s) + (\lambda + \varepsilon\sigma)s \int_{w_i}^{\bar{w}} \left[W(w) - W(w_i) \right] dF(w) \right\},$$

whereas the search intensity s^* of the workers who do not invest is given by (9.4). Given that the cost function is convex and the optimal condition, $s^{**} > s^*$ and obviously the job arrival rate of better job for workers who invest is higher than that of the others, that is $\lambda s^{**} \left[1 - F(w_i) \right] > \lambda s^* \left[1 - F(w_i) \right]$.

16. Note that the same argument applies if we allow for learning from the profitability of the investment.

17. A similar scheme is implemented by Shimer and Smith (2001) in a different framework.

18. The fiscal authority may want to reduce excessive turnover rates that in some cases are shown in literature to be inefficient. The linear tax rate on search effort has the same effect as a linear tax on the net gain associated to moving to a new job, that is $W(w) - W(w_i)$, where $W(w)$ is the lifetime utility associated to the new job.

19. Note that we implicitly assume that workers must be either taxed or subsidized. For those who do not pay ηw, it is possible to model the choice of refusing the search subsidy (so that they do not experience social stigma), or of accepting the search subsidy. This would happen if the lifetime utility from being subsidized is less than the lifetime utility of not being a recipient, given that $\sigma(w) < \sigma^*(w)$. This would be the case for workers employed at sufficiently high wage rates. However even if we account for this observation, the result which concerns us remains substantially unchanged.

20. It is possible to derive the explicit value of this z. However we avoid the calculation for the sake of simplicity; what we need to know is how z varies with respect to the parameters. Moreover recall that the population is a continuum, $z \in [0,1]$ and that at any instant we approximate the values of the measures of workers with the expected ones.

21. Note that $g' < 0$, then σ^* is increasing with respect to z and due to the fact that $\Phi'[\sigma^*(\cdot)] > 0$, $Q(z)$ is increasing in z.

22. For our model, however, the presence of social norms can make it more difficult to implement the redistribution of opportunities. Indeed now depending on the functional form of g, the effect of disutility of tax and subsidy on the critical level of σ may be dominated by the strength of social stigma.

23. Proposition 4 derives from Lindbeck, Nyberg and Weibull (1999) and applies to our case.

REFERENCES

Alesina, A. and E. LaFerrara (2000), 'Participation in heterogeneous communities', *Quarterly Journal of Economics,* **115**, 847–904.

Aronson, E. (1994), *The Social Animal,* 7th edn, New York: W.H. Freeman and Company.

Bénabou, R. and J. Tirole (2002), 'Self-confidence and personal motivation', *Quarterly Journal of Economics,* **117**, 871–915.

Bowles, S., H. Gintis and M. Osborne (2001), 'The determinants of earnings: a behavioral approach', *Journal of Economic Literature,* **39**, 1137–76.

Burdett, K. and D. Mortensen (1998), 'Wage differentials, employer size, and unemployment', *International Economic Review,* **39**, 257–73.

Camerer, C. (1997), 'Progress in behavioral game theory', *Journal of Economic Perspectives,* **11**, 167–88.

Cawley, J., J. Heckman and E. Vytlacil (2001), 'Three observations on wages and measured cognitive ability', *Labour Economics,* **8**, 419–42.

DiPasquale, D. and E. Glaeser (1999), 'Incentives and social capital: are homeowners better citizens?', *Journal of Urban Economics,* **45**, 354–84.

Dubra, J. (2004), 'Optimism and overconfidence in search', *Review of Economics Dynamics,* **7**, 198–218.

Fang, H. and G. Moscarini (2005), 'Moral hazard', *Journal of Monetary Economics,* forthcoming.

Fong, C. (2001), 'Social preferences, self-interest and demand for redistribution', *Journal of Public Economics,* **82**, 225–46.

Glaeser, E., D. Laibson and B. Sacerdote (2002), 'An economic approach to social capital: are homeowners better citizens?', *Economic Journal,* **112**, 437–58.

Köszegi, B. (2004), '"Ego utility" and task choice', mimeo, University of California, Berkeley.

Larwood, L. and W. Whittaker (1977), 'Managerial myopia: self-serving biases in organizational planning', *Journal of Applied Psychology,* **62**, 194–98.

Lindbeck, A., S. Nyberg and J.W. Weibull (1999), 'Social norms and economics incentives in the welfare state', *Quarterly Journal of Economics,* **114**, 1–35.

Lindbeck, A., S. Nyberg and J.W. Weibull (2002), 'Social norms welfare state dynamics', Cesifo working paper series, no. 931.

Meyer, H. (1975), 'The pay-for-performance dilemma', *Organizational Dynamics,* **3**, 39–50.

Moffitt, R. (1983), 'An economic model of welfare stigma', *American Economic Review,* **73**, 1023–35.

Mortensen D. (2003), *Wage Dispersion,* Cambridge, Mass.: The MIT Press.

Mortensen, D. and C. Pissarides (1999), 'New developments in models of search in the labor market', in O. Ashenfelter and D. Card (eds), *Handbook of Labor Economics,* Vol. 3A, Ch. 9, Amsterdam: North-Holland.

Shimer, R. and L. Smith (2001), 'Matching, search, and heterogeneity', *Advances in Macroeconomics,* **1**, article 5.

Svenson, O. (1981), 'Are we all less risky and more skillful than our fellow drivers?', *Acta Psychologica,* **47**, 143–8.

SECTION FOUR

Public Policy

10. Fiscal policy and economic growth[*]

Renato Balducci

10.1. INTRODUCTION

New Growth Theory[1] has sought to recover – within the framework of the rational and optimizing behaviour of agents – the scope for allocative intervention by the policy-maker that was undervalued or indeed denied by the previous neoclassical theory of growth.[2] Despite the differences in analytical structure and founding hypotheses, the models of endogenous growth explain steady state growth at a positive and constant endogenous rate. This important property depends on some form of non-decreasing returns to scale due to constant marginal return in one or more accumulable factors.[3]

Lucas (1988) argued that investment in education increases the stock of human capital; therefore the public provision of general education modifies the optimal accumulation of human capital and the long-run pattern of economic growth. Similarly, government expenditure on research and development (Romer, 1990), health (Bloom et al., 2001) and public infrastructures can influence the optimal rate of economic growth, introducing an externality in private decisions. Turnovsky (1996, 2000) notes that distorsive taxation can internalize the effect of these externalities, inducing an efficient intertemporal allocation.[4]

The basic hypothesis of Barro's model (1990)[5] is that the government purchases a constant share of private output and uses it to provide free public services to private producers. He considers all public expenditures that produce externalities generalized to the firms' system, such as the defence of property rights, spending on justice, national defence, education, and so on. Public investments $g(t)$ per unit of labour are financed with proportional taxes on income: $g(t) = \tau y(t)$. Hence $(1-\tau)y(t)$ is the income available to the economy for private investments and consumption.

Public spending affects the form of the production function, which is with constant returns to scale in two production factors, $k(t)$ and $g(t)$, and concave with respect to each of them. If the economy is aware of the public budget constraint: $g(t) = \tau y(t)$ and if it perfectly knows that the government will comply with that constraint, then we can obtain a production function at constant returns to scale in the private capital stock.[6]

On maximizing the current value of the flow of future utilities derived from private consumption, one obtains a steady-state growth rate which is influenced by public spending on production services. An increase in the tax rate τ reduces the income available for private consumption and investments, but it increases public services $g(t)$ to firms. Which of the two effects will prevail depends on the functional form of the production function. An increase in the tax rate boosts the growth rate until $\tau < \alpha$, and it reaches the maximum when $\tau = \alpha$ (see Barro, 1990, p. 109). Above this threshold, it reduces the growth rate because of the effect brought about by the reduction in disposable household income.

A natural extension of this important finding has been advanced by Barro (1990) himself (see section V). Because public consumption reduces income net of taxes without increasing the productivity of the capital stock, it slows the economy's equilibrium growth rate: 'But suppose that the government's expenditures also finance some services that enter into households' utility functions',[7] and: 'The growth rate lies uniformly below the value γ, ... , that would have been chosen if $\tau_h = 0$' (see Barro, 1990, p. 117).

However, the growth rate obtained by Barro (1990) (equation 25, p. 117) does not consider the weight β that households give to public consumption as an alternative to private consumption $(1 - \beta)$. Then β close to zero or β close to unity would be the same! But, if $\beta = 0$ (why would it be excluded, as in Barro, 1990, p. 117?), public consumption services would be entirely wasted resources, and a lower rate of growth due to such squandering of resources would be justified. If instead $\beta = 1$, then households want public services only and save and invest all their disposable income, with obvious positive effects on growth.

Equation (25) in Barro (1990) shows no evidence of this, in that it considers only the effects of public spending on the productivity of the global (public and private) capital stock. Nor does it consider that the presence of public consumption in the households' utility function modifies the intertemporal elasticity of substitution. This latter cannot be the elasticity of substitution relative to private consumption alone; it must also evaluate the elasticity of substitution relative to public consumption. Consequently, households' consumption and saving choices are modified, with important effects on private investments.

In my opinion, a correct way to reproduce Barro's (1990) analysis is to consider public expenditures, net of transfers, as useful to households; the exponent β in the utility function defines the relative weight. If public expenditure is useful, it has positive effects on households and workers, and will produce positive externalities on production through greater labour productivity. The exponent α in the production function defines the relative weight of this externality.

This chapter examines whether the results obtained by Barro (1990, in particular in section V, pp. 117–18), are correct. In Section 10.2, I consider, as in Barro (1990), that all public consumption services, excluding expenditures on national defence and public education, enter into the household utility function. Public investment is known to exert an effect on the growth rate through the positive externality in the productivity of the capital stock. Public consumption operates differently: the substitutability between public and private consumption modifies the economy's consumption and saving decisions. Hence, whatever the fiscal policy and the composition of the public expenditure, if households positively evaluate public consumption, a higher growth rate may be obtained. In Section 10.3, I assume that the government adopts the economic policies most desired by the economic agents, and I analyse what are both the optimal tax rate and the optimal allocation of the public budget between productive investments and public consumption. As we will see, a higher income tax rate and a greater public consumption share may produce the same growth rate, that would be obtained with productive investment alone. Section 10.4 is dedicated to some concluding remarks.

10.2. A MODEL OF ENDOGENOUS GROWTH WITH PUBLIC CONSUMPTION

In order to verify the above hypothesis, I shall construct a simple model of endogenous growth with public consumption in the utility function, similar to that originally developed by Barro (1990) in section V. I assume that the government imposes a proportional income tax rate, $0 < \tau < 1$. A share $0 < q < 1$ of the public budget $\tau y(t)$ is allocated to productive investments $g(t)$ which increase the productivity of private capital stock;[8] the remaining share, $(1 - q)$, is used to supply households with public consumption $h(t)$ which increases the utility of private consumption and partly substitutes it.[9]

The production function, in terms of constant labour units,[10] is a Cobb–Douglas function with constant returns to scale in private capital stock and public investment. If the economy knows the exogenous public policy: $g(t) = q\,\tau y(t)$, we can obtain the following production function at constant returns to scale in private capital stock $k(t)$:

$$y(t) = Ak(t)^{1-\alpha}\left[q\tau y(t)\right]^{\alpha} = ak(t)(q\tau)^{\frac{\alpha}{1-\alpha}} \tag{10.1}$$

where $a = A^{1/(1-\alpha)}$.

Disposable household income is spent on private consumption and investment:

$$\dot{k}(t) = (1-\tau)y(t) - c(t) = B(q,\tau)k(t) - c(t) \qquad (10.2)$$

where: $B(q,\tau) = a(1-\tau)(q\tau)^{\alpha/(1-\alpha)}$ represents the share of productivity of the capital stock which benefits the households, net of income tax .

The utility function is hypothesized as being of the CRRA type, its arguments being per capita private consumption $c(t)$, with weight $(1-\beta)$, and per capita public consumption $h(t) = (1-q)\tau y(t)$, with weight $0 \le \beta \le 1$:[11]

$$u(t) = \frac{\left[c(t)^{1-\beta} h(t)^{\beta} \right]^{1-\sigma} - 1}{1-\sigma} = \frac{T(q,\tau)^{\beta(1-\sigma)} c(t)^{(1-\beta)(1-\sigma)} k(t)^{\beta(1-\sigma)} - 1}{1-\sigma} \qquad (10.3)$$

where: $T(q,\tau) = (1-q)a\tau(q\tau)^{\alpha/(1-\alpha)} \ge 0$ represents the share of the productivity of the capital stock that the government spends on public consumption.

The intertemporal optimum problem of households requires maximization of the current value of future utility flows, choosing the optimal consumption path $c(t)$ (*control variable*) in respect of the dynamic constraint constituted by the macroeconomic equilibrium condition (10.2); the non-negativity conditions of the capital stock and consumption: $k(t) \ge 0$, $c(t) \ge 0$; and a positive initial capital stock: $k(0) = k_0 > 0$.

We also assume that the economy considers as given and constant both the tax rate τ and the composition of public expenditure between productive investments q and public consumption $(1-q)$. In other words, *the fiscal policy is exogenous*.

The Hamiltonian function of this problem assumes the following form:

$$H[k(t), c(t), \mu(t)] = e^{-\rho t} u(t) + \mu(t) \left[B(q,\tau)k(t) - c(t) \right]$$

where $\rho > 0$ represents the intertemporal discount rate, and the *costate* variable $\mu(t)$ expresses the present value, measured in terms of marginal utility of consumption, of one additional unit of private investment.

I introduce the first-order maximum conditions obtained by deriving the Hamiltonian function with respect to the control variable $c(t)$ and the state variable $k(t)$:

$$e^{-\rho t} u_c(t) - \mu(t) = 0 \qquad \text{FOC.1} \qquad (10.4)$$

$$-\dot{\mu}(t) = e^{-\rho t} u_k(t) + \mu(t) B(q,\tau) \qquad (10.5)$$

It is also necessary to impose the limit condition:

$$\lim_{t \to \infty} \mu(t)k(t) = 0,$$

which states that the value of the capital stock at the end of the (infinite) time horizon must be zero.

Equation (10.4) defines the optimal time path of the control variable $c(t)$, setting it in relation to the time path of the shadow price $\mu(t)$. Equation (10.5) states that the optimal rate of investment must be equal to the marginal productivity of capital.

To solve the optimum problem, first of all we may rewrite (10.4) as follows:

$$e^{-\rho t}u_c(t) = \mu(t) \tag{10.4a}$$

and substitute in (10.5) to obtain the rate of variation of the costate variable:

$$-\gamma_\mu(t) = \frac{\beta}{1-\beta}\frac{c(t)}{k(t)} + B(q,\tau) \tag{10.5a}$$

where γ represents the rate of growth of a variable.

From the economy's budget constraint, we can obtain the growth rate of capital stock:

$$\gamma_k(t) = -\frac{c(t)}{k(t)} + B(q,\tau) \tag{10.6}$$

In steady state the rate of growth of the capital stock must be constant; by differentiating (10.6) with respect to time, one can demonstrate that it must be:

$$\gamma_c(t) = \gamma_k(t) \tag{10.7}$$

I take the logarithms of the condition (10.4a) and derive it with respect to time, obtaining the following relation between rates of variation:

$$-\rho + \beta(1-\sigma)[\gamma_k(t) - \gamma_c(t)] - \sigma\gamma_c(t) = \gamma_\mu(t) \tag{10.8}$$

Taking account of (10.7), the steady-state rate of growth of consumption is derived:

$$\gamma_c(t) = \frac{1}{\sigma}\left[-\gamma_\mu(t) - \rho\right] \tag{10.9}$$

Substituting (10.5a) in (10.9), we obtain:

$$\gamma_c(t) = \frac{1}{\sigma}\left[\frac{\beta}{1-\beta}\frac{c(t)}{k(t)} + B(q,\tau) - \rho\right] \tag{10.9a}$$

The optimal ratio between consumption and capital can be obtained by equalizing equations (10.9a) and (10.6):

$$\frac{c(t)}{k(t)} = \frac{1-\beta}{\sigma+\beta(1-\sigma)}[\rho - (1-\sigma)B(q,\tau)] \tag{10.10}$$

Note that to have a *positive* private consumption $c(t)/k(t)$, the following very important condition must be satisfied, *for all values of* σ, also for σ less than one:[12]

$$\frac{\rho}{1-\sigma} > B(q,\tau) \tag{10.11}$$

where $B(q,\tau)$ represents the share of productivity of the capital stock which increases the net disposable income of households and can be used for private consumption or investment.

Finally, substituting (10.10) in (10.9a) yields the rate of growth of per capita private consumption, which in steady-state conditions is constant and equal to the growth rates of the capital stock and per capita output:

$$\gamma = \frac{1}{\sigma+\beta(1-\sigma)}[B(q,\tau)-(1-\beta)\rho] \tag{10.12}$$

where:[13]

$$sign\frac{\partial\gamma}{\partial\beta} = sign\left[\frac{\rho}{1-\sigma} - B(q,\tau)\right] > 0$$

$$sign\frac{\partial\gamma}{\partial\tau} = signB_\tau = sign(\alpha-\tau)$$

$$sign\frac{\partial\gamma}{\partial q} = signB_q = sign\alpha > 0$$

Examination of equation (10.12) reveals the various channels through which public investment and consumption influence the economy's rate of growth. Public investments $(q\tau)$ positively affect the productivity parameter of composite capital (private and public), but an increase in taxes (given the composition of public budget q) reduces the disposable income of households and thus reduces private investments. An increase in public investment takes place at the expense of private investment.

Public consumption instead affects household saving decisions. If households regard this type of public expenditure favourably $(\beta > 0)$, then public consumption substitutes private consumption, thus freeing resources to increase private saving and investment (*substitution effect*). The higher the value of β, the lower is private consumption, and the higher is private investment. The highest rate of private investment is for $\beta = 1$. We may calculate the growth rates in the two extreme cases $\beta = 1$ and $\beta = 0$.

(a) In the limit case where the economy evaluated only public consumption positively $(\beta = 1)$, the growth rate of the economy would be

$$\gamma(\beta = 1) = B(q, \tau) \qquad (10.13a)$$

which is an increasing function of q and a concave one of τ, reaching its maximum for $\tau^\circ = \alpha$, and $q^\circ = 1$. In this case, the corner solution foresees null private consumption; all private income, net of tax, is invested and the growth rate is entirely explained by the constant productivity of the composite capital. Note that for $q = 1$, also the public consumption h is null as well as the utility function. Therefore, the fiscal policy $(\tau^\circ = \alpha, q^\circ = 1)$ is not feasible.

(b) By contrast, when the economy does not regard public consumption as useful $(\beta = 0)$, we have the growth rate with only public investments:

$$\gamma(\beta = 0) = \frac{1}{\sigma}[B(q, \tau) - \rho] \qquad (10.13b)$$

Note that to have a non-negative growth rate the following condition must be verified:

$$\frac{\rho}{1 - \sigma} > B(q, \tau) \geq \rho \qquad (10.11a)$$

The case $\beta = 0$ allows comparison with the results obtained by Barro (1990) in the model with public investment alone. It follows from (10.13b) that the economy's growth rate is a concave function of the tax rate which reaches its maximum for $\tau^\circ = \alpha$. Moreover, γ is an increasing function with respect to the share q of the tax yield allocated to public investments, such that the highest growth rate will be obtained at the upper extreme of the range of definition of that variable, that is, for $q^\circ = 1$.

$$\gamma^{\circ}(\tau^{\circ}=\alpha,q^{\circ}=1,\beta=0)=\frac{1}{\sigma}\left[a(1-\alpha)\alpha^{\frac{\alpha}{1-\alpha}}-\rho\right]\qquad(10.13c)$$

In general, the following result holds:

Proposition 1: $\gamma[B(q,\tau),\beta>0]-\gamma[B(q,\tau),\beta=0]>0$ *for condition (10.11)*
That is, whatever the exogenous government's policy (q,τ), if households positively evaluate public consumption, the growth rate $\gamma(\beta>0)$ is always higher than it would be in the case of productive investments alone $\gamma(\beta=0)$.

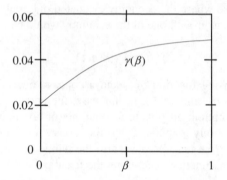

Figure 10.1   The rate of growth $\gamma(\beta)$ in relation to the relative weight of the public consumption. Values of the parameters: $\alpha=0.4$, $\sigma=0.6$, $\rho=0.03$, $a=0.2$, for a given policy (q,τ).

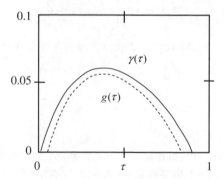

Figure 10.2   Comparison between the rate of growth $\gamma(\tau,\beta>0)$ (solid line) and the rate of growth $\gamma(\tau,\beta=0)$ (dotted line). Values of the parameters: $\alpha=0.4$, $\sigma=0.6$, $\rho=0.03$, $a=0.2$, $\beta=0.3$, $q=0.9$.

When β is positive, the policy $(\tau^\circ = \alpha,\ q^\circ = 1)$, which maximizes the growth rate, implies null public consumption, and the utility function too would be zero. Therefore the following proposition can be maintained:

Proposition 2: *When the economy positively evaluates public consumption, the fiscal policy* $(\tau^\circ = \alpha,\ q^\circ = 1)$, *which maximizes the growth rate, cannot be feasible as the value of economy's utility function is null, that is* $u(\tau^\circ = \alpha,\ q^\circ = 1) = 0$.

In conclusion, also public consumption may be a valid means to promote growth (Proposition 1). The reason is that the availability of public consumption substitutes private consumption, and enables households to save and invest more. The greater the weight of public consumption β in the utility function, the more robust this substitution effect will be.

However, the allocation of the public budget between public investment and public consumption is undetermined and cannot be that which maximizes the growth rate (Proposition 2) even in the extreme cases, $\beta = 0$ or $\beta = 1$. The next section is devoted to analysing this problem.

10.3. OPTIMAL ENDOGENOUS FISCAL POLICY

The above solution of the optimum problem was performed under the following hypotheses: (i) the economy knows perfectly and takes account of the public-sector budget constraint and its composition; (ii) the income tax rate τ and the allocation of public spending between public investment q and public consumption $(1 - q)$ are considered exogenous and constant.

Let us now drop hypothesis (ii), imagining that the electoral choices of the economy – at least in a long-term framework consistent with the treatment of growth problems – may induce governments to establish optimal values for both the tax rate τ^* and the share q^* of the public budget. That is to say, the government may set those values which maximize the present value of the future flows of utility deriving from both private and public consumption.[14]

For this purpose we must zero-set the prime derivatives of the Hamiltonian function with respect to the policy variables τ and q, taking account of FOC.1 (equation (10.4)), which defines the optimal path of private consumption $c(t)$:

$$e^{-\rho t} u_\tau + \mu(t) k(t) B_\tau = 0 \qquad\qquad \text{FOC.2} \qquad (10.15)$$

$$e^{-\rho t} u_q + \mu(t) k(t) B_q = 0 \qquad\qquad \text{FOC.3} \qquad (10.16)$$

From these conditions we obtain the following relation between marginal utilities and marginal productivity of the composite capital stock:

$$\frac{u_q}{u_\tau} = \frac{u_T T_q}{u_T T_\tau} = \frac{T_q}{T_\tau} = \frac{B_q}{B\tau} \ . \tag{10.17}$$

That is, the relative effects of the public policies q and τ on the marginal utilities must be equal to the relative effects on the marginal productivity of the capital stock, net of income tax.

From (10.17), bearing in mind the values of the partial derivatives, we obtain the optimal relation between the income tax rate τ and the share of the public budget allocated to investments q:

$$q^* = \frac{\alpha}{\tau} \qquad 0 < q^* < 1 \tag{10.18}$$

Equation (10.18) suggests two interesting considerations. The share of public investments must diminish as the public budget increases; but the share on income is constant and equal to α. Moreover, because q^* must be less than unity, in order to leave a positive share of public consumption, it follows that τ^* must be greater than α. Recall that $\tau^\circ = \alpha$ and $q^\circ = 1$ are the values which maximize the rate of income growth, γ°, but these values nullify the economy's utility function.

Combining FOC.3 (equation (10.16)) with FOC.1 (equation (10.4)), the optimal consumption/capital ratio is obtained:

$$\frac{c(t)}{k(t)} = \frac{1-\beta}{\beta} B(q,\tau) \frac{\tau - \alpha}{1 - \tau} > 0 \qquad \text{if}: \ \tau > \alpha \tag{10.19}$$

Finally, equalizing equations (10.19) and (10.10), and taking account of equation (10.18), the optimal tax rate τ^* is determined:

$$\tau^* = \alpha + \frac{\beta(1-\alpha)}{\sigma}\left[-(1-\sigma) + \frac{\rho}{a(1-\alpha)\alpha^{\alpha/1-\alpha}}\right]$$

The optimal income tax rate τ^* must be greater than α in order to ensure positive public consumption, $(1 - q^*) > 0$, and less than unity to ensure positive private consumption. But it is easy to verify that $\tau^* > \alpha$ for condition (10.11) and $\tau^* < 1$ for $\beta < \beta_{max} \leq 1$ for condition (10.11a) (see Figure 10.3).

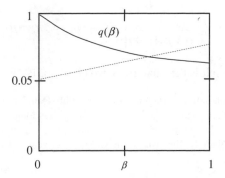

Figure 10.3 The optimal income tax rate (dotted line) and the optimal share of productive investments (solid line). Values of the parameters: $a = 0.5$, $\sigma = 0.5$, $\rho = 0.04$, $a = 0.2$.

Interestingly, the optimal income tax rate depends on the preferences between public and private consumption β, and the intertemporal discount rate ρ:[15]

$$sign\frac{\partial \tau^*}{\partial \beta} = sign\left[\frac{\rho}{1-\sigma} - B(q^*, \tau^*)\right] > 0$$

$$sign\frac{\partial \tau^*}{\partial \rho} = sign\beta \geq 0$$

Hence, as household impatience increases, the economy prefers greater intervention by the government, which implies a greater share of public consumption. This result, however, is closely related to the weight β that households attribute to public consumption. When households are very 'patient', such that they evaluate present and future consumption in the same way, $\rho = 0$, the optimal tax rate is low or zero. For higher values of ρ, as households' impatience to consume increases, the economy is willing to accept a tax rate τ^* greater than $\tau^\circ = \alpha$, and a positive share $(1 - q^*) > 0$ of the public consumption.

In the admissible range of the optimal income tax rate, the solution of the optimum problem can be rewritten thus:

$$\alpha < \tau^* < 1$$

$$0 < q^* = \frac{\alpha}{\tau^*} < 1 \tag{10.22}$$

$$\gamma^*(\tau^*) = \frac{1}{\sigma + \beta(1-\sigma)}\left[a(1-\tau^*)\alpha^{\frac{\alpha}{1-\alpha}} - (1-\beta)\rho \right]$$

Note that this result is the same by Barro (1990, p. 118):

> Combining these conditions for the case of a Cobb–Douglas production function leads to the familiar results: $\tau_g = g/y = \alpha$. That is, as long as $\tau_h = h/y$ is also chosen optimally, the optimal ratio for productive government expenditures is the same as before. Namely, the criterion is still productive efficiency, so that $\phi' = 1$ and $g/y = \alpha$.

But the public budget is greater $\tau^* > \tau^° = \alpha$; it is easy to verify that, if τ^* were equal to α and hence $q^* = 1$, the value of the utility function (equation 10.3) would be null and could not be a maximum.

Moreover, the optimal growth rate $\gamma^*(\tau^* > \alpha, q^* < 1, \beta > 0)$ may be equal to the growth rate $\gamma^°(\tau^° > \alpha, q^° < 1, \beta > 0)$ obtained by maximizing the exogenous growth rate in the case of productive expenditure only. This result contradicts Barro (1990), who maintains: 'The growth rate lies uniformly below the value y, ..., that would have been chosen if $\tau_h = 0$' (p. 117).

Proposition 3: *When households choose the optimal policy* (τ^*, q^*), *an optimal growth rate* $\gamma^*(\tau^* > \alpha, q^* < 1, \beta > 0)$ *equal to the maximum one* $\gamma^°(\tau^° = \alpha, q^° = 1, \beta = 0)$ *is obtained through a different fiscal policy.*

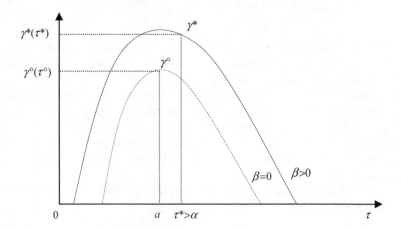

Figure 10.4   The optimal tax rate τ^*, *the optimal rate of growth* $y^*(\tau)$ *(solid line) and Barro's growth rate* $y^°(\tau)$ *(dotted line) in relation to income tax rate.* y^* *and* $y^°$ *are respectively the optimal and maximum rate of growth.*

The two growth rates, the optimal y^*, and the maximum $y°$, may coincide when the optimal income tax rate τ^* is higher than $\tau° = \alpha$, and public spending is partially devoted to public consumption: $q^* < 1$. When this value of the optimal income tax rate has been exceeded, households are willing to accept a lower growth rate provided that an increasing share of the public budget is allocated to public consumption.

10.4.   CONCLUSIONS

The foregoing analysis has enabled me to verify the robustness of Barro's (1990) findings that the most powerful policy instrument to influence the economic growth rate is public spending on productive investments. The latter interact with private productive capital to increase its productivity, giving rise to a positive externality. Consequently, composite capital displays constant returns to scale and the economy is able to grow, in steady state, at a constant rate positively correlated with the tax rate τ until the latter is less than the contribution α of public investments to output. Above this threshold, an increase in the tax rate reduces the growth rate due to the reduction in disposable income (taxation effect).

When we consider that a share of the public budget is allocated to public consumption, which interacts with private consumption to increase its utility, a further channel for influence on the growth rate is opened. Public consumption operates through the economy's decisions of saving and investment (*substitution effect*). Therefore, by applying the same exogenous fiscal policy (that is the same income tax rate τ and the same share of productive investment, it is possible to obtain a higher growth rate than that obtained with public investment only (Proposition 1). The difference between the two rates is due to a different intertemporal elasticity of substitution, which depends on the weight of public consumption β in the utility function. Therefore, the growth rate is an increasing concave function of β.

If we assume that the government adopts the policies most desired by households, one may determine the optimal values of both the income tax rate τ^* and the share q^* of productive investments. The growth rate deriving from them, $\gamma^*(\tau^* > \alpha, q^* < 1)$, may be equal to the maximum one, $\gamma°(\tau° = \alpha, q° = 1)$.

Finally, because the optimal tax rate τ^* depends positively on the discount rate, if the economy looks to the future with confidence and optimism (the discount rate is low), then it prefers a lower level of intervention by the government and a high optimum rate of growth. On the contrary, if the economy is pessimistic about its future prospects (the discount rate is high), then it is well-disposed to a high level of intervention by the government, which also provides for public consumption, although the optimal rate of growth is lower.

NOTES

*   I am indebted to Alberto Bucci, Antonio Ciccone, Fabio Fiorillo, Tommaso Luzzati, Alberto Niccoli, Mario Pomini, Maurizio Pugno, Stefano Staffolani for their useful comments and suggestions. All remaining errors and omissions are entirely my responsibility.

1.   The contributions that have given rise to New Growth Theory are the following: Romer (1986, 1990); Lucas (1988); Barro (1990); Rebelo (1991); Aghion and Howitt (1992).

2.   As regards neoclassical growth theory, reference is made principally to Robert Solow's (1956) model. On the economic policy implications of new growth theory see the following works: Scott (1992), Shaw (1992).

3.   For a different hypothesis, see Jones and Manueli (1990).

4.   For an interesting survey of the literature on fiscal policy and economic growth, see Zagler and Durneker (2003). In a recent paper, Peretto (2003) shows that in a model of endogenous growth that does not exhibit the scale effect, the level and composition of public expenditure have no effect on steady-state growth, but only on per capita income. See also Futagami, Morita and Shibata (1993), Greiner and Hanush (1998), Bajo-Rubio (2000).

5.   Barro (1990). See also Barro and Sala-I-Martin (1992, 1995). Public investments are non-rival and non-excludable, like public goods.

6.   That is, an 'AK' production function as defined by Rebelo (1991).

7.   See also Barro and Sala-I-Martin (1992). Figures from 98 countries in the 1960–95 period show a negative and significative relationship between public consumption and per capita growth rate of GNP.

8.   As in Barro (1990), I assume that the government purchases a portion of the private output and uses it to provide free public services to private producers (infrastructure services, protection of property rights, such as police services and national defence, and so on). In Barro (1990, p. 117), the government determines both the ratio $(h/y) = \tau_h$ of the consumption services, and the ratio $(g/y) = \tau_g$ for productive services; then the total public budget follows: $(\tau_g + \tau_h)y$. In my model, on the contrary, the government chooses the total budget τy and the share of this budget devoted to productive services q; the share of the public budget for consumption services follows as a consequence.

9.   Many public goods are degradable and rival to some extent, or in the current terminology *congested*. For example, a swimming pool is an excludable public service, but when it becomes crowded, customers adversely affect each other's welfare. Analogously, a toll road or a public library may be an excludable public good, but jams happen even these cases. When congestion is taken into account, it is possible to construct an incentive compatible mechanism which ensures the efficient production of public goods and satisfies individual rationality constraints (see Birulin, 2003). However, in our context the problem of the optimal supply of public goods is not considered for the simple reason that phenomena of congestion or performance degradation may also occur in the case of some private goods with externalities (for example: a congested network like the Internet).

10.   For simplicity, the units of population at the initial date are normalized to 1 and the growth rate of the population is assumed to be nil.

11.   In a recent article, Flessig and Rossana (2003) find considerable evidence that private consumption (non-durable goods, services and the stock of durable goods) and government

expenditures (federal defence expenditures, federal non-defence expenditures, state and local expenditures) are net substitutes, even if the elasticity of substitution is not high.

12. As we see later, all signs of the derivatives in the optimum problem depend on (10.11).

13. $\partial^2 \gamma / \partial \beta^2 > 0$; thus the function is increasing and concave; see Figure 10.1.

14. If we wish to state the problem in game theory terms, we may say that the government and the economy have the same utility function and *cooperate* to achieve the common maximum of the same functional objective. This is therefore a *cooperative game* undertaken by a hypothetical benevolent planner.

15. The first inequality is a consequence of inequality (10.11).

REFERENCES

Aghion, P. and P. Howitt (1992), 'A model of growth through creative destruction', *Econometrica*, **60**, 323–51.

Bajo-Rubio, O. (2000), 'A further generalization of the Solow growth model: the role of the public sector', *Economic Letters*, **68**, 79–84.

Barro, R.J. (1990), 'Government spending in a simple model of endogenous growth', *Journal of Political Economy*, **98**, 103–25.

Barro, R.J. and X. Sala-I-Martin (1992), 'Public finance in models of economic growth', *Review of Economic Studies*, **59**(4), 645–61.

Barro, R.J. and X. Sala-I-Martin (1995), *Economic Growth*, New York: McGraw-Hill.

Birulin, O. (2003), 'Public goods with congestion: a mechanism design approach', December 5, Dept. of Economics, The Pennsylvania State University.

Bloom, D.E, D. Canning and J. Sevilla (2001), 'The effect of health on economic growth: theory and evidence', NBER Working Paper no. 8587.

Flessig, A.R. and R.J. Rossana (2003), 'Are consumption and government expenditures substitutes or complements? Morishima elasticity estimates from the fourier flexible form', *Economic Inquiry*, **41**(1), 132–46.

Futagami, K., Y. Morita and S. Akihisa (1993) 'Dynamic analysis of an endogenous growth model with public capital', *Scandinavian Journal of Economics*, **95**, 607–25.

Greiner, A. and H. Hanusch (1998), 'Growth and welfare effects of fiscal policy in an endogenous growth model with public investment', *International Tax and Public Finance*, **5**(3), 249–61.

Jones, L.E. and R.E. Manueli (1990), 'A convex model of equilibrium growth: theory and policy implications', *Journal of Political Economy*, **88**, 1008–38.

Lucas, R. (1988), 'On the mechanics of economic development', *Journal of Monetary Economics*, **22**, 3–42.

Peretto, P.F. (2003), 'Fiscal policy and long-run growth in R&D-based models with endogenous market structure', *Journal of Economic Growth*, **8**, 325–47.

Rebelo, S.T. (1991), 'Long-run policy analysis and long-run growth', *Journal of Political Economy*, **99**, 500–521.

Romer, P.M. (1986), 'Increasing returns and long-run growth', *Journal of Political Economy*, **94**, 1002–37.

Romer, P.M. (1990), 'Endogenous technological change', *Journal of Political Economy*, **98**, 71–101.

Scott, M.F. (1992), 'Policy implications of "a new view of economic growth"', *Economic Journal*, **102**, 622–32.

Shaw, K.G. (1992), 'Policy implications of endogenous growth theory', *Economic Journal*, **102**, 611–21.

Solow, R. (1956), 'A contribution to the theory of economic growth', *Quarterly Journal of Economics*, **70**, 65–94.

Turnovsky, S.J. (1996), 'Optimal tax, debt and expenditure policies in a growing economy', *Journal of Public Economics*, **60**, 21–44.

Turnovsky, S.J. (2000), 'Fiscal policy, elastic labour supply, and endogenous growth', *Journal of Monetary Economics*, **45**, 185–210.

Zagler, M. and G. Durneker (2003), 'Fiscal policy and economic growth', *Journal of Economic Surveys*, **17**(3), 397–418.

11. Government debt, growth and inequality in income distribution: a post-Keynesian analysis

Pasquale Commendatore, Carlo Panico and Antonio Pinto

11.1. INTRODUCTION

Since the 1970s an economic theory in favour of free competition and minimal government regulation has prevailed in the literature. Within the new growth theories, developed since the 1980s, the supremacy of this position has not precluded the analysis of the government sector. Yet this literature has played down the analysis of the effects of changes in government deficits and debt on the inequality in income distribution. It has replaced, in representative agent models, the traditional concept of debt sustainability with the assumption that the present value of government debt must be equal to zero,[1] pushing these models towards focussing on policies carried out with a balanced budget. Some works using overlapping generation models, however, have not followed this line and have reached the conclusion that an increase in government deficits and debt reduces the rate of growth, without examining, in any case, its effect on the inequality in income distribution.[2]

A greater interest in the connection between government intervention and distribution can be found in the Keynesian literature, which has recently seen an intense debate on how government policies carried out with an unbalanced budget can be introduced within the post Keynesian theory of growth and distribution.[3] This debate has focussed on the validity of the 'Pasinetti' and 'anti-Pasinetti' theorems and of the 'Cambridge equation'. In some cases, it has also examined the possibility of reconciling the position on the determinants of distribution proposed by Kaldor and Pasinetti with that of the authors in favour of a monetary theory of distribution, where the money rate of interest determines the rate of profits. Yet the analysis of how changes in government deficits and debt affect the differentials in the distribution of income and wealth among classes has also been neglected by the Keynesian literature.

One important exception to this trend is the article by You and Dutt (1996). They start from the consideration that some economists close to Keynesian positions have jumped on the bandwagon against government intervention and the accumulation of government debt, arguing that 'tax revenues from the working class are used to pay for the interest on the government debt which is owned almost exclusively by a small minority of wealthy individuals, so that government debt contributes to income inequality' (p. 336). According to You and Dutt, this opinion is based on 'impressionistic arguments' since 'the connection between debt and income distribution mentioned above has largely escaped serious economic analysis' (p. 336). They thus try to fill this lacuna by examining a rigorous theoretical model belonging to the Kaleckian tradition.

Making a similar attempt to that of You and Dutt, below we present a model belonging to the Kaldor–Pasinetti tradition, where two classes (workers and *rentiers*) participate in the process of production and distribution.[4] The model considers an economy with similar features to that of You and Dutt. The main differences are that it introduces an explicit relation between the rates of interest and profit and allows the working class to save, so that the income of the workers consists of wages, interests and profits. The fact that a wide range of income sources accrues to each social group is considered by Atkinson (1997) an important feature of modern societies, a feature that, according to Atkinson, makes the analysis of the 'personal' distribution of income the most significant way to study at present the phenomenon of income inequality.

The results achieved in what follows are clear-cut and present some differences with those of You and Dutt. They deal with the effects of government interventions on the distribution of both wealth and income and on the rate of growth. Those on the distribution of wealth are not examined by You and Dutt, owing to the assumption that workers have no wealth. The results achieved in this chapter show that a larger government deficit produces a higher government debt, an increase in the rentiers' quota of wealth and a reduction in the workers' quota. Shifting our focus to the effects on the distribution of income, a larger government deficit produces a higher government debt and an increase in the rentiers' total revenues, measured in terms of the net income of the economy. As to the effects on the total revenues of the working class, measured in terms of the net income of the economy, they are the following: if the rate is stabilized at a given level, the pre-tax total revenues remain constant, while the after-tax ones increase, like those of the rentiers. Thus, a larger government deficit and debt makes both classes better off, as far as their earnings are concerned. However, income inequality increases, since the benefits received by the rentiers are greater than those received by the workers. On the other hand, if the rate of interest is not exogenously given, both the pre-tax and after-tax revenues of the working class decrease. Finally, the model shows that an increase in the government deficit has a positive effect on the rate of growth, while a change in the rate of interest leaves the rate of growth constant.

The economic mechanisms through which the results on the effects on income distribution are achieved in the present model differ from those outlined by the analysis of You and Dutt. First of all, the constancy of the workers' pre-tax total revenues can be seen as a particular application of the Pasinetti theorem to the model considered here. Secondly, the increase in the workers' after tax total revenues is due to the reduction in the tax rate associated with the larger deficit. Thirdly, contrary to what is maintained by those Keynesian economists, mentioned by You and Dutt, who have jumped on the bandwagon against government intervention, the increased income inequality does not stem from the fact that the rentiers own a larger quota of government debt than the workers. It is due to the rentiers' propensity to save being greater than that of the working class. The inequality increases, whatever the quota of wealth owned by the working class. Fourthly the stabilization of the rate of interest at a given level is what allows an expanding fiscal policy to bring about benefits for the working class.

The chapter is organized as follows. In Section 11.2 we present the model used to examine the issue under consideration. Section 11.3 analyses the solutions of the model. Section 11.4 considers the effects of changes in the government deficit and in the rate of interest on the rate of growth, and on the distribution of wealth and income between the two classes.

11.2. THE MODEL

The main difficulty in formulating an analytical model to study the problem under consideration is to increase the complexity of the economy represented without precluding the achievement of analytical results.

The economy considered is similar to that examined by You and Dutt. It is a closed economy with no inflation, two classes (workers and rentiers), and two assets (real capital and government bonds). Workers, unlike what is assumed by You and Dutt, have positive savings. They thus have a positive amount of wealth, invested in real capital and government debt, and earn, beside wages, profits and interests. Rentiers only earn profits and interests. The two classes have the same portfolio structure. The government collects taxes, demands goods and services, funds its deficits by issuing bonds, and pays interest on its debt. Another difference from You and Dutt's analysis is that the rate of profits is related to the rate of interest: the two rates move together in the same direction. Finally, unlike You and Dutt, we follow Pasinetti's approach to the theory of growth and distribution and develop a steady growth analysis where the degree of capital utilization is always at the same normal level. This analysis determines the 'personal' distribution of income, which can be considered the most significant way to study the phenomenon of income inequality.

Let us introduce the model by describing the dynamic equilibrium conditions of the government sector and of the two classes:

$$gb = \delta + R_b b \tag{11.1}$$

$$g\alpha(b+k) = s_r(1-\tau)\pi_r \tag{11.2}$$

$$g(1-\alpha)(b+k) = s_w(1-\tau)\pi_w \tag{11.3}$$

$$\pi_r = \alpha(r_k k + R_b b) \tag{11.4}$$

$$\pi_w = 1 - r_k \alpha k + R_b(1-\alpha)b \tag{11.5}$$

where:
g is the rate of growth of the economy;
b is the stock of government debt measured in terms of the net income of the economy;
δ is the government 'primary' deficit, that is the deficit net of interest payments, measured in terms of the net income of the economy;
R_b is the rate of interest paid on government debt;
α is the rentiers' quota of total wealth;
k is the stock of real capital measured in terms of the net income of the economy;
s_r is the propensity to save of the rentiers ($0 < s_r < 1$);
τ is the tax rate;
π_r is the total revenues of the rentiers, measured in terms of the net income of the economy;
s_w is the propensity to save of the working class ($0 < s_w < s_r < 1$);
π_w is the total revenues of the working class, measured in terms of the net income of the economy;
r_k is the rate of profits;

The investment demand function is described by the following equation, which extends the analysis traditionally proposed by Kaldor and Pasinetti by following the view of J. Robinson on this point:

$$g = a_0 + a_1(1-\tau)r_k \tag{11.6}$$

The rates of interest and profits are linked by the following equation, which maintains the analysis at a simplified level by following the views expressed by the classical political economists and by Marx,[5] according to whom the rate of interest is a portion of the rate of profit:

$$r_k = \beta R_b \quad \text{with } \beta > 1 \tag{11.7}$$

Following Kaldor we then assume that the capital–output ratio is constant

$$k = \overline{k} \tag{11.8}$$

Finally we assume that the authorities fix the rate of interest on government bonds[6] and the government deficit.[7]

$$R_b = \overline{R}_b \tag{11.9}$$

$$\delta + R_b b = \overline{d} \geq 0 \tag{11.10}$$

The previous ten equations contain ten unknowns, that is $b, R_b, \delta, r_k, g, k, \alpha, \tau, \pi_r, \pi_w$.

In the model, the 'functional' distribution of income (that is, the rate of interest, the rate of profits and the wage rate) is unaffected by variations in the government deficit, which depend on changes in the tax rate and in the government demand for goods and services. These variations influence the net output of the economy and the 'personal' distribution of income of the two classes, due to the effect on the tax rate and on interests and profits received on their wealth.

In the analysis of You and Dutt too, variations in the government deficit do not affect the 'functional' distribution of income: the interest rate, the profit share and the wage share of income remain constant. However, the tax rates are given, such that only variations in the government demand for goods and services produce a change in the government deficit and have a direct effect on the net output of the economy. Indirect effects may come about because of variations in the personal distribution of income. Yet these effects only regard the personal income of the capitalist class and are due to the interest payments this class receives for its holding of government bonds.

11.3. SOLUTIONS OF THE MODEL

To examine the solutions of the model we can start by presenting the previous ten equations in a simplified form and then calculate the equilibrium values of the unknowns. From equations (11.3)–(11.9), we can obtain the following equalities, where the rate of growth, the after-tax interest rate, the primary deficit, the workers' quota of total wealth and the total revenues of the rentiers only depend on the value of b, the government debt measured in terms of the net income of the economy:

$$g = g_0 \frac{\bar{k}\beta + b}{\bar{k}\beta(1 - \lambda b)} \tag{11.11}$$

$$\bar{R}_b(1 - \tau) = \frac{g_0}{s_r} \frac{\bar{k} + b}{\bar{k}\beta(1 - \lambda b)} \tag{11.12}$$

$$\delta = \bar{d} - \bar{R}_b b \tag{11.13}$$

$$1 - \alpha = \frac{s_w}{s_r - s_w} \frac{1 - \bar{k}\beta\bar{R}_b}{(\bar{k}\beta + b)\bar{R}_b} \tag{11.14}$$

$$\pi_r = 1 + \bar{R}_b b - \frac{s_r}{s_r - s_w}\left(1 - \bar{k}\beta\bar{R}_b\right) \tag{11.15}$$

where $g_0 \equiv (a_0 s_r)/(s_r - a_1)$ is the rate of growth at $b = 0$ and $\lambda \equiv -[s_r - a_1\beta / \bar{k}\beta(s_r - a_1)]$.

We assume that $s_r > a_1$, hence $g_0 > 0$ and $\lambda \gtreqless 0$ for $s_r \gtreqless a_1\beta$. This assumption is in line with the post Keynesian literature (see Marglin, 1984, and Lavoie, 1992).

Moreover, from equations (11.3)–(11.9), the following equality can be derived:

$$\pi_w = \frac{s_r}{s_r - s_w}\left(1 - \bar{k}\beta\bar{R}_b\right) \tag{11.16}$$

where the pre-tax total revenues of the working class, measured in terms of the net income of the economy, can be directly determined since they depend on the given interest rate, but not on the stock of government bonds.

The fact that the pre-tax income of the working class is invariant with respect to changes in the government deficit and in the stock of government bonds is a preliminary result of the analysis developed here. This can be seen as an application of the Pasinetti theorem to the model presented here. According to this theorem, as equations (11.2) and (11.4) show, the savings of the economy are equal to the savings that the rentiers would generate if they were paid all interests and profits. The dynamic equilibrium conditions thus imply that the workers' savings out of their wages must be equal to the additional savings that the rentiers would generate if the interests and profits paid to workers were instead paid to them:

$$s_w(1-\tau)(1-r_k\overline{k}) = (s_r - s_w)(1-\tau)(1-\alpha)(r_k\overline{k}+\overline{R}_b b) \qquad (11.17)$$

From equation (11.17), taking into account equations (11.7) and (11.9), we can see that what is paid to the working class as interests and profits, that is the term $(1-\alpha)(r_k k + R_b b)$, is constant. Thus, as long as the interest rate on government bonds is exogenously given, the pre-tax income received by the working class is not affected by variations in the government deficit and debt.[8] This result, which is related to the dynamic equilibrium conditions, can be extended to more complex models. It can be extended, for instance, to models with inflation where government deficits are funded through the issue of bonds and money paying no return, provided that equations (11.7) and (11.9) on the relationship between the rates of interest and profits and the exogenous determination of the interest rate are confirmed.

In order to obtain the equilibrium value for the government debt, we substitute equations (11.9)–(11.11) into equation (11.1):

$$-\frac{g_0 b^2 + \overline{k}\beta(\overline{d}\lambda + g_0)b - \overline{k}\beta\overline{d}}{\overline{k}\beta(1-\lambda b)} = 0 \qquad (11.18)$$

Equation (11.18) has two solutions. The non-negative one is

$$b^* = \frac{-\overline{k}\beta(\overline{d}\lambda + g_0) + \sqrt{\Delta_b}}{2g_0} \quad \text{where} \quad \Delta_b \equiv \overline{k}^2\beta^2(\overline{d}\lambda + g_0)^2 + 4\overline{k}\beta\overline{d}g_0 \quad (11.19)$$

The model gives economically meaningful solutions for the other variables when $\lambda b^* < 1$. Moreover, to have $0 < \alpha < 1$, (that is to have an equilibrium with two classes), then $s_w - (s_r - s_w)\overline{R}_b b < s_r\overline{k}\beta\overline{R}_b < s_r$ must occur.

11.4. EFFECTS OF GOVERNMENT INTERVENTIONS ON THE GROWTH RATE AND INCOME AND WEALTH DISTRIBUTION

By comparing different steady growth solutions, the analysis presented in the previous section allows us to evaluate how changes in government interventions affect the growth rate of the economy and the distribution of income and wealth between the two classes.[9]

We consider, in the first place, how changes in the government deficit vary the stock of government bonds measured in terms of the net income of the economy, the tax rate, the growth rate of the economy, and the distribution of wealth and income. Subsequently, we examine how variations in the rate of interest on government bonds produce effects on the same variables.

By calculating the partial derivative of equation (11.19) with respect to the government deficit we obtain the following result, which indicates that the stock of government debt in terms of net output of the economy varies in the same direction as the government deficit:

$$\frac{\partial b^*}{\partial \bar{d}} = \bar{k}\beta(1 - \lambda b^*)\Delta_b^{-1/2} > 0 \qquad (11.20)$$

By calculating the partial derivative of equation (11.12) with respect to the government deficit, we can see that the tax rate moves instead in the opposite direction:

$$\frac{\partial(1-\tau^*)}{\partial \bar{d}} = \frac{\partial(1-\tau^*)}{\partial b^*}\frac{\partial b^*}{\partial \bar{d}} = \frac{g_0(1+\lambda\bar{k})}{s_r \bar{k}\beta\bar{R}_b(1-\lambda b^*)^2}\frac{\partial b^*}{\partial \bar{d}} > 0 \qquad (11.21)$$

Thus, an increase in the overall deficit brings about a reduction in the tax rate. Moreover, if we specify the effect on government expenditure as well, we obtain that it is not determined, that is the sign of the partial derivative of this expenditure with respect to $\bar{d}$ can be either positive or negative.

The effect of changes in $\bar{d}$ on the tax rate and government expenditure follows from the maintenance of steady growth conditions according to which government debt grows at the same rate as the economy. These conditions entail that when the debt/income ratio rises following the deficit increase, the rate of growth must also rise.[10] Owing to equation (11.6), g can only increase if the tax rate diminishes, as shown by the following partial derivative, taking into account that $r_k = \beta\bar{R}_b$:

$$\frac{\partial g^*}{\partial \bar{d}} = a_1 \beta\bar{R}_b \frac{\partial(1-\tau^*)}{\partial \bar{d}} > 0 \qquad (11.22)$$

In the model presented here, therefore, an expanding fiscal policy favours growth, contrary to what is obtained by some recent articles using overlapping generation models within the new growth theories (see Brauninger, 2002). Moreover, the result of expression (11.22) is confirmed when we take, as an alternative way to close the model, the tax rate as exogenously given and the rate of interest as an endogenous variable. In this case, an expanding fiscal policy generates a positive effect on R_b and r_k. This, in turn, produces again an increase in g.

Moving on to effects on the distribution of wealth, by calculating the partial derivative of equation (11.14) with respect to the government deficit, we can see that an expanding fiscal policy increases the quota of wealth owned by the *rentiers* and reduces that of the workers.

$$\frac{\partial\left(1-\alpha^*\right)}{\partial\bar{d}} = -\frac{s_w\left(1-\bar{k}\beta\bar{R}_b\right)}{\bar{R}_b(s_r-s_w)\left(\bar{k}\beta+b^*\right)^2}\frac{\partial b^*}{\partial\bar{d}} < 0 \qquad (11.23)$$

Expanding fiscal policies thus have a negative effect on wealth inequality.

The above results, (11.20)–(11.23), can also be presented through Figure 11.1, drawn for the case $\lambda < 0$, where an increase of $\bar{d}$ is assumed. In the first quadrant we plot equations (11.1) and (11.11); in the second we plot equation (11.6); and in the fourth we draw equation (11.14).

Turning to the issue of income distribution, notice that the total revenue of the rentiers, measured in terms of the net income of the economy, is also positively affected by an expanding fiscal policy, as can be seen by deriving equation (11.15) with respect to the government deficit:

$$\frac{\partial\pi_r^*}{\partial\bar{d}} = \bar{R}_b\frac{\partial b^*}{\partial\bar{d}} > 0 \qquad \frac{\partial(1-\tau^*)\pi_r^*}{\partial\bar{d}} > 0 \qquad (11.24)$$

This positive effect applies to both the pre-tax and after-tax total revenue of this class.

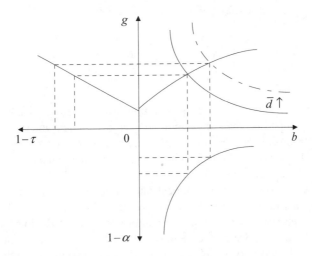

Figure 11.1 Effects of an increase in the government deficit on the rate of growth, the tax rate and wealth distribution

Finally, the effect of an expanding fiscal policy on the total revenues of the working class is null if the pre-tax revenues are considered, and positive if the after-tax revenues are examined. This is shown by the partial derivative of equation (11.16) with respect to the government deficit:

$$\frac{\partial \pi_w^*}{\partial \overline{d}} = 0 \qquad \frac{\partial (1-\tau^*)\pi_w^*}{\partial \overline{d}} > 0 \qquad (11.25)$$

The partial derivative on the left-hand side confirms what was pointed out in Section 11.3 above. The invariance of the pre-tax revenues of the working class comes from the fact that the increase in the workers' holding of government debt is exactly compensated by the reduction in their quota of wealth. What this class receives as interests and profits, measured in terms of the net income of the economy, remains constant. At the same time, the partial derivative on the right-hand side shows that the reduction in the tax rate allows the workers to receive higher after-tax total revenues, measured in terms of the net income of the economy.

Thus, a higher government deficit increases the after-tax revenues of both classes. In relative terms, however, the benefits received by the *rentiers* are larger than those received by the workers, such that, although both classes are better off, income inequality increases, as shown by the following expressions:

$$\frac{\partial}{\partial b^*}\left(\frac{\pi_r^*}{\pi_w^*}\right) = \frac{s_r - s_w}{s_r}\frac{\overline{R}_b}{1-\overline{k}\,\beta\overline{R}_b} > 0 \qquad (11.26a)$$

$$\frac{\partial}{\partial \overline{d}}\left(\frac{\pi_r^*}{\pi_w^*}\right) = \frac{s_r - s_w}{s_r}\frac{\overline{R}_b}{1-\overline{k}\,\beta\overline{R}_b}\frac{\partial b^*}{\partial \overline{d}} > 0 \qquad (11.26b)$$

This result, contrary to what is submitted by those Keynesian economists who have jumped on the bandwagon against government intervention, does not stem from the fact that the *rentiers* own a larger quota of government debt than the workers. The inequality increases, whatever the quota of wealth owned by the working class, as long as $s_r > s_w$.

The assumption of a given interest rate on government bonds is relevant for the effects on the revenues of the workers. Stabilization of the interest rate at a given level by the monetary authorities prevents the increase in this rate and the occurrence of the negative effects on the pre-tax and after-tax revenues of the workers, which are clarified by expression (11.30) below.[11]

To complete the impact of government interventions on growth and distribution, we can now examine how changes in the rate of interest on bonds affect the other variables of the model. First of all, we note, by calculating the partial derivative of equation (11.19) with respect to R_b, that the stock of government debt, measured in terms of the net income of the economy, is not affected by this event:

$$\frac{\partial b^*}{\partial \overline{R}_b} = 0 \qquad (11.27)$$

This apparently counter-intuitive result is due to the fact that in the model examined here the government deficit is constant, such that an increase in interest payment by the public sector is exactly compensated by a reduction in its primary deficit.[12]

An increase in R_b, on the other hand, increases the tax rate, as shown by the partial derivative of equation (11.12):

$$\frac{\partial(1-\tau^*)}{\partial \overline{R}_b} = -\frac{g_0}{s_r} \frac{\overline{k}+b^*}{\overline{k}\beta(1-\lambda b^*)\overline{R}_b^2} < 0 \qquad (11.28)$$

The effect of an increase in the rate of interest on the growth rate is:

$$\frac{\partial g^*}{\partial \overline{R}_b} = 0 \qquad (11.29)$$

This is due to the negative effect on growth of higher tax rates counterbalancing the positive effect of higher rates of profits such that variations in the interest rate do not affect the after-tax rate of profits.[13]

The effect of changes in the interest rate on wealth and income distribution is always in favour of the relative position of the rentiers. Their quota of wealth increases (thus reducing that of the workers), as shown by the partial derivative of equation (11.14):

$$\frac{\partial(1-\alpha^*)}{\partial \overline{R}_b} = -\frac{s_w}{(s_r-s_w)(\overline{k}\beta+b^*)\overline{R}_b^2} < 0 \qquad (11.29)$$

Moreover, both the pre-tax and after-tax total revenues of the working class undergo a reduction when R_b increases, as shown by the partial derivative of equation (11.16):

$$\frac{\partial \pi_w^*}{\partial \overline{R}_b} = -\frac{\overline{k}\beta s_r}{s_r-s_w} < 0 \qquad (11.30a)$$

$$\frac{\partial (1-\tau^*)\pi_w^*}{\partial \bar{R}_b} = -g_0 \frac{\bar{k}+b^*}{\bar{k}\beta(s_r-s_w)(1-\lambda b^*)\bar{R}_b^2} < 0 \tag{11.30b}$$

By contrast, both the pre-tax and after-tax total revenue of the rentiers undergo an increase when R_b increases, as shown by the partial derivative of equation (11.15):

$$\frac{\partial \pi_r^*}{\partial \bar{R}_b} = b^* + \frac{\bar{k}\beta s_r}{s_r-s_w} > 0 \tag{11.31a}$$

$$\frac{\partial (1-\tau^*)\pi_r^*}{\partial \bar{R}_b} = g_0 \frac{s_w(\bar{k}+b^*)}{\bar{k}\beta s_r(1-\lambda b^*)(s_r-s_w)\bar{R}_b^2} > 0 \tag{11.31b}$$

The increased income inequality occurring when the rate of interest rises is also confirmed by the following partial derivative:

$$\frac{\partial}{\partial \bar{R}_b}\left(\frac{\pi_r^*}{\pi_w^*}\right) = \frac{s_r-s_w}{s_r} \frac{\bar{k}\beta+b^*}{(1-\bar{k}\beta\bar{R}_b)^2} > 0 \tag{11.32}$$

Thus, an increase in the rate of interest on government bonds increases the inequality in the distribution of both income and wealth between the two classes considered by the model. Moreover, unlike what happens when the government deficit rises, it reduces both the pre-tax and after-tax total revenues of the working class, measured in terms of the net income of the economy.

11.5. CONCLUSIONS

Analysis of the connection between government deficit, government debt, growth and distribution has been played down by the recent literature on endogenous growth. The post Keynesian literature has instead paid greater attention to this problem. Yet it has not examined the effects of government interventions on income inequality. You and Dutt's analysis (1996) is an important exception. By using a Kaleckian model they examined the view, recently shared by some Keynesian authors too, that a rise in government deficit and in government debt increases income inequality by making the poorer sections of society pay more taxes to provide for the larger interests on government debt earned by the rich.

In this chapter a post Keynesian model of growth and personal distribution, belonging to the Kaldor–Pasinetti tradition, has been presented to deal with the same problems examined by You and Dutt. The results achieved by this post Keynesian model highlight several differences with those of the Kaleckian one, starting with the fact that, unlike You and Dutt's analysis, the effects of government interventions on the growth rate and on wealth and income distribution are not ambiguous. The results obtained can be summarized as follows.

- An increase in the government deficit has a positive effect on the growth rate of the economy.
- A change in the rate of interest leaves the rate of growth constant. This result is related to the dynamic equilibrium conditions and to the fact that the growth rate of the stock of government bonds remains unchanged, owing to the constancy of the government deficit.
- A higher government deficit increases wealth inequality. It produces a larger stock of government debt, an increase in the rentiers' quota of wealth and a reduction in the workers' quota on the distribution of wealth. These effects are not examined by You and Dutt, owing to their assumption that workers are not savers and have no wealth.
- A higher interest rate increases wealth inequality too.
- A higher government deficit produces an increase in the rentiers' total revenues, measured in terms of the net income of the economy.
- A higher interest rate increases the rentiers' total revenues, measured in terms of the net income of the economy too.
- A higher government deficit leaves the pre-tax total revenues of the working class, measured in terms of the net income of the economy, constant. This is due to a particular application of the Pasinetti theorem to the model considered here.
- A higher interest rate reduces the pre-tax total revenues of the working class.
- A higher government deficit increases the after-tax total revenues of the working class, owing to the reduction in the tax rate.
- Although a higher government deficit makes both classes better off, income inequality increases, since the benefits received by the rentiers are greater than those received by the workers. The increased income inequality does not stem from the fact that the rentiers own a larger quota of government debt than the workers. Instead it is due to the fact that the rentiers' propensity to save is greater than that of the working class. Inequality increases whatever the quota of wealth owned by the working class.
- A higher interest rate reduces the after-tax total revenues of the working class and thus increases income inequality.

NOTES

1. This change of perspective in the treatment of government debt can be originally found in Barro (1989, 1990).
2. See Brauninger (2002) and the works referred to therein. This conclusion can be considered in line with the widespread belief that government intervention reduces the rate of growth of the economy due to the poor level of productivity of the government sector.
3. For a review of this literature see Commendatore (1994) and Panico (1997).
4. The approach proposed by Kaldor (1955–56), and further developed by Pasinetti (1962), studies the long-run relationship between effective demand, growth and distribution by assuming full or normal capacity utilization, flexible income shares and an exogenous rate of growth. This approach was extended by Joan Robinson (1956) by introducing a functional relationship between the rate of growth and the rate of profit. The Kaleckian approach instead assumes under-utilized productive capacity, income distribution determined by firms' mark-up procedures and growth driven by profitability and by effective demand.
5. A more complex description of this relationship, which takes for instance into account investor choices among different assets, makes it difficult to obtain explicit analytical solutions from the model.
6. Like You and Dutt (1996), owing to the lack of a monetary base issued by the monetary authorities, the assumption of an exogenous interest rate can only mimic the content of much of the post Keynesian literature on the endogeneity of the money supply and the hint given by Sraffa in *Production of Commodities*, subsequently developed by the works on the monetary theory of distribution. The introduction of central bank money as the third asset of the model hinders the achievement of explicit analytical solutions.
7. The case of a given primary deficit has also been considered. Moreover, the model has been alternatively closed by assuming an endogenous interest rate and an exogenous tax rate. In what follows, the results achieved with these different specifications will be sometimes compared with those derived by the model in the text.
8. On the contrary, when the interest rate is endogenous, π_w changes when there is a variation in the government deficit and government debt. See below.
9. We have examined the local stability of the equilibrium for a simplified case in which the condition $r_k = \beta R_h$ is continuously satisfied, $s_w = 0$ and $s_r = 1$. The following results were reached: a) if the government uses variations in the tax rate in order to maintain the targeted deficit $\bar{d}$ and uses variations in the its expenditure in order to equilibrate the goods market, the equilibrium is locally stable; b) if the government uses variations in the tax rate in order to maintain the equilibrium in the goods market and uses variations in its expenditure in order to maintain the targeted deficit, the equilibrium is unstable. Since savings are more sensitive than investments to changes in the tax rate, the economy is on a razor-edge. Reduction in the tax rate to favour capital accumulation leads to a larger increase in savings, widening the gap between inputs and withdrawals. The government can stabilize the economic system only by acting in a counter-intuitive fashion, by increasing taxation when overall savings exceed investments. Analysis of more general cases is left to further investigation.
10. This can be inferred from the partial derivative of equation (11.11):

$$\frac{\partial g^*}{\partial b^*} = \frac{g_0}{\bar{k}\beta} \left[\frac{1 + \lambda\bar{k}\beta}{(1 - \lambda b^*)^2} \right] > 0 \ .$$

11. When the rate of interest is endogenous an increase in $\bar{d}$ reduces both workers' pre- and after-tax income via an increase in R_b. This strengthens the effect on income inequality.
12. As a matter of fact, when δ, the primary deficit, is exogenously given, we obtain an increasing effect of a rise in R_b on the stock of government debt.
13. A rise in the rate of interest instead enhances growth when the primary deficit is exogenous. In this case, the effect of a change in R_b on the after-tax rate of profits is positive.

REFERENCES

Atkinson, A.B. (1997), 'Macroeconomics and the distribution of income', in P. Arestis, G. Palma and M. Sawyer, *Markets, Unemployment and Economic Policy: Essays in Honour of Geoff Harcourt Volume II*, Routledge: London and New York, pp. 207–22.

Barro, R.J. (1989), 'The neoclassical approach to budget deficits', in R.J. Barro, *Modern Business Cycle Theory*, Oxford: Basil Blackwell.

Barro, R.J. (1990), 'Government spending in a simple model of endogenous growth', *Journal of Political Economy*, **98**(5), S103–25

Brauninger M. (2002), 'The budget deficit, public debt and endogenous growth', Universität der Bundeswehr Hamburg, Economic Theory Discussion Paper N° 2/2002. http://ssrn/com/abstract=362940, forthcoming in *Journal of Public Economic Theory*.

Commendatore, P. (1994), 'Sulla esistenza di un'economia a due classi in un modello Post Keynesiano di crescita e distribuzione con settore pubblico e attività finanziarie', *Studi Economici*, **51**(3), 5–38.

Kaldor, N. (1955–56), 'Alternative theories of distribution', *Review of Economic Studies*, **23**(2), 83–100.

Lavoie, M. (1992), *Foundations of Post-Keynesian Economic Analysis*, Aldershot, UK and Brookfield, US: Edward Elgar.

Marglin, S.A. (1984), *Growth, Distribution, and Prices*, Cambridge, Mass.: Harvard University Press.

Panico, C. (1997), 'Government deficits in post Keynesian theories of growth and distribution', *Contributions to Political Economy*, **16**, 61–86.

Pasinetti, L.L. (1962), 'Rate of profit and income distribution in relation to the rate of economic growth', *Review of Economic Studies*, **29**(4), 103–20.

Robinson, J.V. (1956), *The Accumulation of Capital*, London: Macmillan.

Sraffa, P. (1960), *Production of Commodities by Means of Commodities*, Cambridge: Cambridge University Press.

You, J.I. and A.K. Dutt (1996), 'Government debt, income distribution and growth', *Cambridge Journal of Economics*, **20**, 335–51.

12. Foreign debt, growth and distribution in an investment-constrained system[*]

Massimiliano La Marca

12.1. INTRODUCTION

The discussion of the impact of foreign debt on developing economies, the impossibility of full repayment of debt stocks by crisis-stricken countries and the opportunity of concerted rescheduling or forgiveness have undergone different alternate phases since the first debt crisis of the early 1980s. From an initial position of absolute rejection of debt reduction, to a broad consensus on the necessity of substantial forgiveness for a selected number of countries, the financing vs. forgiving and the 'sustainability' debates have been influenced by political feelings and backed by alternative theoretical approaches.

Debt paths are 'unsustainable' if regarded as too costly or 'excessive' for the viability of the system. The analysis of sustainability has been mostly developed within the internal debt management discussion, while for external debt analysis it has too often taken the very simplistic connotation of the ability and willingness to pay back foreign investors. Foreign debt contracts involve firms and/or governments of sovereign countries. Coupled with the predominance of the MIRA (methodological individualism-rational agent) paradigm across virtually all fields of mainstream economics, this has shaped the way of addressing the problem: countries would be homogeneous entities that interplay through imperfect contracts that, given moral hazard and hidden action, suffer mainly from an enforcement problem. In this case rational debtors would 'promise' to invest loaned funds, but would have the incentive to consume them or invest them abroad. Therefore, mainstream discussion has favoured mostly financial, incentive-based approaches and contract theory as the *exclusive* means of analysing sovereign debt.[1]

Heterodox models, in general, describe an economic system as the composition of different – at times contrasting – forces. A general framework suggested in Foley and Taylor (2004) underlines and sums up some salient features of some non-mainstream models. Economic actors are grouped into institutional sectors which have a distinct and well-specified behaviour. Transactions between sectors are represented in an accounting system that provides a great deal of necessary conditions for the model solution; behavioural equations are not necessarily the outcome of fully maximizing behaviours since limited rationality and uncertainty are pervasive. Demand is at centre stage both in the short and long run, and interplays with financial markets and international capital flows.

Therefore, recognizing that countries are systems of interacting actors, sustainability, illiquidity and insolvency issues become elements of a more complex macroeconomic scenario.

As far as the prevailing policy orientations are concerned, debt rescheduling, refinancing, concerted and 'involuntary' lending was the preferred strategy in the aftermath of the 1982 crisis. It was soon recognized that a country suffering from 'debt overhang' – the existence of inherited debt stock sufficiently large that cannot be expected to be repaid in full – could be objectively solvent but nonetheless incur liquidity problems. Single creditors would have the incentive to withdraw first, while it would be in the overall creditors' interest to prevent the value of the existing loans from falling. Concerted lending would 'socialize' the debt problem and provide a better solution for both parties. This would be typically conditioned by 'austerity' measures such as reduction in aggregate expenditure and in labour costs and real devaluation.

According to some proponents of partial debt forgiveness, rolling over larger amounts of debt can only postpone the problem of repaying its stock in the hope of better macroeconomic domestic and external conditions. Various theoretical frameworks find adverse linkages between indebtedness and growth: debt-ridden countries have no incentive to earn the additional income that would benefit only creditors (Krugman, 1988, 1989). A sort of Laffer curve would characterize the rescheduling vs. forgiveness trade-off where, for high levels of indebtedness, forgiveness would be in the interests of creditors as much as a tax cut would be in the interests of the tax recipient. Rescheduling would be another self-defeating strategy.

The effect of foreign debt on growth, distribution, wealth, capacity utilization and employment is the main theme of this chapter. Starting from the intuition that effective demand can be negatively affected by debt servicing whenever interests do not accrue to domestic households, we suppose that *exogenous capital inflows* have already extinguished their impact effect and that the existing debt endogenously evolves affecting demand, distribution and growth. We set up a model to describe and analyse (i) the relation between foreign debt and main macro variables such as distribution, terms of trade, wealth, capacity utilization and growth in investment-constrained economies, (ii) whether highly-indebted countries can become insolvent even when they 'behave properly' in terms of savings and trade balance or attempt expenditure contraction by cutting wages, (iii) whether partial debt forgiveness, temporary transfers or a reduction in interest rate can push the system on a virtuous path that can lead it to repay its remaining debt with its own resources. More specifically, we allow relative output shares and international competitiveness to be determined as the composition between workers' nominal wage demand and nominal prices set by imperfectly competitive firms, and to feed back on domestic and foreign demand of domestic goods and foreign debt dynamics.

Section 12.2 describes the model including all sets of accounts: aggregate demand and wealth decomposition, output shares, goods and financial transaction between sectors, and stock-flow consistent accumulation of foreign debt and productive capital. In Section 12.3 we look at the short- and long-run dynamics and investigate the sustainability of debt paths and some policies for improving possible economic outcomes. Section 12.4 draws some conclusions.

12.2. MODEL DESCRIPTION

Production requires capital, labour and imported intermediate inputs. Technology and production coefficients are given and, for any constant capital–capacity ratio, the output–capital ratio becomes an index of capacity utilization.

There are three institutional sectors: households, firms and the foreign sector; and three assets: productive capital, equities and foreign debt.

Households hold only equities whose unit price is determined as the present value of firms' net profits; they save a fraction of total income which comprises wages and dividends and buy new equities. A productive sector called firms includes enterprises and the domestic financial business; it finances production through equities and foreign loans in 'dollarized' or exchange rate-indexed debt certificates, and it invests and distributes a fraction of their net profits to households. The 'Foreign Sector' finances excess national expenditure over income: the real exchange rate affects domestic firms' competitiveness and the debt value, and hence aggregate demand, utilization and employment rates.

The balance sheets of the three sectors are reported in Table 12.1, while Table 12.2 gives the social accounting matrix (SAM) in units of capital: most of our model relations are consistently derived from this accounting framework and will be explained in the next sections.

12.2.1. A Relative Price Theory

12.2.1.1. Endogenous capacity utilization

Firms set prices charging a fixed mark-up m over variable costs which include wages as well as imported intermediate inputs

$$p = (1+m)(wl + x\pi a) \qquad (12.1)$$

where w is the wage bill, l the labour input coefficient, x the nominal exchange rate, π the foreign good price, a the coefficient of the imported intermediates per unit of output. Let us define the real wage, the wage share out of total output and the real exchange rate as $\omega \equiv w/p$, $\psi \equiv \omega l$, and $e \equiv x\pi / p$, respectively.[2] The mark-up pricing rule can be expressed in real terms as

$$1 = (1+m)(\psi + ea). \qquad (12.2)$$

Firms' profits are the residual of sales net of variable costs; a profit rate over capital value is simply

$$r = \frac{pX - (wl + x\pi a)X}{pK},$$

where homogeneous capital and a uniform price for capital and consumption goods are assumed.

Defining $u \equiv X/K$, using (12.2) and the other definitions, the profit rate is the product of the profit–output ratio and the output–capital ratio

$$r = m(\psi + ea)u, \qquad (12.3)$$

or

$$r = \frac{m}{1+m}u$$

where $\mu \equiv m/(1+m)$ is the profit–output ratio, that is the profit share. Therefore, assuming a fixed mark-up is tantamount to assuming a fixed profit share on total output, from (12.2), (12.3), and the definition of μ we obtain

$$X = \mu X + \psi X + eaX$$

or, in units of capital,

$$u = r + \psi u + eau \ ;$$

output value is distributed between profits, wages and intermediate inputs (column 1 of Table 12.2). For any constant profit share or mark-up, $1 - \mu = \psi + ea$, there is a trade-off between the real exchange rate and wage share.

Log differentiation of (12.1), for a fixed m, yields

$$\hat{p} = \hat{w} \frac{\psi}{\psi + ea} + \hat{x} \frac{ea}{\psi + ea} : \qquad (12.4)$$

if firms have sufficient market power domestically and abroad, they can preserve profit margins by passing through factor price inflation $\hat{w}$ and $\hat{x}$ according to the factors' shares on variable costs.

Nominal wage inflation, on the other hand, is determined by conflict between workers and firms: even neglecting a distinction between pure workers and rentiers (households can both work and hold shares), a natural hypothesis is that the household-workers defend their wage purchasing power in the face of inflation and changing labour market conditions. Plausible assumptions confirmed by data are that nominal wages respond positively to capacity utilization (increasing production is not accommodated by perfectly elastic labour supply) and negatively to the wage share level because of firms' rising resistance to workers' claims; a lineal specification of that could be

$$\hat{w} = \theta_0 + \theta_u u - \theta_\psi \psi \qquad (12.5)$$

(a specification analogous to Taylor, 2004, and Taylor and Barbosa-Filho, 2003), where $\theta_u, \theta_\psi > 0$ give the wage acceleration required to expand output and the degree of firms' resistance to wage demands, respectively. If labour productivity is constant, labour share and wage rate dynamics coincide

$$\hat{\psi} = \hat{\omega} = \hat{w} - \hat{p} \ .$$

Using (12.4), (12.5), given $1 - \mu = \psi + ea$, and setting $\hat{x} = 0$ for simplicity, we obtain

$$\hat{\psi} = \left(\theta_0 + \theta_u u - \theta_\psi \psi\right)\left(1 - \frac{\psi}{1-\mu}\right) \qquad (12.6)$$

where the last factor is positive for $ea > 0$. Differentiating (12.2) we observe that for any constant mark-up, there is a trade-off between the real exchange and the wage rate: $\dot{e} = -\dot{\psi}/a$. The real exchange rate is an actual 'distributive variable' operating on the factor cost side.

Equation (12.6) defines the dynamics for the labour share as the result of workers and firms bargaining power and price and nominal wage inflation. Since $\psi, ea > 0$, stability is obtained for $\theta_\psi > 0$. An equilibrium capacity utilization-wage share (and profit share) relation, that is, the distributive curve, is given by

$$\theta_0 + \theta_u u - \theta_\psi \psi = 0.$$

12.2.1.2. Capacity utilization boundaries

There are some natural limits to capacity utilization such as non-production and the technologically given capacity–capital ratio, or some more stringent constraints induced by the institutional and economic context. We can, therefore, plausibly assume a fixed mark-up rule only between a given range of capacity utilization $u^L \le u \le u^F$, where u^L is a non-negative lower bound and u^F an upper limit no larger than the full employment utilization rate. These boundaries provide additional constraints to the pricing mechanisms and, once reached, induce mark-up adjustment. (The alternative resulting short- and long-run system is sketched in the Appendix.) However, as confirmed by some exemplificative simulations at the end of the chapter, indebted countries can afford a positive level of capacity below full employment and these non-binding constraints can be safely neglected in the following analysis.

Table 12.1   Balance sheets

Household Sector		Firms		Foreign Sector	
$p_E E$	Ω_p	K	eB	eB	Ω_f
			$p_E E$		
			Ω_b		

Table 12.2 Social Accounting Matrix (SAM)

	Output Costs (1)	Households (2)	Firms (3)	Foreign (4)	Cap. Form. (5)	Home Equities (6)	For. Bonds (7)	Totals (8)
Output (A)		$(1-s_h)[(1-s_b)(r-jeb)+\psi u]+c(r-jeb)]/\rho$	$(1-s_b)(r-jeb)$	εe	g			u
Incomes								
Households (B)	ψu							Y_h/K
Firms (C)	r							Y_b/K
Foreign (D)	eau		jeb					Y_f/K
Flows of Funds								
Households (E)		$s_h[(1-s_b)(r-jeb)+\psi u]-c(r-jeb)]/\rho$				$-p_E\dot E/K$		0
Firms (F)			$s_b(r-jeb)$		$-g$	$p_E\dot E/K$	$e\dot B/K$	0
Foreign (G)				S_f/K			$-e\dot B/K$	0
Totals (H)	u	Y_h/K	Y_b/K	Y_f/K	0	0	0	

244

12.2.2. Firms: Investment and Asset Price

12.2.2.1. Investment under uncertainty

Firms earn gross profits at a rate r and pay foreign debt interest jeb, where $b \equiv B/K$ is the 'foreign-good indexed' real loans in units of capital whose domestic real value changes with the terms of trade: a relative price increase in foreign goods raises the burden of debt repayment in the same goods. The exogenous interest rate, j, comprises a risk-free international interest rate, ρ, a LIBOR or a USD bond rate with the same maturity and characteristics of the debt certificate, and a country-specific risk premium κ:[3]

$$j = \rho + \kappa .$$

Investment decisions are made by looking at their expected future profitability: the stream of net profit rates under static expectations is the main argument for an investment function that can be specified in capital units as[4]

$$g = \gamma + \alpha(r - jeb) ,$$

or

$$g = \gamma + \alpha \mu u - \alpha jeb \qquad (12.7)$$

where γ is an autonomous component reflecting the entrepreneurial 'animal spirits' on investment demand. Therefore, investment demand responds to net profitability of productive capital and is stimulated by capacity utilization and depressed by debt payments.[5]

12.2.2.2. Firm finance and asset and liability valuation

If the domestic asset markets value equities according to their net profitability, stock real prices are obtained capitalizing current net profit rate at the international discount rate ρ – a measure of the opportunity cost of financing production:

$$p_E = \frac{r - jeb}{\rho} \frac{K}{E} , \qquad (12.8)$$

where $(r - jeb)/\rho$ is the valuation of a unit of productive capital in the asset market.

Firms' balance sheets (Table 12.1) give information on the composition of their capital sources: if productive capital is valued at the replacement cost K, the net worth of the firm – the difference between its assets and debt and equity capital – is a non-zero residual that absorbs all the slack between productive capital and debt and equity valuation:

$$K = eB + p_E E + \Omega_b .$$

Combining all sectors' balance sheets we observe that the value of domestic real assets is shared between the two domestic sectors, firms and households, and the foreign

$$K = \Omega_h + \Omega_b + \Omega_f .$$

Investment is financed by retained earnings and newly issued bonds and equities. A fraction s_b of their net profits are retained while the remaining $1 - s_b$ is distributed in the form of dividends (line F of the 'flows of funds' account, Table 12.2)

$$g = s_b (r - jeb) + p_E \frac{\dot{E}}{K} + e \frac{\dot{B}}{K} . \tag{12.9}$$

This tells us that excess investment over firms saving is financed by households and foreign investors. Since foreign loans are accumulated according to the current account (below), equation (12.9) gives the issues of new equities as a residual.

Differentiating firms' balance sheets

$$\dot{K} = e\dot{B} + \dot{e}B + \dot{p}_E E + p_E \dot{E} + \dot{\Omega}_b$$

and using (9) and rearranging we obtain

$$\dot{\Omega}_b = s_b (r - jeb) - \dot{e}B - \dot{p}_E E , \tag{12.10}$$

that is, net worth responds to changes in the net profitability and the real exchange rate.

The latter analysis of price and stock variation gives us an anticipation of the unambiguously depressing effect of a growing debt value on asset prices, households' wealth and accumulation. Large debt values reduce the asset market valuation of capital (12.8) and therefore household wealth; on the other hand, growing debt reduces capital accumulation and firms' net worth and therefore the country's overall wealth.

12.2.3. Households: Distribution Matters

Households receive both wage and profit income through distributed net profits (line B, Table 12.2). Savings are a constant fraction of disposable income out of wages and distributed net profits. If, moreover, households' consumption demand depends on a fraction c of their wealth $p_E E$ and recalling that $p_E E = K(r - jeb)/\rho$, we can include a wealth effect in households' consumption equal to $cK(r - jeb)/\rho$ (column 2, Table 12.2). Defining $v \equiv c/\rho$ household total savings in unit of capital is

$$\frac{S_h}{K} = s_h\left[(1 - s_b)(r - jeb) + \psi u\right] - v(r - jeb)$$

Total domestic savings, the sum of households' and firms' savings, is therefore

$$\frac{S_h}{K} + \frac{S_b}{K} = s_h\left[(1 - s_b)(r - jeb) + \psi u\right] - v(r - jeb) + s_b(r - jeb),$$

which defining $s_p \equiv s_b + s_h - s_b s_h - v$ becomes

$$\frac{S_h}{K} + \frac{S_b}{K} = s_p(r - jeb) + s_h \psi u \tag{12.11}$$

the domestic savings (aggregate demand) effect of a redistribution between wages and exchange rate depends on the debt ratio.[6]

12.2.4. External Balance

12.2.4.1. Competitiveness
Home production and investment is financed both by domestic households and the foreign sector which holds claims on domestic output in the form of bonds. Consolidating all its internal accounts, its foreign assets net worth, Ω_f, equals the home foreign debt, eB, in domestic good units. Its savings correspond to the domestic current account deficit (G, recalling D and 4, Table 12.2)

$$\frac{S_f}{K} = e\frac{\dot{B}}{K} = eau - e\varepsilon + jeb \tag{12.12}$$

where $e\varepsilon$ are the 'competitive' net exports simply specified as a linear function of the real exchange rate with a positive unitary elasticity. Trade balance, $T = e(\varepsilon - au)$, improves with a devaluation whenever $u < \varepsilon/a$, that is when the balance is in surplus and vice versa (Figure 12.1). This extreme specification emphasizes the role of demand on trade balance as apparent from its log differentiation

$$\hat{T} = \hat{e} - \frac{au}{\varepsilon - au}\hat{u} \; ;$$

therefore, we assume for simplicity a unitary elasticity effect of devaluation on the trade balance, while we let capacity utilization play the crucial role in determining how export competitiveness and the real exchange rate affect one country's ability to improve its net external balance. Indeed, high debt/low income countries are typically forced into costly trade surpluses and devaluations which nonetheless may not suffice to stabilize their debt at sustainable levels.

From (12.12) we obtain the dynamic equation of the share of foreign currency denominated debt as a function of capacity utilization and growth rate.

$$\dot{b} = au - \varepsilon + (j - g)b \qquad\qquad (12.13)$$

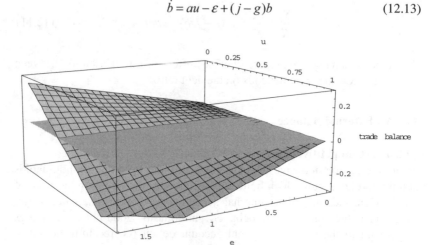

Figure 12.1   Example of trade balance with ε/a set to an exemplificative 0.5. The partial effect of a devaluation is to improve (worsen) the trade surplus (deficit). Both capacity utilization and exchange rate are however a function of the wage share; their joint dynamics are analysed in the following sections.

12.2.4.2. Nature of the debt

Assuming that the debt law of motion is causally determined by the macroequilibrium trade balance plus interest payments instead of, for instance, the investment–saving or expenditure–income gap has strong theoretical implications. Alternative theories of the current account such as the 'intertemporal approach' posit consumption decisions taken by a utility maximizing representative agent as the main determinant in the foreign asset/debt intentional accumulation.[7] In an investment-constrained system such as ours instead, growth, effective demand and distribution combine to determine the foreign balance and the country's own debt dynamics consistent with the assumption that the small economy is not subject to external capital flow shocks.

Our assumption of a consolidated productive and financial system called 'firm' and absence of domestic monetary policy allows us to neglect any distinction between accumulation of reserves and other capital flows.

Firms' debt accumulation is the difference (sum) between the debt payments and the commercial surplus (deficit) with the creditor country. This however does not imply that firms' debt has a sole commercial nature: by postponing principal payment and rolling over debt, foreign investors allow capital accumulation and generation of profits from which interests are paid (equation (12.99). Therefore debt is a financing source for capital, which however can have a depressing effect on capital accumulation if increasing debt payments reduce the expected firms' net profitability (equation (12.7)) and capital own return.

Another major issue is the maturity structure of sovereign debt. Equation (12.13) would easily be consistent with both debt certificates with infinite maturity and short-term loans rolled over as long as there is a perception of solvency and liquidity.[8]

12.3. SHORT- AND LONGER-RUN DYNAMICS

12.3.1. Temporary Equilibrium

Asset and liability stocks are given by history at any single point in time and can be taken as state variables. In the short run, output and distribution variations jointly lead to the macro adjustment of supply and demand in the goods and labour market, while new equities are issued by and loans supplied to firms in the asset market. Total savings supply is the sum of domestic (12.11) and foreign (12.12) savings supply (E, F, and G, recalling D and line 4, Table 12.2);

$$\frac{S}{K} = \frac{S_h}{K} + \frac{S_b}{K} + \frac{S_f}{K} = (s_p\mu + s_h\psi + ea)u + (1 - s_p)jeb - e\varepsilon . \quad (12.14)$$

If output adjusts to clear the goods market, excess demand is a function $f(\bullet)$ of the difference between investment demand (12.7) and aggregate savings (12.14)

$$\dot{u} = f\left\{\left[(\alpha - s_p)\mu - s_h\psi - ea\right]u - (1 - s_p + \alpha)jeb + \gamma + e\varepsilon\right\},$$

with $f'(\bullet) > 0,$ and the equilibrium capacity utilization is therefore a function of distribution

$$u = \frac{\gamma + e\varepsilon - (1 - s_p + \alpha)jeb}{(s_p - \alpha)\mu + s_h\psi + ea}, \quad (12.15)$$

where $e = e[\psi],$ as from (12.2). The wage increases/exchange rate appreciation now has an additional effect on effective demand by reducing competitive exports, import values and interest payments. The condition that savings are more responsive to output changes than investment, $(s_p - \alpha)\mu + s_h\psi + ea > 0$, is required for stability in the goods market and together with $\gamma + e\varepsilon > (1 - s_p + \alpha)jeb$ assure a positive level of capacity utilization setting one upper ceiling to the debt ratio.[9]

Substituting $e = (1 - \mu - \psi)/a$ into (12.15) and simplifying, and recalling (12.6), we obtain the dynamic system between wages and capacity utilization leading to the short-run equilibrium.

$$\dot{u} = \left[(1 - s_p + \alpha)\mu + (1 - s_h)\psi - 1\right]u +$$
$$-(1 - s_p + \alpha)j(1 - \psi - \mu)\frac{b}{a} + (1 - \psi - \mu)\frac{\varepsilon}{a} + \gamma \quad (12.16)$$

$$\dot{\psi} = \psi\left(\theta_0 + \theta_u u - \theta_\psi \psi\right)\left(1 - \frac{\psi}{1 - \mu}\right) \quad (12.17)$$

The system comprises six variables $g,$ $u,$ $\psi,$ $e,$ $\dot{\psi},$ and $\dot{u},$ and six equations (12.17), (12.16), (12.2), (12.8), $\dot{\psi} = 0,$ and $\dot{u} = 0.$ The latter two conditions are required for the equilibrium in the labour and goods market: they determine the capacity utilization and wage share and consequently the real exchange rate and the growth rate.[10]

12.3.1.1. Profit- and wage-led effective demand and growth

The *effective demand function* (12.15) depends on both the distribution, through ψ and $e = e[\psi]$, and the share of debt on capital, b; the former are short-run endogenous variables, the latter is a state variable which changes in the longer run according to its own law of motion (12.13).

Since capacity utilization rises with demand injections generated by consumption, investment and the trade balance, a redistribution towards wages and the resulting appreciation is expansionary whenever the increase in consumption and investment induced by rising households' wage and net profit income and firms' net profitability outweigh the effect of the loss of competitiveness on net exports. Therefore profitability and consumption responsiveness, import dependence and export capacity affect together with the debt ratio the sensitivity of the capacity utilization to changes in the real wage, as apparent from the derivative of the effective demand function

$$\frac{\partial u[\psi;b]}{\partial \psi} = \frac{a\gamma(1-s_h)+\left[jb(1-s_p+\alpha)-\varepsilon\right]\left[s_h(1-\mu)+(s_p-\alpha)\mu\right]}{a\left[(1-s_p+\alpha)\mu+(1-s_h)\psi-1\right]^2}. \quad (12.18)$$

For plausible values of parameters (such as but not necessarily $1 > s_p - \alpha > 0$), the effective demand curve tends to decrease (increase) in the wage share at low (high) levels of debt; Figure 12.2 below plots a family of effective demand curves in the (u,ψ) plane at different debt ratios.

For increasing values of b, the whole demand schedule shifts leftward and the economy becomes wage-led for $b > b°$, where $b° \leq 0$ for $[s_h(1-\mu)+(s_p-\alpha)\mu]/(1-s_h) \leq a\gamma/\varepsilon$. This implies that while in general the increase in the debt ratio can switch a profit-led system into a wage-led system, more specifically a low saving indebted country with large intermediate import over export share would be wage-led, while a creditor high saving country with a favourable import–export ratio would be most likely profit-led.

If the economy is profit-led – that is when the country not only has large savings propensities, and low investment sensitivity to profitability, but also enjoys a favourable export–import ratio and debt is not too large – increasing the ratio of profits to wages stimulates effective demand by reducing the aggregate saving rate (savings out of net profits fall because of rising debt value), increases exports through devaluation and then raises consumption and investment.

In the likely event of a combination of lower savings and larger import–export ratios, such effects are reversed for most positive debt ratios and the system is wage-led: higher wages lead to a real exchange rate appreciation

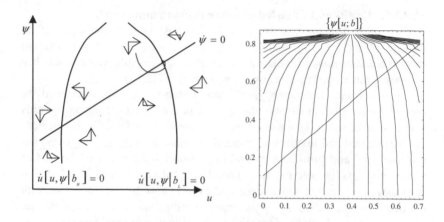

Figure 12.2   The shape and position of the aggregate demand curve in the
(u, ψ) *space depend on the saving propensities, export, import, and the debt*
ratio, b. The left hand panel shows a phase diagram with a profit-led/low-
debt system (downward sloping) and a wage-led/high-debt system (upward
sloping). The combination with the upward sloping distributive curve gives
the short-run equilibrium. In the right hand panel, we assume low saving
rates and a large export ratio, ($s_h = 0.1$; $s_b = 0.3$; $c = 0.01$; $\rho = 0.03$;
$\alpha = 0.1$; $\gamma = 0.03$; $a = 0.4$; $\varepsilon = 0.2$; $\mu = 1/7$; $j = 0.13$; $\theta_0 = 0.01$; $\theta_u = 0.1$;
$\theta_\psi = 0.1$) *and plot a family of curves corresponding to different levels of*
debt.

which, although weakening competitiveness, helps contain the value of the
intermediate imports and debt costs. Devaluations, on the contrary, have a
contractionary effect on aggregate demand regardless of their impact on the
trade balance: the Marshall–Lerner condition can hold but the negative effect
of redistribution on domestic demand is stronger than the positive effect of
foreign demand.[11]

12.3.1.2. Distributive curve

As described in the previous section nominal wage and price dynamics
interact to obtain the real wage and real exchange rate consistent with the
desired mark-up of firms and labour market conditions. The $\dot{\psi} = 0$
equilibrium is represented by the distributive curve $\theta_0 + \theta_u u - \theta_\psi \psi = 0$
which, assuming that larger real wages are associated with slower wage
inflation, is both stable in ψ and upward sloping in the (u, ψ) plane. Figure
12.2 combines aggregate demand and distributive curve to give a
representation of the possible solutions.

12.3.1.3. Equilibrium

The analytical solution of the equilibrium values of the capacity utilization, growth rate, exchange rate and wage share for any given explicit saving, investment and wage inflation function is non-linear:

$$u^*(b) = -\frac{1}{2\theta_u}\left(\theta_0 + \frac{\xi_1(b)+\xi_2(b)}{a(1-s_h)}\right)$$

$$\psi^*(b) = \frac{\theta_0 + \theta_u u^*(b)}{\theta_\psi}$$

$$e^*(b) = 1 - \mu - \psi^*(b)$$

$$g^*(b) = \gamma + \alpha\mu u^*(b) - \alpha j e^*(b)b$$

where

$$\xi_1(b) = jb\theta_u(1-s_p+\alpha) - \varepsilon\theta_u - a\theta_\psi\left[1-(1-s_p+\alpha)\mu\right]$$

and

$$\xi_2(b) = \left\langle 4a(1-s_h)\theta_\psi\left\{jb(1-s_p+\alpha)\theta_u - \varepsilon\theta_u(1-\mu) - a\gamma\theta_u - \theta_0\left[1-(1-s_p+\alpha)\mu\right]\right\}+\right.$$

$$\left.+\left[jb(1-s_p+\alpha)\theta_u - \varepsilon\theta_u - a(1-s_h)\theta_0 - a\theta_\psi(1-s_p+\alpha)\mu\right]^2\right\rangle^{\frac{1}{2}}$$

are increasing functions of b. It is apparent that higher levels of debt reduce the wage share, the capacity utilization, and depreciate the real exchange rate. Both the resulting fall in the gross profit rate and an increase in the domestic value of debt depress the growth rate. This explains why for increasing debt ratios, domestic consumption and investment are relatively more important than foreign demand and are more sensitive to wages, while at the same time falling utilization rate and imports and rising competitiveness may or may not help slow down debt accumulation.

Note that the use of *per output* shares μ and ψ in our analysis may seem to hide the real and more interesting dynamics of the profit $\mu/(1-ea)$ and wage share $\psi/(1-ea)$ in *GDP units*, respectively. Expressing distribution in GDP shares in equilibrium,

$$\frac{\psi^*}{1-e^*a} + \frac{\mu}{1-e^*a} = 1,$$

we observe that a fall in capacity utilization and in the output wage share is associated with a real exchange rate depreciation and net output $(1 - e^* a)$ contraction and therefore a larger profit rate in GDP units; signs are preserved shifting from one to the other normalization while the profit share in GDP units shows the usual trade-off with the wage share. Moreover, the wage share and net output correlation – wage recipients get less of a smaller pie – reduce the relative fall of the wage share to GDP.

12.3.1.4. Stability

The Jacobian of the system is as follows

$$J = \begin{bmatrix} \dfrac{\partial \dot{u}}{\partial u} & \dfrac{\partial \dot{u}}{\partial \psi} \\[2ex] \dfrac{\partial \dot{\psi}}{\partial u} & \dfrac{\partial \dot{\psi}}{\partial \psi} \end{bmatrix}$$

where

$$\frac{\partial \dot{u}}{\partial u} = (1 - s_p + \alpha)\mu + (1 - s_h)\psi^* - 1,$$

$$\frac{\partial \dot{u}}{\partial \psi} = (1 - s_h)u^* + jb\frac{1 - s_p + \alpha}{a},$$

$$\frac{\partial \dot{\psi}}{\partial u} = \psi^*\left(1 - \frac{\psi^*}{1 - \mu}\right)\theta_u,$$

and

$$\frac{\partial \dot{\psi}}{\partial \psi} = \left(\theta_0 + \theta_u u^* - 2\theta_\psi\right)\left[1 - \frac{\psi}{1 - \mu}\left(1 + \frac{\theta_0 + \theta_u u^* - \theta_\psi}{\theta_0 + \theta_u u^* - 2\theta_\psi}\right)\right].$$

The term $\partial \dot{u} / \partial u$ is negative for reasonable values of the investment sensitivity to profits and profit share including $s_p > \alpha$ and also considering that $\psi^* < 1 - \mu$. Similarly, the $\partial \dot{\psi} / \partial \psi$ term is negative since $\psi^* < 1$ implies $\theta_\psi \psi^* = \theta_0 + \theta_u u^* < \theta_\psi$, while the second bracketed factor is positive.

Stability also requires a positive determinant of the Jacobian. Given $\partial \dot{u} / \partial u < 0$, $\partial \dot{\psi} / \partial \psi < 0$ and $\partial \dot{\psi} / \partial u > 0$, a negative $\partial \dot{u} / \partial \psi$ implies a positive determinant and a downward-sloping (profit-led) aggregate demand curve in the (u, ψ) plane. Also a positive $\partial \dot{u} / \partial \psi$ implying an upward-sloping (wage-led) aggregate demand curve allows for stability if $(\partial\dot{u}/\partial u)/(\partial\dot{u}/\partial\psi)<(\partial\dot{\psi}/\partial u)/(\partial\dot{\psi}/\partial\psi)$, that is the aggregate demand curve is steeper than the distributive curve in the vicinity of the relevant equilibrium, which happens to be the case as shown in the previous sections.

Moreover, cycles can arise if $(\partial\dot{u}/\partial u-\partial\dot{\psi}/\partial\psi)^2<-4(\partial\dot{u}/\partial\psi)(\partial\dot{\psi}/\partial u)$ which is not excluded for negative values of $\partial\dot{u}/\partial\psi$ in low-debt profit-led economies.

12.3.2. Longer-Run Dynamics: Foreign Debt and Steady State

The law of motion of foreign debt is obtained by the current account equation at the equilibrium values

$$\dot{b}=au^*(b)-\varepsilon-f+\left(j-g^*(b)\right)b\,. \tag{12.19}$$

We introduce f, a transfer from abroad as a measure of the temporary flow effect of partial debt forgiveness. Steady state is obtained when debt, capital and all flow variables grow at the same rate g, obtained at the current account balance $\dot{b}=0$. If risk-averse foreign creditors have an opportunity cost of lending equal to j, this interest rate is just enough to obtain debt rollover at the ongoing growth rate. Forward iterating the current account and integrating we obtain the debt value at time T as the sum of the current debt b_t and trade deficits, in units of capital, capitalized at the variable growth-adjusted interest rate

$$b_T=b_t\beta_T^{-1}+\int_t^T\left(au^*(b_s)-\varepsilon-f_s\right)\beta_s^{-1}\ ds \tag{12.20}$$

where

$$\beta_s=\exp\left\{-\int_t^s\left(j-g^*(b_\tau)\right)d\tau\right\}.$$

The standard *solvency* condition requires that the present value of all future resource transfers to the foreign sector (trade surpluses) is no smaller than the existing debt in units of capital which implies that no Ponzi debt rollover is allowed over an infinite time horizon

$$b_t=\int_t^\infty\left(\varepsilon+f_s-au^*(b_s)\right)\beta_s\ ds\,.^{12} \tag{12.21}$$

Therefore a convergent path that implies $\lim_{T\to\infty}b_T\beta_T=0$ would satisfy the solvency constraint.

12.3.2.1. Rescheduling at different rates

Equilibrium and stability can be easily analysed representing (12.19) in the $(b,\dot b)$ plane corresponding to output capital ratios between an exemplificative range such as [0, 0.7]. We temporarily assume $f = 0$. Figure 12.3 shows some benchmark examples in debt dynamics at different interest rate levels and how low- and high-saving countries may find an equilibrium (if any) at a high and low debt/capital ratio, respectively.

The left panel shows that at high interest levels a 'prodigal' country may not reach a stable external balance and will supposedly be forced to change its saving and investment policy with or before defaulting. The economy can however converge to a steady-state debt ratio which increases with the *borrowing* interest rate. Higher savings propensities can lead to the accumulation of net foreign assets and under certain conditions turn the country into a foreign creditor (Figure 12.3, right panel). However, as in most demand-constrained models, a rise in the saving rates can have a negative impact on capacity utilization, employment and growth: a *paradox of thrift* applies in our context for reasonable values of b and j although mitigated by the reduction in the consumption leakages due to debt payments, as shown in equation (12.15). Hence, rescheduling at lower rates would reduce the need for aggregate expenditure contraction by increasing the speed of debt reduction at any level of the propensity to save (Figure 12.3, right panel).

Another limit of expenditure reduction policy is that an indebted high-saving country, despite constantly running up trade surpluses, can be trapped into a growing debt/current account deficit, falling growth, profit rate, wage share and depreciation spiral. This is the case if output contraction is not enough to drive a trade surplus that can improve the current account at high

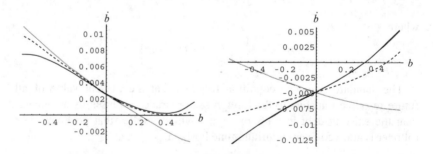

Figure 12.3 Interest rate reduction. $c = 0.01$; $\rho = 0.03$; $\alpha = 0.1$; $\gamma = 0.03$; $a = 0.4$; $\varepsilon = 0.1$; $\mu = 1/7$; $j = 0.13$; $\theta_0 = 0.01$; $\theta_u = 0.1$; $\theta_w = 0.1$ and $s_h = 0.1$; $s_b = 0.3$; for the low saving (left panel) and $s_h = 0.2$; $s_b = 0.3$; for the high saving (right panel). Interest rates are $j = 0.13$ solid line; $j = 0.10$ dashed; and $j = 0.03$ dotted line, respectively.

debt values; if the steady state debt rate is unstable and if the existing debt happens to be larger than the equilibrium (right side of the equilibrium in Figure 12.3, right panel), debt will become explosive and the country insolvent.

Note that perfect foresight would exclude *illiquidity* problems as long as the *solvency* condition is satisfied. Uncertainty plays a crucial role in affecting the expected present value of future repayments and therefore the rise of liquidity problems for otherwise solvent countries. Under our simple hypothesis of static expectations, for instance, solvency is associated with $b_t \le \left(\varepsilon - au^*(b_t)\right)/\left(j - g^*(b_t)\right)$ that is the present value of trade surpluses at the current debt level projected over an infinite horizon is at least as large as the current debt. Recalling (12.19) we find out that this condition is satisfied as long as $\dot{b} \le 0$, which implies that indebted countries approaching higher but stable debt rates can be expected to be insolvent and run into illiquidity and debt crisis. This is because growing debt has a positive effect both on trade surplus and the discount rate (with the former prevailing over the latter) through output and growth contraction, while growing trade surpluses are underestimated by myopic creditors. Debt growth can be a source of 'irrational' macroeconomic fragility both for high-saving and low-saving countries.

12.3.2.2. Rescheduling with labour cost reduction

A country wishing to reduce excess expenditure and free resources for debt repayment may expect a wage cut to be an effective policy with immediate relief for firms, a deflationary effect on aggregate consumption and an improvement in competitiveness. Figures 12.4 and 12.5 show the effect of falling θ_u on low- and high-saving countries, for a profit-led and wage-led system, respectively, providing a combination of expenditure and cost reduction policies. From Figure 12.2 and equation (12.18) we note that a change in the wage share has a greater effect in the profit-led than in the wage-led system.

A fall in θ_u raises temporarily capacity utilization in the profit-led system for any given debt level: imports increase more than growth and worsen the current account (equation (12.19)). Debt accumulates faster, reducing output, growth and wages but also output sensitivity to distribution. Trade balance improvements due to output reduction and fall in the growth rate have opposite effects on the current account; at sufficiently high levels of debt the latter can prevail over the former and there can be a turning point with acceleration in debt levels, leading to non-converging debt ratios. While the well-known *paradox of cost* consists of an inverse relation between labour cost and output in a wage-led system, here a similar phenomenon affects output levels through debt dynamics in the longer run even in a profit-led system.

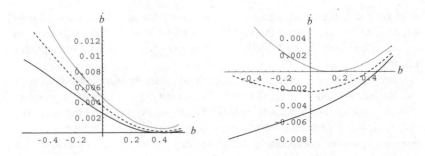

Figure 12.4   Weakening wage demand in a profit-led system. c = 0.01;
ρ = 0.03; α = 0.1; γ = 0.01; a = 0.4; ε = 0.1; μ = 1/7; j = 0.13; θ₀ = 0.01;
θ_ψ = 0.1 and s_h = 0.1; s_b = 0.3; for the low saving (left panel) and s_h = 0.2;
s_b = 0.3; for the high saving (right panel). Wage coefficients are: θ_u = 0.1
solid line; θ_u = 0.07 dashed; and; θ_u = 0.03 dotted line, respectively.

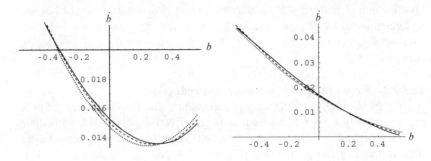

Figure 12.5   Weakening wage demand in a wage-led system. c = 0.01;
ρ = 0.03; α = 0.1; γ = 0.03; a = 0.4; ε = 0.01; μ = 1/7; j = 0.13;
θ₀ = 0.01; θ_ψ = 0.1 and s_h = 0.1; s_b = 0.3; for the low saving (left panel)
and s_h = 0.2; s_b = 0.5; for the high saving (right panel). Wage coefficients
are: θ_u = 0.1 solid line; θ_u = 0.07 dashed; and; θ_u = 0.03 dotted line,
respectively.

Figure 12.5 shows a similar exercise for a wage-led economy: low sensitivity
of the aggregate demand function to wage shares weakens the negative effect
of θ_u reduction on imports and growth, making this policy scarcely effective
on the debt front and regressive on the distributional one.

12.3.2.3. Rescheduling vs. partial forgiving

The previous analysis showed that the convergence towards a high level of debt is both costly in terms of employment, growth and distribution and is risky in terms of the likelihood of a debt crisis. Expenditure and labour cost reduction can be the only options a country can implement with its own short-run policy instruments.[13] Under certain conditions, however, those corrective measures may be neither necessary nor sufficient or even worsen the outcome.

What is the role of according concessional interest rates or forgiving part of the existing debt in such scenarios? We observe that both lower interest rates and temporary transfers ($f > 0$) associated with debt forgiving lower the current account curve when the country is a net debtor, reducing the speed of convergence to a level of the long-run debt equilibrium for low-saving countries and increasing the speed of debt reduction for high-saving countries (a downward translation of the debt dynamics schedule in any of the above represented scenarios). In the latter case it may also prevent the explosive debt paths scenario mentioned above by increasing the value of the unstable equilibrium and allowing the country to fall to the left of it.

Small coordinated efforts for the concerted implementation of policies such as temporary reduction of the interest rate and partial debt forgiveness can have greater, permanent effects, allowing the country to repay the debt with its own resources.

12.4. CONCLUSIONS

The model provides an alternative and comprehensive framework to analyse the relation between macro dynamics and endogenous foreign debt accumulation and its effect on the main elements of a country's welfare, such as growth, capacity utilization *cum* employment, wealth, terms of trade and distribution.[14]

Most discussion nowadays distinguishes between the illiquidity caused by a fall in the expected value of debt service payments and the *ex-post* solvency of a country. *Expectations* of a repayment failure *can be the cause* of a sudden stop of capital flows and make repayment itself an impossible event regardless of the actual stability of the system. Identification of the proper contractual mechanism or domestic policy correction to enforce repayment is often believed to guarantee sustainable debt paths.

We argued that the effectiveness of different standard policies differs from system to system; such policies have radically different social costs which feed back to the ability to repay it. In fact, the concept of sustainability as the convergence to a steady growing state does not capture the real impact of debt burden on wealth, distribution and employment: not only can an illiquidity barrier be hit due to both convergence to and divergence from a steady state, but also even if debt is rescheduled, letting the system converge to a steady state debt to GDP ratio, the latter may not be 'sustainable' for it can be socially unbearable if associated to low employment, regressive distribution and unfavourable terms of trade. Moreover, standard medicines such as contracting expenditure by rising savings and cutting wages can have both short-run and longer-run adverse effects. A weakening of workers' bargaining power (besides the immediate regressive distributional effect) typically has a positive impact on output in profit-led systems and then adverse feedbacks on trade balance and growth and therefore on debt, growth, output and distribution. On the other hand, higher savings do not always prevent explosive paths but under certain conditions can allow convergence towards lower debt ratios through a costly adjustment involving capacity utilization, employment and growth reduction at the onset.

Some policy tools such as partial debt relief and concessional rescheduling have gained wider international consensus in recent years within an alternative theoretical framework. The present analysis can help understand the desirability of internationally concerted policies over standard adjustment advice both in terms of effectiveness and from an often neglected social perspective.

APPENDIX

At the capacity upper u^F or lower bound u^L, nominal wage and price dynamics combine to determine the mark-up rate. For debt ratios $b > b^L$, where $u^*(b^L) = u^L$ and $b < b^F$, where $u^*(b^F) = u^F$, we can presume that excess demand (supply) leads to increasing (falling) mark-ups

$$\dot{\mu} = \left[(1 - s_p + \alpha)\mu + (1 - s_h)\psi^i - 1 \right] u^i +$$
$$-(1 - s_p + \alpha)j(1 - \psi^i - \mu)\frac{b}{a} + (1 - \psi^i - \mu)\frac{\varepsilon}{a} + \gamma$$

(12A.1)

Where

$$\psi^i = \frac{\theta_0 + \theta_u u^i}{\theta_\psi},$$

and $i = L, F$.

This leads to a temporary equilibrium with

$$\mu^i(b) = \frac{\left(1-s_p+\alpha\right)\left(1-\psi^i\right)jb - \left(1-\psi^i\right)\varepsilon + au^i\left(1-\psi^i+s_h\psi^i\right) - a\gamma}{\left(1-s_p+\alpha\right)\left(jb+au^i\right)-\varepsilon},$$

or, rearranging,

$$\mu^i(b) = \left(1-\psi^i\right)\frac{\left(1-s_p+\alpha\right)jb+au^i-\varepsilon}{\left(1-s_p+\alpha\right)\left(jb+au^i\right)-\varepsilon} + \frac{au^i s_h\psi^i - a\gamma}{\left(1-s_p+\alpha\right)\left(jb+au^i\right)-\varepsilon} \quad (12A.2)$$

which is a decreasing function of debt.

The equilibrium exchange rate, growth rate and current account become

$$e^i(b) = 1 - \mu^i(b) - \psi^i,$$

$$g^i(b) = \gamma + \alpha\mu^i(b)u^i - \alpha je^i(b)b,$$

and

$$\dot{b} = au^i - \varepsilon - f + \left(j - g^i(b)\right)b. \quad (A.3)$$

Therefore, as in the endogenous capacity case, increasing debt depreciates the real exchange rate and reduces growth, but unequivocally worsens the current account and debt accumulation.

NOTES

* I would like to thank Arrigo Opocher and Carlo Panico for their useful comments on an earlier version of the paper, Duncan Foley and Lance Taylor for their advice, and Giammario Impullitti and Mika Kato for our friendly and fruitful conversations. The usual caveats apply.

1. Summaries of recent mainstream literature can be found in Obstfeld and Rogoff (1996, ch. 6) and Agénor and Montiel (1999, ch. 14). The issue of internal debt sustainability in a growing system has been pragmatically examined by Blanchard et al. (1990), and Pasinetti (1998 and 2000); dynamic relations and the possible trade-off between external debt and growth tackled by Bhaduri (1987), financial fragility and foreign capital flows by Foley (2003), a synthesis of some macro mainstream views can be found in Pattilo et al. (2002), while a concise critical summary of real exchange models and competitiveness and financial integration can be found in La Marca (2004a and 2004b).

2. Given our assumption of a single (composite) consumption/investment domestic good and of a single (composite) foreign good, the natural definition for the real exchange rate is the

price of the foreign output per domestic output units: a devaluation consists of a rise of foreign good prices in terms of the domestic ones.

3. If the risk premium increased with the stock of debt or foreign assets, such as for $\kappa(eb) = \delta \cdot (eb)^{\varphi}$, with φ an even number, due to increasing country risk or increasing risk of foreign investment, it would only symmetrically enhance the interest rate effect on growth and capacity utilization of increasing absolute values of b.

4. Static expectations are a simplifying assumption as far as interest rate dynamics are concerned (present rates are good proxies of future rates under uncertainty). However, since Meese and Rogoff (1983) showed that a random walk outpredicts any fundamental based model in forecasting the exchange rate, static expectation may be regarded as an extremely rational response to nominal exchange rate unpredictability.

5. Note that both profit margins and capacity utilization enter in the function, though as a product. This has been criticized by Bhaduri and Marglin (1990) on the grounds that it does not distinguish well between mark-up and capacity utilization effects on investment. Assuming constant mark-up, however, minimizes this inconvenience.

6. For small values of c the composite propensity to save out of profit income, s_p, is larger than the propensity to save out of wage income, s_h. This implies that for a given capacity utilization and real exchange rate a redistribution between factors of production would affect aggregate savings along Kaldorian lines (Kaldor, 1956). However the wage-exchange rate trade-off and variable capacity utilization allow for both a positive and negative affect of wage increases on domestic savings as emphasized by the aggregate demand analysis below.

7. The intertemporal approach to the current account has been widely popularized by Obstfeld and Rogoff (1995, 1996) and constitutes the open economy extension of growth and business cycle new classical models.

8. More structure in debt maturity could be easily introduced without any significant change in the debt accumulation law. For example (12.13) would become $\dot{b} = \delta(au - \varepsilon) + (j - g)b$, where δ is a constant that depends on debt maturity and j an 'effective' rate determined as an average of $\rho + \kappa$ and the number of maturing certificates.

9. Note that while the former condition depends on distribution, the latter depends also on the debt ratio, and that $f(\bullet)$ in the excess demand function can be linearized and normalized to 1 without loss of generality.

10. The extended system embracing all the entries of the SAM would include the determination of stock variations, $\dot{E}$ and $\dot{B}$ for instance, valuation p_E and wealth. The latter two are however direct functions of net profitability and we leave them implicit to concentrate on the main flow dynamics in the short-run and long-run stock ratio dynamics.

11. See Krugman and Taylor (1978), Taylor (1991, Ch. 7) and La Marca (2004b), for examples of possible contractionary devaluations.

12. Condition (12.21) is obtained by multiplying (12.20) by β_T, taking the limits and assuming that creditors are not willing to allow infinite and unlimited borrowing: $\lim_{T \to \infty} b_T \beta_T = 0$.

13. Note that although we have not included the government sector we can interpret a rise in the savings propensities as an effect of a budget deficit reduction and other contractionary policies which traditionally would be the first policy advice for a debt-stricken country.

14. This multi-dimensional way of analysing a country's welfare becomes necessary once we acknowledge that no representative agent is available for utility measurement in real economies.

REFERENCES

Agénor, P. and P. Montiel (1999), *Development Macroeconomics*, Princeton, NJ: Princeton University Press.

Bhaduri, A. (1987), 'Dependent and self-reliant growth with foreign borrowing', *Cambridge Journal of Economics*, **11**, 269–73.

Bhaduri, A. and S. Marglin (1990), 'Unemployment and the real wage: the economic basis for contesting political ideologies', *Cambridge Journal of Economics*, **14**, 375–93.

Blanchard, O., J. Chouraqui, R. Hagemann and N. Sartor (1990), 'The sustainability of fiscal policy: new answers and economic questions', *OECD Economic Studies*, No. 15.

Foley, D. (2003), 'Financial fragility in developing economies', in A. Dutt and J. Ross (eds), *Development Economics and Structuralist Macroeconomics: Essays in Honor of Lance Taylor*, Cheltenham, UK and Northampton, MA, USA: Edward Elgar.

Foley, D. and L. Taylor (2004), 'A heterodox growth and distribution model' unpublished paper presented at the Conference 'Economic Growth and Distribution', Lucca, June, 16–18, 2004.

Kaldor, N. (1956), 'Alternative theories of distribution', *Review of Economic Studies*, **23**, 83–100.

Krugman, P. (1988), 'Financing versus forgiving a debt overhang', *Journal of Development Economics*, **29**, 253–68.

Krugman, P. (1989), 'Market-based debt reduction schemes', in J. Frenkel, M. Dooley and P. Wickhan (eds), *Analytical Issues in Debt*, Washington: International Monetary Fund, pp. 258–78.

Krugman, P. and L. Taylor (1978), 'Contractionary effects of devaluation', *Journal of International Economics*, **8**, 445–56.

La Marca, M. (2004a), 'Financial integration, growth, and macroeconomic volatility', *New School Economic Review*, **1**, Fall, New York.

La Marca, M. (2004b), 'Real exchange rate, competitiveness and policy implications: a formal analysis of alternative macro models', CEPA Working Papers, New York.

Meese, R. and K. Rogoff (1983), 'Empirical exchange rate models of the seventies: do they fit out of sample?', *Journal of International Economics*, **14** (February), 3–24.

Obstfeld, M. and K. Rogoff (1995), 'The intertemporal approach to the current account', in G.M. Grossman and K. Rogoff (eds), *Handbook of International Economics*, Amsterdam: North Holland, volume 3, ch. 34, pp. 1731–99.

Obstfeld, M. and K. Rogoff (1996), *Foundations of International Macroeconomics*, Cambridge, Mass.: MIT Press.

Pasinetti, L. (1998), 'The myth (or folly) of the 3% deficit/GDP Maastricht "parameter"', *Cambridge Journal of Economics*, **22**, 117–36.

Pasinetti, L. (2000), 'On concepts of debt sustainability; a reply to Dr. Hark', *Cambridge Journal of Economics*, **24**, 511–14.

Pattillo, C., H. Poirson and L. Ricci (2002), 'External debt and growth', *IMF Working Papers*, WP/02/69, Washington, DC.

Taylor, L. (1991), *Income Distribution, Inflation and Growth*, Cambridge, Mass.: MIT Press.

Taylor, L. (2004), *Reconstructing Macroeconomics: Structuralist Proposals and Critiques of the Mainstream*, Cambridge, Mass.: Harvard University Press.

Taylor, L. and N. Barbosa-Filho (2003), 'Distributive and demand cycles in the US economy – A structuralist Goodwin model', CEPA Working Papers, New York: New School University.

13. Saving capitalism from capitalists: inequality, taxation and growth in a concentrated economy[*]

Guido Cozzi

13.1. INTRODUCTION

This chapter suggests an additional explanation for the negative correlation often found between inequality and growth, and the positive correlation between taxation and growth (see for example, Alesina and Rodrik, 1994, Persson and Tabellini, 1994; Perotti, 1996; Benabou, 1996): the corporate channel.

Endogenous growth theory (for example, Shell, 1966, 1967, and 1970; Romer 1990; Grossman and Helpman, 1991a, 1991b and 1991c; Aghion and Howitt, 1992 and 1996) recognizes the importance of purposeful investment by firms in the research and development (R&D) of better products and processes as a major cause of the growth in the wealth of nations. Cumulated R&D investments generate higher profits and higher wages, in proportion to the productivity advances they bring about.

While the models of 'creative destruction' (see Aghion and Howitt, 1998) develop and extend some important Schumpeterian insights, this chapter seeks to analyse the growth consequences of inequality and taxation in an economic framework perhaps more similar to what Schumpeter (1942) thought should prevail at an advanced stage of capitalism. In the economy of this chapter R&D is a routinized and incremental activity that gains a decisive competitive advantage from the firm's production experience, long-term customer/seller or borrower/lender relationships, so that no potential rival would find it profitable to challenge the incumbent firm on its own terrain. Needless to say, there is ample empirical evidence of incremental and successful R&D carried out in large firms' laboratories, as well as evidence of breakthrough innovations realized by small new entrants, and a more complete model should consider both aspects of the industrial world.

Who decides the amount of R&D carried out in this economy? Those who control the firms, that is, in the model, their owners.

Now, if different individuals are differently 'rich' in terms of firm ownership, they will likely have different opinions as to the 'ideal' R&D investment their firms should carry out. For example, someone who owns no share of any firm and whose income only comes from her labour will like all firms in the economy to invest in R&D as much as possible in order to reap the gains in terms of higher wage income, which increases with the economy-wide productivity. At the other extreme, consider an unrealistically rich 'capitalist' who completely owns all the firms in the economy, and whose income mostly derives from the aggregate profits and in very little proportion from her wages. She would be happy to have aggregate productivity grow, but at the same time she would worry about the R&D investment as well: the R&D expenditures have to be deducted from her profits and they crowd out resources from final output. Though total factor productivity advances benefit the labour and profit components of aggregate income in the same proportion, the 'capitalist' will desire a lower R&D investment than the 'labourer'. Her losses would be direct and indirect: even if someone else (a benevolent *deus ex machina*) paid the wages of the workers employed in the labs, the capitalist would still be worried that these workers are diverted away from the production of the outputs whose sale yields profits to the firm.

If instead of one 'capitalist' we had a group of them spanning the property of all the horizontally differentiated monopolists of a Schumpeterian 'advanced capitalism', their common interest would be to carry out less R&D investment than would be in the common interest of the pure workers.

By the same argument, it is easily understood that groups of individuals whose income comes from intermediate shares of profit/labour sources will have intermediate common interests, with the 'richer' (that is those with higher share of income coming from profits than from labour) desiring a lower aggregate R&D investment, and the 'poorer' desiring more R&D investment and growth.

In a perfectly equal economy, as in a representative agent model, every individual would own the same share of the firms' property, while the more 'unequal' a society the more concentrated firm property would be in the hands of the richer individuals. If property confers control rights, it seems reasonable to assume, as this chapter does, that higher inequality is represented by control over firms by people whose income is more profit-biased. We will then assume that the more concentrated the property, the more the decisions taken by firms aim to satisfy the preferences of the profit earners.

In the models of the political channel (for example, Bertola, 1993; Alesina and Rodrik, 1994; Persson and Tabellini, 1994) for the negative link between inequality and growth it was individual votes for fiscal policy measures that mattered, with different effects depending on the relative wealth characteristics of the pivotal voters (Benabou 1996). In this model of the 'corporate channel' it is the 'pivotal shareholder' that decides R&D investment and growth. If the pivotal shareholders in all the firms in the economy have the same wealth compositions they will all prefer the same aggregate R&D investment and the same economy-wide growth rate. If they are able to achieve collective action to pursue their common interest they will all force their controlled firms to undertake the R&D investment that maximizes their lifetime wealth.

To enforce collective action in a simple way, this chapter will assume a large conglomerate group that concentrates the property of all the firms in the economy in the hands of the same holding, whose shares accurately represent the ownership structure in the economy. This may result from a series of mergers and acquisitions by horizontally differentiated monopolistic firms. The 'corporate channel' is then easily explained: in our hypothetical extremely concentrated Schumpeterian advanced economy, the richer the wealthy groups that dominate the corporate decisions the lower the amount of R&D their firms will undertake, and therefore the lower the aggregate growth of their economy.

This is a simple way to guarantee common action, but it is clear that other indirect forms of coordination may work as well. For example, firms may spontaneously want to cooperate at the R&D level to exploit complementary knowledge: what we really need for our results is effective coordination of the R&D activities of firms with similar ownership structure.

The main point of this chapter is that in a concentrated market economy in which producer's R&D is the main source of technological progress and in which the capital market allows households to have perfectly diversified portfolios, the richer are more unfavourable to growth, while the poorer favour innovation more. The ability of individuals to implement their preferences via their control rights over firms is only a stylized, but consistent, way of finding a channel through which to aggregate their wills, but, similar to politico-economic models, real-world channels could be more indirect and less smooth.

The channel from more inequality to slower growth is studied in Sections 13.2 and 13.3 in a pure *laissez faire* economy. Government intervention is assumed in Section 13.4, under the form of a kind of progressive taxation. It is shown that if profits are taxed, the higher the tax rate the higher is aggregate growth. The intuition is that profit taxation makes the interest of the 'capitalist' more similar to the interest of the 'labourer', with her desiring more intense R&D investment and faster growth. To the extent that her 'desires' are transmitted, through the share ownership channel, to her firms, the latter will invest more and the economy will grow more. Importantly, taxation is distortionary, but it need not be redistributive: unlike Aghion and Bolton (1997), what has to be corrected here is not the negative incentive to underinvest of the poorer, but of the richer.

13.2. THE MODEL

We assume that each of a continuum of infinitely-lived individuals chooses their consumption plans so as to solve

$$\max_{x_h(\cdot,\cdot) \in PC([0,1] \times R_+, R_+)} \int_0^{+\infty} e^{-\rho t} \left[\int_0^1 x_h(i,\ t)^\alpha di \right]^{\frac{1}{\alpha}} dt \qquad (13.1)$$

subject to

$$\int_0^{+\infty} \left[\int_0^1 x_h(i,\ t) p(i,\ t) di \right] e^{-\int_0^t r(s) ds} dt \leq \qquad (13.2)$$

$$\int_0^{+\infty} Lw(t) e^{-\int_0^t r(s) ds} dt + W_h(0) \qquad (13.3)$$

where $x_h(i,\ t)$ is individual $h \in [0,\ 1]$'s time t's rate per unit time of consumption of good $i \in [0,\ 1]$, $p(i,\ t)$ its price, $w(t)$ is time t's wage rate, $W_h(0)$ is her initial non-human wealth and $r(s)$ the capital market's interest rate at time s, and L is her flow labour endowment bearing no disutility.[1]

Linearity of instantaneous utility in the CES consumption index $[\int_0^1 x_h(i,\ t)^\alpha di]^{1/\alpha}$ implies that the real interest rate is constantly equal to ρ. From equations (13.1) and (13.3), and aggregation, it follows that the instantaneous demand for each good i is given by:

$$\int_0^1 x_h u(i,\ t) dh \equiv x(i,\ t) = E(t) \frac{p(i,\ t)^{-\frac{1}{1-\alpha}}}{\int_0^1 p(j,\ t)^{\frac{-\alpha}{1-\alpha}} dj} \qquad (13.4)$$

where $E(t)$ denotes the rate per unit time of aggregate nominal expenditure.

Each good i is produced at each instant $t \geq 0$ by monopolistically competitive firms under a linear technology using labour as the only primary factor, hired at wage $w(t)$, whose average and marginal productivity is denoted by $f_i(t)$. Product varieties do not change over time. Entry and exit is free, but there is instantaneous Bertand competition and a, albeit small, positive fixed cost stemming from overhead labour $n < L(1-\alpha)$: therefore there will be only one firm at each location in the product space $[0, 1]$.

Labour productivity can be increased by firm-specific R&D investment in a flow of labour $u_i(t)$ allocated to the innovative activity. Firm-made technological advances are generated according to the following law of motion:

$$\dot{f_i}(t) = \frac{a'}{\beta} f_i(t)^\beta u_i(t)^\beta \qquad (13.5)$$

for all $i \in A$, where $\beta \in (0, 1)$, and $a' \in R_{++}$ is a scalar productivity parameter. Note that we assume decreasing returns to ideas and decreasing returns to R&D investment, thus ruling out implausible scale effects (see Jones, 1995a, 1995b, and 1999). This particular specification helps calculations, but our qualitative results can be generalized.

In (13.5) we made the strong assumption that innovation is 'firm-specific', instead of 'sector-specific': this rules out 'business stealing' in a drastic way. Similar results would have been obtained by assuming a competitive advantage in R&D of the firm that has developed previous inventions and accumulated the additional practical knowledge of the goods whose production and distribution they control all the time. The previous innovators may have a better innate ability to innovate in that sector, or have better R&D cost conditions (Barro and Sala-i-Martin, 1995). Incumbents may have accumulated a competitive advantage in other dimensions, such as the control of distribution channels (Stein, 1997). These ingredients could make our model generate the same equilibrium outcomes. Moreover, the very fact that innovations are incremental at infinitesimally small steps implies that even if no firm had a cost advantage in R&D, profits would last only one instant (in the absence of patent breadth), and in equilibrium only one firm would occupy each location in the product space; by adding an, albeit small, positive 'entry fee' (installation cost) we would obtain a unique persistent monopoly along the equilibrium path.

From a motivational perspective, this chapter departs from the Schumpeterian models of 'creative destruction' in order to focus on a kind of 'advanced capitalism' (Schumpeter, 1942) in which routinized R&D activities are better carried out by the incumbent monopolist firm run by managers.[2]

We will focus on a symmetric setting for simplicity's sake, and therefore we will assume a common initial technological stock $f_i(0) \equiv f_0$.

Since bonds are perfect substitutes in their return and risk aspects, while equities confer control rights, equity holding weakly dominates bond holding, and hence we will concentrate on equilibria where only equities are held by households.

Moreover, we will work under the assumption that there exists a perfectly efficient system of financial intermediaries that operates at no cost and that completely diversifies firms' property across the population so that every individual has a perfectly balanced portfolio of firm equity. The fact that 'firms are equally owned by all individuals in the economy' (Aghion, Dewatripont and Rey, 1996, p. 8, footnote 3) allows us to index individual wealth in terms of a scalar instead of an infinite dimensional vector: in fact individual $h \in [0, 1]$ owns $\theta_h \in R_{++} \cup \{\infty\}$ shares of every firm's capital in her portfolio, and her non-human wealth will be simply described by scalar θ_h, which will not change over time.[3]

Note that there are infinitely many individuals and firms in this economy, and therefore the ownership of each firm is dispersed among an infinity of agents, while the portfolio of each individual is diversified in the same proportion over the infinity of firm assets. Moreover, since, without loss of generality, we have normalized *both* populations of individuals and firms (consumer product varieties) to the unit interval, a share of $\theta_h = 1$ means that individual h has mean ownership,[4] whereas $\theta_h > 1$ and $\theta_h < 1$ denote above average and below average asset ownership, respectively.

13.3. EQUILIBRIUM

Since firms are perfectly identical as to their quantitative characteristics[5] and their ownership structures we can concentrate on equilibria in which their choice variables take on the same values. Along a symmetric equilibrium every firm proves to invest the same amount in R&D and therefore the evolution of their technological stocks shall satisfy

$$\dot{f}(t) = \frac{a'}{\beta} f(t)^{\beta} u(t)^{\beta},$$

where $f(t)$ and $u(t)$ are their numerically identical labour productivity and labour R&D employment.

It follows that the symmetric instantaneous equilibrium prices are $p(i,t) = [w(t)]/[f(t)\alpha] \equiv p(t)$. Hence real wages are equal to $f(t)\alpha$. Firms' real gross – of R&D expenditures – profit rates per unit time will all be equal to:

$$\pi(i,\ t) = C(t)(1-\alpha) - nf(t)\alpha \tag{13.6}$$

where $C(t) \equiv E(t)/p(t)$ denotes instantaneous aggregate real consumption.

Firm i can improve its technology by hiring workers at rates $u(i,\ t)$ for doing R&D. Therefore its instantaneous cash flows will be $\pi(i,\ t) - u(i,\ t)f(t)\alpha$.

In this hypothetical economy the firms are intended as units that specialize in the production of a consumption variety, but that also contribute to technological improvement by hiring workers to undertake research: therefore specialization in production involves a firm-specific ability to innovate.

Note that this rules out 'creative destruction' (Aghion and Howitt, 1992), because only a firm that produces product variety j can successfully improve its productivity and/or the quality of its product[6] and challenge the firm that is actually producing j, but this is discouraged by instantaneous price competition, and overhead and labour costs. Therefore whoever is most productive at a given date will be the only monopolist at all future dates.

In this model firms are production and research units at the same time, while no other research units can effectively challenge their monopolistic position. However, firms cannot be really regarded as independent players. They are connected to each other by their ownership structure. Thanks to our perfectly efficient financial market all firms are owned by the same individuals in the same way. It is as if all firms were different production and R&D units of the same large conglomerate group: the reader can imagine that the owners of all firms operating indifferent product lines exchanged their stock for that of a holding company. In fact, given our assumption of perfectly competitive financial intermediaries with no overhead cost, the behaviour of the financial sector is identical to the case where only one zero profit financial intermediary owned all of the firm assets in the economy, with the θ_h s representing individual h's ownership of this intermediary. In such a case the individual stockholders would possess shares of the holding company that governs the entire economy.

This leads us to the question of who takes the relevant decisions on the firm's actions. In an economy with costless information, perfect rationality, perfect property rights, and perfect control rights, it must be the stockholders that give the relevant indications to the production units about the strategies they should carry out. Of course there are some institutional limitations: for example, shareholders may desire all of their firms to collude horizontally by jointly fixing prices to maximize joint profits, but this monopolistic behaviour would be found unacceptable by antitrust legislation. In our model rich shareholders would clearly benefit from having all firms set an infinite nominal price/nominal wage ratio for their product in order to drive the real wage to zero and to enjoy maximal real dividends: this would entail excessively strong social tensions in the presence of inequality, as people with $\theta_h = 0$ might threaten the whole social contract. Hence we will assume that horizontal collusion is made unfeasible by a perfectly efficient antitrust authority.

In principle, banning horizontal collusion does not preclude other forms of strategy coordination among firms. In this model firms have to decide their R&D investment, and this analysis is facilitated by the symmetric structure. If all shareholders had the same idea about the optimal R&D investment in the economy, the financial intermediary would transmit it to the controlled firms, which in turn would fix their R&D investment accordingly. This would likely maximize aggregate welfare and would not deserve any antitrust intervention.

Industrial concentration coupled with legal prevention of horizontal collusion between different product lines allows the cooperative behaviour of firms on other dimensions not considered harmful from a social point of view: among them is R&D cooperation. R&D cooperation typically entails efficiency gains in the form of avoided duplications, internalized externalities,[7] and exploited complementarities between the experience of horizontally differentiated firms, as reported by a large body of literature. In this chapter we can simply assume that coordinated R&D activities bring about an efficiency gain in the form of a cost saving in the research technology, for example due to better information spillovers that reduce duplications, and that can be represented by a different law of motion of technology given by

$$\dot{f}(t) = \frac{a}{\beta} f(t)^\beta u(t)^\beta, \tag{13.7}$$

where $a > a'$ summarizes the efficiency gains from coordinated R&D, and motivates a favourable disposition of the antitrust authorities towards interfirm R&D coordination, as witnessed by the National Cooperative Research Act of 1984 in the US and successive amendments, and by the exemption from Art. 85 in the antitrust regulation of the European Community for cooperative agreements in R&D.

Therefore it seems reasonable to adopt here the assumption that all firms in our stylized economy act as *independent production* units (for antitrust reasons), but as *coordinated research* units: the main reason for such centralization of decisions and concentration of property is not to reduce competition, but to internalize positive pecuniary externalities among different sectors and to gain higher efficiency in the research and development of ways to improve the quality of the products and the economy-wide productivity of labour. Due to this behaviour, the assumption that all firms belong to the same economy-wide large conglomerate group becomes unnecessary: a perfectly functioning research association between symmetrically-owned independent firms suffices.

As we shall shortly see, in the presence of unequal individual wealth distribution, unanimity of ideal R&D investment fails. While in a representative agent economy cooperative R&D investment is decided, similar to Cozzi's (1999) representative agent model,[8] by finding a common value function $V_C(f)$ as the solution to the following optimization problem:

$$V_C(f) \equiv \max_{u(\cdot)} \int_t^{+\infty} \{C(s)(1-\alpha) - u(s)f(s)\alpha - nf(s)\alpha\} e^{-\rho(s-t)} ds \quad (13.8)$$

Subject to: $\dot{f}(s) = \frac{a}{\beta} f(s)^{\beta} u(s)^{\beta}$, $f(t) = f$, $s \geq 0$, here we need to take into account that individuals who own different properties have different objective functions.

In this chapter individuals only differ in their firm property, that is in the non-labour component of their wealth, while their labour income is the same. Hence we can rewrite time t's non-human wealth of an individual h with property $\theta_h \geq 0$ as:

$$\theta_h \int_t^{+\infty} [C(s)(1-\alpha) - u(s)f(s)\alpha - nf(s)\alpha] e^{-\rho(s-t)} ds. \quad (13.9)$$

In addition to their share of the present value of the economy's future profits every individual works and earns the same wage income $Lw(t) = Lf(t)\alpha$.

Therefore total individual wealth at time t is given by the discounted value of the sum of her profit and labour income streams

$$\int_t^{+\infty} \{\theta_h [C(s)(1-\alpha) - u(s)f(s)\alpha - nf(s)\alpha] + Lf(s)\alpha\} e^{-\rho(s-t)} ds. \quad (13.10)$$

The ownership of all the firms in our stylized economy is represented by the factors θ_h, $h \in [0, 1]$, that is the market is entirely possessed by the private families through a unique financial intermediary.[9] The board of this financial intermediary will decide on the best possible path for $u(\cdot)$. But 'best' in what sense? Clearly it is not guaranteed that all shareholders' optimal choices of R&D investment coincide: what is trivial in the representative agent world – that is maximizing the economy's present value – becomes controversial in a world with unequal property.

We work here under the assumption that every individual is rational and able to figure out the general equilibrium effects of all possible R&D investment paths. This replicates the extreme assumption on the rationality of voters typically made in the politico-economic models (Bertola, 1993; Persson and Tabellini, 1994; Alesina and Rodrik, 1994; Benabou 1996, etc.), with the only difference that here it is not the political vote that matters, but the corporate vote: it is not the median voter that matters, but the pivotal voter is the stockholder whose equity ownership is decisive. With perfect equality $\theta_h = 1$; hence inequality can be represented by a distribution of holdings such that the pivotal voters are characterized by $\theta_h > 1$, that is they are richer than average.

We obtain:

Proposition 1: *Individual* h*'s optimal value of her wealth is given by*:

$$V_h(f) = \frac{(L - n - L\alpha)\theta_h + L\alpha}{\rho} f + \theta_h^{\frac{-\beta}{1-\beta}} \frac{1-\beta}{\rho\beta}\left[\frac{(L - n - L\alpha)\theta_h + L\alpha}{\rho} a\right] \quad (13.11)$$

and the corresponding ideal feedback rule for R&D is:

$$u_h^*(f;\theta_h) = \left[\frac{L - n - L\alpha(1 - 1/\theta_h)}{\rho} a\right]^{\frac{1}{1-\beta}} f^{-1}. \quad (13.12)$$

Proof: Using the instantaneous resource (labour) condition $[C(s)/f(s)] + u(s) + n = L$, household's h's maximization problem can be written as:

$$\max_{u(\cdot)} \int_t^{+\infty} \{[L - u(s) - n - L\alpha]\theta_h + L\alpha\} f(s) e^{-\rho(s-t)} ds \quad (13.13)$$

subject to law of motion (13.7). The Hamilton–Jacobi–Bellman equation of this problem is then

$$\rho V_h(f) = \max_{u \geq 0} \left[(L - u - n - L\alpha)\theta_h + L\alpha\right] f + V_h'(f)\frac{a}{\beta} f^\beta u^\beta \quad (13.14)$$

By deriving w.r.t. u and equating to zero we get:

$$u_h = \left(\frac{aV_h'(f)}{\theta_h} \right)^{\frac{1}{1-\beta}} f^{-1} \qquad (13.15)$$

Replacing (13.15) for u_h for u into (13.14) yields:

$$\rho V_h(f) = \left[(L-n-L\alpha)\theta_h + L\alpha \right] f + \theta_h^{\frac{-\beta}{1-\beta}} \frac{1-\beta}{\beta} [aV_h'(f)]^{\frac{1}{1-\beta}} \qquad (13.16)$$

which is solved by (13.12). Plugging (13.12) into (13.15) implies (13.11).

Q.E.D.

Remark. From (13.12) we immediately see that $\partial u_h^*(f; \theta_h)/\partial \theta_h < 0$. Therefore the higher the firm share controlled by household h the lower her/his ideal R&D investment: the richer prefers less R&D investment than the poorer because a lower proportion of her wealth comes from labour; and driving more workers from the plants to the research laboratories brings about an increase in the labour share of output at the expense of the profit share. In fact, the wage income $L\alpha f$ increases proportionally with labour productivity, while profits $(L-n-L\alpha)f - uf$ increase less than proportionally with f, and it is strictly decreasing with R&D effort u. The cost of R&D is the sum of the wages paid for R&D workers and the forgone production of the commodities whose sale generates profits: labour in the labs is costly not only directly (wages) but also indirectly, as R&D workers are not producing a final output that can be sold. Workers do not feel any difference, insofar as they are paid the same real wage and the same real interest rate, but profit earners do. Hence the larger the share of the individual income stemming from profits, the lower the incentive to carry out R&D investments.

Obviously, given the individual's share of the firms' equity, her ideal R&D investment path is entirely determined regardless of the way the firms finance such investments, such as retained profits, outside financing through bonds, new equity issuance, or any combination of these. In the case of debt, it does not matter who finances the firm either: it may be the individual whose optimal R&D we are analysing, other individuals or entities, or any combination of them.

Clearly, if the poorer are those who make decisions about R&D investment, they will want more investment and growth than they would if property were equally divided: hence an egalitarian economy grows faster than an unequal society where the investment decisions are in the hands of the rich, but it grows more slowly than an unequal society where the investment decisions are in the hands of the poor. By the same argument, we can say – somewhat paradoxically – that under the assumptions of our model, a capitalist economy where R&D decisions are dictated by the 'proletarians' grows more than a socialist economy, while it grows less if R&D decisions are dictated by the 'capitalists'.

13.3.1   Capitalism Saved by Competitive Finance

In our previous analysis a crucial role was played by the fact that firms coordinated R&D activities in order to pursue the interests of their owners. In this sense cross stockholding facilitated the collective action of the owners in our economy. This led the owners to internalize the negative pecuniary externalities of each other's R&D investment on their profit incomes and the positive externalities on their wage incomes.

If instead each firm was owned by different people who were unable to coordinate actions with the owners of other firms, the R&D decision within each firm would not depend on how rich the decisive shareholder is.

In fact, assuming that individual h only possessed share θ_h of firm i, her lifetime real wealth would be given by:

$$\int_t^{+\infty} \left\{ [x(i,s)p(i,s)(1-\alpha) - u_i(s)\alpha f(s) - n\alpha f(s)]\theta_h + L\alpha f(s) \right\} e^{-\rho(s-t)} ds =$$

$$\int_t^{+\infty} \left\langle \left\{ [L-u(s)-n](1-\alpha)f(s)^{\frac{1-2\alpha}{1-\alpha}} f_i(s)^{\frac{\alpha}{1-\alpha}} - u_i(s)\alpha f(s) - n\alpha f(s) \right\}\theta_h + L\alpha f(s) \right\rangle e^{-\rho(s-t)} ds$$

$$(13.17)$$

where we have assumed for simplicity that all other firms have equal productivity f, and we have made use of the demand function (13.4).

Expression (13.17) is maximized by the same control $u_i(\cdot)$ for any $\theta_h > 0$, that is all of the owners of a firm have unanimous ideal R&D investment for their firm. This emphasizes the role of property concentration in deriving our previous results about inequality and growth. The more 'capitalistic' someone is, the more she feels the *negative* externality of aggregate R&D investment on her firms' profits. Instead, the more 'proletarian' someone is, the more she will feel the *positive* externality of aggregate R&D investment of her wage income.

The following holds:

Proposition 1:   *There is a unique equilibrium feedback rule for R&D adopted by all firms and it is equal to:*

$$u(f) = \left(\frac{L-n}{\rho}a\right)^{\frac{1}{1-\beta}} f^{-1}. \tag{13.18}$$

Proof: Firm i's current value Hamiltonian, after dropping time indexes, is:

$$(L-u-n)(1-\alpha)f^{\frac{1-2\alpha}{1-\alpha}}f_i^{\frac{\alpha}{1-\alpha}} - u_i\alpha f - n\alpha f + \lambda_i\frac{a}{\beta}f_i^{\beta}u_i^{\beta}. \tag{13.19}$$

The optimal control has to satisfy:

$$u_i^{1-\beta} = \frac{\lambda_i a}{\alpha}\left(\frac{f_i}{f}\right)^{\beta} f^{\beta-1} \tag{13.20}$$

The adjoint equation is:

$$\dot{\lambda}_i = \lambda_i\rho - (L-u-n)\left(\frac{f}{f_i}\right)^{\frac{1-2\alpha}{1-\alpha}}\alpha - \lambda_i a f_i^{\beta-1}u_i^{\beta} \tag{13.21}$$

which in a symmetric equilibrium becomes:

$$\dot{\lambda}_i = \lambda_i\rho - (L-u-n)\alpha + \lambda_i a f_i^{\beta-1}u_i^{\beta} \tag{13.22}$$

Applying symmetry to (13.20), plugging it into (13.22), setting $\dot{\lambda}_i = 0$ and solving for u_i finally gives:

$$u_i = \left(\frac{(L-n)\ a}{\rho}\right)^{\frac{1}{1-\beta}} f^{-1} \tag{13.23}$$

Q.E.D.

Note that (13.23) does not depend on individual firm market power (inverse) index α. This is a property of the simplified specification adopted.

This result implies that the more 'developed' a financial market, in the sense of its achieving a higher degree of diversification of households' portfolios over the entire economy, the more opposed the richer individuals will be to innovation and growth. The more they are able to implement their common interest by an efficient use of their property and control rights, the lower the level of R&D investment and the poorer the growth performance of the economy. This suggests a negative effect of ownership concentration on growth.

All our results would continue to hold if we assumed that firms were owned by different individuals but had the same proportional representation of each wealth group, and they only coordinated their R&D activities. The advantage of this interpretation of our model is that with cooperation only at the R&D level, non-cooperative price setting would be the most natural outcome.

Under this alternative interpretation, firms would join the R&D association in order to achieve two results:

1. Increase the efficiency of their R&D by using complementary knowledge from firms operating in different sectors.
2. Maximize the collective interest of their dominant wealth group by internalizing the negative pecuniary externality of R&D investment.

The first positive efficiency effect may or may not overcome the second strategic effect, and should be one of the main arguments in the likely controversies that would arise at the antitrust level.

13.4. PROFIT TAXATION

In this section we introduce a very simple form of progressive taxation and show that the higher the tax rate on profit incomes the higher the R&D investment and growth in the presence of inequality.

Since the pretax income of individual h is $[(L-n-u-L\alpha)\theta_h + L\alpha]f$, we decompose it into an 'average' income $(L-n-u)$ plus an 'excess' income $(L-n-u-L\alpha)(\theta_h-1)f$, and assume that this part of income is taxed at rate $\tau \in (0, 1)$ if $\theta_h > 1$, while average income is not taxed. Recall that inequality is defined as an above average firm ownership – $\theta_h > 1$ – by the pivotal share holder. We assume for simplicity that the tax proceeds are simply destroyed.

It follows that the post-tax income of individual h becomes

$$\{(L-n-u-L\alpha)[\theta_h(1-\tau)+\tau]+L\alpha\}f, \qquad (13.24)$$

and we can repeat the very same steps as in the proof of Proposition 1, arriving at:

Proposition 1: *Individual* h's *optimal value of her wealth is given by:*

$$V_h(f,\theta_h,\tau) = \frac{(L-n-L\alpha)[\theta_h(1-\tau)+\tau]+L\alpha}{\rho}f+ \qquad (13.25)$$

$$+[\theta_h(1-\tau)+\tau]^{\frac{-\beta}{1-\beta}}\frac{1-\beta}{\rho\beta}\left\{\frac{(L-n-L\alpha)[\theta_h(1-\tau)+\tau]+L\alpha}{\rho}a\right\}^{\frac{1}{1-\beta}} \qquad (13.26)$$

and the corresponding ideal feedback rule for R&D is:

$$u_h^*(f;\theta_h,\tau) = \left[\frac{L-n-L\alpha\left(1-\dfrac{1}{[\theta_h(1-\tau)+\tau]}\right)}{\rho}a\right]^{\frac{1}{1-\beta}} \qquad f^{-1} \equiv \psi(\theta_h,\tau)f^{-1}. \quad (13.27)$$

Note that $\partial u_h^*(f;\ \theta_h,\ \tau)/\partial\theta_h < 0 < \partial u_h^*(f;\ \theta_h\tau)/\partial\tau$, and therefore:

Corollary 4: *The richer the pivotal shareholder, the lower the R&D investment and growth, and the higher the profit taxation, the higher the R&D investment and growth.*

Remark. The previous corollary shows that in this model we obtain the well-known empirical negative correlation between a measure of inequality and growth, but at the same time we obtain a *positive* correlation between the average and marginal tax rate on personal income and growth, found by Perotti (1996). Unlike Galor and Zeira (1993), Perotti (1993), Benabou (1996, 2000), Aghion and Bolton (1997), and Piketty (1997), we do not require limited enforceability of obligations, missing markets, or asymmetric information. Not only are credit and labour markets perfect here, but taxation is *not redistributive*, and therefore it is not aimed at improving the incentives for the poor or the middle class to invest. Taxation is only aimed at reducing the incentive for the richer agents to oppose their firms' investment in R&D; and this is achieved by altering the composition of their post-tax incomes toward the labour component.

The economic intuition for Proposition 2 is that since profit taxation reduces the profit share of individual income, it also weakens the adverse incentive effect on R&D investment described in the previous section. Therefore the interest of the shareholders becomes more similar to that of the workers if taxation is higher, which spurs R&D investment and growth. Contrary to the Laffer curve results of previous models, here the relationship between tax rate and growth is *monotonic*: in the limit, as $\tau \uparrow 1$ the individually optimum R&D investment tends to its upper bound $L - n$.

Note that the result of Proposition 2 carries over to a case of redistributive profit taxation with no change. This proves that in the presence of inequality, redistribution is not necessary for tax rates to positively affect growth, but it is not harmful either.

It is again interesting to compare economic regimes in the light of the previous proposition. In the previous section we showed that a market economy where R&D investment decisions are taken by the rich and with no redistribution would grow more slowly than an ideal equally efficient socialist regime that maximizes the welfare of the representative individual (perfect equality), whereas a market economy where those decisions are taken by the poor (a populistic capitalist economy) would grow faster. The results of this section prove that a market economy with strong taxation does better, in terms of growth, than an equally efficient socialized economy: somehow paradoxically, a strongly pro-labour government in a capitalist economy by maximizing redistribution would maximize growth, and would make that economy grow faster not only than a similar economy governed by a pro-wealth regime, but also faster than any purely socialist regime.

13.5. CONCLUSIONS

This chapter has shown that perfectly diversified household portfolios generate a common preference toward innovation (through R&D investment) among individuals who have the same wealth level, and different interests between individuals with different wealth levels. In particular, the poorer like innovation more than the richer. Hence the different interest groups are indeed the different wealth groups.

Individuals have the same labour endowment, but differ in their stock ownership, that is, they differ in the share of income coming from firm profits. But wages are paid a fraction of their marginal productivity, that in turn increases with the accumulated R&D. Profits are a fraction of aggregate expenditure, that is a fraction of the aggregate supply of final products. This means that having more workers in the research sector does not instantaneously reduce current wages, while it does instantaneously reduce current profits via an aggregate expenditure spillover: if less final output is produced each firm will sell proportionally less. Therefore, profit earners like R&D relatively less than do wage earners.

Though both income sources (wages and profits) benefit in the same proportion from total factor productivity growth, only profits suffer from the fewer resources available for final production as a result of R&D investment.

This is the basic mechanism that explains why the larger the profit share of someone's income the less intense her desire for aggregate R&D.

If a wealth group is able to impose its interest on firms, it is clear that the richer this group the lower the R&D investment and hence economic growth.

The most natural way that shareholders can control the decision of their firms is to simply exercise their control rights. That is, wealth is not only dividends, but also economic power. Consequently, in this chapter we have assumed that in an economy with high inequality it is the rich shareholders that can impose their preferred R&D investment path and thus their preferred economic growth rate: this generates a negative relation between inequality and growth. Interestingly, in this model the *de jure* right to influence the economy's decisions correlates perfectly with the dislike for economic growth.

Somewhat at odds with commonsense beliefs, in this model profit taxation proves beneficial to growth because it reduces the incentive for the rich influential shareholders to resist growth, because it links their interest more to the worker's interest: if the government takes away a larger fraction of someone's dividends, it will at the same time take away a larger fraction of the cause of her opposition to higher R&D investment.

It is worth remarking that in this chapter taxation need not be redistributive in order to be growth enhancing: wasteful profit taxation would do a good job for growth in our economy. What seems even more paradoxical, the equilibrium growth rate always increases with the marginal tax rate of the richer incomes: as in Perotti's empirical findings (1996), there is no Laffer curve in our model, as tax rates appear to be monotonically good for growth.

Of course, taxation may not be efficiency enhancing: the trade-off is between lower taxation and higher aggregate growth, but it is not claimed that growth is beneficial *per se*. For example the growth rate desired by the pure workers is higher than the growth rate obtained by a utilitarian social welfare functional.

Unlike Galor and Zeira (1993), Aghion and Bolton (1997), Piketty (1997) and Benabou (1996, 2000), there is no limited enforceability of contracts, nor asymmetric information, nor missing markets in this economy. Perhaps there is too much enforceability and information and markets are too perfect, in the sense that property, though extremely dispersed and diversified, still confers perfect control over firms' actions and perfect agents' coordination in pursuing their common interests: we have outlined a too perfect corporate democracy where the industrial power of individuals is proportional to their property.

The kind of advanced capitalist economy assumed here is perhaps more 'advanced' than Schumpeter's (1942) vision itself, set aside from the contemporary real world. However, the effects outlined here may be working on a smaller scale in more realistic economies and with the kinds of imperfections that enrich the analysis. The common interest of the wealth groups may be pursued with more indirect means.

Moreover, a side benefit from the analysis can be that dealing with limited enforceability and asymmetric information, albeit important, may not be sufficient to rule out a negative effect of inequality on growth and a positive role for progressive taxation. Compared to the models such as Galor and Zeira (1993), Aghion and Bolton (1997), Piketty (1997), a limitation of the present chapter is that it does not have non-trivial dynamics of dynasties' wealth distribution, which instead remains unexplained and unchanged over time. It would be very interesting and challenging to incorporate the effect highlighted in our simple stylized model in their more complex and realistic distributional dynamics.

NOTES

*   I would like to thank Mario Caminati and Stephen Turnovsky for helpful suggestions and seminar participants at the University of Padova, Lucca and Pisa for comments.
1.   Therefore labour is inelastically supplied in this model, but the qualitative results of the chapter do not depend on that.
2.   In any case, ruling out 'creative destruction' by drastic or sophisticated means is useful to make our new causal channel from inequality to growth more transparent, and maybe gets closer to an intuition of Schumpeter's about the future of the capitalist economy; however, in the real world experience we observe several cases that fit our assumption as well as several cases of pure 'creative destruction'. A more complete model should incorporate both.
3.   'This dispersed ownership structure entitles individuals to the whole flow of output (net of production and innovation costs) and not just to the wage fraction of it' (Aghion, Dewatripont and Rey, 1996, p. 8, footnote 3): though Aghion, Dewatripont, and Rey's (1996) model is totally different and uses this assumption only for its welfare analysis, it turns out that their assumption is a key ingredient for the results of our 'frictionless' model.
4.   If $\theta_h = 1$ for all individuals $h \in [0, 1]$ then there is perfectly equality, and we are in a representative agent's economy. If somebody owns all the firm's assets she will have $\theta_h = \infty$, while if $\theta_h = 0$ she only owns her labour endowment.
5.   With enough weak complementarity in the instantaneous utility function it can be shown that in equilibria starting from any asymmetric profile of technological levels across industries the equalization of all sectoral productivities will be reached in *finite time*: bang-bang optimal strategies guarantee technological catch-up.
6.   Under an obvious quality interpretation of $f_i(t)$ as the flow of utility services stemming from time t's version of consumer good i.
7.   For a recent empirical confirmation of the existence of inter-sector externalities of the R&D in US industries, see Kelly and Hageman (1999).
8.   Despite this formal similarity, the economics of Cozzi (1999) is very different. That paper studies the conditions for enforceability of various forms of R&D cooperation under non-

rival R&D and imperfect information. Setting aside the different technological framework, individuals are assumed perfectly identical in that model, while here the main focus is on inequality.

9. Of course this financial intermediary will not be in a monopoly position, because the assumed technology allows new entrants to 'contest' it, and it will be forced to maximize the utility of the aggregation of its shareholders. It would make no difference if we segregated by shareholders' wealth the different financial intermediaries, as they would have to confront each other at the single firm level. The crucial assumption is that every firm is equally owned by 'the market'.

REFERENCES

Aghion, P. and P. Bolton (1997), 'A Trickle-down theory of growth and development with debt overhang', *Review of Economic Studies*, **64**, 151–72.

Aghion, P. and P. Howitt (1992), 'A model of growth through creative destruction', *Econometrica*, **60**, 323–51.

Aghion, P. and P. Howitt (1996), 'Research and development in the growth process', *Journal of Economic Growth*, 1, 49–73.

Aghion, P. and P. Howitt (1998), *Endogenous Growth Theory*, Cambridge, Mass.: MIT Press.

Aghion, P., Dewatripont, M., and P. Rey (1999), 'Competition, financial discipline, and growth', *Review of Economic Studies*, **66**, 825–52.

Alesina, A. and D. Rodrik (1994), Distributive politics and economic growth', *Quarterly Journal of Economics*, **109**, 465–90.

Barro, R. and X. Sala-i-Martin (1995), *Economic Growth*, New York: McGraw-Hill.

Benabou, R. (1996), 'Inequality and growth', in B. Bernanke and J. Rotemberg (eds), *NBER Macroeconomics Annual*, pp. 11–74.

Benabou, R. (2000), 'Unequal societies: income distribution and the social contract', *American Economic Review*, **90**, 96–129.

Bertola, G. (1993), 'Factor shares and savings in endogenous growth', *American Economic Review*, **83**, 1184–98.

Cozzi, G. (1999), 'R&D cooperation and growth', *Journal of Economic Theory*, May, 17–49.

Galor, O. and J. Zeira (1993), 'Income distribution and macroeconomics', *Review of Economic Studies*, **60**, 35–52.

Grossman G. and E. Helpman (1991a), 'Quality ladders in the theory of growth', *Review of Economic Studies*, **58**, 43–61.

Grossman G. and E. Helpman (1991b), 'Quality ladders and product cycles', *Quarterly Journal of Economics*, 557–86.

Grossman G. and E. Helpman (1991c), *Innovation and Growth in the Global Economy*, Cambridge, Mass.: MIT Press.

Jones, C. (1995a), 'Time series tests of endogenous growth models', *Quarterly Journal of Economics*, **110**, 495–525.

Jones, C. (1995b), 'R&D-based models of economic growth', *Journal of Political Economy*, **103**, 759–74.

Jones C. (1999), 'Growth: with or without scale effects?', *American Economic Review*, **89**, 139–44.

Kelly, M. and A. Hageman (1999), 'Marshallian externalities in innovation', *Journal of Economic Growth*, **4**, 39–54.

Perotti, R. (1993), 'Political equilibrium, income distribution, and growth', *Review of Economic Studies*, **60**, 755–76.

Perotti, R. (1996), 'Growth, income distribution, and democracy: what the data say', *Journal of Economic Growth*, **2**, 149–87.

Persson, T. and G. Tabellini (1994), 'Is inequality harmful for growth? Theory and evidence', *American Economic Review*, **48**, 600–621.

Piketty, T. (1997), 'The dynamics of the wealth distribution and interest rate with credit rationing', *Review of Economic Studies*, **64**, 173–89.

Romer, P. (1990), 'Endogenous technical change', *Journal of Political Economy*, **98**, S71–S102.

Schumpeter, J. (1942), *Capitalism, Socialism and Democracy*, New York: Harper & Row.

Shell, K. (1966), 'Toward a theory of inventive activity and capital accumulation', *American Economic Review*, **16**, 62–8.

Shell, K. (1967), 'A model of inventive activity and capital accumulation', in K. Shell (ed.), *Essays on the Theory of Optimal Economic Growth*, Cambridge, Mass.: MIT Press, pp. 67–85.

Shell, K. (1970), 'Inventive activity, industrial organization and economic growth', in J.M. Mirrlees and N.H. Stern (eds), *Models of Economic Growth*, London and New York: John Wiley & Sons, 1973, pp. 77–100.

Stein, J. (1997), 'Waves of creative destruction: firm-specific learning-by-doing and the dynamics of innovation', *Review of Economic Studies*, **64**, 265–88.

14. Economic growth and poverty traps: a simple geometry of intergenerational transfers[*]

Luciano Fanti and Luca Spataro

14.1. INTRODUCTION

There is renewed interest in the relation between economic growth and income distribution. However, while the literature has mainly focused on the issue of the functional distribution of income between classes, social groups and so on, and of individual distribution, less attention has been devoted to the relation between growth and intergenerational distribution.

In addition, the recent literature on economic growth has highlighted the role of multiple equilibria and poverty traps in explaining the different long-run performance of rich and poor countries.[1] However, again, the role of the intergenerational distribution of resources and of redistributive public policies has been overlooked in this stream of literature.

We recall that a loose definition of a poverty trap concerns the existence of a stable 'poor' steady state equilibrium (low levels of per capita output and capital stock) which assumes the feature to be a trap in that, notwithstanding the efforts of the agents to escape from it, the economy shows a tendency to return to such a poor equilibrium.

At least three canonical models of poverty traps in the framework of the neoclassical theory of growth have been largely discussed: 1) models with non-constant returns to scale in technology, due for example to externalities such as learning-by-doing or, from a historical point of view, due to the transition from an agricultural era at diminishing returns to an industrial era at increasing returns; 2) models with a non-constant rate of population growth, for instance corresponding historically to the 'stylized fact' of the so-called demographic transition; 3) models with non-constant saving rates. All these models share the feature of an S-shaped form for the relationship between both technology or population growth or rate of saving on the one side and growth on the other. Likewise, all these models share the other feature that a positive shock of technical progress or the saving rate or, alternatively, a negative shock of the population growth rate may lead to escape from poverty traps.

On the other hand, while the role of public policy in influencing the optimal growth in the neoclassical models has been extensively investigated since Diamond (1965), less attention has been devoted to the role of public policy on the theme of poverty traps.

In the present work we depart from the works on poverty traps mentioned above in that our contribution aims to investigate the role of public intervention via intergenerational transfers in causing or in escaping from the poverty trap in the canonical context of two-period overlapping generations à la Samuelson (1958)–Diamond (1965). Moreover, unlike Diamond (1965), we allow for poverty traps. Our results show that a taxation policy plays a role in the poverty trap issue, which can be added to the role of the shocks mentioned above and so far pointed out in the literature.

In such models a redistributive public policy is known to be able to generate a welfare improvement due to the fact that the market equilibrium can be dynamically inefficient. Subsequent literature, by introducing altruism in this overlapping generation framework, has shown that the market allocation is the optimal allocation and that it is not affected by lump-sum intergenerational transfers.[2] Since in this chapter we analyse the issue of the presence of multiple equilibria and poverty traps and possible remedies, we do not address the problem of the dynamic inefficiency of the market equilibrium, such that we leave the analysis of poverty traps and dynastic altruism to future research.

The work is organized as follows: in Section 14.2 we present the model and characterize the general equilibrium of the decentralized economy in the presence of redistributive public policies; in Section 14.3 we discuss the occurrence of poverty traps and the qualitative effects of such policies in determining the long-run outcomes of the economy. In Section 14.4, we provide an analytical discussion of two alternative policies and suggest some policy implication of the results. This is followed by some concluding remarks.

14.2. THE MODEL SETUP

The economy is populated by two-period living individuals, who maximize a utility function U, defined over c_1 and c_2, that is consumption in the first and second period of life; hence, in their youth the N_t agents born in period t must choose how much to save out of their income, which is comprised of the wages received from their fixed labour supply (which is normalized to 1).

The population P_t grows at a constant growth rate, n, so that $N_t = N_{t-1}(1+n)$.

Moreover, in this closed-production economy perfect competition is assumed. As a consequence, firms owning a CRS technology can hire capital and labour by remunerating them at their marginal productivities.

Finally, the government can levy lump sum taxes/subsidies on the young (τ_1) and/or on the old (τ_2) for redistributive purposes.

14.2.1. Households

Individuals, at time t, choose their optimal intertemporal allocations of consumption/savings. By assuming for simplicity a logarithmic utility they solve the following problem:[3]

$$Max \ U_t = \log c_{1t} + \beta \log c_{2t+1}$$

$$sub \ c_{1t} + \frac{c_{2t+1}}{(1+r_{t+1})} = w_t - \tau_1 - \frac{\tau_2}{(1+r_{t+1})}.$$

First order conditions deliver the following equations:

$$c_{1t} = \frac{1}{\lambda} \tag{14.1}$$

$$\frac{c_{2t+1}}{\beta} = \frac{1+r_{t+1}}{\lambda} \tag{14.2}$$

where λ is the Lagrangean multiplier, so that: [4]

$$c_{1t} = \frac{1}{1+\beta}\left(w_t - \tau_1 - \frac{\tau_2}{1+r_{t+1}}\right) > 0 \tag{14.1'}$$

$$c_{2t+1} = (1+r_{t+1})\frac{\beta}{1+\beta}\left(w_t - \tau_1 - \frac{\tau_2}{1+r_{t+1}}\right) > 0 \tag{14.2}$$

$$s_t \equiv w_t - \tau_1 - c_{1t} = \frac{\beta}{1+\beta}(w_t - \tau_1) + \frac{\tau_2}{(1+r_{t+1})(1+\beta)} > 0 \tag{14.3}$$

14.2.2. The Production Sector

We assume a competitive market with identical firms: thus, firms hire capital and labour by remunerating them according to their marginal productivity. Moreover, due to the homogeneity of degree one of the aggregate production function $F(K,L)$ and defining $k \equiv K/L$ and $f(k) \equiv F(K,L)/L = F(k,1)$, it follows that:

$$F_K' \equiv f_k' = r_t \text{ and } F_L' \equiv f - f_k'k_t = w_t, \tag{14.4}$$

where r_t and w_t are the interest rate and the wage in period t, and the subscript of the derivative functions F' and f' indicates the derivation variable.

In the numerical examples of the subsequent sections we use a CES production function of the following type:

$$F(K,L) = A\left[\alpha K^{-\rho} + (1-\alpha)L^{-\rho}\right]^{-\frac{1}{\rho}}, \ \rho > -1, \ \rho \neq 0, \ A > 0, \ \alpha \in (0,1) \tag{14.5}$$

which, in per worker terms, has the form:

$$f(k) = A\left[\alpha k^{-\rho} + (1-\alpha)\right]^{-\frac{1}{\rho}}, \tag{14.5'}$$

with

$$f_k' = \alpha A^{-\rho}\left(\frac{f}{k}\right)^{(1+\rho)} \text{ and } f - f_k'k_t = (1-\alpha)A^{-\rho}f^{(1+\rho)}. \tag{14.6}$$

14.2.3. Public Sector and the Goods Market Clearing Condition

The government levies lump sum taxes or subsidies on both young and old individuals. The public sector displays the following budget constraint

$$-(\tau_1 N_t + \tau_2 N_{t-1}) + r_t D_t = D_{t+1} - D_t \tag{14.7}$$

where D stands for debt. For the sake of simplicity we assume that the policy keeps the budget balanced in each period, so that, in per worker terms, we get:

$$\tau_1 + \frac{\tau_2}{1+n} = 0. \tag{14.8}$$

Finally, the equilibrium implies the satisfaction of individuals' and firms' optimality equations and the good market clearing condition, whereby aggregate savings (S_t) must equal the capital of the subsequent period:

$$S_t = K_{t+1} \tag{14.9}$$

In per worker terms, and substituting s_t for equation (14.3) and equation (14.8) one gets:

$$k_{t+1} = \frac{1}{1+n}\left[\frac{\beta}{1+\beta} w_t - \frac{\tau_1}{1+\beta} \frac{\beta(1+r_{t+1})+(1+n)}{1+r_{t+1}} \right] \tag{14.10}$$

or

$$k_{t+1} = \frac{s_t(w_t, r_{t+1}, \tau_2)}{1+n} =$$

$$= \phi(k_t, k_{t+1}) = \frac{1}{1+n}\left[\frac{\beta}{1+\beta} w_t + \frac{\tau_2}{1+\beta} \frac{\beta(1+r_{t+1})+(1+n)}{(1+r_{t+1})(1+n)} \right]. \tag{14.10'}$$

Two comments are worth making.

First, by substituting equation (14.8) into the individuals' budget constraint, or, in other words, when individuals 'internalize' the public budget constraint, one can realize that individuals' optimal choices remain unchanged. Indeed one gets:

$$c_{1t} + \frac{c_{2t+1}}{(1+r_{t+1})} = w_t - \frac{\tau_2(n-r_{t+1})}{(1+r_{t+1})(1+n)}.$$

Hence, one can observe that the redistributive policy will affect consumption in both periods if and only if $n \neq r_{t+1}$. In fact, in this case the introduction of such a policy, from a current 'young' perspective, will represent a net lifetime wealth change, in that the current tax payments (equal to τ_1) do not coincide with the actuarial value of future transfers (equal to $\tau_2/(1+r_{t+1})$). Precisely, equations (14.1) and (14.2) become:

$$c_{1t} = \frac{1}{1+\beta}\left[w_t - \frac{\tau_2(n-r_{t+1})}{(1+r_{t+1})(1+n)} \right] \tag{14.1'}$$

$$c_{2t+1} = (1+r_{t+1})\frac{\beta}{1+\beta}\left[w_t - \frac{\tau_2(n-r_{t+1})}{(1+r_{t+1})(1+n)} \right]. \tag{14.2'}$$

Hence, for example, if τ_2 is negative (that is a subsidy), both $dc_{1t}/d\tau_2$, $dc_{2t}/d\tau_2 > (<)0$ *iff* $n > (<)r_{t+1}$. Of course, when the future interest rate exactly equals the population growth rate (so that the Golden Rule of accumulation is satisfied), consumption in both periods will remain unaffected by a tax change.[5] The second comment, related to the previous one, is the following: for whatever value of n and r_{t+1}, private savings will always be affected by the introduction (or increase) of the redistributive policy. Indeed, the optimal saving equation is:

$$s_t = \left[\frac{\beta}{1+\beta} w_t + \frac{\tau_2}{1+\beta} \frac{\beta(1+r_{t+1})+(1+n)}{(1+r_{t+1})(1+n)} \right] \tag{14.3'}$$

which is equivalent to (14.3) such that $(ds_t/d\tau_2) \neq 0$: as standard in OLG models, even when the Golden Rule is satisfied, savings will be crowded out (crowded in) by an increase (decrease) of future transfers.[6]

14.3. POVERTY TRAPS

In this section we analyse the possibility of poverty trap occurrences in an OLG economy without and with public policies, respectively.

14.3.1. Poverty Traps without Intergenerational Transfers

In the absence of public policy (that is τ_1, $\tau_2 = 0$), an OLG economy with logarithmic preferences and CES technology has been extensively discussed by De La Croix and Michel (2002, section 1.6.2, pp. 32–3 and Fig. 1.11). We limit ourselves to considering the case of $\rho > 0$, which appears of some empirical relevance (Rowthorn, 1999a, 1999b).[7] The equation summarizing the entire dynamics of the model is

$$k_{t+1} = \frac{1}{1+n} \left[\frac{\beta}{1+\beta} w_t(k_t) \right]. \tag{14.11}$$

The existence and number of the steady states emerge from the analysis of the implicit equation

$$k - \frac{1}{1+n} \left[\frac{\beta}{1+\beta} w(k) \right] = 0, \tag{14.12}$$

which provides the following possible outcomes:

w1) *one equilibrium: the trivial one (k = 0);*
w2) *two equilibria: k = 0 and a stable one (tangent) (this is obviously a very special case);*
w3) *three equilibria: k = 0, one (unstable) and one stable.*

As for the stability issue, we recall that: 1) when the zero equilibrium is the only equilibrium, it is globally stable; 2) if there are two positive equilibria, the higher one and the zero equilibrium are locally stable. These features are due to the property of the CES technology in the case of low substitutability. In the latter case: 1) $f(0) = 0$, which is an equilibrium point, in contrast with the case of high substitutability where $f(0) > 0$, which is not an equilibrium; 3) since

$$\lim_{k \to 0} f'(k) > 0$$

and finite and

$$\lim_{k \to 0} f''(k) = 0 ,$$

and, under Cobb–Douglas preferences $s_w > 0$ and $s_r = 0$, it can be shown that

$$\lim_{k \to 0} \frac{\partial k_{t+1}}{\partial k_t} = -f'' \frac{k s_w}{(1+n) - f'' s_r} = 0 .$$

In this sense, the violation of one of the Inada conditions (whereby $\lim_{k \to 0} f'(k) = \infty$) implied by the low substitutability is a sufficient condition for the zero equilibrium to be a catching point and, thus, is the basic ingredient for the existence of a poverty trap.

This dynamic analysis allows for the definition of the poverty trap:[8] 1) when only the trivial equilibrium exists the poverty trap is said to be inescapable (for whatever initial capital stock the zero point is a catching one); 2) when a positive k value (namely k^+) exists corresponding to the lowest positive steady state, then the poverty trap can be escaped provided that the initial capital stock is high enough ($k(0) > k^+$).

Figure 14.1 illustrates cases w1)–w3); *en passant* we note that the increases in the technological index A (that is positive technological shocks) can only lead to escape from the inescapable poverty trap situation, although the zero equilibrium remains a local attractive point.

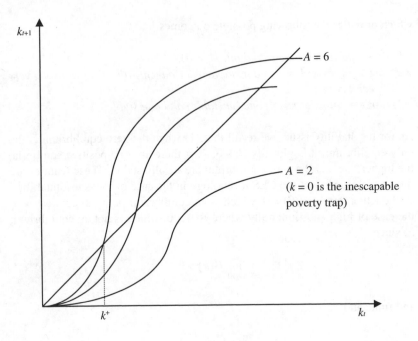

Figure 14.1   Multiple equilibria and poverty trap: $\beta = 0.6$ $\alpha = 0.3$, $n = 0.4$, $\rho = 2$, $\tau_2 = 0$.

14.3.2. Poverty Traps with Intergenerational Transfers

In the presence of intergenerational transfers (that is $\tau_1, \tau_2 \neq 0$), the dynamics of the model is represented by the equation (14.10′).

Note that analysis of the existence and number of the equilibria can be carried out by studying the implicit equation:

$$(1+n)k - s(w,r,\tau_2) = 0 \qquad (14.13)$$

that is

$$k - \frac{1}{1+n}\left\{ \frac{\beta}{1+\beta}w(k) + \frac{\tau_2}{1+\beta}\frac{\beta[1+r(k)]+(1+n)}{[1+r(k)](1+n)} \right\} = 0 . \qquad (14.13′)$$

Comparison of the dynamic equations (14.12) and (14.11) and the two implicit equations (14.13) and (14.10′) highlights the effects of public policies both on stability issues and on the (existence and number of) steady states.

We neglect, for brevity, to derive some (necessary and/or sufficient) conditions for the existence of a poverty trap situation, and resort to some simulations and to their graphical representation.

This simulative analysis shows that six cases may exist, according to whether τ_2 is greater or less than zero:

$\tau_2 > 0$

a1) *three positive equilibria: the lowest and highest are stable, the middle one is unstable;*

a2) *two positive equilibria: the lowest, which is tangent (this is obviously a very special case) and the highest stable;*

a3) *only one positive equilibrium, which is also globally stable.*

Possible configurations of cases a1)–a3) are illustrated in Figure 14.2a.

$\tau_2 < 0$

a4) *no equilibrium;*

a5) *only one positive equilibrium (tangent, this is obviously a very special case);*

a6) *two positive equilibria: the lowest, which is unstable, and the highest which is stable.*

Cases a4)–a6) are presented in Figure 14.2b.

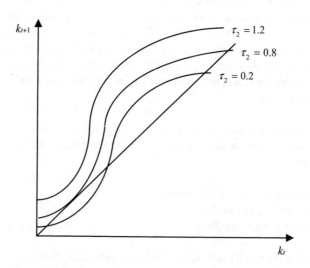

Figure 14.2a Multiple equilibria with $\tau_2 > 0$: $\beta = 0.6$, $\alpha = 0.3$, $n = 0.4$, $\rho = 2$, $A = 6$.

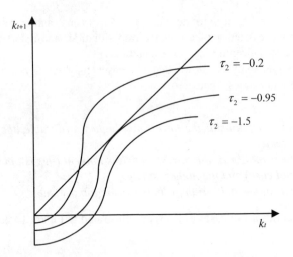

Figure 14.2b   Multiple equilibria with $\tau_2 < 0$: $\beta = 0.6$, $\alpha = 0.3$, $n = 0.4$, $\rho = 2$, $A = 7$.

As to the existence of poverty traps we see that:[9]

1) when no equilibrium exists (case a4) the economy is not existing (for whatever initial capital stock the economy 'explodes'); 2) when a finite k value (namely k^+) exists corresponding to the lowest (case a6) or middle (case a1) positive steady state, then the poverty trap emerges, but the latter can be escaped provided that the initial capital stock is high enough ($k(0) > k^+$); 3) when only one positive equilibrium exists (case a3), it is globally stable and the poverty trap disappears independently of the initial capital stock.

Some comments are worth making. Comparison of cases w1)–w3) and a1)–a6) shows that, in the presence of a public policy, the following new features emerge:

1) *the zero equilibrium disappears;*
2) *the economy may 'explode';*
3) *the poverty trap may disappear independently of the initial capital stock.*

In particular, points 2) and 3) highlight the relevance of the introduction of the public policy: on the one hand, policymakers should be cautious in order to avoid the explosion of the economy; on the other, an opportunely implemented policy may definitely eliminate the poverty trap problem.

For illustrative purposes we show, in Figure 14.3, the role played by the value of the tax (subsidy) on the old in determining the possible long-run dynamics of the economy. In this figure the combinations of τ_2 and the long-run equilibrium capital stock are reported.

In particular, the level of the lump sum tax on the old originates three long-run equilibrium regions, according to the following parametric 'windows' of τ_2 :

$\tau_2 < \tau_2^* < 0$: *non-existence (explosion) of the economy;*

$\tau_2^* \le \tau_2 \le \tau_2^{**}$: *poverty trap situations (the escape from which depends only on the initial (or on the shocks on) capital stock;*

$\tau_2 > \tau_2^{**} > 0$: *no poverty trap; only one 'rich' equilibrium exists.*

What is the economic rationale behind the role of τ_2 in generating the above long-run results? One explanation may be as follows: in an economy stuck in a poverty trap, taxing the young will crowd out private investments and consequently reduce the accumulation rate of resources. Should such a tax be too high, the accumulation path will be even insufficient to replace the capital consumed by the old generations, such that the capital stock will progressively decumulate, going to zero in a finite time. Hence, the introduction of a negative τ_2 has a twofold effect: 1) it reduces the level of income and 2) enlarges the region of instability, rendering the economy more vulnerable to negative temporary shocks, which can, for a sufficiently high level of redistribution, become disruptive for the economy.[10]

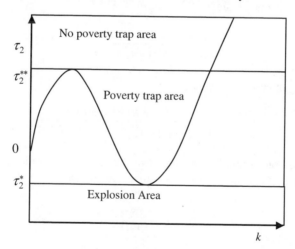

Figure 14.3   Long-run dynamics in the presence of a redistributive policy: equilibrium combinations of k and τ_2. $\beta = 0.6$, $\alpha = 0.3$, $n = 0.4$, $\rho = 2$, $A = 5$.

On the other hand, when τ_2 is positive, the economic intuition behind the result of escaping the poverty trap can be the following: the intergenerational transfer reduces the disposable income of the 'first old generations' through taxation and redistributes the revenues to the young through a negative tax. By doing this the government boosts private savings and, by favouring the formation of new capital, lets the economy escape from the poverty trap (if the latter exists) and, in any case, allows convergence to a high steady state level of capital.[11]

14.4. THE EFFECTS OF PUBLIC POLICIES ON ECONOMIC GROWTH AND ON POVERTY TRAPS

We now focus on the analysis of the effects that public policies may have on poverty traps. First of all, let us analyse the effect of a change in the level of τ_2 on the existence of a steady state value of the capital intensity: it is evident from equation (14.10′) that a sufficiently negative τ_2 value may render the function ϕ negative for whatever value of k_t, and therefore no economy may exist (see case a4).

Secondly, we consider the cases where multiple (non-special) equilibria exist (one, two or three, that is, respectively, cases a3), a6) and a1)). In this case we are able to derive analytically the effects of small changes in τ_2 on each equilibrium. In fact, by implicitly differentiating equation (14.13′), exploiting equations (14.4) and recalling that the factor price frontier implies $dw/dr = -k$, one obtains:

$$\frac{dk}{d\tau_2} = \frac{s_{\tau_2}}{(1+n) - f_k'' s_r + f_k'' k s_w} \tag{14.14}$$

which, in our case, becomes:

$$\frac{dk}{d\tau_2} = \frac{\beta/(1+n) + 1/(1+r)}{(1+n)(1+\beta) + f_k'' \tau_2/(1+f_k')^2 - \beta f_k'' k}. \tag{14.14′}$$

In addition, stability analysis can be easily performed. In fact, by differentiating equation (14.10′) it can be shown that:

$$\frac{dk_{t+1}}{dk_t} = -\frac{f_{k_t}'' k_t s_{w_t}}{(1+n) - f_{k_t}'' s_{r_{t+1}}} \tag{14.15}$$

which, under our assumptions on the utility function, becomes:

$$\frac{dk_{t+1}}{dk_t} = -\frac{f''_k k_t [\beta/(1+\beta)]}{(1+n) + \left[f''_{k_t} \tau_2 / (1+\beta)\left(1+f'_{k_{t+1}}\right)^2 \right]}.$$ (14.15′)

Clearly, when τ_2 is negative (that is a subsidy), since f''_k is negative, this locus is always positive around the equilibrium; on the other hand, when τ_2 is positive, the denominator of equation (14.15′) must be set to be positive.

Finally, the following inequalities will hold:

$$0 < \frac{dk_{t+1}}{dk_t} < (>)1$$

according to whether the equilibrium under analysis is stable or unstable, respectively.

Hence, taking account of the comparative static equations (14.14) and the stability equations (14.15) the following proposition holds:

Proposition 1: *If the equilibrium is stable (that is either the poor or the rich equilibrium), then an increase in the tax on the old increases steady state capital intensity.*

If the equilibrium is unstable, then such an increase reduces steady state capital intensity. This means that the basin of attraction of the rich (poor) equilibrium is enlarged (reduced).

Hence, in the presence of the poverty trap problem, an increase in the tax (or reduction of the subsidy) on the old is always positive for the long-run performance of the economy.

Proof: Since the numerator of equation (14.14′) is strictly positive, the sign of $dk/d\tau_2$ is univocally driven by the sign of the denominator; now, calculating that the denominator is the difference between the denominator and numerator of equation (14.15′), under stability $(0 < dk_{t+1}/dk_t < 1)$, such a difference is positive so that $dk/d\tau_2$ is positive; on the other hand, when the equilibrium is unstable $(dk_{t+1}/dk_t > 1)$, the denominator of equation (14.14′) is negative, so that $dk/d\tau_2$ is negative as well.

The content of Proposition 1 is shown by Figure 14.4.

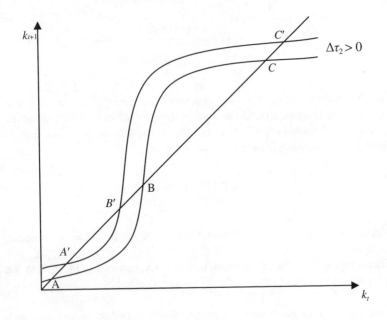

Figure 14.4   The effects of an increase of τ₂ on the stable and unstable equilibria

On policy grounds, an interesting interpretation of our results is to consider the intergenerational transfers as a PAYG social security scheme, but this is beyond the scope of our chapter.

Two final comments are worth making. First, our analysis does not depend strictly on the assumption of lump sum taxes/transfers. However, if both taxes and transfers were proportional to the production factor incomes (either wages or capital income), this would lead to the persistence of the inescapable zero equilibrium. Nevertheless, this device would still play a role in escaping/worsening any poverty trap, possibly generating non-trivial dynamics of the accumulation path. In fact, it is the presence of an independent-of-incomes component in the transfers among cohorts which ensures the disappearance of the poor equilibrium. All things considered, given the ease of implementation, 'pure lump sum policies' are most likely to be used in developing countries; moreover, policies adopting a mixture of proportional taxes/transfers and lump sum elements can be found in mature economies. Hence, our assumptions do not limit the generality of the results.

The other point is the question of what would happen to our results if intergenerational links were introduced, such that a sort of 'Ricardian equivalence result' emerged. In fact, the presence of any of the well known hypotheses invalidating the Ricardian equivalence theorem would suffice for intergenerational redistribution to play a role. In particular, as far as OLG models are concerned, Blanchard (1985), Weil (1988) and Buiter (1988) have shown that the presence of altruism in OLG frameworks does not necessarily imply that policies redistributing among generations are ineffective. In any case, this extension represents an interesting avenue for future research.

14.5. CONCLUSIONS

In this chapter we have adopted the traditional competitive OLG model à la Samuelson (1958)–Diamond (1965) with two-period-living individuals, logarithmic preferences, CES technology with low factor substitution and exogenous fertility rates, where the government can pursue redistributive policies between generations by levying lump sum taxes/subsidies. We show through a simple geometry of the equilibrium analysis that the taxation of the old can be used: 1) to escape from a poverty trap; 2) to increase the per capita income in the positive high steady state. Conversely, the taxation of the young worsens the stationary per capita income and may lead to the explosion of the economy.

Hence, we reveal that the introduction of a redistributive policy enriches the range of possible long-run dynamic outcomes and in particular, that while such a policy should be cautious in order to avoid the explosion of the economy, if opportunely implemented, it could definitely eliminate the poverty trap problem.

These results were obtained under simplified assumptions: lump sum taxation, no government spending and no debt, labour supply and fertility choices exogenously given. Relaxing any of these hypotheses may open up interesting avenues for future research.

NOTES

* We thank Renato Balducci and Alberto Bucci for their comments on a previous version of this work. Although the present chapter is the result of a common research, Sections 14.1 and 14.3 should be attributed to L. Fanti, while Sections 14.2, 14.4 and 14.5 should be attributed to L. Spataro.

1. For recent surveys and works on poverty traps see Galor (1996), Azariadis (1996, 2005), Hoff (2000), Hoff and Sen (2004), Matsuyama (1995, 1997), Easterly (2001), Bowles, Durlauf and Hoff (2004) and Mookherjee and Ray (2001).

2. For a survey on the theoretical and empirical aspects of this topic, see Seater (1993). See also De La Croix and Michel (2002, section 5.1), for OLG models with dynastic altruism.

3. More general individual preferences may be introduced through the CIES utility function. This extension, on the one hand, confirms the qualitative results of this chapter about the role of intergenerational transfers in a world with poverty traps and, on the other, enriches the spectrum of dynamic results, but it goes beyond the scope of the present work; however, we thank an anonymous referee for suggesting this fruitful extension.
4. Note that the inequalities (14.1'), (14.2) and (14.3) require that the net income of the young be always positive or, in other words, that the lump sum taxes cannot be greater than wage. For all the results of this chapter this requirement is always satisfied.
5. The satisfaction of the Golden Rule is a very special case in OLG models, as Diamond (1965, p. 1135) has shown. Needless to say, this occurrence is indeed a very special case also in our OLG model with CES production function.
6. It is easy to show that, when $r_{t+1} = n$, equation (14.3') becomes $s_t = \{[\beta/(1+\beta)]w_t - \tau_1\}$: *the one-to-one crowding out of an increase of the tax on the young (transfer to the old) is evident.* Whether such a transfer to the old (tax on the young) crowds out private saving more or less than one for one depends on the magnitude of the difference between the interest rate and population growth.
7. Rowthorn (1999a) reports the results for the elasticity of substitution $\sigma = 1/(1+\rho)$ of 33 econometric studies, according to which the overall median of the summary values (median of the medians) is equals to 0.58 (and only in 7 cases is the elasticity greater than 0.8). Rowthorn (1999b) estimates indirectly the elasticity of substitution (based on some empirical values of the labour demand elasticity, profit share and price elasticity), generating the following examples for the parameter ρ.

	Italy	UK	France	Germany	Sweden	Japan	USA
ρ	13.3	3.95	15.6	1.63	24	5.25	13.2

8. For an extensive discussion of multiple equilibria see Galor (1996) and Azariadis (1996).
9. The two special tangent equilibria cases (a2 and a5) are not considered for brevity.
10. These arguments can be easily recognized by observing Figure 14.2b.
11. This explanation may resemble the argument developed by De La Croix and Michel (2002, pp. 226–8), according to which nationalizing part of the capital stock held by the first old generation and subsequently redistributing the dividends to the young may help to escape from the poverty trap situation.

REFERENCES

Azariadis C. (1996), 'The economics of poverty traps–part one: complete markets', *Journal of Economic Growth*, **1**(4), 449–86.

Azariadis C. (2005), 'The theory of poverty traps: what have we learned?', in Bowles, Durlauf and Hoff (2005).

Blanchard O. (1985), 'Debt, deficits, and finite horizons', *Journal of Political Economy*, **93**(2), 253–63.

Bowles S., S.N. Durlauf and Hoff K. (eds) (2005), *Poverty Traps*, Princeton: Princeton University Press.

Buiter W.H. (1988), 'Death, birth, productivity growth and debt neutrality', *Economic Journal*, **98**(391), 279–93.

De La Croix D. and P. Michel (2002), *A Theory of Economic Growth*, Cambridge, UK: Cambridge University Press.

Diamond P. (1965), 'National debt in a neoclassical growth model', *American Economic Review*, **41**, 1126–50.

Easterly W. (2001), *The Elusive Quest for Growth: Economists' Adventures and Misadventures in the Tropics*, Cambridge, Mass.: MIT Press.

Galor O. (1996), 'Convergence? Inferences from theoretical models', *The Economic Journal*, **106**(437), 1056–69.

Hoff K. (2000), 'Beyond Rosenstein-Rodan: the modern theory of coordination problems in development', Proceedings of the World Bank Annual Conference on Development Economics.

Hoff K. and A. Sen (2004), 'The kin system as a poverty trap', in Bowles, Durlauf and Hoff (2005).

Matsuyama, K. (1995), 'Complementarities and cumulative processes in models of monopolistic competition', *Journal of Economic Literature*, **33**, 701–729.

Matsuyama K. (1997), 'Complementarity, instability and multiplicity', *Japanese Economic Review*, **48**(3), 240–66.

Mookherjee D. and D. Ray (2001), *Readings in the Theory of Economic Development*, New York: Blackwell Publishing.

Rowthorn R.E. (1999a), 'Unemployment, wage bargaining and capital–labour substitution', *Cambridge Journal of Economics*, July.

Rowthorn R.E. (1999b), 'Unemployment, capital-labor substitution, and economic growth', IMF Working Paper No. 99/43, March 1.

Samuelson P.A. (1958), 'An exact consumption-loan model of interest with or without the social contrivance of money', *Journal of Political Economy*, **66**, 467–82.

Seater J. (1993), 'Ricardian equivalence', *Journal of Economic Literature*, **31**(1), 142–90.

Weil P. (1988), 'Overlapping families of infinitely-lived agents', *Journal of Public Economics*, **38**(2), 183–98.

Index